THE LIFE
AND WORKS OF
BEETHOVEN

THE LIFE

AND WORKS OF

BEETHOVEN

BY JOHN N. BURK

THE
MODERN LIBRARY
NEW YORK

Random House IS THE PUBLISHER OF

THE MODERN LIBRARY

BENNETT A. CERF · DONALD S. KLOPFER · ROBERT K. HAAS

Manufactured in the United States of America

By H. Wolff

CONTENTS

Contents

THE LIFE OF
BEETHOVEN

CHAPTER ONE

ALL LIFE in the town of Bonn during Beethoven's childhood centered upon the Palace which was the Residence of the Elector of Cologne. The peasants paid their tribute from the fields of waving grain and the fruit-clustered vines. The townsfolk were still more closely implicated in the miniature monarchy, as one may see by taking a rough census of the Bonngasse, the little street of two blocks leading from the Market Place northward toward the Cologne Gate. There was Johann Baum, Master of the Electoral Cellar, Franz Ries, Court Violinist, Nicholas Simrock, Court Horn Player. There was Conrad Poll, Electoral Footman, Johann Salomon, another Court Violinist. Of the dwellers in the street, the *Hofkapellmeister* Ludwig van Beethoven (grandfather of the composer) was easily the most distinguished, and probably the least so was his son, the Court Tenor Johann van Beethoven, who lived in miserable lodgings at the rear of the house of Herr Clasen, a lace maker. Three of the Bonngasse neighbors were later to become widely known— Simrock as a music publisher, Salomon as a London impresario, the son born here to *Hofmusicus* Johann van Beethoven as a figure for eternity. But these developments were for a later time. In 1770, when Beethoven was born, all were servants together, conscious only of their small steps of rank and eager for the nod of his radiant Highness.

When the Elector had guests and spread a feast before them, his musicians vied with his Electoral cooks by providing an accompaniment of "table music." If there were a ball, the same musicians mounted their balcony. A choir was maintained for all the chapel services, and when an opera of Grétry or Philidor was prepared, again for the edification of guests, the choristers

3

changed from the surplice to the period costume, and the fiddling and tootling lackeys assembled in the theatre as an opera orchestra. The pieces chosen were usually of the light and entertaining variety, sometimes of local extraction, and the quality of performance was provincial and makeshift. But the Rhine Electors were genuine cultivators of the art. Whatever their share in the making of Beethoven, they are to be credited with having nurtured a considerable musical life in the cultural hinterland of the German principalities.

His Serenity Maximilian Friedrich, of the Suabian line of Königsegg Rothenfels, under whose scepter Beethoven was born, was next to God in his absolute control of the life and fortunes of his subjects. If anyone hoped for redress or betterment, his closest approach was a letter headed with an array of titles, and couched in groveling words that put a universe of space between writer and receiver. The petition was answered by a decree handed down through the minister—perhaps in three days, perhaps in three months.

The Rhinelanders in Bonn and the country near by were not discontented. They managed to live, even after the Electoral tax collectors were through with them. When courtly spectacles ravished the eye and warmed the heart, the populace were being rewarded with a show for which they had paid well, and when cannon mounted on the town wall that buttressed the Rhine were touched off in salute by the Electoral Guard, they grew excited and cheered him who kept them secure and at peace with this small display of soldiery, never impressing them and marching them off to foreign wars, as the lay princes did.

The daily round at Bonn must have filled the boy Beethoven for the most part with contentment. Music was all about him at Court, and when he needed musical advice, there were kindly and patient musicians to give it to him. There was miserable poverty at home; nor was the status of the Beethovens in any way improved when, in their son's fifth or sixth year, the family moved from Herr Clasen's to Master Baker Fischer's house on the Rheingasse. But the boy could lean on the window sill of his little attic room and lose himself in contemplation of the housetops of the clean little town, its spires to the northward and the

4

fair and peaceful valley beyond. The Rhine itself was only a stone's throw away. Its craft struggled up or floated down stream; it had a "flying bridge," a cable ferry, which plied from shore to shore. The meadows and vineyards continued beyond the opposite bank, and the craggy peaks of the Siebengebirge in the distance, though familiar, remained unreal. The town itself had its interests. On a church-festival day all the bells seemed to peal at once over the heads of the gentry, the clergy, the peasantry, and the scene became a pageant of costly silks, ecclesiastical robes, and the bright woolens of peasant costumes. The humble folk made way for the carriages that drove under the flowering chestnuts to the Palace that the elegant beings of another world might kiss the lace-cuffed hand of His Excellency. Beethoven at thirteen had his pride of rank in these spectacles. As a *Hofmusicus* in official standing he must have worn on dress occasions a flaring silk coat and knee breeches, with a sword at his side and a three-cornered hat.

Very likely there were no stirrings of rebellion or mockery in the young heart which later could be so rebellious. Childhood accepts its universe, and only when it finds powers to deal with it, begins to question. There could have been no questioning the awesomeness and unapproachability of the near deity that enveloped the life of his family, and of everyone he knew. If he could have looked beneath the archbishop's robes he would have beheld an inconsequential little man, who as a stranger on the street would not have attracted a second glance. Whatever else Maximilian Friedrich may have been, he was quite unconvincing as a minister of God and the Church. The office was bestowed by the clergy, necessarily approved by Pope and Emperor. It was a mummery, won by self-insinuation into power for the pomps and vanities that were in it.

Beethoven's monarch varied the tedium of his ritual duties by affixing his signature to petitions and recommendations, while saving his best energies for the playing of lord and host at balls, hunting parties or theatrical performances designed to be at least a little more splendid than the best his neighbor Elector could turn out. If the entertainments were a little less splendid, if there were lurking marks of inescapable shabbiness in upkeep, then

5

the whole grand effect was punctured, and all that an Elector really lived for was lost. Henry Swinburne, English visitor to the courts of Europe, went to Bonn with his wife in 1780, dined at the Palace, and wrote about his host:

"He is 73 years old, a little, hale, black man, very merry and affable. His table is none of the best; no dessert wines handed about, nor any foreign wines at all. He is easy and agreeable, having lived all his life in ladies' company, which he is said to have liked better than his breviary. The captains of his guard, and a few other people of the court form the company. . . . The palace is of immense size, the ballroom particularly large and low. . . . The Elector goes about to all the assemblies and plays at *tric-trac*. He asked me to be of his party but I was not acquainted with their way of playing. There is every evening an assembly or play at court."

The family of Beethoven felt the thrift from above in the quarterly payments which were barely enough to keep them alive. It should be added in fairness that Beethoven's father was worth no more than his salary.

The Court musicians had included two Beethovens when the Elector Max assumed the "crook and scepter" in 1761. They were Ludwig and his son Johann, aged forty-nine and twenty-one respectively, the destined grandfather and father of the composer. Both were singers, although the elder man need not have been, for he was Master of the Court *Kapelle* and a dignitary in his own right. This elder Ludwig has been held up as the one among Beethoven's kin who showed the origins of his grandson's dominant personality. The *Kapellmeister* brought to Beethoven the only non-German strain in his blood. He was born in Malines, Flanders, in 1712, the son of a baker who later became a dealer in laces. The name Beethoven was common in Belgium, first traceable around Louvain, and is still found in Holland. *Beethoven* derives from "beetfield," and the Flemish pronounced the vegetable root as we do. The composer's father, who was none too literate, at different times wrote his name several ways: Biethoven, Bithof, Biethoffen, but tended to keep the Flemish vowel sound on the first syllable.

The elder Ludwig had had a good musical training and experience as an organist and as a choir singer when, in 1733, he journeyed from Liége to Bonn to become Court Musician to the Elector of Cologne, singing bass in the chapel and theatre. He had been in Bonn only five months when he married Maria Josepha Poll, a German girl of nineteen. He had found his home and was to remain at the court in Bonn for the rest of his years. Two children of the couple died in infancy; a third, Johann, was the only surviving child. History leaves no information about Maria except that she became addicted to drink and that when she survived her husband she was boarded by her son in a convent in Bonn. The son, too, was to become an alcoholic. Trouble clung to the Beethovens and kept them down, while one of them, the straight-living *Musicus* from Flanders, remained erect and prospered. Enterprising in more ways than one, he took to the bartering of Rhine wine as a side line, selling it at a favorable rate in the Low Countries.

The Flemish inheritance in Beethoven has been labored. Ernest Closson wrote a full book on the subject, developing the thesis that intractability, love of freedom, stubborn assertiveness are as markedly Flemish as conformity and obedience are German. *Kapellmeister* Beethoven knew his own mind; of that one may assure oneself by a contemplation of his portrait by the Court painter, Radoux. He is wearing a rich green, fur-edged robe, and the full velvet cap of an artist. The brow is intelligent, the eyes penetrating, the nose straight and handsome. The features of the grandson are coarse by comparison; only the animated glance of the elder Ludwig directly suggests the younger one. Beethoven's boyhood friend Wegler wrote years later of Beethoven's lifelong veneration for his grandfather—and how "little Louis" had "clung to him with the greatest affection." But when, on Christmas Eve of 1773, the grandfather had died, "little Louis" was three years and one week old. What Beethoven must have remembered was the portrait which hung prominently in the parlor. The family decorated it with a laurel wreath on the name day, and, this being the grandson's own, he was filled with a pride of kinship. This Beethoven of the clear, appraising gaze and easy bearing gave reassurance to the boy when he was

7

shamed by the conduct of his weak father and by the poverty which weighed upon them all.

Johann van Beethoven, the *Kapellmeister's* unpromising son, never acquired any abilities except those essential to his position and livelihood. To write properly was not essential—to sing acceptably was—and Johann learned early from his father to sing and to play the violin. At sixteen he was granted an *"accessit"* as Court Musician and sang a regular tenor in the choir and operatic performances, when he often appeared on the stage with his father. His artistry was undistinguished, tolerated rather than praised, and this was as high as he ever rose. Perhaps it was another case of the mediocre child who is shamed by a brilliant and mentally vigorous parent and so driven into a defiant ineffectuality.

At twenty-seven, Johann van Beethoven married a girl from Ehrenbreitstein, the little town which lies on the opposite shore of the Rhine from Coblentz, a few miles up the river from Bonn. Her name was Maria Magdalena Kewerich; she was twenty-one, and the daughter of the head cook of the Elector of Trèves. The Herr *Kapellmeister* was not pleased at receiving a daughter-in-law of lesser station, even though all three of them came within the boundaries of Electoral servanthood. The irregular habits of his son and the peasant humility of the young wife must have been equally distasteful to him, which would account for the fact that he would not live with them, but had his own rooms near by on the Bonngasse. His rooms were as spotless and elegant as his person. The cupboards shone with silver, the linen was fine enough, so said a neighbor, "to draw through a ring."

One must further disagree with the disapproving father-in-law in failing to see much social disparity between a Court Musician who has fallen short of his intellectual opportunities and a Court Chef's daughter who has never had any. Cäcilia Fischer, with whom the Beethovens later lodged, could not remember ever having seen Frau Beethoven laugh: "She was always serious." Indeed, she could have had little time to be anything else. At seventeen she had married a valet, had been widowed (without children) and married again at twenty-one, a not too happy interlude in her progress from cook's daughter to singer's drudge.

8

She had lost her father, and, shortly after her second marriage, her mother too. It is hard to imagine, within this succession of heavy events, any place for the measure of coquetry and inconsequential gaiety which make up a normally carefree young girlhood. When she stepped from the Church of St. Remigius on the Market Place as Maria Kewerich van Beethoven, her position was hardly improved. She found herself the wife of a good-looking, good-natured, but vain and pretentious singer. When he came home from the tavern garrulous with brandy and empty of pocket, it fell upon her to keep the little household in respectable standing, the landlord and grocer paid. This became increasingly difficult as she took on the burdens of childbearing. She bore six children between the years 1769 and 1781, and three survived. The first, baptized Ludwig Maria on April 2, 1769, lived six days. The second, baptized December 17, 1770 (he may have been born the day before), the parents again named Ludwig, as if they were determined to make the most of the honor and dignity the grandfather had brought to that name. He had acted as sponsor on both occasions. There was a baptismal feast at the house of the other sponsor, the wife of *Kellermeister* Baum, suggesting that their own quarters in the rear of the Clasen house were too confined, too miserable for a celebration. Kaspar Anton Karl was baptized April 8, 1774, and Nicholas Johann, October 2, 1776.

By that time, the Beethovens had moved to the Fischers' house on Rheingasse, a little street leading down to the water's edge. There Ludwig was to spend his boyhood from the age of five or six. Poverty pinched the Beethoven family with increasing sharpness as its number increased, and as the father drank more heavily. He petitioned in vain to his "Most Gracious Elector and Lord" for an increase in position and salary to meet expenses. The Elector was lenient toward his better subjects such as the elder Ludwig, who had held his post and continued to sing in stage performances until the year of his death at 61. Exceptional talent was well paid. But when mediocrity was both aging and declining, as in Johann's case, a rigid economy was brought to bear.

The wife could barely manage to keep her sons in trousers and shirts, or to put enough stew and potatoes or the table for their

9

health and growth. The boys ran rather wild and unkempt, as the children of overdriven mothers are apt to do. But no one could say that the Beethovens were less respectable than any other family in the little community. She accepted her lot quietly. The boy Ludwig knew a serious, rather grimly busy mother who looked worn and drawn for her years, yet who could be patient with his moody or stubborn ways. He would sometimes press her to speak of his grandfather, and she could find it in her heart to praise the qualities of the dignitary who had once received her grudgingly. So wrote Wegeler, stressing her "piety and gentleness." With all her docility, she was quite capable of standing up for her rights and those of her family. "Madame van Beethoven," wrote Fischer, "was a clever woman; she could give converse and reply aptly, politely and modestly to high and low, and for this reason she was much liked and respected. She occupied herself with sewing and knitting. They led a righteous and peaceful married life, and paid their house rent and baker's bills promptly, quarterly and on the day." Fischer adds that she did not pay drinking debts. "She was a good, a domestic woman, she knew how to give and also how to take in a manner that is becoming to all people of honest thoughts."

Her son would surely have liked to confide in her, to turn to her with his perplexities and curiosities. But she could have had no answer for problems of the mind; she had never had any time for such things. Unable to give him this kind of companionship, she must have made amends with her practical philosophy of necessity, her sense of right living and her simple-hearted affection. These saving comforts the boy clung to the more closely because he missed them in his father.

Johann van Beethoven has been made out as a good deal more of a brute than the sifted evidence warrants. He seems to have had pleasant-spoken ways, preferring to make himself agreeable elsewhere than to face miseries at home. He would return late at night, filled with large talk and jovial swagger. We are not told that Frau van Beethoven allowed herself to be imposed upon. She was vanquished in the end by the simple reason that she could not prevent her husband from drinking up the family income. Fischer, a direct observer, has left a milder picture than the usually imagined one of Johann in liquor: "If the father, through the opportunity offered by company (which did not often happen) had drunk a little too much and his sons perceived it, they were all three greatly concerned, and managed with the finest art to prevent him from making any display. They would persuade him to go home quietly, and he would submit. He had no bad temper in drink, but was gay and lively, and so we in the house were hardly aware of these incidents."

Johann taught his eldest son to play the violin and the piano, and did so as a matter of course, just as he had had instruction from his own father. There is some evidence that the two brothers were similarly taken in hand, in which case the father must have looked upon Karl as a doubtful, Johann as a hopeless prospect. With Ludwig, things were different. The boy took to his notes so naturally that his parent was reminded of the recent fruitful exploitation of the infant Mozart. A project for the solution of all money troubles reached the point where, in 1778, Johann arranged a joint recital of his son and his pupil Mlle. Averdonck, "Court Contralto." An announcement in the principal Cologne paper, the *Zeitung*, stated that his "little son of six years" (two years less than the truth) would "give complete enjoyment to all ladies and gentlemen" with "various clavier concertos and trios. . . . Both have had the honor of performing to the greatest delight of the entire Court."

It would so appear that he had been showing the prodigy around, even while pushing his development to the utmost. The neighbors Ries and Simrock each remembered that the father taught the boy both pianoforte and violin from his earliest childhood. When the Beethovens moved to the Fischers' house there was piano practice every day, prolonged beyond young endurance, and in spite of tears. Wegeler was accustomed to play with a schoolmate in the house backing upon the Fischers', and often looked across at the "doings and sufferings of Louis." Cäcilia Fischer, sister to the landlord, remembered him as "a tiny boy, standing on a footstool in front of the clavier to which the implacable severity of his father has so early condemned him," and Burgermeister Windeck, calling on the Fischers, also remembered him "standing in front of the clavier and weeping."

His lessons at school took second place, and were always inadequate. He is known to have attended a little public school on the Neugasse, also the Münsterschule, and later the Latin school "Tirocinium," where he learned enough Latin to serve him later, but carried no further his spelling and arithmetic, and so remained inadequate for life in those subjects. French was a language considerably used at Court, in opera texts for example, and Beethoven could speak French, and write it after a fashion. Italian, too, became familiar to him through operatic usage. Whatever else he learned, he probably picked up of his own accord later. Wurzer, a pupil at the Tirocinium, remembered Beethoven as "distinguished by uncleanliness, negligence, etc." Beethoven's brothers were the only companions with whom he occasionally roamed and played. He was an ungainly lad, short, but sturdy. He acquired the nickname of *"Der Spangol"* (*"Spagnol"*) on account of his swarthy complexion and mop of black hair. He was remembered as moody, seclusive, a dreamer. Soon his music became his whole life.

Johann noticed that the boy took less driving as he progressed, that he even lingered at the piano which had been his cross. Still, the execution did not reach the required professional smoothness. He would give him scales and studies, the high road to the subjection of ten fingers into one smooth mechanism. But the fingers would wander from the prescribed exercises, explore aimlessly, and so get nowhere, wasting time. Then, according to Fischer, the father, to whom music was a job to be mastered like any other craft, would read him a lecture:

"You've not reached the point of making up your own notes; practice the piano and violin thoroughly; learn to play the notes accurately. When you've learned to do that you may think of playing out of your own head; but that must come later."

Johann thereupon kept him at his violin; perhaps he would take better to fiddling. He did not. He had the feeling, the sense of the instrument at once, but instead of reaching the point of ease in the study before him, he would again depart from the cut-and-dried text of repetitious notation. This time Johann would lose his temper and shout. Again according to Fischer:

"What stupid stuff you are scraping at now; you know I can't

12

stand hearing it; play the notes in front of you, or all your scraping will amount to nothing."

Johann could not possibly have understood what was going on in the boy, what was trying fumblingly to come forth. He was acting quite reasonably, according to his lights. The Beethovens learned to fulfill a certain bread-winning routine at Court. They made music as became their place, instead of presuming to compose it. Not even his father, the illustrious *Kapellmeister*, had done such a thing. The present *Kapellmeister* Luchesi had written an opera or two, but Herr Luchesi was an eminent musician of wide and long experience. This young and overweening product of the family of Beethoven knew nothing; he was at the very beginning of his apprenticeship. Later, when he had learned his craft, let him try his hand at writing if he still wished. Meanwhile he had better devote himself to playing one acceptable scale without raucous squeaks. The boy's remarkable quickness to grasp anything musical that was explained or even put before him seemed to carry him only a certain way and no further. The father, with a sharp disappointment, saw his hopes for prosperity collapse.

This dull attempt at exploitation must have hung heavily upon the boy's sensitive spirit. He could not quite hate his tasks, for music, in whatever shape it was hammered into him, was still music. Sometimes he hated his father. The lesson hours hung over him like a threat. It is hard to take reprimands from a taskmaster who is himself slovenly, whom one holds in secret contempt. When Johann, with his judgment clouded by alcohol, mocked sarcastically at his pupil's first attempt to master a new position, the boy, not daring to retort, would glower in silence at the injustice and stupidity of the teacher he did not respect, who was covering his own incompetence with a show of overbearing authority. An average child builds up an imperviousness, learns to evade tyranny. The sensitive Beethoven was defenseless before every wounding word. Injustice was a terrible thing he could not meet, could not forget. The father saw nothing but the boy's tears. He had not the intelligence to know that Beethoven needed no driving whatever. What he did need was the true discipline of orderly instruction, and this he did not have. The

13

result was that he became impatient of performing facility, and allowed his inquisitive imagination to leap ahead of his technical equipment. He was beyond any possible aid from the capacities of the petty professional *Musikant*. The time had come to look elsewhere for guidance.

Trying to find out what he studied and with whom, we run into the foggy memories of his friends, who vaguely mention names. The conclusion is that he picked up scraps of instruction here and there, where he could, learning something of the viola as well as the piano and violin. There was, for example, Tobias Pfeiffer, a tenor, who came to Bonn with Grossman's operatic troupe in 1779, struck up an acquaintance with the Court Tenor Beethoven, and probably lived in the same house with him. Being a good pianist, he was brought into service as teacher. "Often when he came with Beethoven the father from the winehouse late at night the boy was roused from his sleep and kept at the pianoforte until morning."

Ludwig was eight years old when he went to the Court Organist Van den Eeden, and the old man, then nearly seventy, probably initiated him into the marvels of that instrument. It is further told that when he was hardly grown enough to reach the manuals and pedals of an organ at the same time, he found his way into the Franciscan Monastery at Bonn, was befriended and taught by Friar Willibald Koch; that he was similarly befriended by the organist of the Minorites Cloister, where the instrument was larger, and of greater interest. He even ingratiated himself with Organist Zenser of the Münsterkirche; this at the age of ten. He must have done well and inspired confidence, for each of the two friars allowed him to take over an occasional service.

So Beethoven's training continued haphazard and patchy, while through it all there are definite indications. The desire in him to master each aspect of music was so strong that it somehow found its end. The mastery of a single instrument was not his aim, for he was in pursuit of four. This kind of eagerness always finds a helping hand—it is what teachers live for. Musicians round about grew devoted to him, and there was no thought of pay. What he was really after, of course, was definite direction in composing, but even as he asked questions his musical nature had of itself found the way. "I never had to learn to avoid errors," he wrote years later, "for from my childhood I had so keen a sensibility that I wrote correctly without knowing that it had to be so, or could be otherwise." There has come down indirectly from his fellow pupil under Zenser that he surprised his teacher with an organ composition which his childish hands could not manage. "You can't play that, Ludwig," said the teacher, and Ludwig answered: "I will when I am bigger." But more often he improvised. When he was substituting for Van den Eeden at a mass service, he preluded before the credo at such length and so elaborately that the orchestra stared at him in amazement.

We have no means of knowing when Beethoven became the pupil of Christian Gottlob Neefe. Neefe became Court Organist in 1781, at the death of Van den Eeden. He may have taught Beethoven before that, for he had been in Bonn two years. Neefe was probably the very influence Beethoven most needed. He was young and spirited. He had painstaking method, and brought it to bear upon the wild and roving imagination of the young provincial. His touch of Leipzig conservatism gave the impetuous, untutored and groping Beethoven something to beat against and so strengthen himself.

Neefe brought with him from Leipzig musical treasures far more bracing and deeply satisfying than the operettas and general run of trivial music at Court. They were the sonatas of Emanuel Bach, the Bach of Hamburg, and the Preludes and Fugues of Sebastian Bach, who at that time was less thought of than his son, and little more than a dim memory at Leipzig. The teacher was pleased with the boy's skill and ability to read at sight, and rewarded him by giving him *The Well-Tempered Clavichord* as his "principal" music to work upon. Beethoven never lost his enthusiasm, and although he later mentioned Handel and Mozart as his two prime favorites among composers, he was to plunge deeply into Bach again, near the end of his life.

Neefe further encouraged the boy by the publication of three piano sonatas, elaborately dedicated to the Elector, and when he was called away, he turned his duties as organist over to his "vicar," namely the eleven-year-old Beethoven. A year later

15

Neefe was needed by the Elector for operatic drilling, and once more the "vicar" was put to good use. Soon the boy was made regular "cembalist in the orchestra," a responsible position which involved accompanying at opera rehearsals, and keeping the orchestra together at performances. There could have been no better point of vantage for learning the ways of opera and orchestra.

In February, 1784, Beethoven made his first petition to the Elector, asking for official recognition as Assistant Court Organist. He had made himself indispensable; he was yet without salary, and the family conditions were more miserable than ever —three good reasons! The petition was granted. All would have been in order if the Elector had not delayed in affixing the salary. This was unfortunate, for six weeks later, he died.

CHAPTER TWO

THE SUCCESSION to the Cologne Electorship was already cared for. Four years before, Maria Theresa had cast her eye about for a sinecure for her youngest and favored son, the Archduke Maximilian Franz. Cologne and Münster, along the German Rhine, were favorable; Maximilian Friedrich, who held both archbishoprics, was aging and feeble. The thing could be managed, and was. The son of the watchful Empress was, in 1780, elected Coadjutor in Cologne and Münster. Duly assuming office in 1784, he retired into a seminary in Cologne for three weeks in December, and emerged from this short course in godliness a consecrated priest. Three days later, on Christmas Eve, he took his robes for the mass in the Florian Chapel at Bonn.

The new Elector was good-natured and affable. A hearty eater, he was fast acquiring immense size, when, at twenty-eight, he went to Bonn. Max Franz was more engaging in private conversation than imposing on courtly parade. In fact, he was impatient of etiquette, and when he visited his sister Marie Antoinette at Versailles and emphasized his awkward figure by his disregard for conformity, the anti-Austrian faction at that court was delighted at the spectacle.

If Max Franz was unimpressive on his own account, his Empress mother, adept at preparing her offspring for royal office, had taken good care that he was properly groomed. Little more need be expected from an Elector if he knows enough to appoint in the first place good ministers in each department, and not to interfere with them. A proper education in Vienna had taught him enough of the arts and sciences so that he could do something far more important than practice them, and that was to implant and nourish them in the community. His descent upon Bonn was like

17

a fresh renovating breeze from a larger world blowing across a small one. It was thanks to him that Bonn became an important university town.

What Max Franz brought with him was an aura of Vienna, and an aura of Vienna postulates a lively portion of music. He is said to have had a passable singing voice and played upon the viola; not well enough to bring about an embarrassingly frequent use of his talents, but well enough to make a great point of his devotion to the art. He collected a large library of music and encouraged its performance. If the budget did not permit the maintenance of a first-rate opera company, it did permit the importation of one for three carnival seasons. Bonn, having been quite complacent with numerous operettas by composers now forgotten, was probably treated to such serious and inspiring tragedies as *Orfée* and *Alceste,* new and arresting pieces which were shaking Paris with controversy over the reforms of the Chevalier Gluck. It is easy to imagine how the adolescent Beethoven, avid for experience, responded to this flowering of the arts.

One of the Elector's first acts was to require a written report on the status and ability of each of the Court Musicians. Of the "tenorist," Johann Beethoven, he was told:

"His voice is very much worn, he has been long in the service, is in very poor circumstances, of fair deportment."

The investigator has this to say of the assistant organist:

"Ludwig van Beethoven, aged thirteen, born at Bonn, has served two years, no salary—but during the absence of the *Kapellmeister* Luchesy he played the organ; is of good capability, still young, of good and quiet deportment and poor."

The same report recommends the dismissal of Neefe on the grounds that "he is not particularly versed on the organ," and is "of the Calvinistic religion." The Elector seems to have known what to do. He kept Neefe, Calvinism and all, took a third from the father Beethoven's salary, and awarded it to the son.

Beethoven at the organ or pianoforte was apparently never at a loss. If there were any trouble it was in keeping him down to his text. The young organist was feeling his strength, was capable of

18

overstepping his office, and was tolerated rather than put in his place. He had a remedy for the tedium of constant duties as accompanist. He would embroider, let his fancy play upon the dull chord successions, until the singers needed all their alertness not to be thrown off. Wegeler tells how, in Holy Week of the same year, the boy offered, as a dare, to unseat the singer Ferdinand Heller in the *Lamentations of Jeremiah*. Beethoven took his place at the piano, and faithfully gave the singer his Gregorian line with his little finger. But meanwhile he rambled so adroitly, and with such smooth but unexpected modulations that Jeremiah missed his last cadence altogether. Luchesi, presiding, would have smiled if the dignity of his office had allowed him. "In the first access of rage, Heller entered a complaint against Beethoven with the Elector, who commanded a simpler accompaniment, although the spirited and occasionally waggish young prince was amused at the occurrence." So wrote Schindler, who had the story from Beethoven years later. Beethoven added that the Elector "reprimanded him very graciously and forbade such clever tricks in the future."

His obvious talent for composition interested his associates and led them to speculation. In 1781, he had composed a funeral cantata at the death of Cressener, English Ambassador to the Court, who had befriended the Beethoven family. *Kapellmeister* Luchesi was frankly puzzled by the score, but performed it. "At the first rehearsal," writes the 'cellist Mäurer, "there was great astonishment at the originality of the composition, but approval was divided; after a few rehearsals the approbation grew and the piece was performed with general applause."

In the spring of 1787, Beethoven, who had never been more than a few miles from Bonn save for a brief and unproductive trip with his mother down the Rhine into Holland for the purpose of concerts in 1781, journeyed alone to Vienna to visit and play for the great Mozart. This is one of those episodes in Beethoven's life which is lacking in evidence and heaped with conjecture. Did his father hope that Mozart would usher him into a career as boy virtuoso, at the age of sixteen, though passing for fourteen? Was the Elector behind it? Did Beethoven hope for instruction in piano or in composition, and how long did he intend to stay? Otto

Jahn, Mozart's biographer, gives a plausible report of the first meeting:

"Beethoven was taken to Mozart, and at his request played something for him which he, taking for granted that it was a show piece prepared for the occasion, praised in a rather cool manner. Beethoven, observing this, begged Mozart to give him a theme for improvisation. He always played admirably when excited, and now he was inspired too by the presence of the master whom he reverenced greatly; he played in such a style that Mozart, whose attention and interest grew more and more, finally went silently to some friends who were sitting in the adjoining room, and said, vivaciously, 'Keep your eyes on him; some day he will give the world something to talk about.' "

Mozart, if we are to believe this account, showed no enthusiasm in the presence of the boy, as if the stiff-backed young Rhinelander needed a little taking down. The far from first-hand story may be misleading; it is probable that the master's "cool manner" gave Beethoven an air of defiance, and incidentally put him on his mettle.

The visit to Vienna came to a premature and pathetic end after no more than two months. The father wrote in July, urging his son to hasten home as quickly as possible. His mother was sick; she lay helpless and was ailing rapidly. There were additional expenses and no way to meet them; Johann was pawning or selling the few pitiful household effects which would bring any price at all. Beethoven managed to reach Augsburg, but he lacked the coach fare to go farther. He was forced to borrow from a friend whom he had recently met there.

Back in Bonn after the anxious, wearisome journey, he found his mother frail and motionless on her bed. A baby girl a year old, named Margareth, lay in its cradle whimpering, too feeble to cry lustily. The infant looked as sick as its mother. The rooms were dirty and uncared for; there was no money in the house. The two boys were hanging idly about while the father, not knowing what to do, did nothing. Frau Beethoven was past worrying; drudgery, undernourishment and childbearing had conquered her at last. A daughter, Anna Maria, had been born in 1779, and had lived four days. A son, Franz Georg, had been born in 1781,

20

and had lived two years and a half. The new little sister was thus the seventh child and the fourth doomed not to survive infancy. Tuberculosis took the last convulsive breath from the body of Beethoven's mother on July 17, 1787. On November 25th, the baby was dead also.

This was the lugubrious ending of the pilgrimage of a hopeful country lad to the world's most important musical center, and the world's most important composer. He had had the chance neither to hear music, to meet people, nor to make himself known. Mozart probably had given him a few half-preoccupied lesson hours which could have led to nothing in particular. He had returned home to watch the death of the one person whom he had ever deeply and tenderly loved. He speaks of her passing in a letter to Dr. Schaden, his kind friend of Augsburg, who had seen him through on his return to Bonn, and whom he was compelled to ask for further time. The letter is one of the earliest from the hand of the composer which has survived. Its neatly formed script and spaced lines prove that Beethoven's later scrawling ways were a careless lapse and that he once knew better. This interesting letter has that combination of romantic effusiveness and obvious sincerity which is characteristic of the young Beethoven:

"I must tell you that from the time I left Augsburg my cheerfulness as well as my health began to decline; the nearer I came to my native city the more frequent were the letters from my father urging me to travel with all possible speed, as my mother was not in good health. I therefore hurried on as fast as I could, although myself far from well. My longing once more to see my dying mother overcame every obstacle and assisted me in surmounting the greatest difficulties. I found my mother still alive but in a most deplorable condition; her disease was tuberculosis, and about seven weeks ago, after much pain and suffering, she died. She was such a kind, loving mother to me, and my best friend. Ah, who was happier than I when I could still utter the sweet name 'mother' to one who could hear it? And to whom can I now utter that name? Only to the silent image which my imagination calls up."

Johann's discouragement took him more than ever to the tavern. He was little or no use at Court—at home only a cause for humiliation. Stephan von Breuning, a fellow pupil of

Beethoven, remembered how his friend had to rescue his carousing father from a police officer on a public street. And now Beethoven took his mother's place as the responsible head of the family. He found cheap quarters in the Wenzelgasse, moved the two boys and his father there, and hired a housekeeper to look after their needs.

Beethoven at nineteen had to submit a suit to the Elector that the quarterly payment might come directly to him. A decree under date of November 20, 1789, "graciously commanded" that the "suppliant" be paid half of his father's salary, 100 thalers, besides his own of like amount, together with the usual "three measures of grain for the support of his brothers." The father's services were to be "wholly dispensed with, and he was to withdraw to a village in the electorate." Since he continued to live with his sons, this last clause can be looked upon as a precautionary threat held over his head to keep him sober. Karl was occupied in taking music lessons with an eye to an appointment as Court Musician; Johann was apprenticed to the Court Apothecary. So, the burden of support lay upon Ludwig.

22

CHAPTER THREE

A NEW world was opened to Beethoven through the years that immediately followed the death of his mother. Ambitious, looking about him, he was fast becoming something more than an assistant Court Organist fulfilling a petty job. His improvisations, which were causing general wonderment, were an evidence of new growth, and, what was still more important, he was putting his musical thoughts more busily upon paper. He was still bound to his humdrum household and his three charges, but his life was elsewhere.

Beethoven was fortunate in his Elector. Maximilian Franz was rapidly building his Court into a true center of arts and letters. Having put his budget in order he began to expand musically. In the season of 1788, he assembled an opera company of permanent standing. Singers were chosen with care, players no less so. The reorganization shows how valuable Beethoven had made himself. He appears as organist in the *"Toxal"* (the chapel), and presently as a Court Pianist and virtuoso, while Neefe is assigned the duties of accompanying. Beethoven took a regular seat as viola in both the Theatre and Chamber Orchestras, of which the former numbered thirty-one players. He found good company among his fellow musicians in livery. The cousins Andreas and Bernhard Romberg, for example, whom the Elector had engaged at Münster, were master players of the violin and violoncello, respectively, and both composers. Anton Reicha, a nephew of Joseph Reicha, the concertmaster, was a flutist and a composer just Beethoven's age, and his companion through many seasons. Beethoven must have been stimulated by such friendships. He was in a strategic position to gain excellent knowledge of instruments and their possibilities. To know a flutist well is a long step toward knowing the flute. To play viola in a string group is to stir thoughts of what strings might do. The operas in which he performed offered the kind of experience which could have wedded Beethoven permanently to the theatre, had his nature and inclinations been different. The repertory included Paisiello, Martini, Cimarosa, Dittersdorf, Salieri, Grétry, even Gluck. Maximilian of course insisted upon Mozart, whom he had ardently patronized in Vienna, with the result that the German *Die Entführung aus dem Serail* came in the first season, followed in the second by the then new operas *Don Giovanni,* and *Le Nozze di Figaro,* each several times repeated. That prolonged communion with Mozart taught Beethoven, as he sat in his place at viola, far more than he ever could have learned in his brief lessons with the composer in person.

The operatic routine must have been useful to Beethoven when he wrote two cantatas, and to these he added another commissioned piece, a ballet. The *Ritter Ballet,* secretly ordered by Count Waldstein and passed by him as his own according to a custom not then considered too dishonorable, was called a success. These were Beethoven's only largely planned works at that time, save for fragmentary movements of a Piano Concerto in D and a Violin Concerto in C, which have not survived. Beethoven was evidently dissatisfied, for he refrained from further attempts at orchestral writing for a long while. He composed busily enough in smaller forms: piano pieces for his own use, most of them sets of variations, songs, chamber combinations. The Elector possessed an octet of wind players, took pride in them, and found good use for *"tafelmusik"* when entertaining. There is intermittent charm in these works; experimentation is within bounds. They served their purpose well, but went no further; their composer took no steps toward publication while he remained in Bonn. Some of the Bonn manuscripts were to be used in later works; some were subsequently to appear in print through the mercenary zeal of Beethoven's brother Karl.

The Elector, visiting near-by Courts, sometimes took his orchestra with him. Beethoven went along, attired like the rest in a periwig, wearing a red uniform with heavy gold braid. The young viola player was sometimes coaxed to the piano, particularly when there were musicians present who had not heard him. When the orchestra gave a concert in the princely chapel at Kirchberg, Beethoven, according to Junker, a musical amateur who was present, would not play in public, but was persuaded "to extemporize in private." Junker was delighted and could hardly say enough in praise of "the greatness of this amiable, light-hearted man." He had heard the Abbé Vogler at Mannheim, but placed Beethoven distinctly above him. "Bethofen, in addition to the execution, has greater clearness and weight of ideas, and more expressiveness—in short, he is more for the heart—equally great, therefore, as an *adagio* or an *allegro* player. Even the members of this remarkable orchestra are, without exception, his admirers, and all ears when he plays. Yet he is exceedingly modest and free from all pretension." It might be closer to the truth to say that he was shy and diffident before strangers, loath to be exhibited as a curiosity.

Four of the electoral musicians, Ries, Romberg, Simrock and Beethoven, journeyed to Aschaffenburg in November, 1791, to visit the Abbé Sterkel, a pianist of high reputation. Sterkel played for them in his characteristic elegant, transparent, finely shaded style—"somewhat ladylike," Ries afterward called it. Beethoven was astonished, for he had never heard this type of playing. He stood by the performer "at strained attention." He was then asked to play, but excused himself. The Abbé remarked that he was acquainted with Beethoven's variations on *"Venni Amore,"* but had doubted whether the composer himself could manage the most difficult of them. The ruse worked. Beethoven took his place at the piano, played as many of the variations as he could remember, and added new ones, imitating with much success the light, nuanced style of his host. The imitation was not entirely contemptuous. Beethoven was always alien to the finer graces of dexterity, but he had something to learn from them. He had had far too much his own way at Bonn, and had not so much as heard the best piano playing. He always regretted that he had not heard Mozart play.

Beethoven thrived on popularity and esteem, even while they emphasized an unsolved conflict in his nature. Human warmth and sympathy engendered music in him, and a gathering about

25

the piano stimulated him. But his thoughts, once started, needed solitude for their working out. He was sensitive to intrusion. Just now he needed a kind of friendship he had never had. He was leaving the last remnants of his small professionalism behind, emerging from his awkward, furtive ways as the artist of sensibility. His trend of thought was entirely at odds with his surroundings; his tendency to idealize must find elsewhere a responsive chord. The cultivation of his ardent moods in music sought a counterpart in his human relationships. He needed those who could awaken and broaden his understanding, and in so doing draw out his affection.

People who could do this were being drawn to Bonn by the reforms of Max Franz, particularly by the University into which the Palace had been transformed, and which must have its faculty. Beethoven's last five years at Bonn, the years from seventeen to twenty-two, were blessed with every warming influence which could induce his shy spirit to come out of its retreat, to expand, to explore, to sample. He was soon to leave behind the ways of the taciturn, ill-educated Court underling, and emerge as an artist literate enough to take his place in a company of distinction.

A social life which cultivated the mind and the arts had indeed sprung up in the little town. In certain houses there were musical evenings, recitations from the poets, metaphysical discussion. Beethoven was encouraged to drift into these houses. There was something about the boy that won him friends quickly. He was acquiring some of the social amenities, was even neat and careful in his dress. Beneath an occasional moodiness one could find an engaging dreamer, a talent erratic, unpredictable, but entirely fascinating. Beethoven soon found himself very much "taken up" by the well-to-do musical dilettanti and the intelligentsia of Bonn.

The pianist who would, when in the vein, give an impromptu tone characterization of each person present and then, forgetting the company, wander into exquisite melody, was of course welcome to any house. There was the Zehrgarten on the Market Place, a sort of boarding house for the titled, kept by the widow Koch, a gathering point for professors, for secretaries, councillors

26

and other Court dignitaries. Beethoven was often seen there, sometimes in the company of his friend Wegeler, who was then an enterprising student of medicine, and who years later was to write what he saw and remembered of Beethoven the social lion.

The family who had most influence upon Beethoven, who did most for him, were the von Breunings. Stephan von Breuning, one of the three sons of the house, he had known even before his mother died, for both had studied violin with Franz Ries. The two were very unequal; Stephan was four years younger, and no musical wizard in any case. Presently he entered the law college at Bonn. Beethoven soon came to know his two brothers and his sister. Christoph, the eldest, was also studying law. Lorenz, the youngest, known to all as "Lenz," was only ten years old in 1787, the year Beethoven found himself motherless. Eleonore, their affectionate and adored sister, whom they called "Lorchen," was then fifteen. Beethoven taught piano to both Lorchen and Lenz. The four children were from one to seven years younger than he. He could look upon them as a big brother might, as he looked upon Karl and Johann, with the difference that the young Breunings had been raised with every protection, insulated from the uglier realities of life and made adept in its gentler ways. Christoph, for example, wrote poetry, and Stephan was already trying his hand at verses. Even Lorchen could meet such an occasion as a birthday with an apt literary allusion.

These attainments were a reflection of the lively and witty tone set by the elders in that household, the mother in particular. The charm, intelligence and tact of Frau von Breuning radiates through all the spoken memories of those who were about her. In 1777, at the age of twenty-seven, she had lost her husband, Court Councillor Emmanuel von Breuning, in the Palace fire. Fires were not so quickly extinguished in those days. As this one raged into the second night, Hofrath von Breuning, seeing the documents of state threatened, rallied a group of volunteer townsmen to fight back the flames. A wall fell upon them and all perished. So, the girl widow was left with her four small children (Lorenz was born after the death of his father). Courageous, undismayed, she gave them all of her attention. She was never left alone, for her brother, Abraham von Kerich, Canon of the Archdeanery of Bonn, took her into his house, and presently her husband's brother Lorenz, Chancellor of the same institution, came to live with them. These two were fine scholars and genuinely spiritual men, more so than certain near-by ecclesiastics with higher titles.

Beethoven found both social and intellectual stimulation in this company. Wegeler has written: "Soon he was treated as one of the children of the family, spending in the house not only the greater part of his days, but also many nights. Here he felt that he was free, here he moved about without constraint; everything conspired to make him cheerful and develop his mind." Canon Lorenz read Homer and Plutarch with the young people in the original languages. Beethoven, listening with a translation close at hand, acquired his lifelong enthusiasm for those two authors.

So Beethoven's acquaintance with literature had its first real guidance. His growing up had been surrounded with a profusion of prose and poetry good and bad—mostly bad. He had worked among opera libretti of all sorts, and various specimens of the *Singspiel*. He had had access until his fourteenth year to spoken dramas of Schiller or Lessing, Shakespeare or Sheridan in German adaptation. Neefe, who was a widely cultured man, may well have led him to Klopstock or Herder as well as Sebastian Bach. Although Beethoven was contemptuous of the very word "Romantic," his music was sympathetic to the poetic ardors then current, and, strange to say, before he had consciously recognized this impulse, it illuminated his playing. He had not needed, would not need the laborious road of scholasticism, nor did he take the plodding paths of erudition, syntax or linguistic mastery. He had no use for them, for he possessed that strange power already long observable in the growing artist: an intuitive grasp which went directly to the heart of a subject. He caught at once the heroic splendor in Homer, the universal human penetration in Shakespeare, or the intoxicating individual self-assertion of Goethe. He took the powerful current of their thought and allowed it to lift and sweep his music.

It was Frau von Breuning who, in her subtle way, obviated the boy's feelings of awkwardness in dress, manners or learning. She befriended him, made him feel free and at home by including him with her flock as if he were her own. He was softened and tamed under her influence as he was always to be by appealing femininity. She was four years younger than his mother would have been. The protection of wealth must have kept her younger still in appearance.

The von Breunings had everything to give Beethoven that the lad needed. Sometimes he did not take his blessings easily. It is hard to step from the harsh crudities of a wretched condition of life into a family circle accustomed to ease, without a sense of disadvantage and unreasoning resentment. The fantastic contrast was a humiliation. Beethoven was still ignorant on many matters, and it hurt his pride to reveal to his own pupils blanks in his education. He was already, at seventeen, given to lone brooding, to outbursts of violent anger which he himself could not explain. The condition of poverty which had degraded his father and killed his mother while he looked on had done something dark and twisting to the soul of the sensitive child. In spite of himself he would turn woundingly on anyone, even those whom he most loved. When Frau von Breuning's children were as tactless as children are bound to be, the mother could in her gentle way ease the tension and soften the hurt. Beethoven would fling out with some rudeness in company, and succeeded only in injuring himself; often he would try to dodge giving lessons by sending some transparent excuse. The gentle lady alone could coax him to reason. She would never press a point beyond some light admonition. Her reprimand became a pleasure. It did not provoke obstinacy, and he usually yielded so as not to appear a boor. When, lost in his musical thought, he remained silent and unresponsive, she would shrug her shoulders and say, "He has his *raptus* again," an expression Beethoven never forgot. Beethoven remembered the von Breunings vividly and gratefully all his life. Schindler was reporting reminiscences of Beethoven's later years when he wrote: "He still called the members of this family his guardian angels of that time and remembered with pleasure the many reprimands which he had received from the lady of the house. 'She understood,' said he, 'how to keep the insects off the flowers.' " The "insects" could have been those shallow and noisy

29

individuals who at a musical evening affect great emotional understanding, and push themselves forward to match the true coin of sensibility with the false. He could well have remembered his dear lady as shielding him from the slights of the over-riding rich folk, or as a refuge for confidences when his touchiness kept all others at a distance.

The constant visitors at the Breuning mansion brought Beethoven, probably for the first time, in contact with young girlhood. He succumbed quickly enough to their charms, nor did he lose time in shy and speechless adoration. He found ways of declaring himself, musically and otherwise, which had quicker effect than the more conventional approach of handsomer suitors. "There was never a time," says Wegeler, who may once have envied his successes, "when Beethoven was not in love, and that in the highest degree. His passion for the Fräuleins d'Honrath and Westerholt fell in his transition period from youth to manhood, and left as fleeting an impression upon him as upon the beauties themselves. In Vienna, at all events so long as I lived there, Beethoven was always in love and occasionally made a conquest which would have been very difficult if not impossible for many an Adonis."

The Fräulein d'Honrath whom Wegeler mentions was Jeannette, the companion of Eleonore, who would journey from Cologne to spend weeks with the von Breunings. "She was beautiful," adds Wegeler, "vivacious, blonde, of good education and amiable disposition; she enjoyed music greatly, and possessed an agreeable voice." Beethoven, of course, was often on hand when Jeannette was there. Before her return to Cologne she would sing him a pathetic little song to the effect that their coming separation was "more than her heart could bear," and leave him wondering how much she meant. Her heart was consoled and presently won by an army captain in Cologne. Fräulein Maria von Westerholt was Beethoven's piano pupil, the daughter of a Court *Geheimrath*. She is pictured with long, dark curls resting upon her bosom. The passion of Beethoven for Maria was "violent," says Romberg. She married a Baron in 1790. Babette Koch, one of the prettiest and most sought girls in Bonn, was the daughter

30

of the intellectual landlady, and so came under Beethoven's favorable eye. He seems to have survived her charms as well and without too much difficulty.

A romance with Eleonore would have been the most natural thing in the world. The friendship between the teacher and pupil with only two years between them was deep enough to bring forth tender expressions of sentiment on both sides. But the big-brotherly basis seems never to have been lost sight of. Rhymed verses, prettily turned, on his twentieth birthday, are signed "Your true friend and pupil." The last couplet begs for his "for-bearance and patience," as if their lessons had not always been of the smoothest. Before Beethoven left Bonn (and the von Breuning household) forever, a quarrel sprang up between him and Lorchen, and went to such lengths that he broke with the family. The subject of it will doubtless never be known. There was a reconciliation, brought about probably by her mother, and Lorchen sent him a neckcloth as a peace offering. Beethoven, overcome with remorse, dedicated a set of variations to her and wrote:

"The neckcloth worked with your own hand came to me as a great surprise. It awoke in me feelings of sadness to mingle with my pleasure in the gift. It reminded me of former times; also your magnanimous behavior filled me with shame. In truth, I did not think that you still considered me worthy of your remembrance. Oh! if only you could have seen how this incident affected me yesterday you certainly would not accuse me of exaggeration, if I now say to you that your token of remembrance caused me to weep and feel very sad. I entreat you, however little I deserve faith in your eyes, to believe, my friend (let me continue always to call you so), that I have deeply suffered and still suffer, through the loss of your friendship. Never shall I forget you and your dear mother. Your kindness was so great that it will be long before I can make good my loss. I know what I have forfeited, and what you were to me."

But the reconciliation was not complete. When Beethoven saw the von Breunings, including Lorchen, in Vienna, there was a constraint between them. We recognize the Beethoven we are later to know, harboring imagined grievances, nursing them out

31

of all proportion, finding his sense of obligation suddenly unbearable, saying rude things that cannot be unsaid, realizing, too late, that his words have been his unpardonable response to a true and loyal friendship. Through the first year in Vienna a smoldering pride, persistently justifying itself, held him back. Then he saw clearly his own error, realized his outrageous ingratitude to these good people, in particular Lorchen, his dear and patient friend, and he poured out his heart in a rush of repentance. The letter is long. The opening pages run as follows:

Vienna, November 2, 1795.

Honored Eleonore, my dearest friend,

I shall soon have been in this capital a whole year, yet only now do you receive a letter from me, but you were certainly constantly in my thoughts. Frequently, indeed, did I hold converse with you and your dear family, but, for the most part, not with the tranquillity of mind which I should have liked. Then it was that the fatal quarrel hovered before me, and my former behavior appeared to me so abominable. But the past cannot be undone, and what would I not give if I could blot out of my life my former conduct so dishonoring to me, so contrary to my character. Many circumstances indeed kept us at a distance from each other, and, as I presume, it was especially the insinuations resulting from conversations on either side which prevented all reconciliation. Each of us believed that he was convinced of the truth of what he said, and yet it was mere anger, and we were both deceived. Your good and noble character is indeed a guarantee that I have long since been forgiven.

The adolescent Beethoven at Bonn did not lack ranking friends. The Elector himself does not seem to have gone out of his way to favor his talented subject with any special largesse or attention. Others of noble blood more than atoned for any listlessness on his part, and there was plentiful acclaim around him as the Court Pianist propounded a concerto of his own. Count Ferdinand Ernst Gabriel Waldstein, of Austrian blood than which there was none rarer, a close companion of the Elector, was not to be outdone in his championship of Beethoven. It was through no fault of the Count that the Elector did not more readily extend a gracious hand, unless it was from weariness at having the lad's praises poured into his ear. Waldstein came to

Bonn to be made Knight of the Teutonic Order, and at the age of twenty-four received his accolade from its *Hochmeister,* the Elector himself, on June 17, 1788. In the intervals of fulfillment of this illustrious office, he sent a piano to the dingy lodgings in the Wenzelgasse, and betook his high-born self there continually to listen to Beethoven play. Waldstein did all that he could to guide him; he put money in his way, sparing his friend's feelings by making it seem to come from the Elector. Again we may turn to Wegeler, who watched the acquaintance grow and could not speak of it too strongly: "It is due to Count Waldstein that the first sproutings of Beethoven's genius were not nipped; so we may thank this Maecenas for Beethoven's later fame."

Very probably it was Count Waldstein who first urged Beethoven to go to Vienna in 1792 and, since Mozart had died the year before, submit himself to the great Haydn for instruction. He may well have figured that the eaglet needed a broader expanse than a Rhine town for the spreading of his wings. He may also have prevailed upon the Elector to give Beethoven leave of absence with continuation of salary, so that he would not proceed to starve in great, impersonal Vienna. There was good reason to believe that Haydn perceived a striking talent in Beethoven. When Haydn passed through Bonn on Christmas day, 1790, accompanied by his impresario, Johann Peter Salomon, and bound for London, the hopeful but obscure Beethoven may or may not have been introduced to him. On his return from London at the expiration of the season, Haydn passed the same way, and was entertained at Godesberg by the Electoral orchestra. Beethoven then laid before him a cantata, which he is said to have warmly commended. Whatever the degree of warmth, Haydn, for a consideration, was ready to give the young man lessons. Beethoven certainly felt the need of learning a great deal more about his art. His venture was looked upon as no more than an absence on leave, an opportunity to study before venturing forth as a touring pianist. There was no livelihood in composition.

Count Waldstein showed a clearer understanding; indeed, he was remarkably prophetic for an amateur. The album presented to Beethoven by his friends on the eve of his departure contained an inscription which remains arresting, even when one has discounted the rosiness of sentiments born at such moments:

Dear Beethoven! You are going to Vienna in fulfillment of your long frustrated wishes. The Genius of Mozart is mourning and weeping over the death of her pupil. She found a refuge but no occupation with the inexhaustible Haydn; through him she wishes to form a union with another. With the help of assiduous labor you shall receive Mozart's spirit from Haydn's hands.

Your true friend

Waldstein

Bonn, October 29, 1792

Such high-flown thoughts would not have occurred to others at all. Beethoven alone must often have dreamed them, to the point of believing them. Vienna was still to require a good deal of convincing.

CHAPTER FOUR

At the moment when Beethoven started off on his journey, forces unleashed in France, forces ill-disposed toward the nobility, were spreading Rhinewards. The citizen army was on the move. Many of the proscribed class had already made their retreat, and the Elector of Cologne was one of them. The Electoral treasury had been removed to Düsseldorf, where it would be more secure against looting. Beethoven, no doubt, was far more intent upon the momentous step he was taking than upon the implications of social upheaval. Only at Coblenz was he forcibly reminded of hazardous conditions. The Rhine town was occupied by Hessian troops, anticipating the French advance. Beethoven entered this expense item in his memorandum book: *"Trinkgeld* at Coblentz because the fellow drove like the devil right through the Hessian army, at the risk of a cudgeling—one small thaler." Crossing to Ehrenbreitstein, the town where his mother had been born, he looked upon his beloved river for the last time. Traveling by day and night coach, crossing Bavaria through Nürnberg, reaching the Austrian border at Passau, the Danube at Limburg, he was probably the greater part of a week on his journey to Vienna.

The brave and elegant city was a dazzling vision to a citizen of Bonn. The princely palaces, the Imperial Library and University buildings, glittering white, were far more splendid than anything along the Rhine, and the fair spire of St. Stephen's Cathedral, dominating everything, was a marvel, seeming almost as close to heaven as the Cathedral at Cologne. Beethoven took an economical lodging in the house of bookprinter Strauss in the Alser suburb, as if making a cautious approach upon the old fortressed town, with its ramparts and bastions in places fifty feet high. He gazed upon Vienna across the Glacis, an encircling meadowland which, with paths and lanes of trees, gave breathing space to the Viennese, offering a leisurely promenade, or an easy three-mile circuit for a horseback rider. Mingling with fashion and giving the whole scene an agreeably rural air were farmer's carts creaking under their loads. If one passed beyond the low outer wall which enclosed the *Vorstädten,* the ring of suburbs, one found the open pastures and the hillside vineyards of the Danube valley, suggestive of the Rhine valley but less abundant.

Beethoven's first concern was the town and what it might hold for him. He hired a piano, bought a writing desk, firewood and coffee (so the account book shows), and fitted himself out for his first calls with a coat, wig, shoes and silk stockings. He was far better equipped to make his entrée than he had been five years before, for he was now less obscure than other young musicians who were forever gravitating from the provinces toward the great center of musical life. No longer shy and tongue-tied, he had learned at twenty-two to walk into a noble house with assurance, and play his way into attention and favor. He could hardly have been without credentials. Count Waldstein at least must have given him an introduction to Viennese friends, and there were those who had visited the Court at Bonn and must have carried back word of the young extemporizer. The commendation he had extracted from Haydn was in itself an introduction. At any rate, Beethoven did not have, as before, to walk the streets unnoticed, creep back to his lodgings and count his dwindling *groschen.*

The boy was not prepossessing to the eye, with his short stature, his coat and breeches of drab cloth, and his ruddy pock-marked features. The high neckcloth then in vogue gave him a stiff, almost defiant air. He conceded in part to fashion, but not to rank; he apologized to none for his cheap woolens and his thick Rhenish speech, and so was looked upon as cocksure for his age and station. His head of hair, black, shaggy and unconfined, was as a standing reproach to the slick sheen of a wig. A challenging solemnity in a boy of twenty-two sometimes raises a smile. In this one there was a smoldering intensity which commanded respect. The Court Pianist whom an Elector had sent across two countries to Haydn was accepted on his face value.

He was not the sort who would be kept indefinitely in an ante-room, awaiting the pleasure of a Somebody. The spell of his powers as pianist was instantaneous. The doors of inaccessible houses were swung back for him by lackeys in attendance.

In the same letter which Beethoven wrote to Lorchen from Vienna after a year there, he mentioned the remote possibility of his return, and added: "You will then find your friend a more cheerful being, for whom time and his better fortune have smoothed down the furrows of a terrible past."

What Beethoven told Lorchen with a characteristic touch of romantic floridity is confirmed by every available detail of his life. A "better fortune" did indeed smile upon Beethoven in Vienna, as if to atone for the bitterness of his childhood. Fortune now went out of her way to heap upon him the largest measure of happiness possible to an artist whose sensitive nature bears permanent marks of neglect and abuse. Fits of bad temper were exceptional in the first Vienna years, so his friends report. He was kept busy going from house to house where music was made, measuring his strength with the strength of others, and swaying people to his will. He was finding what his heart desired. The tragedy, the suffering which are thought of as the constant under-current of his life were nowhere in evidence.

Wegeler arrived in Vienna in 1794, having fled there before the French army which had by then swept down the Rhine valley and abolished its electorates forever. He was surprised at the condition of Beethoven. This friend, whom he might have expected to find stranded by the loss of his quarterly payments from Bonn, was standing firmly upon his own feet; he was being asked everywhere; and he had money in his pocket. He was no longer weighed down by his family. Within a month of his arrival in Vienna his father had died (in November, 1792). The only written comment on the event that has come down to us is the Elector's remark in a letter that the liquor revenues would suffer by his absence. Karl Kasper and Johann followed their brother to Vienna, but Wegeler did not find them hanging upon his neck, living with him in some grubby alley, as they had in Bonn. On the contrary, Johann had set himself up as apothecary; Karl was doing his best to walk in his brother's footsteps as musician; and

37

Ludwig was faring very well indeed. Looking him up, Wegeler found him dressed in the fashion, consorting with the best. He was even known to have trotted on horseback down the Prater, although few had actually seen him in this strange situation. He was living, almost in state, in the house of Prince Karl Lichnowsky, a young musical enthusiast.

The Prince could play both the violin and the piano; with his brother Moritz, he had been a pupil of Mozart. His charming wife, too, was a pianist, as "noble" pianists went. She was Marie Christine, two years younger than Beethoven, one of the "three graces," so called, the daughters of Count Franz Josef von Thun. Music was Prince Karl's hobby, almost his life, and he lavished money on it in a way which gave the more prudent Marie Christine good cause to be anxious for the family fortune. Music parties large and small happened daily at the Lichnowskys'. The best musicians in Vienna, without exception, were to be found there at one time or another. A principal attraction was the youthful but talented quartet which he had gathered together to perform every Friday morning. Ignaz Schuppanzigh, the first violin, was a stout young man of sixteen when, in 1792, Beethoven first made the acquaintance of the group. Schuppanzigh was an excellent player, and, in spite of his weight, conducted the Augarten concerts for a season with success. Louis Sina, the second violin, Franz Weiss, the viola, and Nicholas Kraft, the violoncello, were about the same age or younger, the latter only fourteen. Sometimes the Prince sat in at second violin, sometimes Zmeskall took the place of Kraft, and sometimes Kraft's father obliged. Anton Kraft was the illustrious 'cellist lately at Esterház with Haydn. With such players always at hand, a fount for the baptism of any quartet, Beethoven was looked to expectantly. But he was wary of the form, and content to listen and mark. Trios, or duo sonatas, the piano part played by himself, must suffice.

Wegeler found Beethoven an important part of the Lichnowsky household. The Lichnowskys were accustomed to dine at four. Beethoven, whose tastes did not run to formal dress or fixed hours, would wander off to a tavern to buy his own meals. There was a clash when the Prince and his guest called for the man-servant at the same moment. Beethoven made some sharp remark, whereupon Lichnowsky, with a bow, ordered the servant always to answer Beethoven's summons first. Beethoven, on his dignity, engaged a servant of his own. When the Prince offered him his horse to ride, Beethoven felt patronized and again hired one of his own. He was affluent enough to nurse his pride in these ways. He could even have his own summer quarters when his wealthy friends moved to theirs.

The Lichnowskys' house was one of many where Beethoven was made quite at home. There was the establishment of Prince Joseph Kinsky, later director of the *Theater-auf-der-Wien,* who was to become his loyal supporter; the wealthy Esterházys, Count Franz in particular, who made known the choral music of Handel, Pergolesi and Emanuel Bach; Court Councillor von Kees, who gave concerts at his house twice a week. Haydn, Mozart, Dittersdorf, in their time had gathered there to hear their own symphonies. But the most symphonically minded of the music patrons was the Baron Gottfried van Swieten, son of the physician to the late Empress Theresa. He had even composed twelve symphonies of his own which were, according to an aside once caught from the lips of Haydn, "as stiff as himself." When at last Beethoven came to the point of writing a symphony, the Baron was to receive the dedication.

Given to logic and order, the Baron was addicted to music in the severe style. "My chief comforters are Handel and the Bachs," he wrote, "when I am discouraged by fresh proofs of the degeneracy of the art." He had organized Sunday morning concerts when he was the Austrian Ambassador at Berlin in the seventies, and upheld artistic morals by confining the programmes for the most part to Handel and Bach. Mozart was obliging enough to write strict fugues for these concerts. His purse-tight patron repaid him none too well upon his death by giving him a pauper's funeral at eleven florins, thirty-six kronen. The dictatorial Baron carried his library of Handel and Bach to Vienna, and treated his guests to organ fugues which they neither knew nor liked. However that might be, he exacted the closest attention. He sat always in the first row, and at any sign of whispering during the performance rose slowly, stood in all the ponderous authority of his wig and double chin, gazed long and pointedly at the disturbers, and slowly sat down again. The overbearing ways of van Swieten might have struck sparks from Beethoven, had he not happened to fall in with them. Audience discipline, Bach fugues and an enormous musical voracity were all to Beethoven's taste. "Come at half past eight," wrote the *Freiherr* in a note of invitation, "with your nightcap in your bag." And he made his meaning clear by asking Beethoven, after a long musical evening, to give the company a half dozen preludes and fugues from *The Well-Tempered Clavichord* as a final "blessing." Beethoven then profited by what Neefe had taught him in the Bonn days.

Beethoven's friends of van Swieten's generation, even the less hidebound of them, were often unsympathetic to Beethoven's innovations, and shook their heads over his perverse and freakish ways. He marred his most beautiful thoughts, so they held, by meaningless interpolations, sudden, extraneous modulations, palpable errors of judgment. The younger men, such as Moritz Lichnowsky, Karl Amenda, Prince Lobkowitz, were far more receptive. Lobkowitz and Beethoven fought and made up with the readiness of intimate friends. This idealistic amateur was impulsive in the way that Lichnowsky was, pouring his money into the giving of music.

The prodigious amount of music, public and private, which took place in that extraordinary capital offered ideal opportunities to a young man bent upon experience. Opera was plentiful, particularly opera of the gay variety. Public concerts were scarce, but private ones were always happening somewhere; they were the rage of society. Every large house kept some sort of musical establishment. If a valet knew how to fiddle on the side, or if a footman could fill in with a bassoon, a dozen positions were open to him. A wealthy nobleman boasting an orchestra of thirty or so need only augment it from other houses, and an oratorio or a symphony concert would result. If he could manage to keep no more than eight musicians in his employ, he could at least provide a wind octet for dinner music; if only four or three, he had a quartet or a trio. The result was a great demand for music in small combinations. There was less call for symphonic music.

Symphonies were played as chamber music, a treatment favored
by the intimacy of the gatherings and the size of the private
theatres and ballrooms. Players were never lacking. Nobles from
smaller centers would flock to Vienna for the height of the winter
season, often bringing their musical retinue with them. There
were enough to fit out several orchestras. Instrumental music
flourished nowhere in Europe as it did in Vienna—not in Paris,
not in Mannheim, not in London. The abundant, facile and ever-
stimulating symphonies and quartets of Mozart and Haydn were
largely responsible for this condition, but it must also be said that
Vienna first drew both composers to its bosom, and nurtured their
ambition. The Viennese aristocracy may have had an imperfect
idea of the importance of the music they were hearing, but at
least they insisted upon hearing it. The Vienna of 1792 could still
set us an example in its honest appetite for quartets, trios or
sonatas.

Certain anecdotes are often—too often—told to illustrate
Beethoven's contempt for the aristocracy as a class by his open
defiance of them. The picture is quite false. Beethoven may have
said in effect to Lichnowsky: "You are only a Prince, I am
Beethoven." If he did, he was in one of his passing rages which
were brought on by any slight, imagined or otherwise, upon his
position as an artist. At such times he was violently scathing
about his opponent's pretensions to importance, whoever he
might be. Beethoven's social theories, if he really had any, were
far from specific. He talked against tyranny, but his tyrants were
the ruling royalty or the bringers of war—certainly not the
aristocracy as a class. His generalized pronouncements were always prompted by his personal advantage or the deprivation of
the moment, and from this point of view the service to him of
his aristocratic entourage was beyond counting. His Elector had
given him livelihood, experience, freedom sufficient for development. The Breunings and Waldstein had awakened the artist and
sent him on his way. His circle of aristocrats in Vienna had done
even more. They provided his main support by fees, subscrip-
tions and outright contributions, in which Lichnowsky led the
way with an annuity of 600 florins. What was equally important
they became his most understanding audiences, his most loyal

41

friends. He accepted their bounty, as he had that of his Elector, as a matter of course, and where custom dictated a formal deference, he complied as a matter of course, just as he had from childhood. He was answerable to them by a bond stronger than official requirement, and that was his obligation of honor. If he had responded with consistent hostility it would have been an unpardonable breach of friendship. Nothing could have been farther from his thoughts.

It will be seen how intimately these people figured in his life and growth. Their respect for him and his music eventually raised the social status of his profession; it could not have been otherwise. But Beethoven did not have to exact social recognition in Vienna. He found there an already established respect for music, which the genius of Mozart and of Haydn had prepared. The fostering of music was more than a fashion, more than a craze. It was a religion, a point of honor. Music was the first accomplishment of gentlefolk, and many of them played or sang. Houses vied with each other to give elaborate concerts, whatever the cost. The young pianist from Bonn did not need to show published music or even his manuscripts as credentials. What he could do at the piano was enough. The musical idealism of Vienna sensed the extraordinary in him, took him on faith, and quietly put up with the tantrums and gaucheries they were by no means obliged to endure. Soon he was surrounded with adoration. He was found acceptable in every way—short of marriage with one's daughter. All things were coming in Beethoven's direction. He heard music in abundance; he played, composed and taught. Beethoven derived far more from the gentry of Vienna than their money. Needing a bolstering faith, as all creators do, he accepted their liberal applause. That sweet sound nourished a self-esteem which in him was not a weakening conceit, but a keen pride of purpose.

CHAPTER FIVE

BEETHOVEN, during his first three years in Vienna, alternated his successes as pianist and his engagements as teacher with hours as pupil in counterpoint, patiently fulfilling his assignments of copybook exercises. His main purpose in going to Vienna should not be lost sight of. Beethoven never lost sight of it; he always knew where his music could be improved and spared no pains to improve it. If he expected, as Count Waldstein had just expressed it, in some mysterious way "to receive the spirit of Mozart from Haydn's hands" through sessions with paper and pen, he was soon to be disappointed. An aged composer, famous, preoccupied, graced with a musical idiosyncrasy which was the ultimate point of many years of ripening—such a composer could be of little direct help to a young one who was already using that slowly achieved style as a springboard to new and untried musical thoughts.

What Beethoven had from Haydn by carrying further what Haydn had begun—the introductions which he deepened from ceremonious portals into dreamy preludings, the slow movements which he pushed to emotional liberation, the swift rondos where he transformed the play of wit into the thrust of daring—these inheritances, for so they were, were never transmitted by the going over of technical or textual points. The cue that Beethoven picked was of the mood and not the letter; it was that tentative quality in Haydn's last symphonies and quartets which reaches beyond engaging gravity or sparkle to the threshold of open fervor. Beethoven's indebtedness was so deep that, listening to Haydn, one often has a deceptive sense of prophecy. That kind of communication can be aided by friendship if it is based on complete artistic congeniality. Such a friendship Mozart and

43

Haydn knew—Haydn and Beethoven did not, nor was that elusive spark conveyed by copy-book agonies.

Beethoven did not go to Haydn to learn how to compose. He was then already a composer, a skilled and finished one. He had brought many manuscripts with him from Bonn, music that would have here and there unsettled Haydn's cosmos and made him peevish. But Beethoven kept his sketches closely to himself. He knew that his expressive powers would be increased by increased flexibility in his inner voices. He wanted to be put through the paces of composition and counterpoint from first to last. Haydn was, needless to say, a poor choice for this purpose. The great and venerated composer was far less interested in teaching than in his own career. Beethoven was not a disciple to whom he could hand down a master's tradition, nor was Haydn's subtle skill deliberately communicable. He had long left behind conscious attention to rules; as for Beethoven, he had grown beyond rules, but still felt the need of them, because he wanted double certainty in his equipment. Beethoven always flouted rules, recognizing no law but the contingency of the moment. Now he was ready to submit to pedantry with entire meekness, and to subject himself to elementary scrutiny, a difficult thing to do when the habits of practice are laid. The ordeal would call upon his enormous store of patience and pertinacity.

Hardly had the pupil arrived in Vienna when Haydn began to receive him for lessons in his rooms. He soon put him to work on simple exercises in counterpoint based on plain chants in the old church modes. Before that, if the guesses of Nottebohm are right, he may even have taken him through the principles of harmony. After six months there were signs of trouble. Things were progressing too slowly; Haydn, busy and important, glanced over Beethoven's exercises and did not trouble to correct them. Beethoven seems to have had enough discretion not to make a scene or cause a break. He confided in van Swieten, who was concerned for him, but helpless to do anything about Haydn. Beethoven persuaded a friend to take him to the house of Johann Schenck, who was an expert on the subject. The composer extemporized in the way he could when his future was at stake, and

Schenck was completely astounded, as he relates in his autobiography:

> "The first thing that I did the next day was to visit the still unknown artist who had so brilliantly disclosed his mastery. On his writing desk I found a few passages from his first lesson in counterpoint. A cursory glance made it clear that, brief as it was, there were mistakes in every part."

Haydn, having returned, glory-laden, from London, was at the moment deep in the composition of symphonies for a second visit, and Beethoven, all impatience, was left with nothing to do. Schenck, realizing the boy's deficiencies, gave him Fux to work upon, and admiration deepened into affection. "I was now eager to become the helper of the zealous student." For the sake of peace and concord among professionals, he first made Beethoven promise to keep the secret close that Haydn was being doubled and amended. Schenck was to correct Beethoven's exercises; then Beethoven was to write them out in his own hand and submit them to Haydn. This went on for the larger part of a year, until it became apparent to Beethoven that Schenck's usefulness to him had passed. Haydn, departing for London in January, 1794, left his pupil in the hands of the famous pedant Johann Georg Albrechtsberger. Albrechtsberger was apparently as conscientious and painstaking as Haydn had been inattentive. He put his pupil once more through the elementary requirements of counterpoint, as if he had not just been through them. Albrechtsberger started him with many exercises on two-part plain chants, progressed through strict and free writing, imitation, fugue in increasing parts. Fugue possibilities were not deeply plumbed in the year and more of lessons. The lion who could shake his mane and roar, musically speaking, when the occasion warranted, was extraordinarily pliant before the stern and arbitrary logician who hedged in his pupil with all the narrow prohibitions of Catholic ritual tradition. Beethoven did what he was told, "creating musical skeletons," as if he were not already far more adept at voice leading than his teacher. He must have benefited by this self-imposed course in tonal calisthenics; otherwise he would not have held to it. Ries, who knew the teachers of Beethoven,

was told that this pupil was often intractable and self-willed, taking nothing on faith and insisting upon arriving of his own accord, often laboriously, at rules laid down by tradition.

Even that which was concocted in the driest possible spirit, the imagination of Beethoven was disposed to enliven, and turn into the forms of beauty. The contrapuntists set forth the super-annuated Church modes as subject matter simply because the forgotten ancients had used them. They set up fugal problems because they were tough and knotty; conquering them, one became a master through desperation. Beethoven did not despair. He welcomed the play of ingenuity. Posing and solving a canon was always to be a diversion for him. Intent upon the process of subtle strengthening, he was not for the time being tempted to exhibit himself in full fugal involutions. At the end of his career the fugue form, implanted long since, was to emerge in great structural strength. Modal church writing, in Beethoven's time utterly archaic so far as the world was concerned, was later to color his musical thinking.

There is no evidence that Beethoven submitted to Albrechts-berger anything more serious than exercises for correction or approval. With Salieri it was different. The Imperial *Kapell-meister,* no longer a conductor at the Opera, but still called upon as a composer, respected for the expertness and experience of many years, was sought by Beethoven for advice on vocal writing, and the setting of Italian texts in particular. The lessons were gratis. Beethoven probably wanted further guidance in the ways of opera, despite the many points his quick ear must have picked up at Bonn. He went laboriously through examples of expression and accent in declamation—the matching of music and text. He wrote Italian arias, such as were then found useful at concerts, and brought them to Salieri for criticism.

Haydn was consulted on Beethoven's instrumental prowess by being asked to hear the three Trios, the destined Opus 1, at their first trial at Prince Lichnowsky's house, in 1793. The old man could scarcely have been shown the sketches before this moment, for when the Trios were played he listened with interest as to something unfamiliar, while the company watched to see how each would affect him. Ferdinand Ries, the son of Franz, and later the pupil of Beethoven, was told of the *soirée* by his master, and so reported it in his own words:

"Most of the artists and music lovers were invited, especially Haydn, for whose opinion all were eager. The Trios were played, and at once commanded extraordinary attention. Haydn also said many pretty things about them, but advised Beethoven not to publish the third, in C minor. This astonished Beethoven, inasmuch as he considered the third the best of the Trios, as it is still the one which gives the greatest pleasure and makes the greatest effect. Consequently, Haydn's remark left a bad impression on Beethoven, and led him to think that Haydn was envious, jealous and ill-disposed toward him. I confess that when Beethoven told me of this I gave it little credence. I therefore took occasion to ask Haydn himself about it. His answer confirmed Beethoven's statement; he said he had not believed that this Trio would so quickly and easily be understood and so favorably received by the public."

If jealousy did not color Haydn's opinion, there was always something grudging about his admiration. The free conception, a certain aggressiveness, were probably both distasteful and upsetting to his idea of where a reasonable trio should draw the line. Haydn, experimental on his own account, could be hidebound when the innovations of another were in question. Beethoven on his part had far more respect for Haydn's music than gratitude for his teaching. When Haydn asked that Beethoven's name be designated on the printed score as "pupil of Haydn," Beethoven refused, and let it be known, widely enough to reach Haydn's ears, that "although he had had some instruction from Haydn, he had never learned anything from him" (Ries), a remark especially correct when applied to the three Trios, Op. 1. Beethoven kept his manuscripts two years longer before publishing them. It would be interesting to know whether Haydn's advice found its way into the revision. The first three Pianoforte Sonatas came out a year later as his Opus 2, this time with a dedication to Haydn. Haydn's annoyance at the overriding ways of Beethoven may have kept him from fulfilling his expressed intention of taking him to London, where he could have pushed him forward as a pianist. The advantage would have been mutual, as Haydn knew, for Haydn saw clearly enough that there was a future in this difficult young man. A friend named Fischenich had word from him from Bonn on the subject in 1793, and so reported, probably apropos of Beethoven's Trios, Op. 1: "Haydn has written here that he would soon put him at grand operas, and soon be obliged to quit composing!" There was always the note of irony in Haydn's praise.

The old man, correct and elegant, and the young one, parading an entire lack of these qualities, could not meet in a salon without a slight aggravation on both sides. Fräulein von Kissow, a young and talented pianist, used to go to the Lichnowskys' to play and was struck by the incongruous appearance of Beethoven in that sumptuous setting: "His attire was very ordinary and far removed from the choiceness customary in those days, and particularly in our circles. Besides, he spoke in a pronounced dialect and had a rather common way of expressing himself. Indeed, his entire deportment showed no signs of exterior polish; on the contrary, he was quite unmannerly." Equally vivid in her memory was the picture of the two teachers of Beethoven: "I still remember distinctly how both Haydn and Salieri sat on a sofa on one side of the little music-room, both most carefully dressed in the old-fashioned style, with bagwig, shoes and silk stockings, while Beethoven used to appear even here in the freer ultra-Rhenish garb, almost carelessly dressed." One can picture the master and pupil, each bristling at the ways of the other. Beethoven's lively glance seems to scorn the pretentious elegance which has fashioned itself out of origins quite as humble as his own. Haydn is the more annoyed that the young man's arrogance is accepted on all sides without a murmur. The wry smile takes a sarcastic twist. His remarks become barbed. "Our great Mogul," he called Beethoven behind his back.

The Vienna which first knew Beethoven looked upon him as an extraordinary pianist rather than as a composer. It was perfectly usual for pianists to carry about with them useful concertos, sonatas or trios of their own, while interest remained centered upon the performer. Beethoven long so used his Concerto in B-flat, but this, the first orchestral piece which he showed about, never satisfied him, even when, after much revision, he
48

published it in 1801. It then appeared as his Second, for he had meanwhile published his C major Concerto. The C major Concerto, thus really the second in order of composition, was, from his initial performance of it in Prague in 1798, in the hands of its maker quite irresistible. He also delayed the publication of his Third Concerto in order that he might have exclusive use of it. He is described by Ries as seated at his piano before an intent audience, peering closely through iron spectacles at the patchy manuscript of his C minor Concerto, while Ries turns the pages. In reality he is only bending his head down to hear better. He is scarcely looking at the score, for the majority of the notes are not even written in. Ries sits gazing at the scrawled pages in bewilderment and must watch for the composer's nod, while the composer is secretly amused. Meanwhile each passage comes forth in striking brilliance and clarity. There is no improvisation here. Each note is in its place as it will be written and printed.

It was Beethoven's career as pianist that engrossed him until then, and bore more promise of profit. He talked of a concert tour, and attempted one in 1796, but, so far as is known, played in only two cities. Prague received him cordially, and he could take a boastful tone in a letter to his brother Johann: "I am getting on well—very well. My art wins for me friends and respect; what more do I want? This time, too, I shall earn considerable money. I shall remain here a few weeks more, and then go to Dresden, Leipzig, and Berlin."

He reached Berlin, but there are no traces of his having visited Saxony. He played at the Prussian Court more than once. Since Friedrich Wilhelm II was a 'cellist, Beethoven brought his two violoncello sonatas composed for the purpose, and to be published as Opus 5. He played them with Duport, His Majesty's 'cellist. His Majesty sent the composer a gold snuffbox filled with *louis d'or*.

Czerny testifies to the brilliance of Beethoven's playing: "Nobody equaled him in the rapidity of his scales, double trills, skips, etc., not even Hummel. His bearing while playing was masterfully quiet, noble and beautiful, without the slightest grimace (he only bent forward low as his deafness grew upon him); his fingers were very powerful, not long, and broadened at the tips by much

49

playing, for he told me very often indeed that he generally had to practice until after midnight in his youth."

He dominated the field in his first Vienna years, but not without disputing it. Joseph Wölffl of Salzburg, once a violin prodigy, then a brilliant and popular pianist of twenty-six, came to Vienna in 1799, and was at once set beside Beethoven, according to the custom of the time, for comparison. Ignatz von Seyfried, young conductor in Schikaneder's theatre *Auf der Wieden,* witnessed some of these contests, as he called them. The nobility divided into two camps, Lichnowsky heading one as the champion of Beethoven, the Baron Wetzlar leading the opposition. The Baron's villa was usually the field of battle, and there, in the quaint language of Seyfried, "The interesting combats of the two athletes not infrequently offered an indescribable artistic treat to the numerous but thoroughly select gathering." Beethoven did not possess his rival's sentimental mien, his well-cultivated side whiskers, his pianistic bag of tricks, with figures in swift thirds intended to create wonderment. But he had his own resources.

This "revival of the old Parisian feud of Gluckists and Piccinists," so wrote Seyfried, does not seem to have ruffled in any way the equanimity of the pianists themselves. "Now one and now the other gave free rein to his glowing fancy; sometimes they would seat themselves at two pianofortes and improvise alternately on themes which they gave each other, thus creating many a four-hand Capriccio which if it could have been put upon paper at the moment would surely have bidden defiance to time." Beethoven's playing, like Seyfried's language in describing it, "soared into the luminous spaces of the high ether."

The year 1799 brought to Vienna John Baptist Cramer, the German-born, English-reared pianist, who was a pupil of Clementi. Cramer was a finer artist than Wölffl; he was shortly to be accepted as the first pianist in Europe. Comparisons led to similar results: Cramer was admired for his exquisite and finished playing, which nevertheless paled before the power, the daring, the incendiary imagination of the improvising Beethoven. Beethoven respected Cramer, befriended and learned from him. Cramer, a formalist, could not endorse the sudden turns of Beethoven's fancy, but he was too intelligent an artist to condemn them. Once, going to Beethoven's lodgings, he heard his friend dreaming at the piano, stood quietly in the hallway for half an hour, "completely entranced," and tiptoed tactfully away.

Ries relates how Beethoven, in 1797, playing the piano in his Quintet for piano and winds, Opus 16, took advantage of a *fermata*, and began to improvise a cadenza. His companions were displeased, and Ramm, the oboeist, was really angry. "It was comical to see those gentlemen waiting expectantly, ready every moment to go on, continually lifting their instruments to their lips, and then quietly putting them down again. At last Beethoven was satisfied and dropped into the Rondo. The entire audience was delighted."

When Beethoven played at the Prussian Court in 1796, he made a remarkable impression, so Carl Czerny wrote years later. Czerny told how Beethoven could "produce such an effect upon every hearer that frequently not an eye remained dry, while many would break out into loud sobs; for there was something wonderful in his expression in addition to the beauty and originality of his ideas and his spirited style of rendering them. After an improvisation of this kind, he would burst out into loud laughter and banter his hearers on the emotion he had caused them. 'You are fools!' he would say. Sometimes he would feel himself insulted by these indications of sympathy. 'Who can live among such spoiled children?' he would cry." It is easy to imagine Beethoven's annoyance at a general display of tears and sobs. Czerny leaves us in doubt as to whether he called the King's guests fools in the presence of the King.

Beethoven attended a meeting of the *Singakademie* on this visit and was asked to improvise. He told Bettina Brentano in 1810 (if that lady is to be believed) that the audience did not applaud after his performance, but came crowding about the piano weeping. "That is not what we artists wish," Bettina quotes Beethoven as saying; "we want applause!" An artist who had just bared emotions of his own through the dignified medium of his art could well be embarrassed and contemptuous at this bit of emotional exhibitionism.

Beethoven once "improvised marvelously" in the presence of

51

Karl Amenda, according to a story handed down by the Amenda family. Amenda said, "It is a great pity that such glorious music is born and lost in a moment." To refute his friend, Beethoven sat down and repeated his extemporization note for note.

This account, like all the accounts of those who beheld Beethoven conjuring music out of thin air and dismissing it again, seems a little less miraculous to those who have been able to study his habits as composer through his sketchbooks. In a way, it is the least surprising of the improvisation anecdotes. A repetition would have been an easy matter to a composer with an imagination so retentive that he could carry several partly worked-out compositions in his head at once for long periods, with no other memoranda than a few thematic notations. What is surprising is that his deliberating, painstakingly selective mind should have submitted itself so readily to the instantaneous sleight-of-hand of improvisation. He was not, like Mozart, a musical conversationalist, with a trigger-like fantasy, ready to produce anything at any moment, with a prescribed formal pattern and an adeptness in figurations to serve him. Beethoven inherited some of these traditional aids, particularly in the variation form, which he often leaned upon when he exhibited himself as virtuoso. When he varied a theme proposed by someone, he was following custom, largely relying upon his never-failing ingenuity and skill.

But it must have been something not of the eighteenth century, something of the new, incendiary Beethoven which so often moved his hearers to tears. It would be hard to believe that the accumulating intensity of an adagio could be the creation of an instant; still harder to believe that the close logic of development could have been so brought to pass. We have many witnesses for the first case, and a single expert for the second—Carl Czerny. Beethoven improvised in three general forms, says Czerny: the variation form, the free fantasy and the first movement or the rondo forms of the sonata. He would present two themes and proceed to develop them, "giving himself freely to all manner of treatment of the motive." We know that themes came easily to Beethoven; also that as they first occurred to him they were usually weak and loose. The apparent importance of some of his improvisations may have been the personal magnetism of the conjuror working his spell. With several uncompleted works occupying his musical thoughts at one time, growing and strengthening bit by bit, he could hardly have prevented scraps of them, perhaps considerable stretches of them, from finding their way through his wandering fingers.

CHAPTER SIX

THE BONN ties continued in Beethoven's Vienna friendships. The cousins Romberg visited the capital in 1797, stayed with him, played in a concert with him and had an argument with him, which Lenz von Breuning patched up. Lenz and Stephan tarried after their brother Christopher and Wegeler had departed. Beethoven was deeply attached to both of them, and was much affected by the death of Lenz in the spring of 1798. These friends found a Beethoven more arrogant than they had known, but no less companionable. He remained essentially a *Musikant*— however much he was honored in palaces, he was never thoroughly at ease, never relaxed and in the vein until he was with his cronies at a favorite public eating place, or at the home of one of them, making music for hours on end. Stephan von Breuning, visiting Vienna in 1796, wrote home a report of Beethoven, remarking that he found him "somewhat more stable [*etwas solider*] . . . Perhaps it is his greater knowledge of men, obtained through his travels or by the large number of friends he has won since he came here." He found no more of the old shyness. Beethoven knew people on all sides. He was consorting far more freely with his kind, moving about among the musicians of Vienna, learning something of the ways of the world, and holding his own. When Stephan called him "somewhat more stable," he did not go so far as to mean that he had acquired anything like Viennese urbanity or good manners. When he met a musician his esteem, or lack of it, was entirely transparent. Fine qualities in an artist won his quick respect, but petty musicians who acted importantly were apt to run into an open insult. He made professional enemies accordingly.

With congenial musical companions the reserve dropped away.

54

Sometimes his high spirits flowed over and took the form of broad jibes or unkind personal allusions. Most of his friends were entirely good-natured about his "unbuttoned" moods, and even ready to put up with his sudden and unreasonable anger. Beethoven did not hesitate to attach scathing epithets to his aristocratic friends, as when he spoke of Lobkowitz as "Fitzli Putzli," or Lichnowsky as a "princely scoundrel." His social equals, with whom he was naturally a good deal more familiar, came in for a more trenchant raillery. Schuppanzigh, sometimes addressed as "Milord Falstaff," was treated to a song, "Praise to the Fat One," and through his life was addressed by Beethoven in the third person. Court Secretary Zmeskall would offer his house for the trying out of a quartet at any time, and ably served as 'cellist when needed. His willingness to oblige seems to have been boundless. Zmeskall, it should be noted, was not a noble by lineage. Beethoven took delight in calling him "Baron" or "Musikgraf," making fun of his title. The faithful Zmeskall not only received without protest various scribbled notes filled with a half contemptuous humor, but carefully treasured them for posterity. They usually concerned an appointment for supper at the *"Schwann,"* or the need of quill pens, nicely sharpened. He was an ever-willing tool of Beethoven's convenience. He was "Cheapest of Barons," the "Most Noble and Well-born," "Charming Count," the "Scavenger of a Count," and was asked for quills in this wise: "His Highness von Zmeskall is requested to hasten somewhat in the plucking out of his (and among them probably some very strange) feathers. It is to be hoped that they have not grown too firmly on you."

Beethoven's sometimes haughty ways suggest the growing consciousness of mastery. He wrote to Zmeskall: "Yesterday, through your Zmeskall-domanovezian chatter I became quite sad. The devil take you. I don't want any of your whole system of ethics. Power is the morality of men who stand out from the rest, and it is also mine." This exuberant egotism was the sort which a creative artist must have if he is to build a new and self-standing world of tones out of his own nature and judgment.

Beethoven had to believe in the importance of what was developing within him. He spoke as he believed, even before stran▾

gers, without the usual polite pretense of a becoming modesty. He once remarked before a stranger at the house of Prince Lobkowitz that he would like to be on permanent terms with a publisher, with a fixed income so that he could compose as he pleased. He believed that Goethe, and Handel in his time, had had some such arrangement.

The older man felt called upon to take this airiness firmly in hand. "My dear young man," he said, "you must not complain; you are neither a Goethe nor a Handel, and it is not to be expected that you ever will be: for such masters will not be born again." Beethoven withdrew into haughty silence. Lobkowitz tried to smooth him down afterward by explaining that there are always those who rest upon tradition and distrust the future.

"So much the worse," said Beethoven; "with men who will not believe and trust in me because I am not yet famous I can hold no intercourse!" Vainglorious as this speech sounded, it was to Beethoven the simple truth. His conviction of great music impending, his sense of resourcefulness, were so firm that he was aroused by a stranger's assumption to the contrary.

This feeling of strength was becoming more and more his reality. Tones could be controlled, assembled and ordered. They were definite facts which could be handled exactly as he willed, and, once they were right and on paper, would be fixed forever. The tonal cosmos was actual and tangible to him. It was ready to receive the flood of his feelings, the overflow of his energies, and perfectly embody them as they took their place in the harmony of full, masterful functioning. Beethoven at the center of his music was clear-sighted, confident of his ground. There was no shadow of doubt, no conflict in it, for the sense of his music was the sense of exultant overcoming. He was a dreamer who could invariably make his dreams come true.

Perfectly organized as he was for his fulfillment as artist, Beethoven was quite unequipped when he had to meet the contingencies of everyday living. The usual minor encounters of life found him suddenly helpless. He could not deal with reality as most of us do. The world of people, unlike the world of notes, was perplexing because it was elusive and resistant. Not having the understanding and tolerant patience which comes of habitual small traffic with the average ways of average men, he became hostile. Rich people with their material advantage seemed to look down upon his art as if it could exist only at their pleasure; the man in the street seemed to deny it by his sluggish non-comprehension. The merchant type, the publisher in particular, was an unscrupulous exploiter. Servility in others was a mockery of his proud independence of spirit. Consequently, servants were hypocritical rascals; expecting the worst from them, he got the worst from them. So he built about himself a wall of suspicion. The people of indifferent intelligence who cluster about a celebrity encroached upon his privacy, and he knew no way of holding them off except by outrageous rudeness. He had none of the little courtesies which become the armor of the man in the public eye. The ways of self-ingratiation, the easing of strain; these arts he never possessed.

His social hostility was the most obvious contradiction of the visionary Beethoven. His belief in the inherent nobility of men as the highest manifestation of the divine principle, destined to prevail over every tyranny—this faith was not the faith of an ascetic, cloistered from gross reality, writing other-worldly music. His music derived its impulse from the world of men, and the composer required their sympathy accordingly. Unable to meet the world, he could not do without it. He looked for understanding, longed intensely for worldly success, even when something in his nature would not allow him to grasp it by writing down to popular expectations.

He had to have the warmth of friendship about him. His friends were his relaxation, the repository of his moods. They became the outlet for the earthy side of his nature, the side which was denied expression in his music. The accounts of his circle agree in showing traits entirely at variance with the traits we know in the composer. Serenity of spirit was replaced by hostility and finely controlled emotional energies by futile and exhausting storminess. The frowning countenance denotes inward concentration, but also a challenge to the intruder. The taut jaw and lower lip are unable to relax into a smile. He must break into a guffaw. It was only in music that Beethoven could really smile. Blind anger, frenetic hilarity, depression—he was subject to them

57

all. The composer who could regiment with such uncanny certainty the massed detail of his sketchbooks would become hopelessly involved for days in some business dispute, or a minor adjustment of routine. His friends perceived clearly enough through this strange, even ugly exterior, the Beethoven of delicate feeling and generous impulse. They saw his openness and lack of guile, his pure devotion to his art, and his capacity for deep affection. Those who knew him well loved him well. When he flung sudden accusations at the very ones who were dearest to him, they would put up with his strange ways, knowing that tortures of remorse would follow.

Some of his letters give samples of his alternate anger and penitence. Johann Nepomuk Hummel, the pianist, then about seventeen, received from Beethoven, who was devoted to him, these two letters on successive days (1799):

The first:

"He is not to come to me again. He is a treacherous dog, and may the Reaper get all treacherous dogs!"

The second:

"Herzens Natzerl—
You are an honest fellow and now I see you were right. Come, then, to me this afternoon. You'll find Schuppanzigh here also, and the two of us will thump, bump, and shake you [*rüffeln knüfflen und schütteln*] to your heart's delight.

> A kiss from
> your Beethoven
> also called *Mehlschöberl.*"

(This last was a species of Viennese dumpling. Beethoven in the occasional rôle of cook called himself *"Mehlschöberl."*)

He wrote this letter to Wegeler (about 1795):

Dearest! Best! In what an odious light you have exhibited me to myself! I acknowledge it, I do not deserve your friendship. You are so noble, so considerate, and the first time that I ranged myself alongside of you I fell so far below you! Ah, for weeks I have displeased my best and noblest friend! You think that I have lost some of my goodness of heart, but thank heaven! it was no intentional or deliberate malice which induced me to act as I did toward you; it was my inexcusable thoughtlessness which did not permit me to see the matter in its true light. Oh, how ashamed I am not only for your sake, but also my own. I can scarcely trust myself to ask for your friendship again. Oh, Wegeler, my only comfort lies in this, that you have known me almost from my childhood and yet, Oh, let me say for myself, I was always good, and always strove to be upright and true in my actions—otherwise, how could you have loved me? Could I have changed so fearfully for the worse in such a short time? Impossible; these feelings of goodness and love of righteousness cannot have died forever in me in a moment. No, Wegeler, dearest, best, venture again to throw yourself entirely into the arms of your B.; trust in the good qualities you used to find in him; I will guarantee that the pure temple of sacred friendship which you erect shall remain firm forever; no accident, no storm shall ever shake its foundations—firm—forever—our friendship—pardon—oblivion—a new upflaming of the dying, sinking friendship—Oh, Wegeler, do not reject this hand of reconciliation. Place yours in mine—O God!—but no more; I am coming to throw myself in your arms, to entreat you to restore to me my lost friend. And you will give yourself to me, your penitent, loving, never-forgetting

Beethoven again.

No one whom he met in Vienna was favored with this degree of affection and intimate confidence; none save one—Karl Amenda. Amenda went to Vienna in 1798, as a newly graduated divinity student of twenty-six, sworn to a pious calling yet an excellent violinist, and deep in music. He aspired to know Beethoven and contrived to be introduced to him at Beethoven's usual *table d'hôte*. Shyness on the one side, reserve on the other kept their meetings perfunctory. It was music that brought them together, according to a paper written later and handed down by the Amenda family. Karl was once playing first violin in a quartet at a friend's house, when someone reached over to turn his pages. At the end he was terrified to find that it was Beethoven, who now straightened up and bowed. The next day their host hailed Amenda:

" 'What have you done? You have captured Beethoven's heart! He requests that you rejoice him with your company.'

"Amenda, much pleased, hurried to Beethoven, who at once asked him to play with him. After several hours, Amenda took his leave,

59

but Beethoven accompanied him to his quarters, and there was music again. As Beethoven finally prepared to go, he said to Amenda, 'Suppose you come with me?' This was done, and Beethoven kept Amenda till evening, and went home with him late at night. The mutual visiting was kept up, and the two were so constantly together that when people on the street saw only one of them he would remark, 'Where is the other?' "

The two confided in each other directly, speaking of matters near their hearts, confidences possible in that day of awakening romanticism, possible in Beethoven's case only toward those few who won his love and in doing so disarmed him of the masks of ceremony or verbal horseplay or taciturnity or irascibility. Karl left Vienna after a little more than a year, and returned to his native Courland on the Baltic coast.

Wenzel Krumpholz, once pupil of Haydn and violinist at Esterház, gave Beethoven violin lessons out of sheer adoration, so that Beethoven called him "his fool." Beethoven apparently wanted to understand the instrument more fully. He could never play it acceptably. Amenda related how once he persuaded Beethoven to play the violin, with results that sent the two of them into uncontrollable laughter. For violin playing Heinrich Eppinger and also the banker Häring, both talented amateurs, were always obliging. Schuppanzigh must not be forgotten, nor his fellow string players of Lichnowsky's quartet. Schindler tells us that the musicians, Joseph Friedlowsky, Johann Wenzel Stich (otherwise known as Giovanni Punto) and Carl Scholl taught Beethoven the "mechanism" or "proper writing" for the clarinet, horn and flute, respectively. But Schindler spoke from hearsay; he did not reckon the opportunities Beethoven had had to learn the fundamentals of those instruments at Bonn. What Beethoven now did was to make himself more thoroughly at home with them for purposes of his own. The tale is often told how he met the double bassist Dragonetti, put one of the two 'cello sonatas before him, was so ecstatic over what he heard that he embraced player and instrument together, and henceforth wrote bass parts requiring an agility which was the despair of bass players for years to come.

The picture of Beethoven's first years in Vienna would be far from complete without its accompaniment of feminine adoration. "He was frequently in love," wrote Ferdinand Ries, who knew him from 1800, "but generally only for a short period. Once when I teased him concerning his conquest of a pretty woman he admitted that she had held him in the strongest bonds for the longest time, that is, fully seven months." There is no audience more sympathetic than a beautiful girl half captivated, no better incentive than her presence to the mood of a hushed adagio finding its rounded expression, and no straighter road to a fair heart than the playing of it at the right moment. Beethoven's susceptibilities are a good deal clearer than his preferences. The dedications of works then published are unreliable guides, for personal sentiments are often hard to distinguish from titled obligations. The dedicatee, often a pupil, of whom Beethoven had many, would be flattered at the privilege of playing a piece before its publication. It would become favorably known in the manuscript, and when Beethoven would offer the forthcoming edition for subscription he would sometimes collect a neat sum before its appearance. Beethoven was never a good teacher, for he was usually distrait with his pupil, loath to interrupt his own musical thoughts in order to guide inept fingers and dull responses. Youthfulness made a difference, and youth, too, was susceptible. When Wegeler wrote of his friend's "conquests" more readily made than those of "any Adonis," and as readily replaced, he had in mind the first three years in Vienna.

There was Barbara Keglevics, the Hungarian "Comtesse Babette," who was accounted a beauty, and who received the dedication of the early E flat Sonata, and the C major Piano Concerto. For Giulietta Guicciardi he had feelings still more tender. But Giulietta was only sixteen when, in 1800, she first came to Vienna from Trieste. It was through her cousins the von Brunswicks that Beethoven came to know her, and they it was who first held his interest. This delightful family came to Vienna in the previous season from Martonvásár, their ancestral estate in Hungary which Beethoven was often to visit. The fine breeding of the Brunswicks (the name was treaceable to the Crusades) was evident in their sensitive cultivation of mind and

61

heart. Idealism and talent were to be found in each of them—but eccentricity too, a trait increased in the children as they ran wild on their Puszta, left to their own devices. Therese, the eldest, god-daughter of the Empress of Austria, had more character and stability than her brother and sisters. She had been eighteen when her father died, and she caught from him a taste for music, poetry and intellectual pursuits which, with little guidance, developed as she matured. The mother, who became aware in spurts of the need of civilizing her country-reared children, transported them to a hotel in Vienna in May of 1799. Therese was twenty-four, Josephine twenty, her brother Franz twenty-two. Karoline was seventeen. All were passionately devoted to music, but especially Tesi and Pepi, the elder sisters. These were both pianists, an accomplishment by all means to be improved upon in Vienna. They had heard wondrous accounts of Beethoven. But Beethoven was not the kind of music master who would come running at the summons of a countess; he had to be sought out.

Accordingly her Excellency with her two piano-playing daughters gathered up her silken petticoats and humbly climbed flights of stairs steep and dark to the god in his music-strewn Olympus. Therese had brought one of Beethoven's trios with her, and walked in with the music under her arm "like a little girl going to her lesson," says her own account. "The dear immortal Ludwig van Beethoven was very friendly, and as polite as he could be. After a few remarks *de part et d'autre* he placed me at his out-of-tune piano, and I began at once; I played valiantly, and sang the accompaniment for 'cello and violin." Beethoven was not appalled but actually pleased at the spectacle of an elegantly dressed Hungarian Fräulein imperturbably bringing to pass a Trio all by herself. "He was so delighted that he promised to come each day to our hotel, the '*Griffon d'or.*' He kept his word; but instead of staying an hour after midday, he would stay four or five. . . . It was five o'clock before we realized we were hungry. Our good mother fasted with us, but the hotel people were angry."

Beethoven came daily, and imposed pieces to be learned, and exercises for hand position. But when to practice them? Their stay in Vienna was to be short, and there was an obligatory round of social duties—calls, drives, sightseeing, dances, and, to complete an evening, ices on the Graben. It was a true dilemma, for the Master was too beloved to be skimped. On the contrary, he was capable of making a frightening scene, tearing the music across and throwing it on the floor. Tesi, the more conscientious of the two, solved the point by practicing all night. Again, no doubt, "the hotel people were angry." Their anger was far preferable to Beethoven's, for the pain of displeasing him was hardest of all to bear.

Far oftener Beethoven was *"scharmant,"* as Pepi wrote it. He loved to hear them play his sonatas. If anyone was more devoted to their Beethoven than these two it was the brother Franz (who was to receive the dedication of the *"Appassionata"* Sonata). The whole family adopted Beethoven and he enjoyed their charm and cultivation as he had once enjoyed the family of von Breuning. The companionship was to deepen and take an unmistakably romantic turn only in later years. In 1800 it was ruffled when Pepi was hurried by her impetuous mother into a loveless marriage with a Count von Dehm, aged fifty. This was distressing, for Pepi, reaching toward an intenser life, found herself senselessly tied to a shallow one. The child turned to Beethoven, and he read in her glance eagerness and helplessness.

It was near the end of the year that Giulietta Guicciardi arrived upon the scene. Already, at sixteen, Giulietta was a more practiced breaker of hearts than her country cousins. Her neat little figure, petite and alluring, her delicate features, her little black curls, her Italian vivacity, all served her purposes. Therese was comely with a slight deformity of the spine, not quite concealed. Josephine was accounted a beauty. A miniature shows her fine-featured and dainty, a kerchief upon her head tied lightly and becomingly under her chin. But the sisters knew that they could not compete with *"la belle Guicciardi"*—except perhaps at long range, where indeed, as companions in art and in fine feeling, their character would prevail.

For the time being, Beethoven was infatuated by Giulietta. Though the music that came forth when his new pupil bent her curly head over the keys was not all that it might have been, nothing comparable to what either Tesi or Pepi could produce, the teacher became the lover, looking for the time being upon her beauty—and forgave her in his heart. Probably she looked affectionately on him in return. At least Beethoven so believed. His friends saw in this something more than another drawing-room flirtation. When his letter to Wegeler in November, 1801, became known, his disclosure to his friend that he was in love was taken as referring to Giulietta:

"My life is again somewhat pleasanter, for I mix in society . . . This change has been brought about by a dear, bewitching girl, who loves me, and whom I love."

He had thought of marriage as a "way to happiness," but had had to give up the thought, for one reason because "she is not of my station of life."

If Giulietta's parents, like the parents of other titled young pupils of Beethoven, decided against the uncouth and improvident music master of thirty as a son-in-law, we should not be too ready to disagree with them. Those daughters, swept (or almost swept) off their dainty feet by raptures of sensibility and waves of ardor, could have been to Beethoven on any permanent basis nothing but a grotesque encumbrance. Almost invariably the objects of his impermanent affections shortly married within their class and continued in the elegant and circumscribed life to which they were born and raised, while Beethoven, with some alacrity, turned an interested eye upon another. Was the affair with the little Southern coquette more than such a one? It seems to have been. The dedication of the C sharp minor Sonata to her in 1802, the Sonata unwarrantably associated with moonlight, might be deceptive. Beethoven's dedications, which led d'Indy into doubtful assumptions, were hardly the compass of his heart. This dedication was given to Giulietta in exchange for the dedication of the Rondo in G, which he wished to retract. Nor did he himself hold the even then too famous fantasia sonata in the highest esteem. Giulietta met Count Gallenberg, and promptly forgot Beethoven to marry him in 1803. The Count was of her age and class, but had little else to recommend him. He called himself a musician—even a composer—but how puny a composer beside her rejected suitor! On the eve of the wedding Beethoven wrote the despairing words: "Ah, what terrible moments there are in life—and yet we must accept them."

The match was unhappy. As Beethoven divulged to Schindler in a conversation book of 1823, "I was well loved by her, and more than her husband ever loved her." He also wrote, in words never intended for the public eye, that she had come to him long afterward, weeping, but that he had repulsed her. A medallion portrait of her was found among his possessions after his death, the only portrait of a woman he had kept, save an oil painting of Therese von Brunswick bearing this inscription: "To the Unique Genius—To the Great Artist—To the Good Man—From T.B." Giulietta, approached by Jahn on the subject of her attachment to Beethoven years after his death, was extremely reticent. Nor did her descendants ever encourage any such intimation. Marie La Mara extracted this information from a friend of the Gallenbergs as recently as 1909—if not directly authoritative it is characteristic: "I do not think that the *Schwärmerei* for Countess Giulietta Gallenberg-Guicciardi—though it may have been warm and wonderful, for she was a very elegant woman of the world—ever took root in Beethoven's heart as deeply as did his later love for Countess Therese Brunswick."

CHAPTER SEVEN

THE YOUNG composer continued to do well for himself. He was enjoying, on the whole, sturdy health, making more friends than enemies. Above all, he was composing prodigiously and receiving encouragement. He had come to Vienna with an accumulation of music in his portfolio, some in sketched form. Much of it was put to good account, for Beethoven husbanded his sketches. The first trios may have come with him from Bonn, and the sonatas that immediately followed. When he had undergone his self-imposed studies and reconsidered all that he had written, only then was he ready to appear in print. The manuscript of an easy sonata, breaking off in the second movement, which he sent to Lorchen in 1796, gives a sample of the Beethoven who had not quite reached the point of self-sanction. The two movements have suppleness and lyric grace equal to any contemporary standard; they must have delighted his pupil. But this music is both sub-Haydn and sub-Beethoven. Placed beside the pending Opus 1 it appears stilted and thin, tentative.

Simrock, embarking upon his publishing business in Bonn in 1794, received some variations from him. But it was Artaria in Vienna to whom he entrusted his real Opus 1 in 1795, following it with a steady stream of music until, in 1798, the opus number had risen to nine. From then until 1801, Beethoven slighted Artaria and bestowed his works, now more profuse than ever, upon Mollo, Eder, Traeg, and two firms in Leipzig—Hoffmeister and Kühn and Breitkopf and Härtel. When he wrote in that year: "I have six or seven publishers, and might have more if I chose," he was telling the literal truth.

The list of publications is the index of great creative industry, high success. By 1801 he had published his Opus 21, which means that there were twelve piano sonatas to commend him to his public, five violin and two 'cello sonatas, eight trios, chamber pieces in various combinations, numerous sets of variations, and songs. If the three sonatas of Opus 10, the *Pathétique*, the Septet, and the song "Adelaide" had been all, his fame and favor would have been secure enough.

Certain works did not go so promptly to the publisher. One of his reasons for holding back the first two piano concertos may have been his hesitation to commit himself to his first published orchestral scores. The case of a symphony was a matter for even greater circumspection and preparation. Beethoven was not satisfied with his orchestral attempts of Bonn days: the two Cantatas and the *Ritter* Ballet. It is conjectured that van Swieten would have liked a symphony from him, and that, encouraged by his studies with Albrechtsberger, Beethoven made the first sketches of what was to be his C major Symphony in 1794 or 1795, then projecting the subject matter of the last movement as of the first. It was van Swieten who was to receive the dedication of the First Symphony, when at last it went to Hoffmeister's *"Bureau d'Arts"* in Leipzig in 1801. Beethoven arranged a performance on April 2, 1800, to give the Symphony a public hearing, his first venture upon a concert of his own. The only surviving report is an adverse criticism, which in itself proves nothing more than that the first critics of Beethoven awoke slowly to new ideas. They would presently be decrying a later attempt and holding up this conventional one as a model to which its composer should return.

The early critics of Beethoven were musicians of the old guard who generally agreed that the young man was stumbling over his pride, balking his unmistakable talent by "rash and ill-considered steps." What they could not know was that Beethoven was incapable of taking a rash or ill-considered step. This most deliberate of composers was scrupulously careful of his ground; he weighed his impulses and could become bold only when he was sure. What seemed arbitrary or even perverse the passage of time would prove to be quite consistent, of a piece with the whole.

Nothing could have been more gradual and peaceable than

67

Beethoven's displacement of eighteenth-century formalism. He lingered with evident fondness over the purity and clarity of the manner to which he had been raised, and which continued around him. The full glow of expressive ardor and the expanding logic of development eventually obliterated the poised and exquisite, but confining, Mozartean mold. It was bound to happen, just as his range of tempi and dynamics was bound to be increased by the urge of expressiveness. A flood of sentiment possessed the song "Adelaide" in 1796, or the slow movement of the Quintet for Piano and Winds in 1797, or in the next year reached such a point of absorption in the Adagio of the C minor Sonata and the Largo of the D major Sonata of Opus 10, or the opening of the *Pathétique,* that music had become a new and different speech. It was no conscious act of revolution. The keyboard under his searching fingers submitted unexpectedly to his mood of tragic pathos, finding a new, arresting forcefulness in sharp dissonance, broken, theatrical chords, or long phrases of tension and release. These pages were startling, as were occasional gamin-like scherzos with displaced rhythms, but they were sporadic. Beethoven continued in the highway of tradition, reverting in the First Symphony and the six Quartets of Opus 18, all completed in 1799, to Haydnesque ways. His caution was built upon reverence. The ultra-perfection to which Mozart and Haydn had brought the symphony and the quartet was a matter for awe in a young and ambitious heart. Beethoven would not try to improve what could not be improved, and he was incapable of perfunctory imitation. He bided his time. Van Swieten could not hurry him into the completion of a symphony. He would not lay a quartet beside its models until he had accumulated the sketches for six, many times gone over before any other eye had seen them. Living daily in an atmosphere of quartets and quartet playing at Lichnowsky's, Beethoven watched and listened as the delicate and masterly scores of Haydn were many times performed under their composer's eye. The Prince and his players might have urged Beethoven to produce something for them to try; they were probably tactful enough not to press the point. When at last the six of Opus 18 were ready they turned out to be inferior to their models, as judged by eighteenth-century tenets. What seemed strange innovation to their first hearers was the innate character of Beethoven, seizing the music momentarily but not yet ready to take confident possession.

Beethoven was held spellbound by the high glaze and finality of his predecessors. He was still restrained, as they had been, from shattering the poise which was the kernel of beauty. Mozart, being a man of strong emotional experience, as we know, could have allowed the slow movement of his G minor Symphony to become openly convulsive if his sense of fitness had not preserved its special indescribable dignity of clouded beauty. He could have allowed the heartbroken Donna Anna to tear her scene to pieces while he cast aside altogether the set vocalisms of the Italian *opera buffa*, if he had been unwise enough to destroy the essential restraint and charm of his style, which was built upon it. Mozart, like Beethoven, possessed daring tempered by judgment. Daring was a quality Haydn lacked. Writing a symphony, he stood squarely in his pattern while his fancy played over it like a willing captive. Sometimes he seemed about to cut loose, as in the slow movement of his Eighty-eighth Symphony in G major, where melody warms to glowing ardor, or in the *Largo* of the String Quartet in D major (Opus 75, No. 5), which strikingly foretells, note for note, the full-throated lamentation of the *espressivo* theme of Beethoven's *Adagio* in his Quartet Opus 59, No. 1. Here is a direct link between Haydn and the Beethoven of the later emotional outpourings. Haydn opened up the way as he stood at the height of his powers. But a certain sense of propriety kept him from crossing the threshold of a new epoch. As one listens to his revelatory slow movements the formal frame lurks always in the background, while, like the chaperon at a party, it continues to make its presence felt, discreetly but plainly. Haydn's innovation was in adroit detail; it lay in the charm of the unexpected, expertly handled. Beethoven's early advances were also detailed, and respectful of the general pattern. But they were subversive as Haydn's never were. What Beethoven did not take from that master was a certain complacency. Haydn's themes, as such, the phrase lengths, the cadences, continually perform little bows, and get in the way of genuine, heartfelt disclosure.

Beethoven, with all his regard for Haydn's music, was temperamentally more like Emanuel Bach, in that he was working toward a style rather than perfecting one. Beethoven's earlier efforts took Haydn, or the clavier music of Rust, as the point of departure, while they caught from the Hamburg Bach the spirit of quest. The spirit grew with technical assurance until at last it became pervasive. The little stiff places disappeared from Beethoven's music as each part turned freely expressive. The development sections became grounds for perambulation. Beethoven never lost his reverence for Haydn. He never saw fit to abandon the essential movement forms, even when later he expanded them to great lengths by pouring the treasure of his imagination into them. His restless skill clothed them according to his fresh point of view until they were revealed as something quite different. The detail became alive in a new way. The bass turned into melody, and so did the ornamental figures. The music began to sing in every part. A trill ceased to be an embellishment and became a point of suspense; a modulation was elevated from a flick of dexterity to a dramatic change of mood. Chords, once little more than pleasant tonal foundations of melodies, became vital in voice motion, taking on accents exultant, poignant or shaking. With these new attributes, the older ones were forfeited. The new texture was richer—and more opaque. The old transparency was inevitably lost. Beethoven's music shows a reluctance at the sacrifice—a reluctance overcome because the new affirmation was stronger. He could not have argued the point because he could not have explicitly apprehended it—he was always vague as to conscious purpose. What he did possess was a guiding sense unerring and unswerving beyond human credibility.

These innovations, contemplated against the general sluggish background of the musical profession in 1800, have an originality which is overwhelming. Looked upon in relation to contemporary thought and endeavor in a wider sense, Beethoven's originality is diminished. Effusive mood poetry, the exaltation of the expressive were in the air. Goethe's love lyrics, Jean Paul Richter's fantasies, Schiller's heroic dramas were thrilling every well-read household, and, although he was never a literary adept, Beetho-

70

ven as well. The art of music otherwise remained still strangely impervious to the new movement; musicians still echoed a polite past as if there were no such things as heady, liberating thoughts, which made the artist supreme arbiter in his own domain, and started him upon emotional self-examination. Music must have come to this discovery in its own tardy time, even without Beethoven. With Weber, for example, the new point of view took possession of music as if on its own impetus. Weber, conventional at heart, rode a current of popular taste in fervor and transformed it into tone. Beethoven's current ran deeper within himself, at first unseen, and presently changed the whole aspect of music.

He had no defined scheme or goal, but steadily pursued his path as if some inexplicable force were driving him. There was nothing of the theoretical reformer in Beethoven, as there was in Gluck before him, or Wagner after. He delivered no polemics—his letters and reported conversations are quite free of them. Beethoven could not formulate his aims because he could not command words, and because in any case he was incapable of abstraction. His belief was instinctive, noncommunicable except in music, but there it became high and clear, unmistakable. We sense in his music an idealization, an emotional experience which is more than music. The distinguishing quality is as easy to recognize in every line of his more important scores as it is hard to define. We call it directness, naïve purity, elevation, evocation—and then we pause, at a loss. We know that popular concepts of his time appealed to him—God, nature, love, loyalty, individual freedom. Of course it is not these concepts that matter, but his belief in them. His conviction, as it emanates from his music, is so strong that we know at once that life for the dreamer was whole and good, reducing mean and bitter thoughts to inessential shadows.

Outside of music, he had no need of expert knowledge. His knowledge was elementary, idealized, unparticularized—but it was never superficial. His ideas of contemporary or of Platonic republicanism, his understanding of classical literature, or of Rousseau, or of Kant were probably of the vaguest. But he had what he needed from them. To have plunged into the intricacies of politics, or philosophy, or ancient languages would

71

only have muddied his clear vision, and lessened the force of his musical affirmation. Utopian? Art can be as utopian as it pleases. Literature merely awakened what lay already in Beethoven's soul, seeking a name. "For Beethoven," wrote Wegeler, "to know was to create."

Perhaps the strength of his faith lay in its childlike, inexpert, unquestioning acceptance, for there is no faith so strong as the ingenuous, uninstructed kind. Many who met or knew him remarked that Beethoven had the qualities of a child. The poet Wiessenbach wrote: "Never in my life have I met with such a childlike simplicity, in company with so powerful a personality. He has an inner drive towards all that is fine and good, which is far higher than any education." This trait is something that education could have spoiled. His impulsiveness, his forthrightness, his credulity, and his helplessness (which appealed to women) were a part of it. But more than these, his lack of self-consciousness was a part of it. It was because Beethoven's motivations were unstudied that they could attain their true grandeur. They were beyond circumscribing discussion, inscrutable, even more universal than Beethoven himself. Beethoven had one immense advantage over a century to follow of experts in sensibility —the advantage of pristine freshness. His musical experience was too new to know itself. Nothing is more contagious than derived ardor—a malady which was to afflict every later Romantic, making him a play actor cultivating lofty or impassioned moods long since become stock-in-trade. Schiller once praised that quality of simplicity which "lifts to a higher plane the unconscious inspiration and solves without realizing them the knottiest problems." This was precisely Beethoven's simplicity. It was because Beethoven could draw directly from his own nature that his simplest measures, even those which follow the letter of tradition, are sometimes surprisingly personal and pregnantly expressive.

The salient unorthodoxies of Beethoven were completely mystifying to the narrow professional musicians, who were at a loss even to discuss them, and so complained vaguely about stylistic improprieties. Among many laudatory paragraphs on new music by composers now forgotten there appear in the 1798 and 1799 issues of the *Allgemeine Musikalische Zeitung,* Breitkopf and Härtel's periodical, several patronizing reviews of pieces by Beethoven. His piano variations are found "harsh in modulations," proving that he should continue to play the instrument and not write for it. His Clarinet Trio, Opus 11, is considered more promising, but he can never hope to be famous unless he will try to "write more naturally." The three violin sonatas, Opus 12, are "overladen with difficulties . . . Herr Beethoven goes his own gait, but what a bizarre and singular gait it is!" The writer concludes: "To be accurate, there is only a mass of learning here, without good method, obstinacy which fails to interest us, a striving for strange modulations, a heaping up of difficulties on difficulties until one loses all patience or enjoyment." At length there was a glimmer of light, a retraction of the earlier opinion of the same set of violin sonatas: "The critic, after he has tried to accustom himself more and more to Herr Beethoven's manner, has learned to admire him more than he did at first."

Beethoven, who needed no advice, good or bad, was not greatly disturbed by the Leipzig scribblers. What did bother him was to be held up before the world as a wrong-headed intellectual, merely out of step with everybody else. He wrote to Hoffmeister in Leipzig more than a year later (January, 1801): "As regards the Leipzig O—[Leipzig Oxen?], let them talk; they will certainly never make anybody immortal by their twaddle, nor will they rob of immortality those whom Apollo has favored." The firm of Breitkopf and Härtel was mildly taken to task in the following spring: "You should recommend to the Messrs. your critics greater care and wisdom." Their "howls" had given him a moment of humiliation, but he "could not get angry," realizing that "they did not understand their business." Perhaps the crux of the letter was an uneasy "hint" to the effect that his first two piano concertos, then recently off the press, were not among his best works "in this form," and not to be approached with high expectations. With a new concerto in C minor in course of composition, he was painfully aware of the shortcomings of the earlier ones. He could not have understood his critics. If they could have seen the new Third Concerto they would surely have

73

found it impossibly "learned," and would have held up the one in C major as far superior.

Beethoven's outspoken enemy was the leather-necked, traditional attitude in Leipzig and elsewhere, which resented all change and imposed bans to the extent of its authority. Ignatz Moscheles, a musically eager boy of ten, was warned against the music of Beethoven by Dionys Weber, his hidebound master at Prague. When Moscheles came upon a copy of the then new *Pathétique* Sonata and took it to his teacher in rapture, he was sternly forbidden to corrupt himself with such eccentric stuff, and told to base his training on the more solid models of Sebastian Bach, Mozart and Clementi. Moscheles secretly devoured every sonata of Beethoven which appeared, copying them when he had not the pocket money to buy them. Beethoven's music took this sort of immediate hold upon many people, for the fervid line was in full accord with the popular trend. The emotional current overrode the intellectual proprieties, and the fact that an academic minority disapproved did not greatly concern the majority. It certainly did not concern the publishers, whose insatiability is the surest evidence of the popular demand.

Beethoven was now fortified in his fame. The Hoftheater had turned to him for a ballet to compliment Maria Theresa, the consort of the Emperor Francis, and he had written *Die Geschöpfe des Prometheus,* which, mounted in March, 1801, went through performance after performance. Having proved himself able to write for the theatre, he was ambitious to compete with other composers who wrote short cantatas for performance in the Lenten season when the theatres were closed. He was at work upon an oratorio, rather hastily undertaken, *Christus am Ölberg.*

If he had been inclined to rest on his official laurels and to court popular success by exerting the magic power of expressive lyricism, he might have settled into an easy and profitable groove. Continuing to write melting slow movements like the *Adagio Cantabile* of the *Pathétique* Sonata, he could have become wealthy, the permanent idol of every fluttering heart in Europe. It was not in his nature to do this. In his slow movements to come there would be a new deflection of fervor, an apparent abstruseness and obscurity of treatment. The sentimental wor-

74

shippers would be disappointed with Beethoven's obstinacy, his perverse spirit which seemed determined to discourage his best wishers. What they could not understand was that nothing could have been further from perversity than the spirit of Beethoven. He stood in a sort of humility of self-dedication to the purpose of his art. His spirit was searching, testing. It grew impatient at sentiment which tended to become external and strike attitudes He turned his spirit inward, probed his heart and there found a richer voice. Simultaneously, the expressive means, the technique and detail of development, were undergoing a re-alignment. He was aware of something momentous gathering within him. Subtilization was a means to power, power to expansion and dramatic impact. Beethoven wrote to Wegeler in the autumn of 1801: "Day by day I am approaching the goal which I apprehend but cannot describe. It is only in this that your Beethoven can live. Tell me nothing of rest. I know of none but sleep."

One is tempted to linger over the exultant Beethoven of thirty-one, become firm and resilient in musical strength, aware of its pending great increase, swaying men to his will, and bringing praise his way. The felicity would not continue. His first years of untroubled peacefulness were destined to be his last as well. An enemy, insidious, lurking, intermittent at first, threatened to nullify his plans, and eventually undermine the reputation which had been so proudly unyielding before petty attack.

CHAPTER EIGHT

BEETHOVEN HAD first noticed, three years before, a humming in his ears. It had seemed to be connected with a chronic dysentery which had long bothered him. He had spoken of it to no living soul but the Doctors Frank and Vering, and another who made him worse with cold baths. A cure of warm baths seemed to help, but oil of almonds or herb teas applied to his ears brought no improvement. Sometimes the higher tones of instruments, or at a distance the softer passages, became inaudible. Then his hearing would become normal, but a return of the painful colic would seem to start the humming again. He would lose the syllables of a quiet conversation while he could still hear the tones. When voices were raised, the sound became acutely painful. For a long time his friends knew nothing of this, for they were accustomed to his absent-minded ways, and thought him inattentive. He went secretly to his doctor. Vering shook his head over the likelihood of a complete cure, and Beethoven, no longer able to dismiss a prospect which was unthinkable, was filled with despair.

At first he tried to shut from his mind any thought of interference with his music. He felt his musical power imperious and vibrant within him, and relied upon it, fighting off a turmoil of fears. The loss of ready converse with those about him was a more immediate specter, and it was terrible enough. His pride recoiled from the necessity of enduring the pity and constraint, even the involuntary contempt of his friends. For a long time he would tell no one. Then at last the weight of his secret became too great to bear.

He turned first to Karl Amenda in Courland; it was natural, for he and the gentle curate had most freely confided one in the other. Even so, he could not at first bring himself to tell Amenda

the truth. His letter, written in the spring of 1801, was an affectionate greeting, with a promise that he would write again about
his "present condition," and all else that might interest him.

"A thousand times my thoughts dwell upon the best of the men
whom I have known. Yes, after the two who have possessed my
whole love, and of whom one still lives, you come as third, as one of
whom my recollection can never fade."

Of the two who possessed his "whole love" one was undoubtedly Lenz von Breuning, who had died two years before. The
other was just as surely Wegeler. Lenz he might have told;
Stephan, who was then visiting Vienna, he probably did not.
He was drawn to Wegeler by a double bond. Wegeler could receive his secret as doctor as well as friend. Yet two more months
had passed before, within the month of June, he poured out his
heart in long letters to his two friends.

He wrote to Amenda on June 1:

"How often do I wish you were with me, for your Beethoven is
living an unhappy life, quarreling with nature and its creator, often
cursing the latter because he surrenders his creatures to the merest
accident, which can break or destroy the most beautiful blossoms.
Know that my noblest faculty, my hearing, has greatly deteriorated.
When you were still with me I felt the symptoms but kept silent;
now it is continually growing worse, and whether or not a cure is
possible has become a question; but it is said to be due to my bowels,
and so far as they are concerned I am nearly restored to health. I
hope indeed that my hearing will also improve, but I am dubious
because such diseases are often incurable. . . .

"Oh, how happy I would be if my hearing were completely restored;
then would I hurry to you, but as it is I must refrain from everything,
and the most beautiful years of my life must pass without accomplishment of the promise my talent and powers hold. I must resort to
a sad resignation, although I am resolved to rise superior to every
obstacle. But how will that be possible? Yes, Amenda, if in six
months' time my malady shows itself to be incurable, I shall appeal
to you; you must abandon everything and come to me. My affliction
stands least in my way of playing and composing, most in conversation with others, and you must be my companion. I am sure fortune
will not desert me. What might I not attempt? Since you went away

'77

I have written in every form except operas and church music. You will not deny me; you will help your friend bear his cares and affliction.— I have received all your letters, and in spite of having answered so few, I have you always in mind and my heart beats for you as ever. I beg of you to keep secret what I have told you about my deafness and *confide it to nobody, no matter who it is.*

"Now farewell, my dear, good fellow; if you think I can do something for you here, command me as a matter of course.

Your faithful and truly affectionate

L. v. Beethoven."

It is strange to behold a desperate clinging in the independent spirit of Beethoven. Someone dear to him must live with him, stand at his side, and replace society, if need be, with a single friendship. He turned to Wegeler in the same way, for the doctor was associated with all his happier days at Bonn. Childhood memories leaped up and filled him with yearning. "My true, good, brave friend," he wrote. "Do not believe that I could forget you who were always so dear to me. No. There are moments when I long for you and to be with you. My fatherland, the beautiful region where I first saw the light, is still as beautiful and clear before my eyes as when I left you. In short, I shall look upon it as one of the happiest events in my life when once more I can see you and the mighty Father Rhine. When this shall be I cannot tell you now, but I want to say that you will see me again only as a great man." He stands proudly on his achievements, speaks of his successes in Vienna, and then comes to his tragedy: "The trouble is that my evil demon, my health, has gotten in my way; what I mean is that my hearing has grown steadily worse for three years." He gives the doctor his history of symptoms and attempted cures, but ends sadly: "It is true that I am stronger and better; only my ears ring and buzz continually, day and night. I am living a wretched life; for two years I have avoided almost all social gatherings because it is impossible for me to tell people—'I am deaf.' If I belonged to any other profession it would be easier, but in my profession it is an awful situation, the more so because of my enemies, and they are not few—what would they say? . . . I have often cursed my existence; Plutarch taught me resignation. If possible I will bid

78

defiance to my fate, although there will be moments in my life when I shall be the unhappiest of God's creatures. . . . If my condition continues I will go to you next spring; you could hire a house for me in some pretty place in the country, and for half a year I would be a farmer. This might bring about a change. Resignation! What a wretched refuge—and yet it is the only one open to me." He enjoins Wegeler to tell no one of his condition, not even Lorchen von Breuning, since become Wegeler's wife. But he sends messages to Lorchen and to her mother "the good *Frau Hofräthin,* and tell her that I still occasionally have a *'raptus.'* "

On November 16th he wrote again. He thanked his friend for his advice, reported on his condition, but could not honestly say that it had improved. "I am living more pleasantly since I live more amongst men. You will scarcely believe how lonely and sad my life was for two years; my bad hearing haunted me everywhere like a ghost and I fled from mankind and seemed like a misanthrope though far from being one." Then a companion gently probed his secret, and led him out of his solitary brooding. "This change has been brought about by a dear, bewitching girl who loves me, and whom I love. There have been a few blessed moments within the last two years, and this is the first time that I feel that marriage might bring me happiness. Alas! She is not of my station—and now—it would be impossible for me to marry." The "dear, bewitching girl," now doubly barred from him, was supposed by Wegeler and others to have been Giulietta Guicciardi, and she it must have been. Giulietta's infatuation, born of the ardor of an affecting moment, could not stand the cold light of reason. Giddy, flirtatious, pleasure-bent, bolstered by her round of fashionable activities, the dainty Giulietta was hardly to be pictured as the mate of a boorish musician, who above all else was deaf and so must be ministered to in seclusion.

Beethoven now learned to accept the bitter fact that no one on this earth, not his best friend, not even a girl who would be ready to sacrifice all her gaiety to become his wife, could help him face what he must face entirely alone. Wegeler had invited him to come to him and Lorchen, but Beethoven answered: "Do not believe that I could be happy with you. What is there that could make me happier? Even your care would give me pain. I would see pity on your faces every minute, and be only still more unhappy." Nor does he dwell any more upon Rhineland memories; it is the present and future which must be met. "Oh, if I were rid of this affliction, I could embrace the world! I feel that my youth is just beginning, and have I not always been ill? . . . My physical strength has for a short time past been growing steadily, and so have my mental powers. . . . Grant me but half freedom from my affliction and then—as a complete, ripe man I shall return to you and renew the old feelings of friendship. You must see me as happy as it is possible to be here below—not unhappy. No! I cannot endure it. I will take fate by the throat; it shall not overcome me. Oh, it is so beautiful to live—to live a thousand times! I feel that I was not made for a quiet life."

Indeed he was not—nor, just now, for meek "resignation." There is no further mention of that word.

When Dr. Vering, who had promised "an improvement if no complete cure," failed to bring about either, Beethoven went to another, a Dr. Schmidt, who recommended a quiet dwelling place where his hearing would be spared. Beethoven accordingly took lodgings, in the spring of 1802, in a peasant house at Heiligenstadt, then a verdant and peaceful suburb of Vienna, a short walk over a ridge from Döbling. The place was suitable for a dreamer who needed only to wander undisturbed through tranquil woods and meadows, and yet be within easy call of friends.

There was no letting up of the daily musical round; the sketch books seldom lagged. His friends often saw him. Ferdinand Ries, then seventeen, the son of Franz Ries of Bonn memories, went frequently to Heiligenstadt for morning lessons. "At times, at 8 o'clock in the morning after breakfast he would say: 'Let us first take a short walk.' We went and frequently did not return till 3 or 4 o'clock, after having made a meal in some village. On one of these wanderings Beethoven gave me the first striking proof of his loss of hearing, concerning which Stephan von Breuning had already spoken to me. I called his attention to a shepherd who was piping very agreeably in the woods on a flute made of a twig of elder. For half an hour Beethoven could hear nothing, and though I assured him that it was the same with me (which was not the case), he became extremely quiet and morose. When occasionally he seemed to be merry it was generally to the extreme of boisterousness; but this happened seldom." Seyfried, Zmeskall, Reicha, those who saw much of him in that year, could not help noticing when he missed familiar sounds and glowered in silence, or when he could not follow their conversation and pretended to be preoccupied. They were embarrassed at the difficulty of pretending not to notice, and of raising their voices without being pointed about it. Unlike Wegeler at Bonn, or Amenda at Courland, they knew nothing of his despair.

Despair came as he watched his friends joke and gossip, and could not follow, or as he sank into fearful thoughts of the world's mockery when it would surprise his secret from him. Then he left them, strode his Heiligenstadt paths, while music teemed within him as never before. This was the herculean strength that would enable him to "seize fate by the throat." He gloried in his strength, and wrote both to Amenda and Wegeler of how his music was demanded on all sides, bringing him fame and money. The writing of letters, he said to Wegeler apologetically, was never his forte, but with music it is a different matter. "I live only in my notes and when one composition is scarcely ended, another is already begun. As I work at present I am frequently occupied with three or four compositions at the same time."

His friends knew, in the summer of 1802, a Beethoven much occupied with playing and making music, sometimes jovial, sometimes splenetic, but for the most part high spirited. Posterity knows a very different Beethoven of that summer. He experienced that moment when a man must tell himself irrevocably that he is to be a creature apart, a subject for meaningful glances interchanged, an outcast from all intercourse with man save by a laborious trickle of shouts or signs. That unspeakable moment came when autumn had descended upon Heiligenstadt. His summer's industry seemed the futile postponement of this realization. The return to the daily round in Vienna could no longer be put off. But what had that round come to be? From

81

brooding, he saw his plight as worse than it was. He saw himself misunderstood because of his enforced silence and put down as a hater of his race, which would have been a cruel injustice.

At his death there was found among his papers a large folded sheet, closely written, and dated "Heiglnstadt [sic], October 10, 1802." It was folded in and inscribed on the last page: "For my brothers Carl and [the omission throughout of the name of Johann has never been explained], to be read and executed after my death." No study of Beethoven would be adequate without its full quotation:

"You men who think or say that I am malevolent, stubborn, or misanthropic, how greatly do you wrong me, you do not know the secret causes of my seeming so, from childhood my heart and mind were inclined to gentleness and goodwill, I was always eager to accomplish great deeds, but reflect now that I have been in a wretched condition aggravated by senseless doctors, while year after year I was deceived in my hopes of improvement, and finally faced with the prospect of a *lasting malady* (whose cure may take years or turn out to be impossible); born with an ardent and lively temperament, even susceptible to the diversions of society, I was compelled early to keep apart, to live in loneliness; when at times I tried to live this down, O how harshly was I defeated by the doubly tragic experience of my bad hearing, and yet I could not say to people, speak louder, shout, for I am deaf. Ah, how could I possibly admit an infirmity in the *one sense* which should have been more acute in me than in others, a sense which I once possessed in highest perfection, a perfection such as surely few in my profession enjoy or have ever enjoyed —O, I cannot do it, therefore forgive me when you see me draw back when I would gladly mingle with you, my misfortune is doubly painful because it must lead to my being misunderstood, for me there can be no refreshment from association with my fellows, no subtle intercourse, no ready flow and exchange of thoughts, only the barest needs of communication will be allowed me in society, I must live like an exile, if I come near people a hot terror seizes me, a fear that my condition may be noticed—so it has been during the half year I have been spending in the country, as ordered by my intelligent physician that my hearing might be spared as much as possible, this was in accord with my inclinations, although I sometimes longed for society, but what a humiliation when one stood beside me and heard a flute

82

in the distance, and *I heard nothing,* or someone heard *a shepherd singing,* and again I heard nothing, such incidents brought me almost to despair, I almost reached the point of putting an end to my life— only art it was that held me back, ah, it seemed impossible to leave the world until I had brought forth all that I felt called upon to produce, and so I endured this wretched existence—truly wretched, a sensitive body which a sudden change can throw from the best into the worst state—Patience—that is what I now must choose for my guide, I have done so, may my determination endure until it pleases the inexorable Parcae to break the thread, perhaps I shall get better, perhaps not—I am prepared. Forced already in my 28th year to become a philosopher, O, it is not easy, and harder for an artist than another—God, thou lookest into my inmost being, Thou knowest that love of man and desire to do good live in me. O men, when some day you read these words, reflect that you did me wrong, may I in my misfortune be consoled by finding one of my kind who, despite all obstacles of nature yet did all that was in his power to be accepted among worthy artists and men. You my brothers Carl and ____ as soon as I am dead if Dr. Schmid is still alive ask him in my name to describe my malady and attach this written sheet to the history of my illness so that so far as is possible the world may become reconciled with me after my death. At the same time I declare you two to be the heirs to my small fortune (if so it can be called), divide it fairly, bear with and help each other, what injury you have done me you know has long been forgiven. To you brother Carl I give special thanks for the attachment you have shown toward me of late. It is my wish that your lives may be better and freer from care than I have had, recommend *virtue* to your children, it alone can give happiness, not money, I speak from experience, it was virtue that upheld me in misery, to it next to my art I owe that fact that I did not end my life by my own hand—Farewell and love each other—I thank all my friends, particularly Prince Lichnowsky and Professor Schmidt—I desire that the instruments from Prince L. be preserved by one of you but let no quarrel result from this, as soon as they serve you to no better purpose sell them, how glad will I be if I can still be helpful to you in my grave—with joy I hasten toward death—if it comes before I have had an opportunity to show all my artistic capacities it will still come too early for me despite my hard fate and I shall probably wish that it had come later—but even then I am satisfied, will it not free me from a state of endless suffering? Come when thou wilt, I shall meet thee bravely—Farewell and do

83

not wholly forget me when I am dead, I deserve this of you, for I
have in life often thought of how to make you happy, be so—

Ludwig van Beethoven.
(Black seal)

Heiglnstadt
October 6, 1802.

Heiglnstadt, October 10, 1802,
so do I take my farewell of you—and indeed sadly—yes, that beloved hope—which I brought with me when I came here to be cured
at least in some degree—I must wholly abandon it, as the leaves of
autumn fall and are withered, so hope has been blighted, almost as I
came I go away—even the high courage—which often inspired me in
the beautiful days of summer—has disappeared—O God—grant me
at last but one day of pure joy—it is so long since real joy has
echoed in my heart—O when—O when—O Divine One—shall I feel
it again in the temple of nature and of men—Never? No—O that
would be too hard."

It is an extraordinary document, this complete confession,
never intended to be seen by another so long as he should live.
The release of his burden is so impelling that two-thirds of the
letter is written before he makes a full stop. In the postscript, the
intensity of his protest and anguish is so great that the rush of
words becomes continuous. The quasi-poetic phrases about the
"Parcae" or the "leaves of autumn" are entirely sincere; they are
the stumbling attempts of a young man whose full heart must
transcend the prosaic, but who has no command of genuine literary eloquence. The desperation which fills the letter makes the
thoughts of suicide ring true, and the twice-mentioned circumstance which held his hand is convincing. He writes of "virtue,"
of his "love of man," his "desire to do good," and the words which
can be lame abstractions, the cheap coin of any ranting evangelist,
are here Beethoven's full Credo, the motive of all his music to
come, which only the music itself will give its full meaning.

Thayer considers the Heiligenstadt document the result of
lone brooding, and blames Dr. Schmidt, who mistakenly sent
his patient to the country to spare him the irritation of sounds,
thereby enabling him "to defer, too long for his peace of mind,
the bitter moment of confession." Could he in any case have

84

been spared that agony? Heiligenstadt, beloved of the composer, had not been a place of idle brooding, but of absorbing activity. The publishers had kept him at his desk with proof sheets, as his music constantly appeared from the press. But the larger number of his days were given over to creative thoughts. Examining the musical fruits of this Heiligenstadt summer, one finds an incredible abundance. The notebooks are brimming with sketches for the Piano Sonatas, Opus 31, the three Violin Sonatas, Opus 30, Variations, Bagatelles, but most important, the Second Symphony, which was completed there.

The Symphony is sunny throughout, its mood unruffled, capturing the peacefulness of the countryside. The first movement is a summons, gleaming with energy, but in the *Larghetto* the composer reins his new powers to the uses of an extended romantic lyricism. The Symphony shows a considerable advance over the First in the use of instrumental color.

When Beethoven wrote in the Heiligenstadt Will: "It is so long since real joy has echoed in my heart," he had forgotten the joy, which, out of the bitterness of his heart, he had found anew in music. It was not the last time with him that personal suffering was to find release in the pure, limpid tones of his art. Beethoven never filled a brace of sonatas with more sparkling grace than the three piano sonatas, Opus 31, which are the product of this summer. The storms which blow through the middle section of the *Andante Grazioso* in the First, and through most of the Second, have no counterpart in the less personal Symphony. But the somberness in these sonatas is no deeper than the lover's melancholy in much of the young Beethoven. The *Allegretto* of the Second Sonata floats on the lightest surface. Coming to the Third, in E flat, he waived the idea of a slow movement and wrote a scherzo, minuet and presto as light-footed as if there were no such thing as care. The Violin Sonatas are in the vein of the Piano Sonatas; the *Adagio Cantabile* of the Second has the ingratiating touch of effusiveness; the Third is without a slow movement.

As the autumnal pall had descended with suddenness, after the idyllic summer, stagnant gloom was thrown off with equal suddenness. Sealing his confession and locking it in his desk, away from all knowledge of man, away from his own thoughts, he plunged in November into the daily round of friends and music-making in Vienna. He gave lessons, accepted invitations and was seen at one house or another. Meanwhile the deeper, the unseen Beethoven underwent a remarkable change. A strange new forcefulness was about to be released. Bitter, degrading misery, which would have marred the spirit of another, gave Beethoven's the bright resiliency of forged steel. Outward adversity built up inward power—a new firmness of hand, a depth and purity of view. On the heels of the Symphony which brought him peace in time of doubt was to come from his deepest anguish the Symphony which, reckless, defiant, was to trample weak thoughts of defeat. Beethoven was exultant in his new power which suddenly showed him the way to capture in tone the noblest aspirations of the human spirit. It was to be a symphony of conquest, but not the conquest of military campaigns. The composer was the conqueror. After many months of travail he had confirmed a faith and found to proclaim it a strength which would be forever invincible, whatever should befall him. He had learned the way at last to "take Fate by the throat."

CHAPTER NINE

THE FRIENDS in Vienna knew nothing of the terrible ordeal at Heiligenstadt as the summer had faded. Back among them, Beethoven seemed in higher spirits than ever, as he indulged in violent hilarity. His fits of rage were correspondingly lusty, as he involved himself in a perplexing tangle with three publishers over his String Quintet. Only his intimate friends who were often alone with him noticed an imperfection in his hearing. Indeed, the fears which filled the Heiligenstadt document were mostly the fears of apprehension, for deafness did not yet bar Beethoven from any of his usual pursuits. Czerny wrote: "Although he had suffered from pains in his ears and the like ever since 1800, he still heard speech and music perfectly well until nearly 1812." That Seyfried made a similar statement only shows how well those about him were deceived.

They were even more in the dark as to what was taking place in Beethoven's tonal scheming. They could have known little or nothing of a great symphony which was occupying the more vital portion of his mental energies, extending through 1803 and into the next year. Beethoven remarked to the violinist Krumpholz, "I am not satisfied with my works up to the present time. From today I mean to take a new road." Krumpholz could only have wondered. Beethoven had every cause for satisfaction with his present ways; he finished his Oratorio "The Mount of Olives" and brought it out at the *Theater-an-der-Wien* in April, 1803, together with his two completed symphonies and his new Piano Concerto in C minor. The concert put a good sum of money in his pocket. The First Symphony was receiving performances in many German towns. A month later than the *Theater-an-der-Wien* concert, the composer had hastily completed a violin sonata (later to be dedicated to Kreutzer) for a performance by the half-African violinist from London, Bridgetower, with a slow movement which completely captivated the audience.

This was no "new road"; it was the brilliant continuation of the road he had been taking. The exuberant words could have come from the creator who may have just projected the first mighty sketch which in a single ebullition of new power captured the bold lines, encompassed the incredible plan of the opening movement of the *Eroica* Symphony. In a hundred continuous bars, wherein a succession of themes appear in embryo, the exposition, and therefore the concept of the first movement, is clearly set down. This sudden manifestation of reaching forcefulness must have been long gathering. Artistic caution cannot explain its holding back in the purling innocuousness of the Second Symphony a few months before.

Beethoven spoke later of "the bad habit which I have had from my childhood of writing down my first thoughts." If the habit was bad, it was extraordinarily effective, for it was his invariable way of finding his bolder innovations. Chance scraps of themes which occurred to him would go into the sketchbooks, many of them coming to nothing. Suddenly, perhaps years later, one would begin to develop. It was then, in the heat of creation, that the magnitude of his conception first showed itself. The initial sketches often give no intimation of this, but appear elementary to the point of insipidity. It was as if Beethoven took quite casually as his point of departure what lay at hand. At white heat he transformed all that he touched.

The idealized heroism of the *Eroica,* music of profound and personal experience, could have been nothing else than autobiographical. The heroism is Beethoven's own indomitable spirit extended and universalized. In the first movement it is the heroism of intrepidity where faith and strength become one, a strength which exalts and purifies. The funeral march soon ceases to be elegiac. Its solemnity has no odor of mortality; death had no place in Beethoven's thoughts as an artist. The spirit which gathers and rises in the middle portion sweeps inaction aside and becomes a life assertion even more penetrating than that in the long crescendos and shattering chords of the opening movement.

88

These two movements are the movements of conquering. The last two are clear and confident—the *Scherzo* serene, the *Finale* joyous. The shouting triumph of the close has no tramp of heavy, crushing feet. It is a jubilant exhortation to all mankind, a foreshadowing of the finales of the Fifth and Ninth Symphonies.

Nothing could have been more incongruous to this picture than the self-vaunting soldier-statesman from Corsica. If Beethoven could have met and spoken to Napoleon even for a few minutes, his quick intuition would have perceived in him the callous despoiler, obtuse to his own pretension of noble aim. What Beethoven knew was a name often spoken by idealists as the destined champion of republicanism, as the "liberator" of Europe from wretched monarchical oppression. Beethoven's ideal hero would have been a commoner, bending his might for the cause of humanity. "Liberation" was a magic word in 1804, a panacea still believed in, despite the persistent bloodshed and failure which had been resulting from its pursuit. Beethoven's belief in that ideal was so powerful that it dominated his art, becoming his patriotism and his religion. This was the motive force of the new symphony. Napoleon was a name standing for it, a convenient popular title.

It was Ries who saw the word "Bonaparte" written on the first sheet of the finished manuscript as it lay on Beethoven's desk in the spring of 1804. When the composer learned a few weeks later that the "First Consul" had crowned himself "Emperor" he angrily tore the title-page in two—so Ries and Lichnowsky have each testified, although the story has an apocryphal odor. He did not in any sense repudiate the intention of his music. He merely removed a name which, so events had shown, no longer stood for the substance of his symphony. Beethoven's idea of Napoleon was probably as vague as his concept of heroism was precise. Being very sure indeed that the score was as he wished it, he was not greatly concerned with what decorative title the publisher might put at the head. When he offered his Symphony to Breitkopf and Härtel on August 24th, he described it almost ruefully as "really entitled Bonaparte," as if still aware that that name might have had selling possibilities. Beethoven remarked to Ries: "He is only a man after all, like any other."

89

But no man on this earth could have fitted the dimensions of the *Eroica*—none save the artist who wrote it, at the moment of writing it. The parts appeared in print with the obviously reconsidered and *post facto* title: "*Sinfonia Eroica, composed to celebrate the memory of a great man.*"

What could be expected of the first audiences of the *Eroica* in the year 1805? Symphonic music consisted of an adroit discourse of pleasant sounds. This was not yet a matter for argument; nothing else had ever been known. When Beethoven had given his hearers affecting sentiment in his slow movements, there was nothing to be disturbed about. But when this *Marcia funebre* spoke in accents restrained, remote, awesome, in a line which was almost static, a sentiment which instead of being pretty was almost frightening, even the admirers of Beethoven's earlier slow movements were alienated. When the movement continued for fifteen minutes, they were bored. The First Movement, alternations of dissonant tension and smooth confluence, proudly striding and mounting, shaking a fist in harsh chords defiantly repeated—this was enough to damn the Symphony in its first minutes. "Music," we can hear them saying, "should be something we can enjoy." The first hearers of the *Eroica* must have said that because audiences always have said it in the presence of the unaccustomed; they are saying it still.

Very few of the early hearers of the *Eroica* would in their hearts have acquitted Beethoven of having taken advantage of his fame and position to inflict upon them harsh and arbitrary sounds exceeding all reasonable lengths. They would still have thought so, even if the contemporary performances had been far less inept, muddy and groping than they were. It has taken many years to bring forth in performances what long lay unclarified by the bewildered fumblings of musicians, and what even Beethoven's most loyal friends could not perceive—the long, surging lines of melody, alive in every voice, essential euphony, superb constructive balance, the pursuit of a single driving idea to a remarkable integration.

The critic of the *Freymüthige* reported the event of the first public performance, and divided its audience into three parts. There were those who failed to find in it any "artistic value," but only "an untamed and unsuccessful striving after singularity," a use of "strange modulations and violent transitions" which achieve the "unusual and the fantastic" at the expense of the beautiful and the sublime, wherein the composer forfeits every merit found in his earlier works. The second faction, to which the writer of the article seems to belong, finds the symphony beautiful in spots but impossibly long, and a regrettable departure on the composer's part from the more reasonable path of the Symphonies in C and D, and the Septet in E flat. The third faction consists of Beethoven's "particular friends" who assert "that it is just this Symphony which is his masterpiece, that this is the true style for high-class music, and that if it does not please now, it is because the public is not cultured enough artistically to grasp all these lofty beauties; after a few thousand years have passed it will not fail of its effect."

This critic would have been surprised if he could have known that by the omission of one word, the word "thousand," this statement of the blind loyalist's case would have been the absolute truth.

Although little other music came forth during the many months in which the *Eroica* absorbed him, Beethoven's spare hours were loaded with smaller duties. There could have been little time for brooding over his deafness; perhaps he welcomed diverting occupations, ponderous or annoying as some of them were. The penalty for the large number of sonatas and smaller works he had been writing was a still continuing stream of proofs to be corrected. Printers' errors became too numerous to be downed. They even persisted in the printed copies, to the great anger of the composer who was always scrupulously exact in his scores. He wrote of one proof: "Errors swarm in it like fish in the sea."

It is plain that his publishers treated him a good deal more casually than they did later, when he was considered a rarer prize. He was constantly protesting with them for bringing out his music in transcriptions for saleable combinations, sometimes falsely attributing the transcriptions to himself. He had more justification than later for calling some of them "arch swindlers." The pirate trade which to this day cheerfully flourishes among music publishers was then carried to bolder lengths. Beethoven would retaliate in anger and be drawn into interminable, exhausting disputations. The affair of the String Quintet, Opus 29, which dragged through two years, was an example of Beethoven's propensity to get himself needlessly, and ever more deeply, into trouble. The Quintet was issued from the press of Breitkopf and Härtel in November, 1802. Simultaneously Artaria appeared upon the scene with copies of a "reprint" edition. Beethoven tried to placate Breitkopf and Härtel with a letter fulminating against Artaria. The Quintet had been bought by Count Moritz Fries for private use until a certain date, according to custom, after which the ownership, for publication, reverted to the author. The rogue Artaria, so said Beethoven, obtained the Count's private copy through oily misrepresentation, and promptly engraved it. All that Beethoven felt able to put upon Artaria was a restraint of delay, eased by the bribe of a new composition. He took the further dubious expedient of asking for the fifty copies which had come from the press of Artaria, for correction, and instructing Ries to make the corrections with such heavy pen strokes that they would be spoiled for sale. He further sought to protect the Leipzig firm by a public statement to the effect that the edition of "Messrs. Artaria and Mollo" had no connection with him and was moreover "faulty, incorrect, and utterly useless to players." The result was legal action by Artaria, whom Beethoven had given a certain technical sanction by his corrections, and by Mollo, who had had no actual part in the affair, and so considered himself libeled. Beethoven countered that he had made only a partial revision—"out of spite to Artaria." He had supposed that Artaria and Mollo were "really one firm," describing them to Breitkopf and Härtel as "a whole family of rascals." Spiteful half-revisions and false suppositions did not help him in the eyes of the law. The *Polizer Oberdirection* decided in favor of both firms, and Beethoven had to publish a retraction, exonerating Mollo.

As the fair copy of the *Eroica* Symphony lay upon his desk at Baden in July, 1804, complete and awaiting a publisher, Beethoven wrote to Ries: "I never believed that I could be so lazy

92

as I am here. If a burst of industry follows, something may be expected." It was not laziness. His idling was dreaming, and his dreaming was gestation, to be followed, as he supposed but was not sure, by a fresh outburst. He was through with his orchestra for the time being. The piano would next receive his complete attention. Seyfried has described his intense industry at this period: "The whole forenoon from the first ray of light was devoted to mechanical labor, i.e., to transcribing; the rest of the day was given to thought and the ordering of ideas. Hardly, at the meal hour, had he put the last morsel in his mouth before he began his customary promenade, unless he had some other excursion *in petto;* that is to say, he hurried in double-quick tempo several times around the city, as if urged on by a goad; and this, let the weather be what it might."

He was now accounted definitely peculiar by all who encountered him. His power of absorption had increased. As he walked the streets or fields, according to the season, his face was a mask, only the smoldering eyes reflecting the life within. The more active, clear and purposeful his inward world, the more disordered became his everyday life. His lodgings, wherever they might be, for he often changed them, were chaos. "Books and music," says Seyfried, "were scattered in every corner; here the remnants of a cold luncheon; here sealed or half-emptied bottles; here upon a stand the hurried sketches of a quartet; here the remains of a *déjeuner;* there on the pianoforte, on scribbled paper, the material for a glorious symphony still slumbering in embryo; here a proof sheet awaiting salvation; friendly and business letters covering the floor; between the windows a respectable loaf of strachino, *ad latus* a considerable ruin of a genuine Veronese salami."

Ries tells of a summer day in 1804, when he went to the master's lodging at Döbling for his lesson. Beethoven wished to take a walk, and led his young companion "so far astray that we did not get back to Döbling until nearly eight o'clock. He had been all the time humming and sometimes howling, always up and down, without singing any definite notes. In answer to my question what it was he said: 'A theme for the last movement of the

93

Sonata has occurred to me.' When we entered the room he ran to the pianoforte without taking off his hat. I took a seat in a corner, and he soon forgot all about me. Now he stormed for at least an hour with the beautiful finale of the Sonata. Finally he got up, was surprised still to see me, and said: 'I can't give you a lesson today, I must do some more work.' "

This was to be the *"Appassionata"* Sonata. Here and in the *"Waldstein"* Sonata of the next year, there was a sweeping impetuosity, as if the lover's sighs of Jean Paul's Titan or Goethe's Werther had suddenly become as overwhelming and convincing as their authors would have liked to make them. He had overflowed his mold, as with the *Eroica* Symphony he had strained the limits of the chamber orchestra of the time, and fairly burst the four elegant walls of Lichnowsky's princely salon, where that music was first tried. His thought had carried him beyond them, and now it carried him beyond the mechanical limits of the piano. The instruments of his day were built for lightness and elegance. A few years later he persuaded Andreas Streicher, the piano maker, to "give his instruments greater resonance and elasticity," this, according to Reichardt, "so that the virtuoso who plays with strength and significance may have the instrument in better command for sustained and expressive tones." The new sonatas, if played according to their plain implications, would have threatened wreckage upon the instruments of the time, close descendants of the harpsichord, nor were the virtuosos then abroad disposed to follow those implications. They were not a species of *"Jupiter tonans,"* to hurl musical thunderbolts, nor could their pale and fastidious temperaments deal with the *Andante con moto* of the *"Appassionata,"* where to sustain the melody and the mood exacted the utmost from contemporary strings, pedals and imagination. The *"Appassionata"* was not attempted in public performance, so far as records show, until its composer had been in his grave a dozen years.

Beethoven, composing, had merely forgotten the virtuosos, and their pianos as well. His imagination commanded; musicians and instruments must adapt themselves as best they may. His heart was full and knew no boundary. Heaven and earth were his space. The artist was free; he had only to take his freedom. He could love, suffer, dream, exult greatly, and pour his feelings into his art. It was an intoxicating egotism, and yet no egotism at all, for it merged with feelings of many, present and to come, and so contained them.

CHAPTER TEN

WHEN BEETHOVEN, in his letter to Wegeler in 1801, spoke of his success in all musical forms except those of "opera and the church," he was revealing an ambition, which, at least so far as the opera was concerned, lay close to his heart. His eagerness when the opportunity came to him in 1804 overrode a certain lack of working experience, for his expertness in theatre craft was necessarily drawn from nothing more substantial than the routine at Bonn, his studies of vocal writing with Salieri, his perusal of available scores by Cherubini, Méhul, or other contemporaries, and his direct observation in the theatres of Vienna, where he was often seen.

The crowded performances were a reminder of the glory which was showering upon talents far less than his own. Cherubini, much applauded in Paris, held his great respect. There was Paisiello in Naples; Päer, lately settled in Dresden. In Vienna Salieri, Vogler, Seyfried, had enjoyed the production of many a stage piece, reaping esteem and reward. Beethoven hoped and strove mightily to do the same. The impresarios of Vienna remembered the success of his Ballet *The Creations of Prometheus*. They were aware that his name would arouse anticipation and they were ready to gamble with it.

Since opera was the only form of music in Vienna which coincided with public entertainment, it alone could bring the ducats rolling in. Cherubini afforded an example of a long famous composer discovered overnight in Vienna to be an effective writer of operas. In 1803, when the operas of Cherubini had been given in Italy and Paris for some twenty years, Schikaneder at the *Theater-an-der-Wien* and Baron Braun at the *Burg Theater* awoke suddenly to the fact that a golden opportunity was at hand. They fell over each other's heels importing his latest operas from Paris, and even came out simultaneously with the same piece, differently titled. Schikaneder offered to provide Beethoven with an opera libretto which he himself would write, and Beethoven received the idea favorably. He moved into the *Theater* building where free lodgings were allowed him, according to custom, and is supposed to have made some sketches for an opera of which not even the subject is known. In the following season, Braun bought out the *Theater-an-der-Wien*. Schikaneder was excluded—so was Beethoven, from his opera project and probably from his lodgings as well. But fortune soon turned his way again. In November, 1804, the Baron put his former rival in charge of the theatre—a tribute to the value of that arch-showman, and presently we find Beethoven back in his lodgings and at work upon another opera. The text was a German adaptation which Sonnleithner, Secretary of the *Burg Theater*, had made of a French piece then six years old—Bouilly's *Léonore*.

There began a struggle intense and prolonged. Beethoven alone with his libretto must subdue to his purpose an adversary far different from the pliant and responsive instruments which had always leapt to serve his greater thoughts. Now there were prosaic stretches of text, stage situations which must become a part of him and would not, the necessity of holding down his beloved orchestra as a background for vocal advantage. To adapt himself to the traditional *Singspiel* of the expired eighteenth century, infusing the stylized airs and ensembles with true and moving dramatic expressiveness, would have required a performer of miracles, a Mozart at the very least. Beethoven sometimes performed miracles, but he was not temperamentally constituted for this one. Mozart had the touch and go of the theatre which could accept an inanity without hesitation and on the instant turn it into music of immortal beauty. Beethoven approached his subject slowly, laboriously, from within. In those parts where the characters and their dilemma took hold of him, the sheer power of his conviction overcame wooden conventions, and the story came to moving life. In none of his works was there a more remarkable manifestation of his will power.

The first libretto proposed to Beethoven (other than what he may have had from Schikaneder, the stage clown who wrote *The Magic Flute* text) was an extraordinarily happy choice. It was not a good piece of literature—no libretto of its day was that. But the subject had sprung from French revolutionary ideals; it played upon the great, all-absorbing motive of liberation from tyranny, and was consequently the one subject that could have set Beethoven on fire. Bouilly, a French lawyer, and the librettist of Cherubini's *The Water Carrier*, had written the original book for Paris in 1798, as *Léonore, ou l'Amour Conjugal*, and Gaveaux had set it. Bouilly let it be known in his memoirs that the tale of the imprisonment of Florestan by a political enemy, and the efforts of his wife, Léonore, to liberate him by disguising herself as a jailer at the risk of her life, had a basis of fact in the days of the Terror. He had also intimated that he had set the scene in Spain for discretionary reasons. The book had been popular enough to make its way, in those days of free borrowing, into three languages. Paër had composed a score for an Italian version, *Leonora*, which opened the Dresden season in 1804, just at the time that Beethoven began to compose his German version. Sonnleithner had been called into service for this translation. The title was changed to *Fidelio*, so as to avoid confusion with Paër's opera; Beethoven naturally much preferred the real name to the assumed name of his heroine, and struggled in vain to keep the title. He showed his preference by naming two overtures "Leonore" when they were separately performed and published.

Beethoven could not rise above those scenes in Bouilly's text which were no more than a typical romantic effusion of the time. But the concept of cruel oppression overcome through a conjugal fidelity all-enduring and all-surpassing was to Beethoven more than the current coin of romantic tale-telling. It was a vitalizing impulse transcending pedestrian dialogue and stock situations. The pity of Florestan wasting away his life in a dungeon with no gleam of hope became something for every generation to feel, whatever its fashion in sentiment. The plight of his fellow prisoners, wan shadows of the men they once were—Beethoven lived and suffered in these with a compassion which too has outlasted all fashions. Leonore was to him woman's love at its noblest, deep and quiet, unfaltering and unquestioning.

98

Beethoven composed the scenes in order, as if to preserve in his own mind the continuity of unfoldment. The many pages of the sketchbooks, an astonishing tangle of notations decipherable only to himself, are proof of his devotion to his task, but proof no less of his labors to subjugate a resistant medium to his expressive intent. He made eighteen beginnings to the famous air *"In des Lebens Frühlingstagen"* before he found what he was seeking: the full sense of Florestan's hopeless vision of the fair world which has been shut out to him. The jubilant final chorus *"O namenlose Freude"* was also arrived at by many stages.

Beethoven retired to Hetzendorf for the summer months of 1805 and between June and September made his last rounding out of the score. Returning to Vienna and his quarters in the *Theater-an-der-Wien,* he was able to hand to Sebastian Meier the complete music in performable shape. The opera was promptly put into rehearsal.

And now began the first episode in the unfortunate early career of *Fidelio*. When the initial performance was announced the attention of all Vienna was distracted by fearful speculations. The armies of France were moving steadily up the Rhine Valley, and across Southern Germany. Austria lay before them, and Austria's capital would be Napoleon's certain objective. Ulm fell on October 20th, and ten days later the news came that the boundary had been crossed. Bernadotte was in occupation of Salzburg. The progress down the Danube continued. Vienna, fair and proud, inviolate through her centuries, lay quite undefended. The nobility packed their jewels in their carriages and joined the trek of refugees which crowded the roads to Brünn or Presburg. The best male singers were not available for *Fidelio*. Demmer, a tenor successful in light rôles, had little idea of the character of Florestan. The villainous Don Pizzaro fell to Sebastian Meier, who was a better stage manager than baritone. Anna Pauline Milder, the Leonore, had an ample voice; it was when she was only fourteen that Haydn had listened to her and exclaimed: "My dear child, you have a voice like a house!" Milder was to become famous in this part, but only later, with maturity and experience. She was now only twenty. The conscientious Seyfried rehearsed the opera, but the rehearsals were hasty and

99

preoccupied. The tension and uncertainty which gripped Vienna made its way to the stage and orchestra.

On November 13th, just a week before the scheduled first performance, the French battalions marched into Vienna. Napoleon had let it be known through his generals that he was the well-wisher of the Austrians, their protector against Russian barbarism. The Viennese were to be treated with courtesy; even the volunteer guards were to be left unmolested. The citizens did not know how to receive the invaders. The procession was a strange spectacle, and they gazed upon it in curious silence. The invaders were silent too. The emblazoned *grenadiers á cheval* were proud figures in their polished cuirasses, but the horses under them looked dejected. The infantry were mud-splashed and unshaven; here and there one carried a loaf of bread or a ham on the point of his bayonet. They seemed to come without end, day and night, some marching on toward Hungary or northward, some pitching camp in the suburbs, the officers taking occupation of the princely mansions in the town. The reports of distant cannon could be heard; it was said that the French were engaged in a terrific battle with the Russians, that the Austrian army to the south was being annihilated by the Italians. But nothing was known. All communication was suppressed and, with it, all news. What could not be concealed was the presence of French wounded who were being brought in on stretchers from the Russian front. Austrian prisoners, too, were herded in. They could give no clear information except that the country was laid waste, the armies were living on it, and the people were starving.

The magistrates as much as ordered the townspeople to ignore what might be going on about them, and to forget their troubles in the pleasures of their parks. The Court Theatres were commanded to be kept open. *Othello* was acted before an empty house on the night before the occupation. Operas of Cherubini or Zingarelli were to follow *Fidelio* at intervals.

There was no excitement over *Fidelio,* no anticipation. Almost all of Beethoven's friends were away, and those who remained had other things to worry about. The rehearsals were listless. In an over-run Vienna the rigid presence of men at arms seemed to make the private misfortunes of a legendary family in Spain dim

100

and unimportant. Beethoven could gaze from his window in the Pasqualati house on the Mölker Bastei toward Hetzendorf and the *Schönbrunn* gardens where, in the heat of recent summer days, he had dreamed out his *Fidelio*. Now Schönbrunn was heavily guarded, for the Emperor Napoleon sat in state at the Palace, receiving delegations. Napoleon knew nothing of an opera about to be•produced, which had been composed a short while before in the paths beneath the Palace window, where his sentries were now pacing. He did not know that the composer, a fiery little man who had once inscribed "Bonaparte" upon a symphony and then thought better of it, was gazing toward the violated Palace and speculating, quite correctly, that his own kind of power was more far-reaching in time and space, its impress upon mankind far more enduring. This proposition would have interested Napoleon not in the least. Music for him had a single function: to soothe and relax. He considered Cherubini taxing, more learned than tuneful. Finding him by chance in Vienna at the time, he patronized him for reasons of good appearance; it was fitting to surround himself with a retinue of culture. He much preferred Paisiello.

On November 20, 1805, *Fidelio* was first unfolded before a scattered assemblage who were mostly French officers, present because the *Theater-an-der-Wien* was open under orders and there was nothing else to do. Even if they had been able to follow the German text, these men of action would have preferred a more elegant and sprightly show to this one with its drab prison sets, and its woeful tale of virtue oppressed. On the second night, a young doctor from Edinburgh, Henry P. Reeve, attended *Fidelio* and described what he saw. "Beethoven presided at the pianoforte. He is a small, dark, young-looking man, and wears spectacles." Reeve found the plot "a miserable mixture of low manners and romantic situations," "the music equal to any praise." This would look like musical acumen had not the Scottish doctor attended Zingarelli's *Romeo and Juliet* the following week, and found it likewise "above all praise." He finally reports that "a copy of complimentary verses was showered down from the upper balcony at the end of the piece." This vain attempt to stir acclaim for Beethoven is attributable to the faithful

Stephan von Breuning. After three performances the public for *Fidelio* vanished altogether and the opera was dropped. Several critics managed to be there, despite conditions, and delivered their post mortems to the effect that Beethoven had written a dull opera without even the interest of his usual startling "singularities." None seemed to suspect that the opera might contain passages of imperishable beauty.

In December, the immediate emergency having passed, Baron Braun decided to give the opera another try; some of the initial expense might be saved, and there was the chance that, given a proper audience, it would after all prove worthy of its composer's reputation. It was generally agreed between the *régisseur* Meier and a group of Beethoven's friends that the first act moved too slowly. It must be cut. A night session was arranged at the Palace of Lichnowsky, at which the act was to be played and discussed with Beethoven. The imperious composer who never permitted questioning of his artistic judgment was strangely meek. He could not afford to be otherwise, for he knew not how to face the problems of dealing with the limitations and vanities of singers, the insistence of the stage director, the behavior of the crowds before the footlights, with their prejudices and their failure to respond at vital moments. All these people must be mollified if the whole venture were to be saved. Compromise on every side for the obdurate Beethoven! A composer like Gluck, who had the theatre in his blood, could follow through his clear intentions to the bitter end. Beethoven knew how to be adamant; but now his unease and inexperience threw him upon the mercy and advice of others.

Treitschke and Meier of the *Theater* were at Lichnowsky's, and Clement, the leader of the violins. Von Collin, author of *Coriolan* and the playwright Lange would give literary advice. There was the tenor Röckel, a young man of twenty; there was Karl van Beethoven, interested in the salvation of a possible money-getter. Seyfried, as conductor at the theatre and friend of Beethoven, must surely have been present.

Röckel has described the scene:

"Meier had prepared me for the coming storm when Beethoven should be advised to leave out three whole numbers in the first act.

. . . I had arrived in Vienna only a short while before, and there met Beethoven for the first time. As the whole opera was to be gone through, we went directly to work. Princess Lichnowsky played on the grand piano from the great score, and Clement, sitting in a corner of the room, accompanied with his violin the whole opera by heart, playing all the solos of the different instruments. The extraordinary memory of Clement having been universally known, nobody was astonished by it except myself. Meier and I made ourselves useful by singing as well as we could, he the lower, I the higher parts. Though the friends of Beethoven were fully prepared for the impending battle, they had never seen him in that excitement before, and without the prayers and entreaties of the Princess, an invalid, who was a second mother to Beethoven and acknowledged by himself as such, his united friends were not likely to have succeeded in an enterprise they had undertaken without confidence."

It must have been doubly hard for Beethoven to throw overboard music written with his heart's blood, some of it incomparably fine, and to yield to the combined pressure of his friends on such a subject. Once reconciled, he fell into a mood of reckless gaiety.

"When after their efforts from seven until after one o'clock, the sacrifice of the three numbers was accomplished, and when we, exhausted, hungry and thirsty, went to revive ourselves with a splendid supper—then none was happier and gayer than Beethoven. His fury had been replaced by exhilaration. He saw me, opposite to him, intently occupied with a French dish and asked me what I was eating. I answered: 'I don't know,' and with his lion's voice he roared out: 'He eats like a wolf without knowing what! Ha, ha, ha!'"

Stephan von Breuning made the necessary condensations of the text, and Beethoven made the necessary excisions in the score. He reduced the acts from three to two. He was urged to re-write the overture. The one then used, and now known as "No. 2," was too symphonic and involved, said the operatic experts. Undertaking a simplification, he became lost in his subject, and quite forgot the grave admonitions that not otherwise could his beloved *Fidelio* make him the successful operatic composer he longed to be. Without a text to cope with, alone with his beloved orchestra, he spoke in his true strength, producing a concert overture which, before the lowered curtain, told far more powerfully than the cumbrous stage could ever tell of loyalty, ringing conviction, joyous release. The new Overture ("No. 3") lost some of the quasi-theatrical directness and impact of the second, and became more symphonically involved. Instead of aiding the illusion to come, it was destined to crush the opening scene between Jacqueline at her ironing board and Jaquino, her loutish lover, into silly puppetry. It was not until he made a fourth attempt at an overture and for a later revival wrote the one which still bears the name *Fidelio* that he found the suitable way lightly to bow in the pleasantly jogging, homely level of the opening scene.

The revised score for the second mounting of *Fidelio* was barely ready for rehearsal. There were signs of a favorable reception at the first performance (March 29th), but things did not go well. Beethoven refused to conduct the second performance, for the orchestra, he complained, paid no attention to the dynamic indications. After two performances, the opera was once more withdrawn. Some remarkable critical statements accompanied the second going down of *Fidelio*—one of which referred to the glorious liberating trumpet call as a "postillion horn solo," and another which waved aside the new overture as "abominable cacophony." Breuning attributed the second failure to cabals against the composer. It is easier to believe that Beethoven, unhappy and angry when he could not bring about an adequate performance with only one full rehearsal, became as usual a disrupting force.

Fidelio was mounted again in the following season; its audience perceptibly grew. But Beethoven now conceived the idea that he was being cheated of his full percentage. He went to the office of the Baron Braun and made his complaint. The Baron, knowing of Beethoven's reputed suspiciousness (Roeckel tells this), protested mildly that his employees were trustworthy, and that if there were any shortage in the accounting he would lose more by it than Beethoven. Very likely the audiences would further increase. Until now they had been pretty well limited to the highest-priced seats—the stalls and first rows of the floor. It was to be hoped that the seats above would later be occupied.

"I don't write for the galleries!" exclaimed Beethoven.

"No?" replied the Baron. "My dear sir, even Mozart did not disdain to write for the galleries."

If the Baron wished to bring to an end his troubles with *Fidelio* and its vexatious composer, he could not have hit upon a surer way to do it.

"My score," Beethoven shouted. "Immediately. There will be no more performances. Give me my score!"

The Baron rang a bell and ordered that the score be returned at once to its author. So Beethoven, closing the door upon the career which had been his fondest ambition, found himself with his much-labored manuscript on his hands. Perhaps what had been most infuriating about the intendant's remark was its entire truth. Beethoven could tell himself proudly that he wrote for those of finer perceptions. So did Mozart, but that pupil of the school of necessity knew that to be a successful operatic composer, one must at the same time write for all and sundry. He had found the way, even before he had begun to grow up. Beethoven had not, so far as his opera was concerned, and nothing could have been more bitter to him than to hear it as a taunt from the lips of the man who controlled its destiny. *Fidelio* was quite without the combination of qualities by which the knowing composer contrives to win the mixed thousands in the dark spaces beyond the footlights—grateful displays of vocalism, incisive declamation, lush melody, spectacle, bright costumes, lively choruses. When Beethoven told Braun that he did not write for the galleries, he should rather have said that when an idea fully possessed him, he was incapable of courting the galleries with broadly externalized effects. His idea could grow and expand within him until it became irresistible, but not by resort to the obvious. The transfiguring power latent in *Fidelio* was so without ostentation that it could pass unnoticed. Only after the revival seven years later would it begin to win popular understanding.

Nevertheless, he labored with all that was in him to achieve adequate performance and general acceptance. It became his intermittent problem through about ten years of his life, from the end of 1803, when he made his first sketches, until 1814, when he made the second complete revision. They were the years of his greatest fertility. Into none of his music did he put more affectionate care. When his last illness was upon him, Beethoven extracted from his confusion of papers the manuscript score of *Fidelio* and presented it to Schindler with the words: "Of all my children, this is the one that cost me the worst birth-pangs, the one that brought me the most sorrow; and for that reason it is the one most dear to me."

CHAPTER ELEVEN

NOT LATER than 1804, there came an unusual addition to Beethoven's small selection of pupils. Rudolph Johann Joseph Rainer, Archduke of Austria, half brother to the Emperor, was then sixteen. Like his late illustrious uncle, Maximilian Franz, Beethoven's Elector at Bonn, he was inclined, while the Church claimed his allegiance, to give his heart to music. Having reached the age where he could choose his own master, he stepped out from under the musical tutor, who as composer to the Imperial Court had been assigned to him, and went to Beethoven. It was natural enough that the boy should be drawn to the master whose praises he must often have heard from the aristocracy of Vienna, and whom he must have encountered at the houses of Lichnowsky, Liechtenstein, Lobkowitz or Rasoumowsky.

Conforming, as an *Erzherzog* must, to what had been laid out for him, Rudolph became before three years had passed coadjutor of the Archbishopric of Olmütz, and in due time would be ordained Archbishop Cardinal of Austria. Meanwhile, he attached himself to the cause of Beethoven, in what was to be a lifelong friendship. Beethoven's motley assortment of friends turned up no stranger relationship than this one between the boy exalted by blood and the man exalted in art, the first unable to bend, the second unwilling. The space between them stirred antagonisms, reared a barrier of etiquette, but the two found a way of getting along with each other, reaching a basis of affection, and avoiding quarrels altogether. Beethoven, reared in the habit of outward respect toward exalted position, met requirements. One can believe that the strong-willed Beethoven often had his way with the noble of the rather weak and effeminate features which a later portrait shows. He took one conspicuous liberty—the privilege of breaking appointments at the Palace when in the throes of composition, and this the royal pupil recognized and had no choice but to accept with good grace.

Plainly, Beethoven liked the boy, while musically he managed to put up with him. As a pianist, Rudolph was as far below Czerny or Ries, Beethoven's principal pupils at the time, as a dilettante is likely to be below professionals. Beethoven was inclined to be indulgent. To the question whether the Archduke really played well, he answered with a laugh: "When he is feeling just right." Beethoven allowed him to perform in his Triple Concerto when he had taught him about a year. The piano part is not insuperable. As time went on, the patron received an array of dedications which showed Beethoven's care to honor him with his best: the Fourth and Fifth Piano Concertos, the *"Lebewohl"* and *"Hammer-Klavier"* Piano Sonatas, the Violin Sonata Opus 96 and Trio Opus 97, the *Missa Solemnis*, and in the composer's last year, the *"Grosse Fugue"* for string quartet. The pupil may have tried the chamber music in Beethoven's presence; latitude is possible in an intimate circle. It is unthinkable that such works as the "Emperor" Concerto could ever have been freely given over to the archducal fingers.

In contrast to Ries, who, if he were fortunate enough to find his teacher at home, was more likely to be put to good use than given a lesson, the Archduke could never go to Beethoven—their respective stations forbade. Since Beethoven would in no case have kept an appointment when music was upon him, there is, through the pages of the published letters, an *ostinato* of excuses, pleading a great variety of ailments, and either postponing a lesson or regretting one which he had missed. The formalities of obeisance thinly concealed the evasive and arbitrary ways of the writer. Rudolph indulgently allowed himself to be set aside, and put up with the neglect which anyone demanding Beethoven's time must certainly have suffered. He was amused at the conflict between ineradicable etiquette and his untamable teacher. When Beethoven was obstructed at the Palace by a succession of liveried servants, bowing and announcing, he lost his temper. The Archduke gave orders that the impatient music master should henceforth be allowed to penetrate directly to the music room. Beethoven, always particular about finger position, once rapped his pupil's fingers, so we are told, and was mildly put in his place. He retorted with a quotation from Goethe, and was so pleased with himself at having chastised royalty that he boasted of the incident years later.

Beethoven's repeated assurances in the letters that his actions were prompted by affection and not "cold self-interest" seem tactless in that both motives were surely present. When warm friendship happens to coincide with easy favor, who can speak with any confidence of the degree of mercenary coloration? Rudolph was his principal benefactor—at times his only regular source of income. There were musical performances at the Palace, and there was the music library to which a manuscript copy of each new score of Beethoven was added, and to which he had ready access. Beethoven was probably as grateful for these blessings as could be expected from one who was inclined to accept such blessings as his due.

The lessons continued for years, and into a period when they became a great encumbrance to Beethoven. He was heard to hint as much to others, but not too loudly. Affection deepened with the years; even while lessons became more irksome and excuses more frequent. Rudolph could scarcely have missed the edge of irony which sometimes showed through in the letters, an inevitable undercurrent of the self-abasing phrases required before royalty. "I am no courtier," wrote Beethoven to his patron. That this was a pun on the name "Hofmann" did not alter its truth. A courtier would have been far less clumsy in his dissimulations. When the pupil, having been assigned a theme by his teacher at a later time, sent him a set of variations upon it with a dedication, Beethoven acknowledged it (tardily) in a New Year's greeting. He called them:

"The masterly variations . . . of my highly honored, exalted pupil, and favorite of the Muses. For the surprise and favor with which I have been honored, I cannot venture to express my thanks either in writing or by word of mouth, as I occupy too *humble* a position; neither, could I, however much I should desire to do so, repay *like with like*. May Heaven hear and truly grant my wish for the health of I.K.H. [*Ihre Kaiserliche Hoheit*]. In a few days I hope to hear

I.K.H. play the masterpiece sent to me, and nothing could rejoice me more than to assist in obtaining for I.K.H. as speedily as possible the place already prepared for you on the summit of Parnassus.

To Your Imperial Highness
with love and deep respect,
From your most obedient servant,
Ludwig van Beethoven.

The humble servant who was unable to "repay like with like" sent the favorite of the muses a little later, perhaps within the month, a new manuscript sonata, to be known as the *"Hammer-Klavier"* Sonata, and spoke of progress upon "A High Mass" in his honor, to be known as the *Missa Solemnis*.

The year of the shelving of *Fidelio* at the *Theater-an-der-Wien* had hardly ended when its direction and that of the two Court Theatres passed out of the hands of the Baron von Braun and into the combined control of the princes Lobkowitz, Schwarzenberg and Esterházy, two Counts Esterházy, and the Counts Palffy, Zichy and Lodron. Time would prove before a year had passed that eight blooded nobles were not wiser than one ennobled man of affairs. But Beethoven must have been well pleased with the turn of events which deposed the hated Baron and elevated to operatic power the more than favorable houses of Esterházy and Lobkowitz. He acted so promptly on his advantage that the new directors received from him early in January, 1807, when they had been in control only a few days, a long petition. The petitioner wished to establish himself in a position of security where he could fulfill his "desire to live wholly for art," which he had been forced to debase on account of the problems of livelihood. He hinted at leaving Vienna and asked for an inducement to remain. That inducement would be a position at the *Theater*, at a salary of 2,400 florins a year. In return for this sum he would undertake to provide yearly "at least one grand opera" and "gratis each year a small operetta, divertissement, choruses, or occasional pieces, according to the wishes or needs of the worshipful direction." He explained that he was making his petition "at the kind suggestion of his Serene Highness, Prince Lobkowitz."

The group of directors, so far as their duty to the theatres was concerned, had no reason to be impressed. Beethoven's expansive promises were well known; the failure of *Fidelio* was remembered, and so was the composer's inability to get along with an opera company and keep the peace with them. What Beethoven was asking for in effect was an honorary post, a living from the state. That expectation was not unreasonable, for the name of Beethoven was indeed the pride of cultured Vienna. But the directors knew that he was unlikely to leave Vienna, and were probably disposed to let well enough alone. They were not all Beethoven partisans like Lobkowitz, who had even tried to organize a private performance of *Fidelio* at his own palace after the second failure. Lobkowitz's fellow directors could not have thanked him for stimulating this petition and so subjecting them all to the displeasure of Beethoven. They (apparently) took the course which would anger him most —that of silence. This was the occasion of his famous written remark to Franz von Brunswick in May: "I can't get along here with the princely theatre rabble [*dem Fürstlichen Theater-Gesindel*]."

When the abused directors dutifully avoided the complication of having Beethoven upon the staff of an opera house, they could have had no dim idea of the deep justice of his expectation of a state subsidy by the extent to which he had been "living for his art" in the months past. If ever Beethoven had a claim by the weight of his offerings to a fixed income which would disentangle his musical plans from the pressure of house rents and grocery bills, it was at the close of 1806. Within the last six months he had poured upon the world a treasure of great music profligate beyond belief. His outward life, as often happens with an artist, showed little of what was going on, nor did those closest to him more than suspect its extent. Stephan von Breuning, apparently thinking that with the collapse of *Fidelio* Beethoven was at the end of his resources, wrote in the early summer: "Beethoven has lost a good deal of his pleasure in and love for work." When he wrote these lines Beethoven had already plunged into adventures new and strange in the long untouched realm of the string quartet. It was noticed that he had not even taken summer lodgings, his one sure stamping ground for the

111

working out of scores. Instead, he lingered in the heart-warming company of the Brunswick brother and sisters at Martonvásár. He allowed Pepi, then a widow of twenty-six, and plainly interested in him, to borrow the parts of his new quartets. They must have remained a puzzle to her. In that adoring circle he completed an extraordinary sonata and promised its dedication to Franz. Therese, who was a better pianist than her brother, was more likely to have divined some of its wild beauty through her intuitive sympathy and loyal zeal. One other was allowed to see the destined "*Appassionata*": Marie Bigot, the wife of the librarian of Count Rasoumowsky. Beethoven took the manuscript to this fair and favored performer on his return to Vienna. The sheets were water-stained, for Beethoven, fleeing from Silesia by night (after a furious quarrel with Lichnowsky), had carried them under his arm as he strode through a driving rain to Troppau. Beethoven was astonished when his friend read the sonata at sight through its corrections and bleared ink; Mme. Bigot was even more astonished at this music of mingled beauty and violence, stormy and stormed upon.

During that summer the following works were in active progress, all to be finished before the year would end: the "*Appassionata*" Sonata, the G major Piano Concerto, the three quartets for Rasoumowsky, Opus 59 (begun in May and completed in November or December), and somewhere in between, where, no one can say, for there seems no possible time left, the idyllic Fourth Symphony. The sketches for this euphonious venture into veiled musing were mingled with those for the C minor Symphony but displaced them. Was it his romantic and relaxed mood of 1806 which prevented him from following that more tense and powerful music to its conclusion? Rolland has called the Fourth Symphony a love song, the outgrowth of the composer's affection for Therese von Brunswick. The felicity of Martonvásár seems to have found its reflection in the Symphony. The gusty lover was in abeyance for the time being. Beethoven dominated the affections of all, but not in a way to ruffle the placid succession of summer days and nights in the Hungarian manor secluded in its immense acres, where a row of lindens was singled out, and one chosen as sacred to each of the little circle, Beethoven included. Beethoven found repose in the intellectual atmosphere, the cultivation of ardor idealized, without flame. Therese sensed Beethoven's mood, and wrote wonderingly in her diary: "What he desires he desires with force; but he desires only good. . . . Toward women he displays an affectionate regard, and his feelings for them are virgin pure." These sentiments bespeak the composing Beethoven; they may have meant that the Symphony in B flat was in full course. His summer dreaming would also have dwelt upon marriage. The fertility in music would have given him confidence, and the fixed income he was soon to ask for would have made the thought of marriage a possibility. His special efforts to obtain a fixed income are an indication of marriage thoughts; they are seen both in his petition at the end of the year, and in his letters to Breitkopf and Härtel in the late summer, proposing the sole German rights to his works on a permanent basis.

But there was probably no avowal at Martonvásár in the summer of 1806. Much has been written about a great romance between Beethoven and Therese von Brunswick. Unfortunately, the diaries of Therese, since examined, reveal that Therese's passions were directed elsewhere, while her feelings for Beethoven were those of a warm and admiring friendship. Pepi, on the other hand, is mentioned by Therese as being interested in Beethoven to the danger point. This summer infatuation may have had a single lasting effect—the agreeable one of stimulating music.

The musical Beethoven of 1806 was far more than the lover; no single mood could have encompassed that outpouring in the most abundant point of his creative life. The *Adagio* in the first of the three quartets is the true love song, the most poignant declaration of that summer. The mood is not repeated; indeed, the twelve movements of the three quartets traverse the gamut of his art. It was as if, taking up that subtly responsive medium after long abstention, he must fill it with his immeasurable growth since 1800. In the tumultuous fugal finale of the third, he seems to have finished his prodigious stint in one long, breathless outburst of controlled strength. What satisfaction in such a manner to complete such a three! Yet these quartets were for a long time greeted with nothing but laughter, and the shaking of heads. As if this display of symphonic, quartet and piano music were not enough, Beethoven added to the list in the autumn his Thirty Variations for Piano in C Minor. The Variations have their points, but Beethoven despised them as soon as they were completed. He could well afford to! In his exuberant state of invention, he was ready to promise anything, whether it was a yearly grand opera for the *Theater-an-der-Wien* with a few minor stage pieces thrown in, or a brace of chamber pieces for George Thomson of Edinburgh. He agreed in a letter to his Scottish client to write three string trios, three string quintets, three quartets, a flute quintet and two duo sonatas! In a postscript he also agreed to make harmonized settings of a collection of Scottish songs, as Haydn before him had set some Irish songs. Only the songs were forthcoming.

A chance offered for the payment of a compliment in a favorable quarter. Franz Clement, leader of the violins at the *Theater-an-der-Wien,* was to appear in a concert on December 23rd. Beethoven produced, barely in time for performance at sight, his one Concerto for the Violin. It has surely some kinship with the Fourth Piano Concerto, with its enchantment of a weaving and dreaming voice which dispels all predilections of glittering bravura.

Even with this recital of incredible activity, the story is not complete. Before the season was over he had written the overture for Collin's drama *Coriolan.* As in the slow movement of the Fourth Piano Concerto, Beethoven here set two opposing voices in conflict, the gentle persuasive theme gradually softening the strong and intrepid one until it is subdued and pliant.

The year 1806 was to have no equal in fertile abundance. It may have been an accumulation of the years previous, the rounding out of musical concepts retarded by the exigencies of *Fidelio.* The productivity was gradually to diminish in the years to follow.

CHAPTER TWELVE

IT WAS at the end of 1805 that the name of Count Andreas Rasoumowsky appeared as full patron of Beethoven in his order for three new string quartets with the first privilege of performance. The Count had dwelt in Vienna as long as Beethoven (except for a short interim) as Ambassador from Russia. His wealth and fame were formidable, even in Vienna. When he ordered the quartets, he was in process of building a new palace on the Donau Canal, overlooking the Prater. The palace had an enormous library, many art treasures, and was the occasion of the founding of a private quartet group which Rasoumowsky intended to be the finest in Europe. The step may have been instigated by his wife, the Countess Elizabeth von Thun, for she was the older sister of that Beethoven idolator, Princess Lichnowsky. The Count derived from Lichnowsky two of his players: Schuppanzigh became his first violin for life; Weiss was his viola. Linke was 'cellist. The part of second violin he usually played himself. The Count's sister-in-law and her husband, themselves unable to continue with their own quartet, would hardly have allowed Rasoumowsky to neglect ordering some new manuscripts from Beethoven.

This time the composer did not lag; as if eager to return to the medium he had left too long untouched, he completed his assignment before either the palace was completed, or the group assembled. Two authentic Russian themes were to be found in them, to meet the current fashion of commissions. If the first public and critics of the quartets expected anything in Opus 59 similar to the popular Opus 18, they were soon to learn their error. When Schuppanzigh received the First and placed the parts on the stands for trial, the players put down their instruments, thinking Beethoven had played some joke on them. For years to come, no players in Russia or England would try one of them to the end. Whichever came up for inspection would be dismissed as "musical madness." The opening of the *Allegretto scherzando* of the First was always greeted with bursts of laughter, as if that light rhythmic motto from the 'cello on a single note were anything else than a bit of sheer, breathless delight. Not until 1812 or 1813 did the realization begin to dawn that the quartets were neither entirely crazy, nor, as some began to say, a patchwork of crazy ideas, with an occasional phrase of genuine beauty.

Commissions continued to come Beethoven's way in 1807, and he continued to accept them. Prince Nicholaus Esterházy ordered a Mass to be performed for the name day of his Princess. Beethoven showed no hesitation in postponing the completion of the Fifth Symphony to devote a precious July and August at Heiligenstadt to his first venture into church music. He managed to be at Eisenstadt in time to prepare and conduct the new work on September 13, 1807. These were the old precincts of Haydn, who in his time had filled just such a commission for such a day, presiding over the performance as Beethoven now did.

The Mass in C made less of an impression than had "Christ on the Mount of Olives." The subject had not deeply taken hold of him, nor could he, as Haydn had done, or as Cherubini could, readily contrive choruses with rounded, sonorous effects and singable solos.

Beethoven was plainly on the defensive when he wrote to Breitkopf and Härtel that he had the piece especially at heart, and would offer it to them "as a present" if they would only publish it. It was less the case of the indulgent parent and the abused child than the pride of the master who cannot bear to take an inferior position in any field of his art. The commissioned work, quickly composed to meet an unchangeable date, occupying two months of his summer, never quite pushed out of mind the Symphony in C Minor, for the sketches for that more deeply engrossing score continued.

Did Beethoven's readiness to accept commissions seriously interfere with the main current of his creative life? The Fifth

Symphony, for example, apparently awaited development from 1805 to 1807, while the more pressing matters of *Fidelio*, the Rasoumowsky Quartets and the Mass in C took precedence. It certainly did not suffer by its postponement, or lose in strength. The vapid and spineless form of the opening theme as it first appears in the sketchbooks would suggest, on the other hand, that he fulfilled other works because he was not ready for this one. There is no suspicion of the concentrated energy of the theme in its first drafts—the direct, clear line which seems so simple, so inevitable, was arrived at by slow and laborious stages. It was as if, when the theme was clarified to the last detail, the creative labors were for the most part accomplished. The evolution of the bare theme must have carried with it, how consciously cannot be known, the development to come, the growth implicit in the seed. One has the sense, in listening to such a movement as the opening one of the C minor, or of the *Eroica* Symphony, that the music is being revealed rather than built up as a construction upon a random unit, in the way of Bach, or even Mozart. The elementary form of Beethoven's themes is often deceptive, especially when he has arrived at them by minute stages. A profile of the common chord—and his themes are often nothing more—could be called characterless if the listener could isolate it from associations of the treatment to come. In the composer's mind the theme which he had shaped to his satisfaction, and which he was about to develop must have been pregnant with meaning; his foresight must have been similar to our hindsight of associations from past experience.

When Beethoven reached this stage, his sense of direction became sure and strong. His imagination was alight, and required no self-goading. A fragment of rhythm, vague and unaccentuated in the early sketches for the Fifth Symphony, suddenly dominated him. It multiplied upon itself, took innumerable shapes, would not release him from its thralldom until it had branched and expanded into the *Scherzo* and *Finale*.

Before that prodigious imagination had warmed to a certain degree of activity, the powers of selection and direction were still vague and fumbling. The sketchbooks are a mass of haphazard and disordered notations. Important matters await their

117

turn while trivial ones are carried out. Many plans come to nothing; there are the beginnings of several times nine symphonies, not to speak of music in other forms. Yet it can be ventured with some assurance that nothing of true importance was lost. Once embarked upon a piece of music, Beethoven could (and this was the most astonishing aspect of his abilities) set it aside for another and take it up again at will. The likelihood is that Beethoven's copious store of musical ideas did not control the occurrence of his symphonies, but lay ready for use when he should need them. In the first eight years of the century, the first six symphonies were completed at fairly regular intervals, as if naturally fulfilling the growing artist. The capacious nature which contained every contrast and extreme, compensating moods, tension and relaxation, found its checks and balances. Periods of intense exertion of will-power would alternate with the effortlessness of potboilers and trivia.

The dual nature of Beethoven, discernible in the two themes of a movement, or in the succeeding movements of a single work, also conditions one work as compared with another shortly following, a phenomenon clearly to be seen in the symphonies. The symphonies alternated (after the First) between driving energy and engaging placidity, as if the paired complements of two of them were necessary in a certain period for wholeness of realiza-tion. Robert Schumann's duality of the "Florestan" and "Eusebius" is nowhere found more conspicuously than in Beethoven. The odd-numbered symphonies have grandeur, flight, daring, innovation. The even ones are more docile, more com-placent with the classical tradition which Beethoven never re-pudiated; they can even relapse into a minuet. The C Minor Symphony would have followed the *Eroica* if Beethoven had carried out his sketches as they came to him. Something in his nature forestalled him until the gentler Symphony in B flat had insinuated itself, fulfilling other needs after the mighty tonal expenditure of the Third. Schumann once referred to the Fourth Symphony as "a slender Greek maiden between two Norse Giants." The Pastoral Symphony followed close upon the Fifth as a contemplative companion, indeed overlapping it in the sketchbooks. After a space of four years there came another pair of complementary affinities, the Seventh and Eighth, both completed in 1812, in close succession. Almost ten years were to elapse before the Ninth, in its lone grandeur.

A sense of balance and assurance pervades Beethoven's creative life. Sometimes he complained loudly when congenial works had to wait for commissioned ones. His annoyance did not prevent him from accepting most orders as they came along. When a subject failed to take hold of him he was quite incapable of turning out anything but lifeless, conventional measures. He did so with equanimity and dispatch, while his invention was never at a loss. The brain was constantly searching. When an idea came to life it would move at its own pace to its consummation, quite without anxious self-questionings or indecisions. Beethoven never had to waste good effort by abandoning a project seriously embarked upon. He never turned back to a completed work to revise (save in *Fidelio,* a case of outward compulsion). No artist ever reached his goal with more scrupulous care and complete finality.

Where he did waste effort was in the outer edge of his mind which received one literary subject after another and, not having reached the point of tonal thinking, was unable to dismiss them at once as impossible. In the very midst of his greatest fertility in instrumental music, impresarios and librettists continued in the illusion that Beethoven would bring forth a miraculous opera. It seems never to have occurred to them, clearly and unequivocally, that the theatre was not his province. It certainly did not occur to Beethoven, who led them on and dissipated precious energies investigating possibilities and trying to reconcile himself to one unlikely subject after another. The desire to gain wealth and to show the world that he could match the success of Weber or Cherubini only served to increase Beethoven's vagueness as, not seeing his way clearly, he would talk in arrogant, worldly terms about propositions still in the abstract.

Beethoven set his particular hopes on Heinrich von Collin in 1808, after the successful collaboration of 1807. Beethoven had been reading Schlegel's translations of the plays of Shakespeare as they had been appearing one after another, and he was eager for a subject from that noble source. Attempts at Tasso's *Jerusa-*

119

lem Delivered and *Bradamante* fell by the wayside, *Macbeth* was proposed, and Beethoven made some notations. Collin, in the middle of the second act, found his subject becoming too persistently gloomy. Beethoven meanwhile had struggled with musical sketches for the incantations of the weird sisters. Fortunately, taking summer quarters at Heiligenstadt, he abandoned the imaginary Scottish heath for the wooded slopes of the Kahlenberg, the blood-besmirched Thane of that play—for the "Pastoral" Symphony!

The enormous desirability of symphonies from Beethoven as compared with operas was not felt by those about him. We find Lichnowsky urging *Alfred the Great* upon him as a fruitful subject, and Schindler extolling a comic-opera text. The symphonies as they appeared were, even now, not yet looked upon necessarily as milestones in Beethoven's career. For one reason, since they had outgrown chamber dimensions, there was no place for them in Vienna concert life. Even his most ardent patrons, Lichnowsky or Lobkowitz, while accepting dedications and obligingly arranging trial performances at their palaces, did not commission them. Beethoven never received a definite order for a symphony in Vienna. Count Oppersdorf, who maintained an orchestra in his Silesian palace, ordered a symphony in 1806, but Beethoven took his own course with his symphonies. The Count was promised the Fifth Symphony, was switched to the Fourth, and, as it happened, received neither, paying in effect 350 florins for a dedication.

Beethoven composed his symphonies as and when he wished, for his own satisfaction. Prospects of a public hearing were few and offered little inducement; the best performance Vienna could muster would have been none too good, and the amateur performances must have been sadly inept and fumbling. Such were the amateur concerts at the Augarten under Schuppanzigh, or the "*Liebhaber*" concerts organized in 1808, where Clement patiently led a group of ladies and gentlemen more ardent than skillful through the mazes of music, while their friends attended. They tried Beethoven's Second and Fourth Symphonies under his own directing hand, and even the formidable *Eroica*. The very existence of these concerts, nobler in intention than result, indicates the dearth of professional symphonic performances. In lieu of the mid-winter charity concerts, which would have brought him nothing, and to obtain at least an orchestral hearing, Beethoven arranged an "Academy" of his own in the same week (December 22, 1808), in the *Theater-an-der-Wien*.

His orchestral pieces unheard and gathered through four years were so numerous that he could announce a full program of his own music "entirely new and not yet heard in public." The program began with the Pastoral Symphony, continued with the Aria *"Ah! Perfido"* and three numbers from the Mass in C (translated from Latin to German to meet regulations about the concert performance of church music). The first part ended with the Fourth Concerto, played by himself. The second part began with the Fifth Symphony, included the Sanctus from the Mass, and a piano solo. As if this were not enough, Beethoven took pains to assure the success of the concert by writing, for the sake of *réclame* at the close, a "Fantasia for the Pianoforte which ends with the gradual entrance of the entire orchestra and the introduction of choruses as a finale." The Choral Fantasia was rushed to its completion. The vocal parts were scarcely dry at the hasty, last-minute rehearsal.

Here was a lavish outlay of new music to commend the prowess of an orchestral composer to his public. A heavy accumulation, ranging from his greatest to his least, from a symphony, which in its concentrated energy was a startling new apparition in the world, to a scratched-off closing piece quite vacuous by contrast. Trouble beset the over-ambitious project from the beginning. There was a great deal too much to prepare. The players were inadequate and no doubt considerably mystified. When Beethoven rehearsed them he became so impatient, and consequently so outspoken, that the musicians would not continue unless he remained in another room, where they would be spared his criticisms. Beethoven paced up and down the anteroom during rehearsal, Röckel at his side. He quarreled with Anna Milder, the solo singer, once his "Leonore," and she refused to sing. A sister-in-law of Schuppanzigh was called in at the last minute. Beethoven led out an inexperienced and terrified *Fräulein*, who made a travesty of the dramatic concert aria. The audiences, of course, could never have absorbed so much that was new and strange, even if it had been clearly and intelligently performed.

What may have happened short of catastrophe during the symphonies we are not told, but Reichardt relates that he sat in a stage box with Prince Lobkowitz. "Many a failure in the performance tried our patience to the highest degree. Singers and orchestra were composed of heterogeneous elements, and it had been found impossible to get a single full rehearsal for all the pieces, filled as they were with the greatest difficulties." The December cold had taken full possession of the hall, and the audience sat shivering from 6:30 to 10:30. The Prince was in delicate health, but on account of his conspicuous location could not leave until the end. The culminating misfortune occurred in the ill-rehearsed Fantasia. Either a wrong entrance in the orchestra or a misunderstanding about a repeat (this point is not clear) brought tonal chaos, with orchestra and chorus at odds. Beethoven stopped the performance, called out orders to begin at a certain point, and after a moment of strained silence resumed. The orchestra was angered again at being subjected to public humiliation. The concert with its earlier treasures is perhaps the most flagrant of the many instances where music of imperishable beauty has made its first bow in a befogged performance to a listless and unsuspecting public.

Incidents like this increased Beethoven's dissatisfaction with Vienna. He continued to chafe at the frivolous preferences of the capital, which became more pronounced under the French occupation. Balls, operas, variety shows, fashion parades in the Prater, flirtations too easy and too brazen—these were the main current of pleasure-seeking, and in them symphony concerts and the serious, aspiring music of Beethoven had no place. It was a circle of the more discerning among the musicians, together with a handful of princes and counts, personal devotees, who followed his music, heard it, and gave it their support. Reports came from other cities that his symphonies were gaining a foothold and a general popularity. Habeneck in Paris performed them at the student concerts of the *Conservatoire*. Salomon in London put them into his subscription concerts, and the Gewand-

122

haus at Leipzig eagerly received, performed and repeated them to loud applause as they appeared. It was the same story everywhere. The learned praised his music with reservations, now putting him in third place after the sanctified Haydn and Mozart. They regretted that measures of outstanding beauty were marred by sudden explosions of gross dissonance. But there were others, a rapidly growing public, who responded with zeal to the idealistic ardor in the music, and were moved to take all of it on faith. Publishers were the barometers, and the Leipzig publishers, especially, registered the musical progressiveness of that town.

These echoes of distant conquests made Beethoven more impatient than ever with the intransigeance of Vienna, and the artist in whom the proud lines of the *"Emperor"* Concerto were taking shape was high-handed about what was due him. He had not forgotten that his petition for a Court post had been ignored; his pique increased, and his friends heard grumbling remarks on the stupidity of Vienna and tightness of the princes. He had made it clearly known that he could be induced to leave Vienna, and that inducement came in the autumn of 1808. He was called upon by an emissary of the "King of Westphalia," Jerome Bonaparte, who at twenty-three was profiting by the ascendancy of his brother Napoleon, and playing ruler in a conquered country It is a little hard to imagine Beethoven as either suiting or liking a royal Kapellmeistership in provincial Cassel. The prospective patron, a weak, effeminate member of that preferentially distributed family, and no more musical than the rest of them, would hardly have known what to do with Beethoven beyond decorating his Court with an illustrious name. Beethoven's friends in Vienna saw the incongruity, but they saw too that he was tempted by the idea of having light duties, plenty of time to compose, and an adequate and dependable living.

The security of Cassel may have appealed to him with particular forcefulness under the immediate shadow of his sorry attempt to make known his Fifth and Sixth Symphonies, for on January 7, 1809, a fortnight after the concert, he wrote Breitkopf and Härtel that he had that very day accepted the offer of "His Royal Majesty of Westphalia." He would be forced to leave "the only surviving German Fatherland," with its "intrigues and cabals and contemptible behavior of all kinds." He describes the unfortunate episode of the December concert in his own words lest a twisted account come to them from another source. His intentions were definite, for he spoke of traveling by way of Leipzig and appearing in concert there.

When it became known that Beethoven was on the point of committing himself to Cassel, an unofficial suggestion came to him that he state his conditions for remaining in Vienna. Beethoven answered, in a carefully worded document, that he would expect an annual payment for life of an amount equal to what had been offered to him by Jerome Bonaparte—4,000 florins. The donors would be considered as "co-authors" in the works they would thus enable him to compose. If he should at any time receive an Imperial post or title such as that of *Kapellmeister*, his annuity would be reduced to the extent of the new salary. He asked for the use of the *Theater-an-der-Wien* for a concert each year, and agreed to conduct a charity concert, or contribute a new work. He would never live outside of Austria.

The terms were agreed to on March 1, 1809, and signed by the following three, who together pledged the amount asked:

His Imperial Highness, Archduke Rudolph	1,500 florins
The Highborn Prince Lobkowitz	700 florins
The Highborn Prince Ferdinand Kinsky	1,800 florins
Total	4,000 florins

It is worth noticing that the pledge of security came to Beethoven not by public action, not by State decree, but from the pockets of three noble admirers, all younger than himself! It was a handsome reply—especially on the part of Lobkowitz, who could ill afford it. The sum was sufficient for all reasonable needs. Adding the fees to be expected from publishers, Beethoven could well allow his thoughts to dwell upon a protected and carefree future.

Elation colored his letter to Breitkopf and Härtel, where he asked them to correct the rumor of his Cassel appointment. He put in a joking postscript, reminding them to mention that he had almost acquired a title: "Do not forget the 'First *Kapell-*

meister.' I laugh at such things, but there are miserables who know how to dish them up in the manner of the cook." He liked to affect scorn of titles or decorations, but always took a childlike pleasure in the glittering badges of power. He was even then nursing the hope of an Imperial appointment at Vienna.

CHAPTER THIRTEEN

A ROUNDED portrait of Beethoven in the year 1806 or the years immediately following is hard to capture, not from any sparsity in the record, but from the abundance and contradictoriness of it. The flood of music, reaching its highest point of fecundity, tells of sheer vitality, lusty and buoyant. The letters would tell a different story if they were exclusively relied upon, for they are pervaded by the growing habit of discontent; complaints over patrons, servants, Viennese taste and the paper currency become more frequent. None of those about him quite escaped the sting of his anger and the heavy ban of his displeasure. These outbursts should be kept in their place as the more vociferous moments of a mercurial disposition. Beethoven was too active, musically and otherwise, for long brooding, nor did deafness yet prevent him from consorting freely with his kind. Almost any day he could be found at the *"Schwann"* joking with friends over a bottle of wine. He was often to be found at the houses of Lichnowsky, Lobkowitz and Rasoumowsky, and at lesser houses where music was afoot. Feminine company interested him more than ever. He would dress up to an occasion and go out of his way to ingratiate himself. His thoughts of marriage had come to the point of definite intention, which in itself goes far to explain his grievance when the expected income failed. He longed to marry, which was no more than any man's right; he had been promised in writing an income which would be sufficient to keep a wife, an income certainly no greater than his supremacy and his industry as a composer warranted. This was his attitude, and, when his income suffered on account of war conditions and the consequent misfortunes of those whose function it was to nurture music, his sense of deprivation was too strong to make any reasonable allowance.

It is certainly doubtful whether marriage would have brought him the happiness he dreamed about. His helplessness sometimes cried out for domestic regulation and protection, and yet the imagination balks at the prospect of captivity for the wild and free Beethoven who would disappear for hours from his house, miss meals, return and shut himself away from everyone, vacillate between Vienna and Baden, hire country lodgings or depart suddenly for Hungary.

These years were full and rich in friendships and in the hopes that love held out. Fame surrounded him and favored his self-esteem. The fundamental satisfaction lay in the constant emergence of symphonies, quartets, sonatas, triumphant assertions of will power, gleaming adventures of the mind, inwardly sounding sure and clear, even though actual performances were poor and in the creator's hardened ears dim and jangling.

Beethoven drank in life with a capacious appetite; no one could have been more avid for experience. He took what was at hand, the highest and the least, but always insatiably. He listened to music as closely as his ears allowed, and his faculty for the inward image, which his infirmity could not touch, devoured all the scores of Handel, Bach, Emanuel Bach or Mozart which he could lay his hands upon. He followed the musical currents of the moment with some praise and, rightly enough, with more scorn. He read voraciously the ancient writers and the poets of his own time, not with literary acumen, not for beauty of language, but for narrative substance, drama, nobility of concept. In this, his search for an operatic subject was constant but incidental; the composer was stirring his own imagination, enlarging and clarifying his vision. The poets were useful to him, and not only in the furnishing of texts for musical settings. Klopstock, whose high-flown pulsations set fire to many a romantic soul, attuned Beethoven to musical moods. Klopstock's particular idealism, his apostrophe to joy, his humanism and republicanism appealed to Beethoven. Above all, there was his luxuriating melancholy, the mood which is music's own, and needs only notes. Beethoven kept the *Oden* and the *Messias* close by him in his youth and even in later life. He admitted to Rochlitz in 1823 that he used to take a volume of Klopstock on his walks and read him continually. Only when he met Goethe did that poet (who too had had his Klopstock phase) replace the storm and stress poet in his affections.

"Goethe killed Klopstock for me. You are surprised? Now you are laughing? Aha, it is because I used to read Klopstock! For years I put up with him, when I took my walks, and elsewhere. Well, then, it is true that I did not always know what he was driving at. He leaps about so much, and starts off at too lofty an altitude. Always *maestoso*, D flat major! Isn't it so? But he is great and uplifts the soul, nevertheless. When I couldn't understand him, I made a guess at it. If only he did not always want to die! That will come soon enough. Well, at any rate, what he writes always sounds well."

Every habit of Beethoven's life could be called preparation for music, even his periods of relaxation. It was at these times that he craved companionship, and his companions were accordingly not of the stimulating sort—not poets, nor even composers distinguished for high intelligence and sensibility. With the poets Grillparzer or Treitschke he was on courteous, formal terms; they served him briefly as he was girding himself for music, but their usefulness was literary; they could not have divined the true character of his inmost musical plans, rare and withdrawn. Only a musician of a more exceptional breadth than then existed could have done that. When Weber, or Rossini, or Cherubini visited him, he showed a far more generous understanding than a great artist will usually find in his heart when the art of a contemporary is before him.

But here again there was no real basis for intimacy. Those whom he consorted with daily were the faithful small souls, humdrum, easy-going, convenient, like Ries, Czerny, Gleichenstein, Schuppanzigh, Breuning. A stranger from another part, visiting the great Beethoven, wondered at the assorted and undistinguished satellites of this great sun. These minor devotees loved him well, giving him all that he needed as he rested from his labors. They provided the latest gossip, the small talk of the profession, surrounded him with affection and loyalty; they were ready to be the butt of his witticisms, and to be useful to him in menial ways, while their lord never hesitated to tyrannize, and abuse his privileges. He drew them into his gross, peasant conviviality, where eating, drinking and joking were joys unpunctured by nice restraint. Beethoven kept the ways of his origin; he would strike a bargain, or maneuver for his advantage with the blunt realism of a commoner. He had the commoner's slight regard for elegant manners, with the difference that he made no attempt to conceal his contempt.

The coarser side of Beethoven has been glossed over or suppressed by the writers who would otherwise have been at a loss to preserve a beautiful picture drawn, quite justly, in the noble and elevated vein of his music. If the character of Beethoven is to be presented whole and so understood, the first requisite is confidence that the essential nobility of the man who wrote *Fidelio* or the *Pastoral* Symphony (to go no further) is unassailable. In such music there is no room for a shadow of hypocrisy or pretending. Those who knew him intimately sensed in his presence his lofty nature, pure to the point of austerity. It should be remembered that their belief in him, unconfirmed by any adequate understanding of his music, was not shaken by the various peculiarities and contradictions in his behavior.

We are told that Beethoven, standing in the street, would leer through his eyeglass at a pretty figure, and we read the endings of his letters where he pokes sly jokes at a friend about his wife. His actions elsewhere bespeak unequivocally his high and puritanically chaste regard for the dignity of womanhood and the sanctity of marriage. The women whom he respected were without exception impressed by the purity of his regard, a purity the more striking in an epoch of general laxity. His idealization of womanhood is of course still more incontrovertible in his music. About women he did not respect, his revulsion was correspondingly strong. But condemnation, in this as in other matters, did not include abstention. We read this observation of his own, extracted from the *Tagebuch*: "Sensual enjoyment without a union of souls is bestial and will always remain bestial; after it, one experiences not a trace of noble sentiment, but rather regret." That Beethoven may have sought gross sexual experience and that what was predominant and immaculate in him recoiled from it is quite in keeping with all that we know about his ways.

Too much has been made of a confidential intimation by one of his doctors, long withheld and finally published, that Beethoven was once infected with a venereal disease. The question of whether he may have had syphilis has already had too much attention, but for that very reason cannot be passed over. The contention that Beethoven's deafness *might* have been caused by the disease, having no other basis than the deafness itself, proves nothing and gets us nowhere. The evidence is this: de Hevesy in 1926 disclosed a memorandum which he believed to have been written by Beethoven in 1819, which speaks of his intention to get a book on the "knowledge and cure of all venereal contagions." Theodor von Frimmel, in 1912, wrote of having had from Thayer years before information about an unnamed "malady" of Beethoven. Thayer in his biography had revealed nothing more specific than his belief that Beethoven's life was not scrupulously chaste. Sir George Grove, principal proponent of the syphilis theory in his dictionary (1879), wrote that he had had from Thayer confidential information which Thayer in turn had had from Dr. Bertolini, about "two prescriptions," otherwise unspecified, which Bertolini had destroyed after Beethoven's death, together with several communications from the composer. These communications and prescriptions would have been made between 1806 and 1815, the years in which Dr. Bertolini knew and was on good terms with Beethoven. Presumably the doctor had a reason to destroy them. His scrupulous delicacy, and that of Thayer, commands respect—but at the same time leads to regret. As so often happens in such cases, veiled disclosures create mystification, and mystification breeds exaggerated attention and broad conjecture. Ernest Newman (in *The Unconscious Beethoven*, 1927) builds a neat theory that Beethoven, under the dreadful shadow of syphilis, showed "morbid sex obsessions" on the subject of "loose" women from about 1796 to the end of his life. The conclusion is interesting, but it by no means justifies the preposterous assumption that he may have been a syphilitic for more than thirty years. Let us sift these grains of tangible evidence. Beethoven may have suffered from a venereal infection at some time between 1806 and 1815. Or he may merely have feared such an infection. There is no reason whatsoever to assume that that infection was specifically syphilis, or incurable. To suppose that he was syphilitic for the greater part of his life would be an infinitely graver indictment, for it amounts to saying that, having been ravaged by the disease to the point of losing his hearing, he contemplated marriage continuously for about four years, proposed it at least three times, and succeeded in restraining completely the garrulous tongues of his friends who would surely have known—not to speak of the other doctors. Nor is the art of Beethoven, wholesome, sane, life-affirming, the product of a social pariah. Common sense will readily dismiss a charge so completely at odds with circumstances.

Incriminations, like excuses, will never explain the duality of Beethoven. The idealists are disconcerted that he could turn from thoughts of the *Missa Solemnis* to write to Hauschka of the *Musikfreunde*: "I wish you open bowels and a handsome and convenient stool." It is perplexing to behold the composer who lifted Schiller's *Ode* to a mighty affirmation of love for mankind treat his servants like despicable beasts, or in sudden anger throw a plate of gravy at a waiter and then roar with laughter at the pitiable spectacle. An artist should be as manifold as his nature and circumstances allow. He will only constrict his art by renouncing his origin and cultivating the fastidiousness of another class. Mozart, whose special delicacy no composer has excelled, allowed his humor to run to unprintable obscenities; Haydn could be scabrous; Schubert was a tippler; Brahms, that rare and refined poet of tone, could revert to the peasant with apologies to none. Roots deep in the soil nourish a sturdy plant which bears the most delicate blossoms. The analogy does not apply to all; it emphatically applies to the artist who captures the full, broad current of life with his art. To do so he must be as whole as life has made him.

The sublimation of Beethoven's art from thoughts where harassment, humiliation, bitterness abounded to a region which is pure faith, noble evocation, radiant beauty, is the true miracle of his character. It is like nature's purifying process, the fragile petal untouched by the slightest fleck of the mud that went into

131

its making. When Beethoven turned to music, conflict was elevated and laughter purified; hostility dropped away. Gusty violence became sheer, buoyant power. It was like a temperamental resolution of futile, clashing dissonance. There could have been no abnegation in the process, no self-imposed asceticism, for these were the properties of weaklings, and not in Beethoven's cosmos.

Beethoven did have one besetting weakness: the pride which wasted his energies in inward strife. His pride prompted the defiant boorishness which lorded it over everyone, from tradesman to archduke, and compelled forbearance. It was never more quickly in arms than when he imagined his ability impugned, and this, unfortunately both for him and his friends, was far too often.

With all his contradictions, there was also in Beethoven an underlying consistency. His behavior, taken for what it was, remained from first to last entirely predictable. Circumstances such as his deafness or his celibacy modified but did not alter him. Always, he was as ill-adjusted for everyday matters as he was well-organized for musical ends. The state of excitation necessary to him when music was in the flux had at other times no outlet and left him a prey to his emotions. Emotion became blind and headlong. He flew out in anger against all that was petty, dull or greedy in men as if they intruded upon and mocked his interior world, and blurred his clear vision. At those moments reason no longer guided him. He could not admit in himself the feelings he despised in others; nor was there any sense in his suspicions and accusations. Often his transports of anger would suddenly become violent hilarity, his scorn turning to humorous rejection. His laughter, ringing out, would startle people in public places. Those close to him must have found his jeering insults more wounding than the livid explosions which had preceded them. They were aware of what lay concealed beneath: a kind heart and a sometimes meek dependence upon friendship and affection.

His arrogance, as one examines it, points always to the protection of his position as artist. He could have afforded to be far more assured and generous, less eager for worldly badges and less on the defensive. Ferdinand Ries, who enjoyed the privilege of being close to the master, witnessing unnoticed his behavior, and recording his observations in his *"Notizen,"* usually escaped the direct wrath of Beethoven. The reason was that he was young and unobtrusive, extraordinarily convenient for a pupil. But there was no one who did not fall from grace at some time. Ries did once, when he aspired to the Cassel position Beethoven had refused, thus seeming to put himself on Beethoven's level. There was another occasion when Lichnowsky, who was often out of favor, was the true cause of the trouble. It was about the *"Andante favori"* which Beethoven composed, probably in 1804, for the *"Waldstein"* Sonata, but was to publish separately. "When Beethoven played it for the first time to our friend Krumpholz and me," wrote Ries, "it delighted us greatly and we teased him until he repeated it. Passing the door of Prince Lichnowsky's house on my way home, I went in to tell the Prince of the new and glorious composition of Beethoven, and was persuaded to play it as well as I could remember it. As I recalled more and more of it the Prince urged me to repeat it. In this way it happened that the Prince also learned a portion of the piece. To give Beethoven a surprise the Prince went to him the next day and said that he too had composed something which was not at all bad. In spite of Beethoven's remark that he did not want to hear it the Prince sat down and to the amazement of the composer played a goodly portion of the *Andante*. Beethoven was greatly angered, and this was the reason why I never again heard Beethoven play."

Even Beethoven's fondness for the boy could not bring him for a long time to the point of relenting. Once when Ries returned after an absence in Silesia, he greeted Beethoven in the midst of shaving and received an absent-minded kiss which smeared him with lather. Both of them laughed over this. But when Beethoven played his opera *Fidelio* for the first time to a company of friends, Ries was sternly excluded from the room, while Prince Lichnowsky, whose tactless idea of humor was certainly more to blame, was allowed to remain. There was nothing reasonable about Beethoven when a sensitive spot was touched.

A friend who made a similar blunder was saved by Beethoven's sense of humor. The man was once playing a march of his own

:omposition when a lady of rank wanted to know who had composed it. "It is a new march by Beethoven," said the gentleman. The lady at once decided that it was beautiful. Later when Beethoven was present, she spoke ecstatically of his new march. "What march?" Beethoven wanted to know, at once suspicious. The lady urged the joker to play it. He hastily whispered to Beethoven what he had done. Beethoven was ready to be furious, but, looking at the lady, he suddenly burst into roars of laughter.

He was quick to take offense at noble houses when rank, accidentally or not, seemed to measure itself against his own importance. At a dinner given to Prince Louis Ferdinand, only the nobility were placed at the table of the guest of honor, which thus excluded Beethoven. He expressed his opinion loudly, seized his hat and strode out. A more serious outburst took place at *Schloss Grätz*, Prince Lichnowsky's Silesian estate. Beethoven was a visitor, and so were a group of French officers, who urged him to play. Perhaps they expected to hear a new manuscript sonata he had brought with him. But Beethoven had no intention of favoring them with the *"Appassionata"* (which it happened to be). He had no liking for French officers, even at their best, and proclaimed that he was nobody's servant to be commanded. Pursuing their joke with, probably, a touch of insolence, they threatened to arrest him if he would not play. Beethoven stamped from the house, though it was late at night and stormy, and walked to Troppau, whence he took the next coach with all speed back to Vienna. Lichnowsky was not soon forgiven.

The long friendship of Beethoven and Stephan von Breuning could not possibly have survived without a quarrel—for one reason because Stephan had a tight-lipped determination and an inflammable temper of his own, for another because he had the temerity to attempt what no other man dared attempt—in 1804, he and Beethoven shared lodgings and a cook, for the sake of economy. There arose an argument at table as to which of them had failed to notify Beethoven's former landlord, and so failed to relieve Beethoven of a double rent. One can well guess Beethoven to have been at fault, for he was constantly involving himself in two, or even three simultaneous rents. There were hot words and recriminations. Friends were present, whereby honor entered into it. Breuning sprang to his feet, Beethoven did the same, knocking over a chair. Both departed, in two directions, leaving their guests hostless. Breuning, soon realizing that it had been a tempest over nothing, sued for peace, and when his letter remained unanswered turned to Ries as intermediary. Beethoven answered Ries with a long letter of indignant self-justification. It was seven months later that he wrote Ries again on the subject: "I have the ability in many cases to conceal my sensitiveness and repress it; but if I am irritated at a time when I am more susceptible than usual to anger, I burst out more violently than anyone else." As if Ries had to be told! But Breuning was not yet forgiven. "He shall never again hold the place in my heart which he once occupied." It was not until almost a year had passed that the two encountered by accident and made up. Beethoven wrote his "Steffen," as he called him, sending a miniature of himself as a peace offering:

"Let us bury behind this picture forever, my dear Steffen, what has in these months passed between us. I know that I broke your heart. The feelings within me which you must have noticed have sufficiently punished me for that. It was not evil that I felt toward you; no, if that were so I should never again be worthy of your friendship; it was passion on your part and on mine; but mistrust of you arose in me; men came between us who are not worthy of you and me. My portrait was long ago intended for you, faithful, good, noble Steffen! Forgive me if I have pained you; I have suffered no less. When I no longer saw you near me I felt for the first time how dear to my heart you are and always will be.

"Surely you will come to my arms again as in past days."

Those who knew Beethoven well simply waited for the storm to pass, little understanding it, aware that forgiveness would follow, and that the lovable, noble-minded, aspiring Beethoven would return. Recognizing danger signals, they would carefully leave him to himself at the irritable moments. In times of repose he would be equable and even polite, so extraordinarily patient that he would answer the most obtuse questions in good nature. Strangers, seeking him out, were sometimes surprised that the reputed ogre received them with kindness and courtesy. Their moment was fortunate. If an importunate visitor had walked in upon him while he was possessed with music, he would have been driven away unceremoniously enough.

It was because Beethoven's nature required the simple and homely level in most intercourse that he almost totally escaped the pitfall of the Romantic artist who feels constrained to adapt his demeanor to his high artist's intentions and so becomes, in spite of himself, a play actor. Beethoven made no attempt to play a superhuman part. Individuals were sometimes favored with conversation in the elevated terms of his art; a mixed company was not. When, seated at the piano, he would forget where he was and uncover before curious spectators a privacy usually withheld, he would counter their *Ohs* and *Ahs* with a burst of rudeness, striking the keys with his open hand. When he confided the progress of a slow movement to a Giulietta or a Therese, the music resulting had a slight cast of affected sentiment which was to disappear when the composing Beethoven became an object never known to mortal eye. It could not have been otherwise if his music were to remain a direct emanation of his secret nature, an immediate reflection of an inmost source of dreaming. The unstudied genuineness of feeling which scarcely knows itself is the measure of his absolute supremacy over the full century of parading Romanticism which was to come.

In the first months of 1809, Beethoven was to be found living in the house of the Hungarian Countess Anna Marie Erdödy, his staunch supporter, who had agitated in high quarters in favor of the annuity, and helped him draw up his conditions. She was then twenty-nine, "a beautiful, fine little woman," so Reichardt describes her, "and a semi-invalid."

The Countess coaxed Beethoven under her roof to deliver him from his interminable succession of lodgings. Beethoven was forever changing his lodgings. He had the restlessness of a bachelor with no ties, and the habit of taking flight at any discomfort or altercation with a landlord. His difficulties over servants seemed to grow progressively worse. When he engaged a married couple to attend to his household, he would send them to the accommodating Zmeskall for the disagreeable discussion of terms and

136

duties. "Today Herzog, who is to be my servant, will come to you," he wrote his friend. "Settle with him and his obbligato wife for thirty florins—hear from them how condescending they are willing to be—she must cook when I want it, also darn, etc.— for this is a highly important matter. I will afterwards come to you and hear the result. Would not the best thing be to ask them what they are willing to do for me?"

We find that Beethoven, living at the Erdödys' two months later, had taken his servants and servant troubles with him. The Countess tried to keep the peace by bribing them to put up with their master, but only brought on her well-meaning head a furious outburst. There was a reconciliation, but her guest departed.

Beethoven was in lodgings again, the Herzogs still on his hands, when, two months later, the storms of war bore down on Vienna once more. The Imperial family took flight on May 4, 1809, Beethoven's Archduke with them, and many other nobles followed. This was the departure which was the subject of Beethoven's Sonata "Farewell, Absence and Return." Rudolph did not return until the January following. The farewells were many. On May 10th, Beethoven found himself without his aristocratic friends in a city prepared for siege. The Erdödys had gone, even Zmeskall had gone, and presently Beethoven was not only unprotected against the miserable Herzog and his "obbligato wife," but he had them helpless on his hands in an occupied city, with prices soaring and food dwindling.

The French stationed their howitzers on the Spittelberg, and at other points in the faubourgs, and at nine o'clock on the evening of May 11th opened fire. The population crowded indiscriminately into every possible underground shelter. Beethoven's windows on the Wasserkunst Bastei, chosen for their outlook, were in direct line of the bombardment. He fled to the house of his brother Karl on the Rauhensteingasse, and crouched in the cellar, holding a pillow over his head to spare his poor, sensitive ears the pain of the concussive reports. Shells were fired into the city without cessation through the night. Many houses burst into flames; wounded civilians were carried through the streets to safety. On the following afternoon, Vienna capitulated—it could have done nothing else—and forthwith endured the French occu-

137

pation for the two months that remained of the campaign. Napoleon set himself up in state at the Schönbrunn Palace once more. General Andréossy had issued a proclamation to the inhabitants of Vienna, assuring them of the good will of his sovereign the Emperor Napoleon, "King of Italy, Protector of the Confederation of the Rhine." On May 15th the Commandant Razout quartered the soldiery upon all lodgings in Vienna. Next, a levy was imposed upon house rentals, whereby a quarter of Beethoven's rent money went to the conquerors.

It was fortunate that two of his benefactors, Lobkowitz and Rudolph, had paid the first installment of their pledge, for now all three had disappeared. The sources of his income were out of sight altogether, while commodities were scarce and currency had depreciated. Beethoven relieved his feelings by railing against the French, the vanished benefactors, the whole miserable situation. "Oh, unfortunate decree, seductive as a siren!" he wrote to Franz von Brunswick. "I ought, like Ulysses, to have stopped my ears with wax and refused to sign anything." He had plenty of time for self-pity, for there was no escape into music. His country haunts were all closed to him; Heiligenstadt was a barracks. Even the public parks were closed. So, sulking in the half-deserted city, he occupied himself through the precious summer season by compiling a musical textbook for his absent Archduke. Young Rust once found him in a sidewalk café, shaking his fist at a passing French officer. "If I knew strategy as I know counterpoint," he said, "I'd show you something!" The war did not lift him to any zeal for national retaliation; it merely left him disgusted with the oppressive stupidity of his race. "What a disturbed wild life all around me," he wrote Breitkopf and Härtel, "nothing but drums, cannon, men, misery of all sorts."

At the end of the summer he was able to get into Hungary and there probably visited the Brunswicks. Musical thoughts were loosened again in two piano works, to be dedicated to Franz and to his sister Therese. They were the Fantasia, Opus 77, and the Sonata in F sharp, Opus 78, completed in October. By February, he was able to offer Breitkopf and Härtel, among other things, the lovely "Harp" Quartet, Opus 74, in E flat, and a new Piano Concerto which put that heroic key to its proudest uses. This was resurgence indeed! Some have tried to connect the *"Emperor"* Concerto with the military experiences of the summer past, as if those experiences could have been anything but a deterrent. He may have composed it with a concert at the *Theater-an-der-Wien* in mind. It may also have been his hopes for such a concert which filled the sketchbooks of 1809 with page after page of notations for what were to emerge later as the Allegretto and Finale of the Seventh Symphony, the first and last movements of the Eighth. There are sketches too for an overture on Schiller's *Ode to Joy*. Thoughts of Schiller were probably stimulated at the Court Theatres in the dramas of the poet not long since dead. In fact Hartl (the new manager, replacing the aristocratic directors whose term had lasted barely a year) planned elaborate productions of Schiller's *Wilhelm Tell* and Goethe's *Egmont*. Beethoven and Gyrowetz were to compose incidental music. It has been claimed that Beethoven would have preferred *Wilhelm Tell* to Goethe's play which was assigned to him. Either poet, or their heroes—the two liberators of their peoples—would have engrossed him. One can even think of the overture to *Egmont* as equally fitting the Swiss patriot. The urgency of the new task caused the plan for a concert to be abandoned. The sketches for two symphonies were laid aside for the time being.

Early in 1810 we find Beethoven living once more in normal comfort. He returned to lodgings on the fourth floor of the house of the Freiherr Pasqualati on the Mölker Bastei. He had lived there intermittently since 1804, and was attached to his landlord—and the view. He was busy and in good spirits. He completed the music for *Egmont* in the first months of the year, and was consulted in the preparations for the performance of the play, which took place in the *Hofburg Theater* on May 24th. He grumbled at the penury of the *Theater*, which gave him no payment for his music. Kinsky, who had been active in the war and who had not returned, was behind in his annuity payment, but Lobkowitz and the Archduke were prompt with theirs. A payment, long unpaid on account of Napoleon's restrictions upon exchange, at last came to him from Clementi's firm in London, and amply filled his pocketbook, as certain free expenditures show. It was not to be a year of much music (after *Egmont*, the

139

"Serious Quartet," Opus 95, composed in the autumn, was the only considerable work); it proved to be a year of romance. Beethoven's thoughts and plans dwelt once more upon marriage He had written to his friend the Graf Ignatz von Gleichenstein a year before when the annuity was under negotiation, jokingly asking him to find him a wife: "If you find a beautiful one who would respond readily to my harmonies, go after her at once. But she must be beautiful; I cannot love what is not beautiful— or I should be loving myself."

Gleichenstein, who was co-secretary of the War Department with Stephan von Breuning, had been for years in the circle of Beethoven's friends. Now the obliging young nobleman was put to use, as if supplementing the Baron Zmeskall. He seems to have been equally ready to serve as companion at the *"Schwann"* or *"Zum Wilden Mann,"* or to produce quills, sealing wax, medicine, or a translation of Tacitus. The rôle of intermediary in love came to him accidentally. He had no choice but to do what was asked of him in a delicate situation.

Gleichenstein introduced Beethoven to a family named Malfatti, with the result that he acquired a pupil—and a doctor, who was her uncle. The Malfattis were one of the many families to be found in Vienna where grace and charm abounded, as the arts, music above all, were quietly cultivated. The two daughters, Therese and Anna, were less than a year apart in age, and children when Beethoven first knew them. In 1810, Therese was probably eighteen; she had suddenly grown up and become disturbingly lovely. The relation of master to pupil is delightful when the pupil, fresh and susceptible, can be led into the wonders of music or literature. She would listen soberly and understandingly, and then suddenly turn aside into the light exuberance of her years.

We have the first sign that Beethoven at thirty-nine was to become the suitor again when he writes to Zmeskall for a mirror and to Gleichenstein with a copious request for the purchase of "linen and nankeen for shirts and at least half a dozen neckties." The letter ends: "Greet everything that is dear to you and me. How gladly would I like to add—to whom we are dear?????" Gleichenstein was included in the wish because he was in love with Anna. Evidently his prospects were far stronger, for Beethoven continued: "The question marks apply to me at least. Farewell, be happy; I am not."

Gleichenstein, according to another note, is to meet him at the tavern *"Zum Wilden Mann"* on the Prater, together with the Malfattis. "I fancy that I shall find no wild men there, but beautiful Graces, and for them I shall don my armor." The Graces, it seems, subdued the wildness in Beethoven, for we behold him basking in the gentle kindnesses which they shed upon him, and allowing himself to be drawn into the domestic interests of the feminine household. Surely he was charmed by Therese's feminine frivolity; in a portrait she flaunts enormous, puffed sleeves and a large brimmed hat, evidently in the height of fashion. Her sister has described her as having "dark ringlets, brown black eyes, nose slightly *retroussé*, intelligent, and of a fiery temperament, capable of application but inclined to the pleasures of life."

"Remember me to them all," wrote Beethoven to Gleichenstein. "I am so happy in their company; it is as if the wounds with which evil people have pierced my soul might be healed through them. I thank you, good Gleichenstein, for having introduced me to them." Never having in recorded history noticed a pet animal, he befriends the dog "Gigon," allows it to sit beside him at dinner and follow him home. He offers to purchase a piano for Therese at a discount, although such favors are against his principles. If, as Dr. Unger conjectures, the little piano piece of that spring, *"Für Elise"* was really inscribed *"Für Therese"* and misread in copying, this trifle, suited to fingers more graceful than skillful, was the offering of a suitor—a suitor, perhaps, who could find real pleasure in the parlor graces of Therese's piano playing and Anna's guitar.

The letters which follow are all undated. Their sequence seems clearly fixed by the contents, which tell a story otherwise unknown. The first was written to Therese by Beethoven about the end of April. She had gone to the country with her family, and Beethoven found himself disconsolate. He wrote meekly and circumspectly, withholding his true feelings and taking the tone of an older friend giving advice to a child. "Pray do not forget the pianoforte among your occupations, or indeed, music gen-

141

erally. You have such fine talent for it. Why not devote yourself entirely to it? You have such feeling for all that is beautiful and good. Why will you not make use of this, that you may recognize in so beautiful an art the higher perfection which radiates its blessings upon us?" This is not a sermon; it is a fond exhortation. Full of *Egmont*, he quotes a line which he has applied to themselves: "Persons are together not only when in each other's company, but the absent and the departed live in us." More than a certain amount of solemnity ceases to make its impress upon Therese's eighteen years. He adds quickly: "Who would think of writing such things to the volatile Therese, who treats everything in life so lightly?" What is on his heart cannot be quite withheld: "I am very solitary and quiet; I may be awakened again, but since you all went away from here, I am conscious of a void which cannot be filled. Even my art, usually so faithful to me, has not been able to gain any triumph." He offers to send her books to fill in her leisure time in the country: Goethe's *Wilhelm Meister* and Schlegel's translations of Shakespeare. "How lucky you are to be able to go so soon to the country; I cannot enjoy that happiness until the 8th. I am as happy as a child at the thought of wandering among clusters of bushes, in the woods, among trees, grass and rocks. No man loves the country more than I; for do not forests, trees, rocks echo that for which man longs?"

This letter, which meekly asks the privilege of a "half hour's visit," was very far from a declaration. But his thoughts were bolder. A few days later at the most (May 2nd), he wrote to Wegeler at Coblenz, asking him to obtain and send his birth certificate. The letter gives no reason, but is urgent, and the intent is plain. He looks back upon his life and considers his present condition, as one who is about to take an important step. And once more his deafness confronts him as a cruel obstacle to what he is about to do: "I should be happy, perhaps one of the happiest of men, if the demon had not taken possession of my ears. If I had not read somewhere that man may not voluntarily part with his life, I should have long since been no more—and by my own hands. Oh, life is so beautiful, but to me it is poisoned."

142

Beethoven evidently did not go to the country to make his proposal, but sent Gleichenstein a letter to present. Perhaps he feared the humiliation of a face-to-face refusal. The mission was delicate for Gleichenstein, for he was intimately attached on both sides; his engagement to Anna was all but sealed.

Beethoven wrote this note to Gleichenstein, enclosing the fateful letter:

"Dear friend, press them all warmly to your heart. Why cannot I be with you? Farewell, we shall meet on Wednesday morning—the letter is written so that the whole world may read it—if you find that the paper covering is not clean enough, put on another one, I cannot tell at night whether it is clean—farewell, dear friend, think and act also for your faithful friend."

The following day he had to relieve his suspense by writing again:

"You are living on a calm and peaceful sea," he began enviously, "or possibly are already in a safe harbor—do you not feel the distress of the friend who is still in the storm—what will they think of me in the star Venus Urania, how will they judge me without seeing me—my pride is so humbled I would go there with you uninvited— let me see you at my lodging tomorrow morning, I shall expect you at about 9 o'clock at breakfast—if only you were franker with me— you are certainly concealing something from me, you want to spare me, and this uncertainty is more painful than the most fatal certainty —Farewell, if you cannot come, let me know in advance—think and act for me—I cannot trust to paper more of what is going on within me."

Another note seems to be the aftermath of an uneaten breakfast at Beethoven's lodgings when the tidings were stammeringly delivered. It must have been a painful scene. Gleichenstein was compelled to wound his friend, bring crashing down the structure his imagination had built, and with it his pride, leaving him with the bitter realization that the fatuous age of thirty-nine can leap to appallingly mistaken conclusions.

"Your news hurled me from the regions of highest rapture to the lowest depths. Why add that you would let me know when there was to be music again? Am I then nothing more than a *musicus* to you

143

and to the other? That seems at least to be the explanation. So, I can seek support only in my own breast; for me there is none from without. No, friendship and all kindred emotions have nothing but wounds for me. So be it then, for yourself, poor Beethoven, there is to be no happiness from without, you must create everything from within; only in the ideal world can you find friends."

Beethoven's despair was very real to him at the moment, but it was not beyond healing. The episode had flared too suddenly not to be outlived. It is a tribute to the tact of the Malfatti family that Beethoven continued to visit them, even after the marriage of Therese, in 1817, to the Baron von Drosdick. Dr. Sonnleithner described Therese in later years:

"She was a beautiful, lively, intellectual woman, a very good piano-forte player and, besides, the cousin of the famous physician and friend of Beethoven, Dr. von Malfatti. Nothing is known of a particular intimacy between her and Beethoven. A relative of the Baroness, who knew her intimately, knows also that she and Beethoven formed a lasting friendship, but as to any warmer feeling on either side, he knew nothing, nor anything to the contrary, but he says: 'When conversation turned on Beethoven she spoke of him reverentially but with a certain reserve.'"

So did the gentle Therese and her family scrupulously keep Beethoven's secret. Wegeler and Breuning knew of his marriage intention through his request for his birth certificate, and they noted his disappointment and dejection afterward; of the identity of the lady they knew nothing. Gleichenstein, marrying Anna in the next year (1811), thus brought Beethoven's letters into the family, where they remained undisclosed for many years.

CHAPTER FOURTEEN

"I CAN seek support only in my own breast; for me there is none from without."

A few days after these words were written, Beethoven sat at his piano in the Pasqualati house, the fresh manuscript of a song in front of him. Two hands were placed lightly on his shoulders, and a young voice said, tactfully close to his ear:

"I am Bettina Brentano."

Beethoven turned and beheld a strange figure. She was a comely girl of twenty-five, with a natural pallor that was accentuated by her dark hair and ringlets, and by the long black robe that she wore, held by a cord about her waist. This was no fashionable *Fräulein*, no sheltered darling of an aristocratic house. Her passing shyness at the abrupt meeting was belied by the intent gaze of her almost black eyes, searching, predatory.

Her name in itself assured her a favorable reception. She belonged to a family well known and dear to Beethoven. She was the sister of his friend Franz Brentano, who had married Antonie von Birkenstock. Antonie had induced her husband to move from Frankfort to Vienna and live with her invalided father. The Birkenstock mansion was famous. The windows looked over the Prater, and the well-groomed gardens of Rasoumowsky. Hofrat Joseph von Birkenstock had retired from a brilliant career, and made the great house a repository for every object which taste, learning, travel and wealth could accumulate. Bettina, arriving, was astonished to find herself surrounded by a profusion of copper engravings, hand drawings, relics of antiquity, exotic curios, books without number. Beethoven was at liberty to walk into that house at any time. Quartet performances drew him there. When, as sometimes happened, "Toni" Brentano, Bettina's sister-in-law, was confined to her room by illness and denied visitors, Beethoven would go directly to her anteroom where a piano stood, improvise at length and depart, without a word. The Brentano children adored Beethoven and would run over to his house with little presents. Beethoven wrote a little Trio for Maximiliane, and, when she grew up, dedicated a sonata to her.

Beethoven had been told at the Birkenstock house of the exploits of Franz's sister. Bettina had gone to Weimar and Goethe in the spring of 1807, and had appeared unannounced before him, as now she had appeared before Beethoven. She had read in letters of the romance many years before between Goethe, at the age of twenty-one, and Maximiliane La Roche, a bride of seventeen with an aging husband. Maximiliane, now long since dead, had been Bettina's mother. Bettina, at twenty-three, had nurtured a passion for the great poet whom she had never seen, and had gone to him to re-enact her mother's part, to revive in the poet of fifty-eight his youth and his past. As it happened, Goethe was going through a phase favorable to reminiscence and rejuvenation. Bettina stirred up memories. Her black curls were very like those upon which Goethe had addressed poetic thoughts many years before. It was like a reincarnation, with the difference that the daughter was more importunate. Resistance by him would have been useless. Before many minutes had passed she had placed her arms around his neck. He had slipped a gold ring upon her finger. In the correspondence which had followed, she had gratified him by reflecting the radiance of his genius. At last the reserve of the poet, well experienced and on guard against the complications of impulsive women, was relaxed to the point of responding in kind to the *du* of her letters.

When Bettina had heard a "Fantasia" of Beethoven (it was probably the *"Moonlight"* Sonata), she had at once decided to come to him. The family had told her that it was impossible, that Beethoven had three lodgings in which he concealed himself, and, even if he could be found, was inaccessible and rude to intruders. Bettina had instinctively gone to his rooms on the Bastion. Her coming was beautifully timed. Beethoven, like her, was under the immediate spell of the poet. *Egmont* was in rehearsal, and about to be produced with his music. He said to her

146

at once: "I have just written a beautiful song for you. Do you want to hear it?" And he sang what he had just completed—a setting of Goethe's *"Kennst du das Land?"* He had the harsh and grating voice of a deaf man but the expression was vivid and effective. He asked whether she liked it, and she nodded gravely without a word. He sang again the dramatic song of Mignon, his eyes fixed upon her, noting the sudden color in her cheeks, and the glow in her eyes. "Aha!" he said. "Most people are touched by a good thing, but they have not the nature of the artist. Artists are fiery; they do not weep." Then he sang as if to prove that tears were in the music alone, his moving song on Goethe's *"Trocknet nicht, Thränen der ewigen Liebe."*

Bettina was completely won by the passion of the song, at once wild and controlled, which came clearly through its crude singing. And Beethoven was carried away by the charm of the girl whose emotional understanding grasped and enfolded his music with an uncanny directness. If her response had not been entirely genuine, if it had been inflated with affectation, she would have had bare toleration or less from Beethoven—never his ready confidence on his deepest aims as composer.

He offered to accompany her home, and when she reminded him that there was to be a large dinner party at the Birkenstock house, he agreed to go with her. She suggested that he put on a more presentable coat, and after some heavy jokes about his wardrobe, he complied. They walked across the city together, he talking loudly and gesticulating, she so intent that she did not notice they were on a public street. She remembered the family's warning that Beethoven was not to be captured, and, with her instinct for spectacle, walked in upon a company of forty hand in hand with him! After dinner, all went up to the tower of the house, to look at the view. When they descended, Bettina lingered, and kept Beethoven with her. "When they were gone and he and I were alone, he drew forth his tablet, wrote and corrected, and then said: 'My song is finished.' He leaned against the window frame and sang it out upon the air. Then he said: 'That sounds, doesn't it? It belongs to you if you like it, I made it for you; you inspired it; I read it in your eyes just as it was written.' " This may have been *Sehnsucht,* or, one must add, the whole incident may

147

have been Bettina's narrative talent overleaping itself. Beethoven's reference to it in a letter two years later would confirm it if that letter, given forth by Bettina, were to be trusted:

"A musician is also a poet, and the magic of a pair of eyes can suddenly cause him to feel transported into a more beautiful world. . . . In the little observation tower during the splendid May rain, that was a fertile moment for me: the most beautiful themes then glided from your eyes into my heart, which one day will enchant the world when Beethoven has ceased to conduct. If God grant me yet a few years, then I must see you again, dear, dear Bettina; so calls the voice within me which never errs. Even minds can love one another. I shall always court yours; your approval is dearer to me than anything in the whole world."

Day after day, the two were in each other's company, she accompanying him on his rambles, stimulating him to speak about his art, pausing to write her leading observations in his conversation book. Bettina was exactly what Beethoven needed at that moment. She diverted him with her eager vivacity; she spoke revealingly of Goethe; and she drew him out upon his artistic beliefs until he talked as he had never talked before.

In August he looked back upon these spring days with her, remembering "your good heart which looks out of your eyes, and your sense, which lies in your ears." He wrote:

"How dear to me are the few days in which we chatted, or rather corresponded with each other; I have preserved all the little bits of paper on which your bright, dear, dearest answers are written. And so I owe it to my bad ears that the best portion of these fleeting conversations is written down. Since you have gone I have had vexatious hours, hours of shadow, in which nothing can be done; I walked about in the Schönbrunn Allee for fully three hours after you were gone, and on the bastion; but there was no angel who might fascinate me as you do."

"He comes to me every day," she wrote to Goethe, "or I go to him. For this I neglect social meetings, galleries, the theatre, and even the tower of St. Stephen's. Beethoven says: 'What do you want to see there? I will call for you toward evening; we will walk through the paths of Schönbrunn.' Yesterday I went with him to a glorious garden in full bloom, all the hot-beds open—the perfume was bewildering. Beethoven stopped in the oppressive sunshine and said: 'Goethe's poems have great power over me, not only because of their contents but because of their rhythm. I am attuned and stimulated to composition by his language which builds itself to lofty heights as if by the work of spirits and already bears within itself the mystery of the harmonies.' "

These conversations stirred a new intent in Bettina. She had found in Beethoven a glorious artist, helpless and misunderstood, and her protective impulses were stirred. He longed to meet Goethe, but did not know how to bring it about. She would bring her two favorites together. Goethe could do much for Beethoven. Her letters to him put praise of Goethe into Beethoven's mouth. She reported how Beethoven had told of the way music grew within him: " 'From the focus of enthusiasm I must discharge melody in all directions; I pursue it, capture it passionately, I see it flying away and disappearing in the mass of varied agitations; now I seize upon it again with renewed passion; I cannot tear myself from it; I am impelled with hurried modulations to multiply it, and at length I conquer it: behold—a symphony! Music, truly, is the mediator between intellectual and sensuous life. I should like to talk to Goethe about this—would he understand me?' " And elsewhere—" 'Music is the one incorporeal entrance into the higher world of knowledge which comprehends mankind, but which mankind cannot comprehend. . . . Every real creation of art is independent, more powerful than the artist himself and returns to the divine through its manifestation.' "

Bettina showed his reported conversation to Beethoven, and Beethoven exclaimed: "Did I say that? Well, then I had a *raptus*!" But he did not protest or prevent her from sending the letter to Goethe.

Bettina has confounded the historians by her voluble pen, her too vivid sense of effect, and her cheerful way of intertwining fact and legend. At least one of the three letters which she gave out as sent to her by Beethoven shows plain signs of "improvement." Viewed by the biographers of Goethe and of Beethoven, Bettina is hardly recognizable as the same person. Emil Ludwig calls her "lascivious" and much more—"the crowning bloom in the hothouse of pseudo-Romanticism." Romain Rolland erects a shrine

149

about her and even defends her quasi-quotations from Goethe or Beethoven: "At least she did not depart from the spirit of the truth." The discrepancy is easily explained. To Goethe, Bettina was one of many, a blossom in the bouquet of loves which he gathered here and there, at Carlsbad or Franzensbrunn, while his stout wife Christiane remained at Weimar in compulsory complaisance. He was never more handsome and winning than now, as, iron-gray and erect, he dallied with feminine friendship and wrote wistful sonnets. Bettina would have liked to be known as the inspiration for "Pandora" instead of Minna Herzlieb, who was younger than herself and more truly a "child." There was Silvie von Ziegesar, "daughter, mistress, darling, white and slim," and a darker aristocrat, the Jewess Marianne von Eybenberg. There were still others. Even the Empress of Austria paid sentimental deference to him at Teplitz—until he turned his attention to her lady-in-waiting.

With Beethoven, Bettina found no rivalry of beauty and rank to stand in her way. She did not even have to pursue him, for he was plainly fascinated. Her penetrating perception of his music in a day when there was no one else to put its character into intelligible words, together with her valiant battle in his cause, have prejudiced the champions of Beethoven in her favor, and even inclined them to look upon her published correspondence with a lenient eye.

Beethoven, reveling in the attentions and transports of Bettina, was no doubt much beguiled by her peculiar mixture of intellectual fermentation and spiritual flirtation. If his letters to her took an ardent tone, they were no more than a gallant response to her own fervid ways. She presented an astonishing contrast after Therese, the light-hearted innocent. Bettina, with all her emotional maturity and solemn ardor of the crusader, was also still a child. She looked less than her twenty-five years. Goethe had called her *"Kind,"* and she proudly wrote that title at the head of their published letters. She was a *mignonne* still, feminine in appearance as well as instinct, no angular intellectual. She was even then engaged to a young man of suitable age— Achim von Arnim. The fiancé must wait, for her loftier mission came first; she incited genius by putting herself boldly upon its

150

plane, serving it with her mind and heart and charms with the zeal of a fanatic. She was beginning her career as a collector of great men, and beginning it by conquering the foremost composer of the opening century, and its foremost poet. At that moment she was progressing very well indeed. On May 10th, while she was with Beethoven, Goethe wrote begging for her attention.

Bettina's love for Goethe was a fixed determination to awaken the past in him, to stir the ardors of his youth by the offering of her own. She offered her physical attractions as an eager sacrifice on the altar of spiritual union. She went to him in August, after leaving Beethoven, and in a moment of intimate confidence told him that no man had looked upon her. When Goethe bared her breast, watching the flush mount in her cheeks, and covered it with fervent kisses, she carried the experience to her boudoir, and wrote: "The memory of it tears me asunder, I long to dissolve in tears, like a cloudy sky!" Now her written thoughts and sentiments fascinated him. She found a stronger bond, for she succeeded in making herself indispensable to the author. She had talked for hours to Goethe's mother, before her death, about Goethe's boyhood. Now Goethe was planning *Dichtung und Wahrheit* and his memory was dim. Bettina was able to furnish him abundant material. And in her diary she wrote (and this time not for the world to see) that she was like "a spider, weaving a net around Goethe, ensnaring him softly, softly . . . And he will not be able to escape!"

But one of her schemes, almost her principal one, had not been successful. She had talked interminably of Beethoven's qualities. Goethe had only smiled upon her eagerness indulgently, and paid little heed. Beethoven had written a polite note, mentioning Bettina, and Goethe had answered in equal courtesy. Beethoven wished to send the score of *Egmont*, but its publication was delayed. The poet did not receive it until January, 1812. Meanwhile Bettina and Goethe had broken relations. She had never ceased to plead Beethoven's cause, even when he had wearied of listening. She had had to contend with Zelter, whom Goethe had lately come to accept as his musical oracle. Nothing could have been more annoying to Bettina than this pontificate of music who, wrapped in the self-assurance of expertness and conservatism, delivered condemnations of Beethoven. *Christus am Ölberg,* said he, was "immoral"; it was "perverted art." Beethoven abused his talent by investing trivial things with importance, "like Hercules using his club to kill flies." Goethe had accepted this solemn rubbish in good faith, and when Bettina saw that she was losing ground, she could not resist some sharp remarks. "The Philistine," she had called Zelter, "with the large bones and the long waistcoat." Spiteful innuendo before Goethe about his friend helped neither Beethoven's cause nor her own.

When she went to Weimar in September, 1811, with von Arním, whom she had married in the previous spring, the situation became awkward. Christiane, who was not in a position to denounce any of her husband's flames, had harbored from the beginning a special dislike for Bettina and her superior intellectual airs. Now her suspicion that Goethe would be pleased to be rid of Bettina gave her boldness. In a picture gallery one day, Bettina goaded her by sarcastic remarks about some worthless paintings she had been naïve enough to praise, and Christiane burst out into a tirade for all Weimar to hear.

The meeting between Beethoven and Goethe at last came about in the following summer (July, 1812). Goethe went unexpectedly to Teplitz, and, learning on arrival that Beethoven was there taking the cure, lost no time in calling upon him. His quick insight caught at once the remarkable qualities of the man. Returning to his rooms (it was Sunday, July 19th) he wrote to his wife forthwith, and summed up Beethoven in a single, illuminating sentence:

"Never before have I seen an artist with more power of concentration, more energy, more inwardness."

It should have been momentous, this encounter between the two boldest spirits of their age, so alike in their individual courage and adventurousness, their breadth of vision held to a firmness of substance through a deep classical reverence.

The two seem to have been drawn to each other at first, for on the next day they walked together to Bilin; on the next, Goethe called again in the evening, and Beethoven played to him. On Wednesday he called once more. But their friendship did not improve. A searching interchange of views was difficult on account

152

of Beethoven's deafness. Beethoven derived more from the acquaintance than Goethe, whose admiration for the composer remained theoretical, tepid and uneasy. Beethoven's veneration for Goethe was beyond bounds, indestructible. But proximity brought up annoying temperamental differences and frictions. Goethe's elegance and circumspection, his suave speech, made Beethoven feel uncouth and ill at ease. Beethoven's bluntness made Goethe withdraw into stiff formality. When Beethoven played for him, Goethe made a show of sentiment which rang false. Beethoven reproached him bitterly: "You yourself must know how gratifying it is to win the applause of those who understand! If you do not recognize me, if you do not consider me as your equal, who will? To what beggarly mob must I play to find understanding?" (This is Bettina's report.) Scenes like these continually increased the constraint between them. When Beethoven later improvised, bending the force of his will to the penetration of the great heart which must lie beneath the elegant waistcoat, Goethe only told him with a formal bow that he had "played charmingly."

Beethoven was bitterly disappointed. The poet whom he had idolized since his boyhood was there, but he could not reach him. He could hardly discern in him a fellow artist. He appeared rather as a Court Official a little too aware of the dignity of a *Geheimrath*. Teplitz was swarming with titles and uniforms, and Goethe, quite at home among them, showed far more respect for rank than Beethoven considered necessary in an artist who from the pinnacle of his achievement had the right to look down upon them all. His bosom was filled with wild rebellion; he made provocative remarks to his companion; and Goethe, not knowing how to meet this strange behavior, stood in embarrassed silence. Beethoven dominated him by assertiveness while Goethe held the superiority of one who meets crude offense with forbearance and restraint.

The two one day encountered in a country lane a select company of promenaders, of which the Empress was one. Beethoven said: "Let us walk on, arm in arm. They will have to get out of our way, not we out of theirs!" But Goethe stood aside, hat in hand, bowing, while Beethoven, his hat upon his head, strode

153

down the middle of the lane, compelling the lords and ladies to make way. All greeted the two men in friendly fashion (amused probably at both of them).

Bettina was the first spreader of this often told tale, through the publication of a letter of her own, and another which was supposedly written to her by Beethoven, but which is in language strangely similar. She was in Teplitz, having arrived on July 23rd, but she was not present. Not being on speaking terms with Goethe, she was barred from witnessing the meeting she had striven so long to bring about.

Beethoven exulted in his triumph and boasted about it more freely and loudly than he need have done. The story became current that Goethe had remarked to Beethoven that he was growing tired of the many bows one must acknowledge in Teplitz. "Don't be annoyed, Excellency," answered Beethoven. "Perhaps they are bowing to me!" He wrote to Breitkopf and Härtel: "Goethe is much too fond of the Court atmosphere, far fonder than is compatible with the dignity of a poet."

Beethoven and Goethe did not quarrel. They were to correspond occasionally. But when Beethoven left Teplitz on July 27th to go to Karlsruhe, he had so far as is known seen Goethe for the last time. He preserved more successfully at a distance his admiration for the poet. Goethe, moderate, gentlemanly as usual, wrote to Zelter a month later:

"I have made Beethoven's acquaintance. His talent amazes me but, unfortunately, he has no self-control whatever. He is, no doubt, quite right in finding the world detestable, but by behaving as he does he really does not make it any more pleasant for himself or for others. We must forgive him a great deal, for his hearing is getting very bad; this interferes perhaps less with his musical than with his social side. He is naturally laconic, and he is becoming still more so as a result of his deafness."

CHAPTER FIFTEEN

OUR NARRATIVE brings us now to the three-part love letter which, Stephan von Breuning accidentally found after Beethoven's death in a secret drawer of his writing desk, the letter which has acquired its too-famous title from the opening of the second post-script: "My thoughts go out to you, my immortal beloved." The letter is written in pencil, "with yours," it says, and is in parts almost undecipherable. How it remained in his possession, whether it was returned to him or was a copy, or was never sent, is one of the many mysteries which surround it.

The two great questions—to whom he wrote it, and at what point in his life—have piqued and balked investigation through a century. In recent years, the second riddle has been answered almost indisputably. The year was 1812. So, Beethoven's most compelling experience of love was no youthful one. It was the cul-mination of the longing for a permanent union which had pos-sessed him for at least six years past, since his increased prospects for a regular income. He yearned for a protecting domesticity with all that was bourgeois in his nature, the more so since his increasing deafness was threatening to shut him in a dreaded soli-tude, and his helplessness in the small transactions of daily life was throwing him increasingly upon the good offices of his friends. He craved the permanent affection of a sympathetic woman, her tact, her ministering touch, her companionship, which, in his bachelorhood, he could only have in snatches. He had connected many with dreams of marriage, proposed to one, two years before. Frustration, which sometimes had found outlet in music, in a case like that of Therese Malfatti only goaded his desire. Now, at forty-one, the fires of the artist lover were at their highest in the emotional nature which had just produced that outburst of exuberant energy, the Seventh Symphony, completed in May. The troubled status of the lovers is unmistakable; the exact circumstances are unknown. From his overflowing heart the words came in an incoherent flood:

On the 6th of July, in the morning.

My angel, my all, my very self,

Only a few words today, and those in pencil (with yours)—till to-morrow I cannot have my room—what waste of time for such a matter —why this sorrow where necessity speaks— How can our love continue except through sacrifices, through not longing for the utmost. Can you change it that you are not wholly mine, I, not wholly yours? Oh! gaze upon nature in its beauty and solace your heart with a sense of the inevitable—love demands everything, and rightly so, thus is it for me with you, for you with me, only you are so apt to forget that I must live for myself and for you as well—were we wholly united you would feel the pain of it as little as I. My journey was fearful. I arrived here only yesterday morning at four o'clock, and as they were short of horses, the mail coach selected another route, but what an awful road; at the last stage but one I was warned against traveling by night; they warned me of wooded country, but that only spurred me on—and I was wrong, the coach must needs break down, the road being dreadful, a swamp, a mere country road; without the postillions I had with me, I should have been left half-way. Esterházy, by the ordinary road, met with the same fate with eight horses as I with four—yet it gave me some pleasure, as successfully overcoming any difficulty always does. Now quickly from outward to inward matters— we shall probably soon see each other. I cannot tell you now all my thoughts during the past few days about my life—if only our hearts were united once and for all I should not have such thoughts. My heart is full of the many things I have to say—ah!—there are moments in which I feel that speech is powerless—have courage—remain my true, my only treasure, my all!!! as I am yours. The gods must send the rest, what for us must be and ought to be.

Your faithful
Ludwig

Monday evening, July 6.

You are suffering, my dearest love. I have just found out that letters must be posted very early—Mondays, Thursdays—the only days when the mail goes from here to K. You are suffering—Ah! where I am, you are also with me; I will arrange for us both. I will manage so that I can live with you; and what a life!!! But without you!!—persecuted by the kindness of people everywhere, which I little deserve, and as little care to deserve. Humility of one man toward another—it pains me—and when I think of myself in relation to the universe, what am I and what is He who is named the Greatest; and yet this in itself shows the divine in man. I weep when I think that probably you will not get the first news from me until Saturday evening. However much you love me, my love for you is stronger, but never conceal your thoughts from me. Good night. As I am taking the baths, I must go to bed [two words scratched through]. O God—so near! so far! Is not our love truly a celestial edifice, and firm as heaven's vault?

Good morning on July 7

Even while still in bed, my thoughts go out to you, my immortal beloved, at moments with joy, and then again with sorrow, waiting to see whether fate will take pity on us. Either I must live wholly with you or not at all. Yes, I have resolved to wander in distant lands, until I can fly to your arms, and feel that with you I have a real home; while you enfold me, I can send my soul into the realm of the spirit. Yes, unfortunately, it must be so. Be calm, and all the more since you know my faithfulness toward you, never can another possess my heart, never—never—O God, why must one part from what one so loves, and yet my life in V. [Vienna] at present is a wretched life. Your love has made me one of the happiest, and, at the same time, one of the unhappiest of men—at my age I need a quiet, steady life—is that possible in our situation? My Angel, I have just heard that the post goes every day, and I must therefore stop, so that you may receive the letter without delay. Be calm, only by calm consideration of our existence can we attain our aim to live together—be calm—love me—today—yesterday—how I have longed for you—you—you—my life—my all—farewell—Oh, continue to love me—never misjudge the faithful heart

Of your Beloved

L.

ever yours
ever mine
ever for one another

The passion which Beethoven so effectually concealed from every friend—and then forgot to conceal from posterity—is far different from those earlier infatuations which would drift into a

157

slow movement, find a poignant accent, and so end. Beside this letter, the earlier affairs are as the heat lightning of passing enchantments. The letter is clouded by the impossibility of a union: Beethoven knows that what is within his grasp he cannot have But the exhilaration of the present dominates him. He loves, not as he loved Therese Malfatti, not as a beggar at a distance, but with the full giving out of a love that is fully returned. This is no longer courtship; it is the mutual understanding which can share all matters, "external" or "internal." Her whom he knew so well he may not have known long. He must certainly have seen her in Vienna. One would expect to find hints and signs of an emotional crisis in the record of his life in 1812. Beethoven, always secretive about his deeper affections, has here completely covered his tracks. Perhaps no third person knew of it.

Truly enough, July 5th, the date indicated in the letter, was the day on which he arrived at Teplitz. Let us follow him once more to the fashionable Bohemian watering place. The little mountain resort with its surrounding meadows and wooded promenades was fairly bulging with titles. The Emperor Franz and his Empress were there, and about them a well-picked bouquet of notables— Marie Louise of France, the King of Saxony, dukes, princes and barons. Those whom Beethoven best knew were the Princes Lichnowsky and Kinsky.

There was a strain upon them, for the political atmosphere was heavy and glowering. The largest army ever assembled, with horses, cannon, provisions beyond counting, had crossed the Polish border, and was moving slowly, tentatively, unopposed, into the wilderness of Russia. The interloper was making his grandest play of all. Napoleon was advancing upon the Czar whom he had befriended and still addressed as his friend. He had no single avowed aim; he was moving upon Russia because the course of his career permitted no turning back and no standing still. Alexander was the last great outstanding king upon the continent. The federated Europe of which Napoleon dreamed could scarcely exist with this immense, unsubdued empire upon its eastern boundary.

These notables at Teplitz had been drawn in spite of themselves into the wake of Napoleon. Marie Louise was his uneager *Épouse de convenance.* The Austrian royal couple were reluctant as parents-in-law. The King of Saxony had been compelled with many of the others to receive in silence his condescension at Dresden. All were his nominal allies; their people were marching with him, hypnotized into submission by his mysterious halo of invincibility.

Beethoven must have felt the tension and muttered anger at Teplitz. He felt alien both to oppressive royalty and to the indiscriminate oppressor of all. Striding about Teplitz alone, deep in his own problem, he was depressed and rebellious. He wrote to his friend Varnhagen: "There is not much to be said about Teplitz, few people, and among the few nothing extraordinary, wherefore I live alone! alone! alone!" The remark might have been no more than a wistful recollection of the good times Beethoven had had at Teplitz just one year before in the company of Varnhagen and many companions. But, looking for an involuntary betrayal of his secret, one re-reads that repeated word—*"Allein! allein! allein!"*—and hears in it a hollow, despairing ring. Here at last is a clue. And there are two others: entries in the *Tagebuch.* The first, of the year 1812, but of indeterminate date, is like a piteous outcry:

"Submission, absolute submission to your fate . . .
"You may no longer be a man, not for yourself, only for others, for you there is no longer happiness except in yourself, in your art. O God give me strength to conquer myself, since nothing must tie me to life. In this way with A everything goes to ruin."

And these lines bear the date of May 13, 1813, heartbreaking proof that even a year later, he could not shake off his longing. Scribbled, chaotic words, despairing thoughts, where the current of brooding had not become clear utterance:

"To forego a great act which may be, and remain so—O what a difference compared with the carefree life which often rose in my fancy —O fearful circumstances which cannot overcome my feeling for domesticity, but whose execution—O God, God look down upon the unfortunate Beethoven, do not permit it to last this way much longer."

Who was the "immortal beloved"? There have been schools of

thought on the subject, each of Beethoven's loves championed by one or more spectacled knights beneath their lamps. Whoever the favored one was, Beethoven shielded her well. The letter, which escaped destruction by some accident, disclosed just enough to set up a glorious perpetual game of ingenious speculation.

Schindler, as the first biographer and proud owner of the letter, turned to Beethoven's one obvious and admitted affair, and named Giulietta Guicciardi, hanging a probable year of 1806 on that assumption. This statement was unquestioned for many years. When investigation started he was forced to abandon either the lady or the date, and chose to remain loyal to the lady. He stated in the latest revision (1860) of his biography: "To which year the letters belong cannot be determined with certainty."

Thayer, focusing his methodical mind on the subject, built up the first of several pretty structures of detective work. The letter showed the dates of Monday July 6th and Tuesday, July 7th, without specifying the year. It was written from a Bohemian watering place, from which Beethoven was about to go to another which he designated as "K," to meet the beloved one. In which summers could Beethoven have been in Bohemia in July? And in which of these summers could any one of those whom he was known to have admired have been at Karlsbad (where Beethoven sometimes went by order of his doctors)? Another solution for K would be Korompa in Hungary where the Brunswicks had an estate. Above all, on which years did July 6th occur on Monday?

Thayer examined a calendar, and found those years to be 1795, 1801, 1807, 1812 and 1818. 1795 was ruled out because Beethoven did not travel to distant watering places in his twenties, and would scarcely have written "at my age I need a steady, quiet life." He spent the July of 1801 at Hetzendorf, of 1807 at Baden, of 1818 at Mödling. This would leave only 1812. Thayer made these eliminations, by other reasoning in some cases, but proceeded to eliminate 1812 as well! Beethoven went to Teplitz in July of that year but, so Thayer figured, could not have reached his destination by the 5th of the month. Having disposed of all the proper calendar years, he had no recourse but to decide that Beethoven had wrongly dated his letter, as he sometimes did. Thayer finally arrived at 1806, which would have meant a misdating by no more than one day, and decided upon Therese von Brunswick, on the strength of Beethoven's visit to Martonvásár in July of that year. The weight of Thayer's reputed probity led many after him into the shifting sands of the wrong-date theory. Krehbiel supported him, and so did La Mara at first, to the extent of accepting Therese von Brunswick. Later she switched to Therese's sister, the Countess Josephine Deym. The biographer Nohl held to Giulietta, and so did Kalischer, insisting upon the year 1801. To make his case tenable this devious scholar was compelled to date Beethoven's letters to Wegeler, obviously of 1801, as of 1800. Krehbiel, as American editor of Thayer's biography, found Therese's case increasingly precarious in the light of new evidence, and, retaining Thayer's arguments in the text, could justify them only as a "working hypothesis."

This prodigious sleuthing was sometimes too preoccupied with its own ingenuity. It was never quite free of the regimentation of evidence to favor a desired result. Each expert suffered from what might be called *"femme fixe."* Every case was a necessarily supposititious structure, built on probabilities and assumptions, and liable to collapse should a single one of them be mistaken.

Two new and more thoroughgoing detectives came upon the scene, and produced books in 1909 and 1910, respectively. They were Dr. Wolfgang A. Thomas-San-Galli (*Die Unsterbliche Geliebte Beethovens, Amalie Sebald*) and Max Unger (*Auf Spuren von Beethovens Unsterbliche Geliebte*). Working independently, they arrived at a similar result—a result which, strange to tell, effectively disposed of both Giulietta Guicciardi and Therese von Brunswick.

Working to establish first of all the year and the place, Thomas-San-Galli, studying one by one every year from 1795 to 1818, found only one which admitted an indestructible case. This was 1812, the year which fitted the dates on the letter and from which Thayer had succeeded in diverting the general attention. Beethoven was certainly in Teplitz on July 5, 1812, and went from there to Karlsbad. Allusions in the letter led to investigations. The rainy weather, muddy roads, the mail and postchaise schedules, the presence of Esterházy at Karlsbad, every scrap of evidence fell into place.

161

Some writers would not give up Therese von Brunswick without a struggle. She had become the object of a good deal of literary romancing. Most of it grew from a book by Mariam Tenger, devoted to the noble passion of Beethoven and Therese, purporting to derive from conversations with the lady herself in her old age. This book has been entirely discredited. De Hévesy, who had access to Therese's diaries in 1909, found there the admission of two *"grandes passions"* in her life, neither being Beethoven, whom, in many volumes, she mentioned in a single sentence of warm regard.

Who was to take the place of the two cousins? Surely not Bettina Brentano. She went to Teplitz while Beethoven was there in 1812. But she had her newly acquired husband with her, and she could scarcely have gone to Karlsbad. Examining the police lists of residents in Karlsbad at that time, our investigators found there the name of no woman whom Beethoven demonstrably knew. At this point, Unger confessed himself beaten. He had solved everything but the mystery itself.

Not so Thomas-San-Galli. A girl of twenty-four came into Beethoven's life the year before—Amalie Sebald. According to Carl Maria von Weber, who was captivated by her a year later, Amalie had an "enchantingly beautiful" soprano voice, and wit to go with it. She was dark-eyed, pretty, well-made. Beethoven was captivated too, as may be seen from a series of notes he wrote to her in September, 1812. Amalie was the obvious candidate. Thomas-San-Galli brought together every scrap of information about the friendship of Beethoven and Amalie, and the pieces fitted together for the most part extraordinarily well. On July 17, 1812, a few days after the famous enigma-letter, Beethoven wrote from Teplitz to Breitkopf and Härtel asking that they send to Amalie in Berlin his Goethe songs and other of his compositions. Other signposts pointed to the same period. Fanny Giannatasio del Rio, who was the tutor of Beethoven's nephew Karl in 1816, overheard a conversation between Beethoven and her father, so she records in her diary, wherein Beethoven revealed that "Five years ago he had made the acquaintance of a person, a union with whom he would have considered the greatest happiness of his life. It was not to be thought of, almost an impossibility, a chimera,

162

nevertheless it is now as on the first day. This harmony, he added, he had not yet discovered! It had never reached a declaration [*Erklärung*] but he could not get it out of his mind!"

This romantic disclosure by a girl of twenty-six is not necessarily to be trusted. It does not identify the "person," but points to 1811, the year of the first meeting between Beethoven and Amalie. Beethoven's denial of any "declaration" is certainly puzzling when compared to the rapturous phrases of the letter itself. Beethoven made another and more applicable allusion when, in the same year (1816), he wrote to Ries: "All kind messages to your wife. Unfortunately, I have none. I found one who will, however, never be mine."

Then, there is the strange line in the diary of 1812, already quoted: "In this way with A everything goes to ruin." This to Thomas-San-Galli seemed the silver nail clinching his case. At the agonized crisis of his love affair, Beethoven writes of "A," using the same initial by which he is to address Amalie six times in his letters of September 1812! Everything might well have gone to ruin if these two had married. A young and talented actress with a career ahead of her, involving much traveling, would have been of little help to Beethoven. Yet even this evidence is suspect. The autograph of the initial letter is not unmistakably an A.

At this point doubts begin to gather. The confident conclusion of Thomas-San-Galli has not been universally accepted. The latest distinguished contributor to the whole complex subject, Oscar G. Sonneck, in his *The Riddle of the Immortal Beloved* (1927), follows Thomas-San-Galli with admiration up to the point where Amalie Sebald enters, and there differs with him. Nor have many others stayed with him until the end. Unfortunately, the few surviving traces of the friendship between Beethoven and Amalie have a discouragingly slight and ephemeral character. Beethoven met Amalie in 1811 through the poet Tiedge, and writing him sent this message to her: "An ardent kiss when nobody sees us." The half-jocular remark might indicate the beginning of an infatuation. Amalie kept in an album Beethoven's rather insipid attempt at a complimentary rhyme, together with a lock of his hair, but no letters save the seven written at Teplitz in September, 1812. There may conceivably have been other letters, destroyed for what they would reveal, but these seven certainly betray no secrets. Here is one of them—a fair sample of the rest:

"Dear, good A. After leaving you yesterday my condition grew worse again and from last night till now I have not left my bed. I wanted to send you word today—and then again I believed it would look as if I wanted to appear important in your eyes, so I refrained. What a dream of yours that you can be nothing to me! By word of mouth we will talk about that, dear A. Always my wish was that my presence might bring you rest, peace, and that you would be more confiding toward me. I hope to feel better tomorrow and, some hours will then still remain for us during your presence here mutually to uplift, to gladden ourselves in nature—Good night, dear A. many thanks for the proofs of your sentiments toward your friends. I will glance through the pages of Tiedge."

The other letters are equally lacking in any strong feeling, nor is there any sign of mastered emotion or a newly controlled basis of tender friendship. They are anticipatory, rather. Beethoven, sick at Teplitz, is being nursed by a delightful girl who tends to his wants, brings him a medicine or a delicacy, keeps his accounts. She calls him her "tyrant," and he protests, though pleased. A light flirtation adds its charm to this relation of the patient and the visiting, solicitous friend. Beethoven is working toward a greater intimacy, but he is careful not to offend her sense of the proprieties. The *"Sie"* form of address is not surprising; it is quite fitting for such a relationship. To conjecture, as some have, that Beethoven had held back the letter of July and not shown his heart to Amalie is to betray a plain ignorance of the ways of the heart. What possible relation is there between these agreeable diversions of the invalid and the indelible phrases of the summer past: "Much as you love me, I love you more." "Is not our love truly a celestial edifice, and firm as heaven's vault?"

So, once more, a nice piece of scholarly research moves brilliantly, with inexorable logic—down the wrong alley! Perhaps it is as well that the *Unsterbliche Geliebte* remains unnamed. Bee-

164

thoven wished it so. The inquisitive will not be deprived of their best pastime—poking into the secret love affairs of others—and the interest of the biographies will not be lessened if the chapter on the year 1812 continues to end with a tantalizing question mark.

CHAPTER SIXTEEN

"DID NOT Daedalus," wrote Beethoven to Zmeskall in 1812, "shut up in the labyrinth, invent the wings which carried him upward into the air? And I too will find them, these wings."

The speedy completion of two symphonies shows how well Beethoven found his wings. The nature of his labyrinth can be easily detected from the string of complaints in his letters, not to speak of frustrated plans of which he told no one. There were his compulsory attentions upon the Archduke, the ill health from which he suffered particularly in this summer, and the distracting commissions, such as the song accompaniments he was writing for George Thomson. But his real discontent was the failure of the income he had counted on. A fixed and dependable annuity was an ever-receding dream which eluded his pursuit. The Austrian *Finanz-patent* had reduced the redeemable value of his promised 4,000 florins to about 1,600. "Our country," he protested, "is a paper fountain." Lobkowitz, having implicated his fortune with the theatres, was tied up in litigation, and unable to pay anything at all. Beethoven, exacting with his benefactors, went to Kinsky in the summer of 1812 and was given a verbal promise of restitution in gold value. But before the year had ended, the Prince was thrown from a horse and killed, which turn of affairs left Beethoven with no recourse but to lay his case at length before the widow. Payments were held up, pending a judicial ruling, until 1815. Only Rudolph remained faithful, promptly meeting the altered rate of exchange, and keeping up his payments.

Money seems to have been particularly scarce with Beethoven at this time. Frau Nanette Streicher, the wife of the piano manufacturer, has told how she found him in a "desolate" condition, "as regards his physical and domestic needs—not only did he not have a single good coat, but not a whole shirt." She and her husband urged him to make a practice of "putting by money against the future," advice to which he meekly listened. Louis Spohr was surprised to learn from him that he had but one pair of shoes, and was compelled to stay home while they were under repair. This sounds like unnecessary misery; Beethoven must have been receiving payments from publishers, who were loaded with his manuscripts. His bachelor's life was more wasteful than costly. If one is as poor as one finds oneself to be, then Beethoven was certainly poor. He wrote to his Archduke about Kinsky, who had left him nothing but a good intention. "And now this must be fought out in the law courts of Prague. What an occupation for an artist to whom nothing is so dear as his art!"

The continuing war aroused in him nothing but disgust and depression. He wrote to Franz von Brunswick: "If the billows of war roll nearer here I shall go to Hungary; perhaps in any event if I must care for my miserable self, I shall no doubt beat my way through—away, nobler, loftier plans! Infinite are our strivings, the vulgar puts an end to all!"

His nobler strivings had first borne fruit in the new Symphony in A major, completed May 13th. Close upon it, within the space of four otherwise eventful months before the composer's return to Vienna in the autumn, the Eighth Symphony was drafted, worked out and completed. As the Second Symphony was the lyric outpouring of Beethoven during a mental agony which had induced thoughts of suicide, the Eighth, which, with the Second, is the most light-hearted, took shape and reached its completion at the very time when he was forced to renounce his dearest attachment, and to give up his dream of finding a loving companion to fill the void of his disordered life.

His increasing deafness still weighed upon him as a humiliation. He now no longer would play the piano before an assemblage of people. He avoided "music parties," for the sounds of a quartet or trio would escape him almost altogether. He had become aware of the curious stares of strangers which his loud voice attracted, and would go to no tavern but the "Swan," where he had his accustomed corner, and could pass unnoticed. He saw himself shut off from society, forced toward becoming a deaf recluse. There

167

was only music left to him, and through it his spirit rose, poised and serene, with the resilience which Beethoven possessed to such an extraordinary degree. Deafness was not altogether blighting. It was a curtain which helped him to shut out more completely the world with its many perplexities and the ties of the heart which were involved with them. Tones were still a refuge where ideal thoughts could remain unobscured, and where every problem could be solved by a mastery that was not to be beaten down.

The Eighth Symphony, falling quickly into shape, became beauty incarnate, tangible, explicit, restoring. Every measure sang joyously, never looking deeply, not pausing for the reflectiveness of a slow movement. The hilarity his friends knew found its way into the score. But it was transformed: the grotesque, abrupt humor was refined into delicate fantasy, which lightly touched the development of the first and last movements, and in the allegretto became extended playfulness.

The manuscript bears the inscription: "Linz, in October 1812." Beethoven went to Linz from Franzensbrunn in that month, and stayed in the house of his brother Johann, the apothecary. Johann has said that Beethoven wrote the Symphony from sketches which he made in "walks to and upon the Pöstlingberg." There is evidence that Beethoven began the Symphony even before Teplitz. At least, he finished it at Linz, and his mission in that little town gives another example of the sometimes incongruous variance between the factual and the dreaming Beethoven.

Johann had taken tenants into his commodious house: a doctor from Vienna, his wife, and his wife's sister. The sister, Therese Obermeyer, was pleasing to look upon; she had risen from Johann's tenant to being his housekeeper, and from housekeeper to a more intimate status. Beethoven heard of this; his sense of rectitude and family honor were outraged, and he went posthaste to Linz. He had the effrontery to establish himself at Johann's house and there indulge in loud invectives against his brother, for all to hear. When Johann refused to alter his life to satisfy his meddling brother, Beethoven obtained a police injunction compelling the odious woman to leave Linz. Of course this piece of blundering intervention in the private affairs of a brother, otherwise respectable and law-abiding, had exactly the opposite effect from the one intended. Johann found himself with the choice of satisfying his brother by giving up his mate, or confounding him by marrying her. He married her with all speed. Beethoven had completely defeated his purpose. The woman of whom he could not think except with fury, he had acquired as a permanent sister-in-law, having made an enemy of her as well. Johann was of course angry, and, when the marriage turned out unhappily, reproached Beethoven, with a certain justice, for having precipitated it.

Thayer, with one of his well-considered exercises in deduction, breaks down the remark of Schindler that the *Allegretto Scherzando* of the Eighth Symphony grew from a canon written by Beethoven for a jolly evening of supper and singing in which the inventor Mälzel took part. The canon and the supper probably came after the Symphony and were in a reminiscent vein, but Johann Nepomuk Mälzel and his invention for measuring tempo, which he worked upon in Vienna in 1812, were the certain source of the movement. The "chronometer," as Mälzel called it, consisted of a little hammer upon a lever released by a cog-wheel, tapping upon a little wooden anvil (the automatic pendulum, which he was to call the "metronome," was a later invention). Musicians visited Mälzel's workshop to gaze solemnly upon the contrivance which aroused their hopes, Beethoven's included, of fixing tempo by numerical symbols as definite as the symbols of notation. Beethoven saw the droll side of it, too, and, when Zmeskall pondered deeply over ways to abolish the lever, addressed him in a letter (of February 8th) as "Most Extraordinary, foremost oscillator of the world, and that without a lever!!!!" The "tock tock," set at the exact beat of an *allegretto*, continued tapping in his imagination until a symphony movement complete had resulted.

It was a strange friendship, this one between Beethoven and Mälzel. They had one thing in common if little else: the lack of ready money. Beethoven was impressed by Mälzel's account of the riches which could be reaped if they should journey to England together. Mälzel was the kind of scientist who is extremely sensitive to ripe moments for profit. The name of Beethoven had aroused wonderment in the world. In England he had become a legendary figure, and, incited to a proper pitch of curiosity, England was a gold mine.

The acquaintance goes back into the previous year. A pianist from Ratisbon, Mälzel had allowed his inventive mind to lead him into projects more remunerative than playing or teaching. It was related that while he was Court Mechanician to the Empress at Schönbrunn in 1809, he mystified the great Napoleon with an "automatic" chessplayer, in which a man was concealed. Next we find him in the city, where he hired a laboratory in the piano factory of Beethoven's friend Nanette Streicher and her husband (Nanette was the daughter of the piano maker Andreas Stein). Mälzel's experiments drew the curious and interested to his shop. Beethoven, for one, was carried away by his mysterious apparatus and his visionary talk. There were bottles with wires attached which could produce miniature lightning. "Electricity" was a strange and magic apparition in the world. It was thought to be the secret of the life force. Bettina had acted as in the forefront of enlightened speculation when she described the divine fount of Beethoven's music as "electric." More particularly, Mälzel was turning his ingenuity to the future benefit of the art of music. Beethoven, Salieri, Hummel, other prominent musicians visited the wonder-working Mälzel and listened to his discourse on what he had done and what he would yet do. The "chronometer," beating out measures to scientific fractions of a second, was much approved. Salieri tried to determine the right tempi of Haydn's "Creation," and Beethoven saw the possibility of forestalling the witless virtuosos of whom a composer was completely at the mercy. Unfortunately, Beethoven never derived anything from Mälzel which proved to be of much use to him. The accuracy of the crude contrivance is certainly open to doubt. In any case, Beethoven could not measure his music in cold numbers. The musical thoughts of the deaf man were out of touch with the practical contingencies of performance. The broad concept of a tempo is its creator's; the niceties lie within the instrument as it responds to the player's touch; they are matters for adjustment between these two. Most of Beethoven's tempo indications are near a reasonable norm; some of them are obviously far from it.

Mälzel worked upon conical instruments to help Beethoven's hearing. He had a "mechanical trumpeter" which executed marches and fanfares while he accompanied it on the pianoforte.

More remarkable still was a newly perfected "Panharmonicon," an improvement on an earlier machine he had shown and sold in Paris. The "Panharmonicon" was a mechanical brass band, all contained in a single case. The instruments were blown through a bellows, and their notes controlled by a revolving brass cylinder with pins. This, together with other curiosities, was exhibited before the public at a fee, and made to perform overtures of Handel and Cherubini, and Haydn's Military Symphony.

Mälzel, watching popular currents, was ready to make the most of a wave of jubilation that swept over Europe, when the battalions of Napoleon, under his brother's command, were routed in Spain by the Allies. The English nation was in the highest fever of enthusiasm over their Duke of Wellington, the hero of Vittoria, who had at last opened a crack in the vise-like tyranny over Europe. Mälzel at once conceived the idea of a battle piece celebrating the victory, to be written especially for the Panharmonicon by Beethoven. To exhibit this in England with the name of Beethoven attached, and to exhibit the composer in person should make a fortune for them both. Once more, Beethoven listened and accepted the inventor's judgment. What could be more intriguing than a contrivance which would grind out fanfares and tattoos of his own making, and simultaneously lay golden eggs? Battle pieces were common enough. There was hardly a life-and-death struggle in recent history which had not been re-enacted upon a piano keyboard or by an orchestra. Now Napoleon's cohorts should be laid low once more by a scientific invention such as had never before been seen.

Docile for once, Beethoven cared little what he put into the patriotic concoction, allowing his intended partner to map out the musical scheme. The tune of "Rule Britannia" should triumph over *"Malbrouck s'en va-t-en guerre,"* and "God Save the King" should cap all, fully fugued. Beethoven accepted complacently this rather appalling bit of banality. He even found it amusing to rest from more concentrated tasks and let his skill casually build up a structure which would take the populace by assault. "It is certain," he noted in his sketchbook, "that one writes most gratefully when one writes for the public; also that one writes rapidly." Beethoven took his sketches and partly written score often to Mälzel in his workshop. Mälzel must advise him, for example, on what the Panharmonicon could and could not do. Meanwhile Mälzel worked upon a panorama depicting, with clever illumination, the burning of Moscow, an event still hardly a year old. By October, 1813, the score was completed and ready to be transferred from written notes to rotating spikes. By this time, Mälzel was by necessity shifting his plans. The making of the cylinders, and the transportation of Beethoven and himself to London, together with considerable equipment, would require money, which neither he nor Beethoven possessed. No more was to be coaxed out of the Viennese public by the display of his automata; they were by now an old story there. All he had was the great Beethoven at his bidding, and money must be found through him. The battle piece could be a stunning affair if Beethoven, freed from the cramping restrictions of the mechanism, should re-write it for full orchestral forces with a double front of brass and drums. What was more, Beethoven had a new and unplayed symphony, his Seventh. An "academy" with this and "The Battle of Vittoria," even though it were performed by flesh-and-blood players, should make a considerable stir. He organized a charity concert (thus avoiding expenses) for December 8th, which, he calculated, would be so successful as to warrant a later performance with profits. The new symphony would draw the musical folk, "The Battle of Vittoria" the crowd. The choice of the beneficiaries—the Austrians and Bavarians wounded at the battle of Hanau—was well calculated to heighten patriotic fervor and good will toward the promoters.

Distinguished musicians then in Vienna were amused at the spectacle of Beethoven producing an unabashed battle number, and volunteered their services. Schuppanzigh led the violins and Louis Spohr took second place. Salieri cued the salvos and fanfares, young Meyerbeer took the bass drum while Moscheles stood beside him with the cymbals. Hummel was the opposing drummer on the opposite side of the stage. Beethoven conducted. Spohr tells us that his deafness made him a ludicrous figure. He would crouch down behind his desk for a pianissimo and rise to his full height for a large crescendo. But he could not hear, and at one of the rehearsals lost his place, towering and shaking his fists while the orchestra was still playing softly. This precarious kind of leadership does not seem to have marred the success of the concert, which was played to a large audience on December 8th and again on December 12th, netting the charity 4,000 florins. The A major Symphony was much applauded, the Allegretto encored. The Battle Symphony caused a sensation. On many in the audience it made more of an impression than would have all the seven symphonies put together. The doubting ones were now ready to accede that Beethoven was a great composer after all. Even the discriminating Beethoven enthusiasts were impressed.

Beethoven obtained the use of the great Redoutensaal in the Royal Palace, admirably suited to "The Battle of Vittoria," for another performance on January 2nd, this time for his own benefit. Again he conducted, and came so close to disaster that *Kapellmeister* Umlauf had to stand up and surreptitiously give the cues. But this did not hinder the performance from being a great popular and financial success. "The applause," wrote the singer Franz Wild, "reached the highest ecstasy." And Schindler says that "the enthusiasm, heightened by the patriotic feeling of those memorable days, was overwhelming."

There was one significant change. Instead of the Mechanical Trumpeter, which had displayed itself between the two symphonies, Beethoven now included numbers from his *Ruins of Athens* music, after which a likeness of the Emperor was disclosed from behind a curtain. This meant that the entire attention and profits were going to Beethoven. The inventor and his invention were being rapidly forgotten. Beethoven filled the same large hall once more on February 27th with "The Battle of Vittoria," this time preceding it with both the Seventh Symphony and "an entirely new, hitherto unheard Symphony in F major," as the press announced. The patriotic piece thus bore in its wake another new symphony, and brought it to the attention of thousands. The Eighth Symphony, coming after the tumultuous Seventh and before the bombarding battle music, sounded tame and disappointing.

Mälzel, still waiting about in hopes of carrying Beethoven

173

with him to London, was not happy to behold his partner riding to glory quite alone. Protests and conferences with Beethoven before a lawyer availed him nothing. Indeed, it would seem that, although Beethoven had not deliberately planned to ease Mälzel out of all participation in the outcome of what they had at least hatched together, events had so turned out that Mälzel had no legal claim. Determined to salvage what he could out of a bad matter, ethics aside, he did a little underground work, obtaining enough parts to reconstruct a semblance of the score which Beethoven was closely guarding. He left Vienna and Beethoven presently heard that he had performed "The Battle of Vittoria" twice in Munich. Beethoven was furious and at once instituted a lawsuit against him. Did Mälzel, to whom the Panharmonicon version indisputably belonged, have any rights of proprietorship in the orchestral version of the piece? This tangled question was the subject of bitter dispute for several years, until at length the suit was dropped, each agreeing to pay half the costs. The significant part of the whole affair, so far as posterity is concerned, is that Beethoven added one more process of law to the two then pending over his claims upon the Kinsky and Lobkowitz estates. There is nothing less conducive to creative labors than indeterminate waiting upon the leisurely progress of the courts, and the bad blood which it usually breeds even in people more reasonable and equable than Beethoven.

One result of the popularity which "The Battle of Vittoria" had heaped upon Beethoven was the unearthing once more of *Fidelio.* Treitschke, then stage manager of the *Kärnthnerthor Theater,* discussed the plan with Beethoven and offered to revise the text for what he considered indispensable changes in the score itself. Beethoven, still hopeful for his operatic child, was amenable once more. He would have entrusted the book to no hands more readily than those of Treitschke. Treitschke had thoroughgoing ideas. A *Singspiel* must be clear and concise as to text, if it is to succeed, and this text he rewrote in many places. The action must hang together and proceed without undue delay. He pointed out that the first act must open and end differently; a duet and terzetto were dropped. The Second Act must end in the courtyard instead of the dark underground cell.

174

This act, too, was variously tightened. Treitschke boldly told the composer that Florestan's aria at the beginning of the act would not do. A man dying of starvation would not convey that effect if he were given a full bravura number. Beethoven came to Treitschke in the evening, and Treitschke handed him a verse he had just written. It was Florestan's pathetic vision of what had been lost to him—the fair world of sunshine and his beloved wife. It was to be a "last blazing up of life before it should be extinguished forever." Treitschke has left a description of its effect on Beethoven.

"What I am now relating will remain always in my memory. . . . He read it, ran up and down the room, muttered, growled, as was his habit instead of singing—and tore open the pianoforte. My wife had often begged him to play; today he placed the text in front of him and began to improvise marvelously—music which no magic could hold fast. Out of it he seemed to conjure the motive of the aria. The hours went by, but Beethoven improvised on. Supper, which he had intended to eat with us, was served, but—he would not be disturbed. It was late when he embraced me, and declining the meal, hurried home. The next day the admirable composition was finished."

The re-working did not otherwise proceed at this degree of heat. Beethoven was pleased with the new text, and wrote: "So I am determined to rebuild the walls of an old castle." But he could not easily open so old and closed a subject for revision. He became dissatisfied both with its former and new state. He could not "surrender to free reflection or enthusiasm," he wrote to Treitschke. "It cannot go as fast as if I were composing something new." He was to write a fresh overture, and this, he predicted, "will be the easiest, because I can compose it entirely new." But this overture, the brief and spirited piece which was henceforth to usher in *Fidelio*, was undertaken at the last minute; it was not ready for the performance on May 23rd. Another had to be substituted. The *Fidelio* Overture was played, and much applauded, at the second performance, two days later. The opera had been given six times before the next month had passed. Another performance was given for the composer, and, though out of season (July 18th), was crowded. Artaria offered to put out a piano score which Beethoven allowed Moscheles to make, to the great delight of his young admirer. Moscheles relates in his diary how he brought his transcriptions to the master, one or two numbers at a time, for correction. The point of the following anecdote hangs upon the fact that Beethoven had recently changed his quarters from the fourth floor to the far less private ground floor:

"Coming early to Beethoven, I found him still in bed; this day he was particularly merry, leaped up at once, and, as he was, went to the window, which opened on the Schottenbastei, to look through the arranged numbers. Naturally the boys assembled under the window until he cried out: 'Damn the youngsters, what do they want?' I smilingly pointed to his garment. 'Yes, yes, you are right,' said he, and hastily threw a dressing gown over his shoulders. When we reached the last great duet, *'Namenlose Frende,'* where I had written down the text *'Ret-terin des Gat-ten'* he crossed it out and wrote *'Rett-erin des Gatt-en'* for it was not possible to sing on 't'. Under the last number I had written *'fine,* with God's help.' He was not at home when I carried it to him, and when he sent it back he had written these words under mine: 'O man, help yourself.'"

CHAPTER SEVENTEEN

VIENNA, SPREADING its elegance to receive the crowns and titles of Europe at the Congress of 1814, pointed to Beethoven as the product of its musical culture. When Count Rasoumowsky gave enormous receptions in his palace, to be exceeded only by the ball which his monarch, the Czar Alexander, gave in that same palace, Beethoven was passed around. "All strove to do him homage," wrote Schindler. "He was presented by Count Rasoumowsky to the assembled rulers, who made known their respect for him in the most flattering terms. The Empress of Russia tried in particular to be complimentary to him. The introduction took place in the rooms of Archduke Rudolph, in which he was also greeted by other exalted personages. It would seem as though the Archduke was desirous always to take part in the celebration of his great teacher's triumph by inviting the distinguished foreigners to meet Beethoven."

Beethoven was not averse to homage, and was ready to respond appropriately. He wrote a polonaise for the Empress of Russia and a cantata on Weissenbach's text, *Der Glorreiche Augenblick*. If this was not in the fullest sense a "glorious moment," it was at least a fruitful one for Beethoven. *Fidelio* was revived in September and repeated in October with much acclaim. Next month, a concert of his music at the *Redoutensaal* of the Royal Palace was attended by a remarkable assemblage of important people. Many white gloved hands were raised high and struck together after the Battle of Vittoria had been fought once more in music. What more appropriate, for were not all in Vienna to rejoice that the arrogant bourgeois had been put down for once and all, shipped away to Elba so that Europe henceforth could become the harmonious dwelling place of hereditary

177

ruler and ruled? They even showed pleasure in the symphony which a paper described as "composed as a companion piece." It was the Seventh Symphony in A major. Between the two, "The Glorious Moment" was performed. The concert was repeated twice in December.

Beethoven was put in such a good mood by the attention which came his way that he did something surprising to all who knew him. A concert in the Imperial *Rittersaal* on January 25th ended with the quartet *"Mir ist so Wunderbar"* from *Fidelio*. Beethoven acknowledged the applause, and suddenly taking his place at the piano improvised before all—kings, queens, ministers, princes. This was his last appearance as a pianist in public.

Guests swarmed through the paths, between the trees and graded lawns of Rasoumowsky's park to the palace with its huge white columns. The immense building was not large enough to accommodate them all, and a wing was specially built for a festivity on December 31st, designed for seven hundred people. At dawn of the new year a fire was discovered in the temporary wooden structure. It raged on, quite beyond control. By midday, a large part of the main building was a mass of flaming ruins. The magnificent library, the art treasures accumulated through twenty years and costing several fortunes, were obliterated. Rasoumowsky's gracious Czar made his Ambassador a Prince and sent him 400,000 rubles to build another palace, but the sum was not enough; a mortgaged prince lacks the proper air. The treasures were quite irreplaceable. There is somehow an impermanence about "glorious moments." The glittering assemblage must have felt so as they shrank from the conflagration and its sooty remains—the intrusion of ugly calamity upon their rounds of entertainment. Soon there was a more sinister intrusion, the unsettling news, whispered through the audience at a dramatic performance, that Napoleon had escaped his island and was even then in France.

When the Congress hastily dispersed, a special era of Viennese culture seemed also to have passed. Certainly there was a dropping away in the palaces of the activities which had been a part of Beethoven's musical subsistence. The private orchestral concerts of Lichnowsky were to be no more; that prince had died

178

in the previous April. Rasoumowsky's munificence was at an end. His quartet had dispersed, gone the way of Lichnowsky's quartet, and there were none to order music in that form. Lobkowitz, to avoid the embarrassment of his indebtedness, had retired to Prague. The Archduke, alone of Beethoven's particular patrons, remained at the Imperial Palace, and Beethoven saw him often—too often for his own peace of mind. The Birkenstock mansion no longer offered the warmth of friendship and music; Franz and Toni Brentano had returned to Frankfort; her father had died. The names of feminine friends, other than Nanette Streicher, do not appear with any regularity in the record of his daily life. Even the Erdödys, to whom he remained devoted, were no longer his near neighbors. They moved in 1815 to Jedlersee, and shortly afterward to Croatia. Beethoven moved from his quarters on the Mölkerbastei, where he had dwelt close to them so long, to a new third-floor perch on the Sailerstätte, where his window received the streaming sun and gave him a fine view across the Glacis and the Wieden to the Danube shores, with the Carpathian range in the distance.

A loneliness settled upon him. "Everything is illusion," he wrote to his lawyer Kanka on April 8, 1815: "Friendship, empire, imperial dignity, everything is mist which is dispersed by every breath of wind and shaped anew!" And four days later he made a more intimate revelation. Some wistful stirring of memories led him to write, after years of silence, to the friend of his youth, Karl Amenda in Courland:

"I think a thousand times of you and your patriarchal simplicity, and how often I have wished that I could have such men as yourself about me—but fate, for my good or that of others, has not granted my desire. I may say that I live almost alone in the greatest city of Germany, and am forced to live apart from all the men I love, whom I could love."

The old contradictory impulses were still tearing at him. He must have friends about him, close friends, but meanwhile he tried to deny the need of them. "Always more alone!" he wrote in the *Tagebuch*. "One is never enough so." And again: "To get away from here, to live in the country—or the sweet quiet of the woods!" But a little later: "Living alone is poison for you!"

He no longer favored adoring circles in aristocratic houses, or instructed the daughters of those houses with the leniency which comes of ardent interest. Romantic affection had no longer an accepted place in his life. Fair friends still hovered about, and were kind, but they secretly shrank from the untidiness of his bachelor quarters. An artist does not duly outgrow his ardent nature. Ardor is the breath of his life, the substance of his imagination. It becomes unbearably vivid as the body lags. He must find recourse in reverie, and in his art. The *Tagebuch* of 1816 has tortured, undefinable allusions. As late as 1818, Beethoven saw a woman he had loved pass in a carriage, and he was filled with despair.

Deafness was still defeating him, hedging him in. He confided to Magister Brauchle, who was then tutor to the Erdödy children: "I am more sensitive than all other men, and with the curse of my bad hearing, I find only suffering when in the company of others."

Chance gathered around him an assortment of friends with whom he could be at ease, even though he could not love them as he loved Amenda. Standing on no ceremony, they had learned to adapt themselves to his habits. With them he had no need to cover his deafness; they had found how to make themselves understood by placing their mouths close to his left ear and speaking in a certain way. "Steffen" von Breuning was not among them; he had quarreled again with Beethoven. Linke was in Croatia teaching 'cello to the young Erdödys. Ries was in London. But there were others to take their places. They had their nicknames and were the objects of much punning. Steiner, a Viennese publisher who had largely replaced Breitkopf and Härtel in receiving his new manuscripts, was the "stony" one, the "Lieutenant General"; his young partner Tobias Haslinger was the "Little Adjutant"; Beethoven called himself the "Generalissimus." Diabelli was "Diabolus." Carl Joseph Bernard, an admiring young poet, was often reminded that in spite of his name he was no saint, while Peters, tutor to the son of Lobkowitz, was called both a saint and a rock. This proposition is set to music in the conversation books—

> *"Sanct Petrus war ein Fels!*
> *Bernardus war ein Sanct??"*

The habit of punning, which became stronger in his last years, was no chance quirk. It was a part of the activity of the garnering and assimilating mind. A scrap of sound would persist in his thoughts, a name or a phrase often falling into notation. His searching imagination would play with words as with rhythms and intervals, making odd combinations, merging symbols, seeking deeper significations. Soon this dalliance became expressive of its creator's wider nature, his general point of view. *"Nothen"* stood for both "notes" and "needs," the opposing banners in the battlefield of his soul where his aspirations and his material wants contended. Similarly, his *"Reich"* was his "kingdom" of tones, and also his quest of "riches" which stood in the way. Bach was the eternal "stream" of his art. Wolf, his opposing lawyer, was a predatory beast, Diabelli, threatening to sue him, a "devil" indeed. Names or axioms would readily become notes, fall into a canon at a moment's notice. He set *"Ars longa, vita brevis,"* the first two words long drawn, the second two lively. But a conversation book of 1820 shows the reverse of the coin: *"Lang ist das Leben nur, kurz die Kunst."*

The little musical jokes had no importance as they stood, but if one of them should happen to persist in his thoughts, it was likely to reach great ends. His tonal imagination was like his sketchbooks, a storehouse of odd bits that had occurred to him, most of them worthless. It was Schumann who said: "Beethoven picked up his motifs in the street, but he re-created them into the most beautiful utterances in the world." One of these street pickings was the homely proposition: *"Muss es sein? Es muss sein."* It began as a tavern joke touched with contempt: the obligation of a stingy acquaintance to pay his fee. Beethoven applied it to himself—his obligation to his landlady. By then it had become a universal observation: man's accountability to his fate. "What is decreed," says the *Tagebuch,* "must be; and so be it then!" But musical growth kept pace with philosophical

181

growth. Three notes became the query, their inversion, with positive accent, the answer, and the musical proposition found its way into the final Quartet, refined into terms of beauty. Words so transformed into tones always became intensified in their meaning. *"Lebewohl,"* as a three-note motto for an instrumental sonata, is more than a personal pang of separation. The name *"Adelaïde"* sounds as melancholy music in the memories of all who have heard the song. Many words in the *Missa Solemnis* became musically indelible in the same way, and here the trait had its most complete realization. *"Gloria," "Miserere," "Benedictus," "In nomine Domini,"* each word was taken to heart and long nurtured there, until it had become a motif in itself, grown from the natural rhythmic inflection. In the full musical setting, the word became embracingly expressive of all that it implied.

Charles Neate, a young and devoted Englishman, arrived in Vienna in June of 1815, and quickly won a place in Beethoven's affections. Another youth, Anton Schindler, now relieved Zmeskall by stepping into his place as principal handy man. Schindler was quite content to bask in the effulgence of the master, boasting a certain proprietorship. He kept in favor by abetting denunciations and encouraging grievances. His stuffy dignity and rather ponderous sense of humor made him the butt of many a sharp thrust from Beethoven in his expansive moments. But Beethoven was usually kind, and would welcome him in his special corner of a favorite beer house, *"Zum Rosenstock,"* whither Schindler would hurry from his afternoon classes at the University, usually to find the master reading the newspaper.

Beethoven looked to his lawyer von Kanka to "resolve a great discord" (the Kinsky suit), and wrote to him continually in the same refrain, "When I find myself in high spirits, when I have happy moments in my art sphere, then earthly spirits drag me down again, and to these belong the two lawsuits." The endless fuming and bickering over his rights and deprivations, his complaints over the shortcomings of men, his negotiations in pursuit of funds—these too often brought the mighty dreamer

182

down to the humdrum plane of petty troubles, and kept him there.

The year following that of the Seventh and Eighth Symphonies produced nothing worthy of the name of Beethoven. In 1814, the new air of Florestan for the revival of *Fidelio,* the *Elegischer Gesang,* written in memory of his landlord Pasqualati's wife, and the Piano Sonata in E minor, Opus 90, written for Moritz Lichnowsky to compliment his engagement, had at least intimations of greatness. The two 'cello sonatas, of 1815, composed for Countess Erdödy, and probably first played in that household by Linke, had some fine pages, notably the *Adagio* of the second, but dry spots as well. These were all written to match occasions, as were two choruses for the theatre, arrangements, dances, which showed nothing more than the readiness of the expert to sell his services.

Beethoven, waiting upon the deliberate processes of the law while three cases hung over him simultaneously, was kept fretting in Vienna through the summer weeks when he might have been roaming the paths of Mödling or Nussdorf, notebook in hand. It is disheartening to behold him lengthily describing the perfidies of Mälzel, or abusing the "disgraceful" heirs of Kinsky. His tone was that of the man who sees himself victimized, and nurses the wrongs done him until each is magnified and still others imagined. He became indiscriminate in placing the blame. He had been promised security, freedom from worry, and had had nothing but worry from that moment. Only the Archduke was exonerated, the exemplary patron who met every promise and even put himself to the embarrassment of interceding in disputes of which he was no part. Beethoven abused Lobkowitz, the "rascally prince," quite unjustly, forgetting that it was his open-handedness in the cause of music which in the first place had tied up his estate. Lobkowitz remained good-natured. Kinsky had behaved in honor, so Beethoven acceded. But he could not forgive the administrators and heirs for not accepting his assurance of Kinsky's verbal promise to meet the gold currency. Had not Kinsky explicitly advised him to refuse Jerome Bonaparte's offer, to "refrain from eating Westphalian ham," and to remain in Vienna where he would be handsomely taken care of? Beethoven could not see that the testimony of the beneficiary as to a verbal promise did not constitute evidence before the law. Was the word of Beethoven to be publicly doubted?

His claim, tangled in the problems of depreciated currency, was settled in court by a compromise in January, 1815, and in March he received the dues which had been accumulating since November, 1812, 2,500 florins in notes of redemption. In the next month another decree was handed down, settling his arrears from the Lobkowitz estate at another 2,500 florins. He was paid from then each year until his death 1,500 florins from Rudolph, 1,200 from Kinsky's estate and 700 from Lobkowitz, a sum of 3,400 florins, the equivalent, with some fluctuation, of about 1,360 in convention silver. Six hundred dollars a century ago was not a fortune; it was a basis for security.

Beethoven's continued protestations of poverty invite speculation upon his probable income before the court rulings. The homage done him during the Congress took the form, if Schindler is correct, of money presents from several sovereigns. The center of his acclaim was of course the battle piece, the only shameless "best seller" he ever achieved. Its success fomented the continuance of *Fidelio,* which reached its sixteenth performance, focused attention upon his other works and made him such a popular figure that the shop windows displayed a new engraving of him made from a portrait by the French artist Latronne. Substantial payments came from Thomson, and from Steiner's firm.

He was able to purchase, in 1816, the seven National Bank shares which made him a property holder until his death to the amount of 7,400 florins, convention coin. Such a sum must have been gathered from gifts and concert profits at the Congress, together with the annuity arrears of a few months later. It puts in serious question Beethoven's remarks in letters to Kanka, Ries and others about his impoverished condition, whatever he may have paid to his ailing brother in 1815, or to his landlords or the tax collector. New obligations of that year must explain the fact that at the moment when he should have felt more affluent than at any other time in his life he was borne down by worry

over money, and borrowed from both Steiner and Franz Brentano.

It was evident that his brother Karl was in the last stages of
tuberculosis, with no more than a few months to live. Beethoven
was moved to compassion by the helpless invalid, slowly wasting
away. His heart went out to his nephew Karl, then a boy of
nine. Charles Neate described him as "a very beautiful, intelligent lad," and remarked upon the uncle's devotion to him, even
before the father's death. Beethoven met the family's indebtedness several times, as we know from his remark in a letter to
Ries that he had given his brother 10,000 florins in notes of redemption "in order to make life easier for him." The incredible
figure is a round one, distributed probably over a period of years,
and so quite beyond the composer's reckoning memory. It points
to his growing interest in the boy, an interest proprietary and
yet apprehensive, for he looked upon the mother with moral revulsion and profound suspicion. Beethoven was unfortunate in
his sisters-in-law. The thought of little Karl as entirely in the
hands of this one was unendurable. His need for affection at a
desolate crossroads in his life was an impulsion stronger than
the perplexity of taking a child into the confusion of his household. It is probable that he made the only money investment of
his life with the boy in mind, and worried over his future income
for the same reason.

The brother Karl died on November 16, 1815. The will, dated
only two days before, reveals Beethoven's handiwork. He had
evidently talked himself into the guardianship. But he had gone
too far, said too much and filled his brother's heart with mis-
giving. A codicil, added the same day, was as follows:

"Having learned that my brother, Hr. Ludwig van Beethoven, desires after my death to take wholly to himself my son Karl, and
wholly to withdraw him from the supervision and training of his
mother, and inasmuch as the best of harmony does not exist between
my brother and my wife, I have found it necessary to add to my will
that I by no means desire that my son be taken away from his mother,
but that he shall always and so long as his future career permits remain
with his mother, to which end the guardianship is to be exercised by
her as well as by my brother. Only by unity can the object which I

185

had in view in appointing my brother guardian of my son be attained, wherefore, for the welfare of my child, I recommend *compliance* to my wife and more *moderation* to my brother.

"God permit them to be harmonious for the sake of my child's welfare. This is the last wish of the dying husband and brother."

So, the dying man left behind him a dilemma beyond the wisdom of a Solomon. His wife was irresponsible, no fit parent, but loved her son, and had a mother's right to him. His brother loved the child likewise, and could do much for him, but was impossible to imagine as a foster parent. It was enough for Beethoven that this woman had been publicly known as adulterous. The "Queen of Night," he called her, after Mozart's captivating villainess. It would have been fantastic to expect any toleration from him. All the stretching in the world of compliance on the one side and moderation on the other would never bring the harmony which the dying man had prayed God to permit. The will was a virtual decree of failure for the boy, heavy care and anguish for the uncle, pain of separation and humiliation for the mother.

Beethoven filed with the Austrian *Landrecht,* eight days after his brother's death, a petition for sole guardianship on the grounds that the mother had been guilty of infidelity and was unsuitable. On the ninth of January, his petition was granted. The next question was what to do with Karl. Beethoven had no conceivable place for a child in his lodgings. He crossed the Glacis holding his new charge by the hand, and visited the private school of Cajetan Giannatasio del Rio in the suburb of Landstrasse. The proprietor introduced his wife and two young daughters, eager admirers of the music of Beethoven. Beethoven liked the family and the school, and the boy seemed willing. On February 2 he was taken out of public school and established in the private one.

Almost immediately trouble began. The mother came to the school to visit her son or take him out. Beethoven appealed to the *Landrecht* to exclude her altogether from seeing him. The *Landrecht* ruled that her visits were to be allowed only in the presence of a third person to be appointed by the guardian. Interpreting this freely, Beethoven and Giannatasio contrived to prevent her entirely from seeing her son. She went to Beethoven's house to protest, and there was a heated scene, with, as always, scant satisfaction from her brother-in-law. Beethoven went to Baden at the end of July, where, when the quarterly term should have been completed, he planned to receive his nephew, taking him out of the private school. This implied no dissatisfaction with Giannatasio, but was part of his previous intention. He had written to the Countess Erdödy in May:

"The death of my brother was a cause of great grief to me, and the effort to save my dear nephew from his depraved mother was a heavy strain. I succeeded, but so far the best thing I could do for him was to put him in a school, and hence beyond my supervision. And what is a school in comparison with the direct sympathy and care of a father for his child, for such I now consider myself; and I am turning over in my mind one and another plan as to how I can manage to have this dear treasure closer to me, so that my influence over him may be more rapid and advantageous; but to accomplish this is no easy matter."

The Countess had good reason to know that there would be difficulty in making a place for a spirited child of nine in the best bachelor quarters Beethoven could set up. It is touching to observe the tone master devoting his precious summer months to the establishment of a smooth-running household. He went deeply into the questions of wages, livery, laundry costs, "boot money," kitchen provision. An elaborate questionnaire has survived, covering these weighty points and submitted for enlightenment to an unknown expert. Zmeskall was pressed continually into service. He was told on September 5th that he must find another servant: "His behavior must be good and orderly, he must have good recommendations, be married, and not murderously inclined, so that I may feel my life is safe; for in spite of various scamps loafing about, I should like to live a little longer." No servant could have straightened out the disorderliness of Beethoven, for he would not have permitted it. Tired of preparing meals for one who either would not eat them, or objected violently, or was not there at all, his cook would soon cease trying to feed him properly. Beethoven would lie in bed sick for hours, unattended, in a cold house, or continue to live amid dusty confusion where he would not permit his papers to be touched. Only devoted women friends, such as Nanette Streicher, could restore order and cleanliness, replenish the composer's frayed linen, and make him for the time being comfortable.

Beethoven wrote from Baden in September, asking Giannatasio and his family to visit him, bringing Karl along—a remarkable invitation from Beethoven, born, perhaps, of a desire to demonstrate his domestic fitness. Fanny Giannatasio has described their reception. Beethoven had made no provision for them and was obliged to take them to a tavern for supper, where "he dickered with the waiter about every roll," this because "owing to his bad hearing he had frequently been cheated by serving people." Shouting in his ear she noticed that it was partly covered by his overgrown grayish hair. He apologized and said, "I must have my hair cut." It appeared at first glance that his hair was "coarse and bristly, but it was very fine and when he put his hand through it it remained standing in all directions, which often looked comical." He apologized too when his overcoat was noticeably out at the elbow. When it came time to put up his guests for the night he apologized again; he had done nothing about it. The girls were obliged to spend the night in the master's music-littered study, where stood his piano. An extra sofa was carried in, Beethoven taking an end.

Giannatasio could not have been surprised when Beethoven wrote from his Sailerstätte lodging in Vienna next month that he was not yet ready to receive Karl. "My household resembles a shipwreck, or threatens to," he wrote and laid the cause to his rascally servants. He suspected them of theft, and told Zmeskall reproachfully: "All projects concerning my nephew have foundered because of these miserable persons."

CHAPTER EIGHTEEN

THE MAGNITUDE of his new responsibility grew upon Beethoven through the first year of his experience in the problems of raising a child. He must surround his nephew with educational advantages, intelligent direction, all that would be necessary to correct wayward beginnings and build a noble character. The letters are pitiful proof of his inability and failure. This note to Giannatasio, after he had taken Karl from the Institute for a few hours, shows the child's already fast-developing hypocrisy, by which the uncle is completely duped: "I have been deeply touched by his feeling for honor. At your house I referred to his lack of diligence. As we walked along, in very serious mood, he pressed my hand with terrible earnestness, but I gave no response. At table he scarcely ate anything, and declared he was very unhappy because he had not been able to show the same diligence as formerly. I now did all I could to soothe him, and spoke in a more friendly way than at first. In this he shows tenderness of feeling, a trait which leads me to hope good things for the future." A boy who is unusually bright, with an ignorant mother and an uncle who is harshly severe, repentant and over-indulgent by turns, taught by each to have no respect for the other, can be counted on to become adept in guile soon enough, playing, foxlike, contradictory forces one against the other for his own advantage.

Beethoven's friends were called upon only too often. Giannatasio had to listen to the unending perplexities of an uncle as if there were nothing else in the world to be thought about. He and Zmeskall helped Beethoven as best they could, submitting to his sharp (and unmerited) rebuke when things went wrong. Beethoven allowed none to oppose him, or criticize Karl. Breuning, in his outspoken way, had advised strongly against the guardianship, and was for several years virtually banned from the presence. There was even a temporary falling out between Beethoven and Giannatasio, at which the Giannatasio sisters, Fanny in particular, were much distressed. They adored the great man the more through their compassion, and were loath to be deprived of easing his troubles in small ways, as Frau Streicher did. All could see that he was deeply shaken, but they could do little more than stand aside, watching his futile, blundering efforts.

His love for his nephew, now dominating his whole life, leaving him a prey to sudden gusts of doubt, was always exclusive and fearful. He continually expected the mother to win the boy over by indulgences, and turn him against his uncle. His attitude toward her was alternately vituperative and conscience-stricken. He was aware of her just claims. She contributed largely to her son's support—before all, she had the claim of motherhood. The quiet protective affection of Beethoven's own mother, which had been dear to him at Karl's present age, was still vivid in his memory. The reasonable wish of Karl's mother to see her son he recognized grudgingly because of his panic of apprehension. He knew that he was interfering with nature. By cutting the boy off from a normal relation, which Beethoven had so far been unable to replace, he was courting danger. He lived in terror that Karl might turn against him.

This was but a part of Beethoven's problem. He was on sufferance, must still prove his right to keep Karl, and yet he could not succeed in laying the barest groundwork of normal surroundings for a child, or providing him with the most elementary needs. Servants seemed to use up all available funds, so that he had to ask patience from the amiable Giannatasio. These phrases in the *Tagebuch* are significant: "I have sacrificed the best of my own for the sake of my precious Karl. . . . Why cannot I follow my heart's inclinations?" He was ready to lay aside all serious musical plans, bending every thought to the possibility of bringing in money, as if music had no other purpose. As usual, he proved to be singularly unsuccessful in the art of writing for profit.

We find him looking about anxiously in every direction. An

opera, of course, was his first thought, and he considered a libretto on Bacchus by a poet friend of Amenda, and another on Romulus by Treitschke, as if either of those dim ancient figures could ever set him alight. At the turn of 1816 we find him writing to Frau Milder, the now highly successful Leonore of the production of his opera in Berlin, asking from the intendant the subject for a new opera suitable for her and for the "exclusive use of the Berlin stage." A few weeks before he had declared through Zmeskall his readiness to provide for the newly formed *Gesellschaft der Musikfreunde* of Vienna a "heroic" oratorio, and spoke of a text in preparation. In each plan the anxious and hard-pressed uncle is far more discernible than the judicious artist.

Simultaneously, and with greater hope, he turned to England, the fabulous country where Haydn had so quickly reaped a fortune. His relation with London, which was to be close and continuous, began, on his part, on a money level; it was to remain a little too mercenary for the comfort of idealism. Hearing of the success of "The Battle of Vittoria" at the Drury Lane Theatre earlier in the year, Beethoven had written to Sir George Smart, who had done well by it, and by the "Mount of Olives." He had offered Smart the English rights, and had written similarly to Salomon who, as leader of the London Philharmonic Society, put Beethoven upon his programs until his death in November, 1815. Ries labored stoutly in Beethoven's cause. Interest in his music spread rapidly in London, and the publisher Birchall became highly receptive.

On the day of his appointment as "associate guardian," November 22, 1815, he wrote to Ries, and also to Birchall, negotiating to the utmost what he had on hand. Neate, first coming to Vienna from London in the summer, had brought with him enthusiastic messages from the London Philharmonic Society of which he was a member. Beethoven had many friends among them. There was Salomon who remembered him from Bonn days. Salomon had laughed at the C minor Symphony when the Society had tried it and later had stood nobly before his fellows to declare himself mistaken. There was Sir George Smart who had made a thousand pounds by bringing to performance the

191

Christus am Ölberg, J. B. Cramer who had been Beethoven's friendly rival as piano virtuoso, Clementi who had been cordially received by him on each of his visits to Vienna. The Society was then three years old. In its twenty-four concerts to date the name of Beethoven had occurred upon the printed programs twenty times. The word "symphony" appears seven times (otherwise unspecified save in the case of the *Eroica*). The first six symphonies, or most of them, may have been played. The Society wished to engage Beethoven to compose three overtures for them, for which they had voted 200 pounds from their treasury.

When Neate returned to his own country in January, 1816, he went laden with scores of Beethoven which he was instructed to promote and sell. The Seventh Symphony was among them. There was also a package of three overtures for the Philharmonic Society, which when opened turned out to be not new at all, but the *Namensfeier* Overture and those to *King Stephen* and *The Ruins of Athens*—occasional pieces which had already fulfilled their purpose, having been performed and sold. The fine overtures to *Prometheus* and *Egmont,* played at the Society's concerts, had aroused expectations, which collapsed when each of the three "new" ones had been played over. When Ries was compelled to report the Society's disappointment Beethoven was surprised. The Overtures for the two plays of Kotzebue had been liked in Pesth. "I by no means reckon them among my best works," he wrote to Neate, adding in remembrance of a score then in Neate's possession, "which, however, I can boldly say of the Symphony in A." Neate was berated for holding too long the scores entrusted to him for sale, and accused, on the strength of a clipping sent to Beethoven from the *Morning Chronicle* ("Morning Cronigle," the composer wrote it), of giving out the Seventh Symphony prematurely for performance. Neate was compelled to explain that he had not violated Beethoven's trust, and that the symphony performed had probably been the Fifth.

About a year later, Beethoven was again to hear from London. Ries wrote him on June 9, 1817, in behalf of the Philharmonic Society. He was asked to journey to England not later than January 8th next, and to bring with him two new "grand symphonies" for the exclusive use of the Society. Unable to raise their offered fee from three to four hundred guineas, he accepted their terms. His days as a public pianist were over, but he looked for profit through the additional concerts he would be allowed to give for his own benefit. The journey could be made, for Karl could be left in the safe keeping of Giannatasio. He might return with a fortune which would fulfill his needs and Karl's for the rest of his days. This commission must have seemed a heaven-given solution to all his troubles. A symphony would combine profit with artistic satisfaction and honor. We have evidence that symphonic thoughts had for him just now a special sanctity putting them quite apart from the *"Brodwerke,"* which might be defined as commissions where the fee was more attractive than the subject. For these, specifications could be cynically accepted from the purchaser. With a symphony, it was a different matter. When an English army officer by the name of Kyd had a little while before offered a hundred pounds for a symphony that would be simpler and more comprehensible than his more recent ones—in the style of his First or Second for example—he suddenly found himself in the street as the door slammed in his face. A symphony could be thought of in one way only—and that was Beethoven's way.

Yet in September, when the particulars for a London journey were agreed upon and the date of departure less than four months away, Beethoven did nothing about writing the two symphonies. Ries and his fellow Londoners should by now have begun to realize the difference between extracting twelve symphonies from Haydn and as many as two from Beethoven. If they had ordered one overture from Beethoven instead of three, they might with luck have had a good one. If they had ordered one symphony instead of two, and if such a symphony had stood, well advanced, in Beethoven's books, as the result of a summer's work, then their hopes might have been rewarded. One wonders whether Beethoven knew more about his capabilities than his friends did when he promised without apparent hesitation a ninth and a tenth symphony within four months, the summer having ended. Subsequent sketches show that he thought of one, possibly two, symphonies for London. He had every inducement in the world to throw himself upon the beloved task, while London would surely wait for a year, two years, whatever time the labor should require.

He was in the mood for composing. Sir Charles Neate, coming to Vienna in the summer of 1815, at the time when the dying brother and the little boy had become a heavy care to Beethoven, followed the composer on some of his walks across the Helenen Thal in Baden, and reported years later how "he had never met a man who so enjoyed nature. He took intense delight in the flowers, in the clouds, in everything. Nature was like food to him, he seemed really to live in it. Walking in the fields, he would sit down on any green bank that offered a good seat, and give his thoughts free course." Why did not the ecstatic mood, the sheer, relaxed delight become indescribable tonal felicity by the alchemy of earlier years, resulting in another Pastoral Symphony? Beethoven would have blamed the "wretched, everyday, unpoetical surroundings" which hemmed him in, as he wrote to a friend in that summer. But that would not have explained the failure of his scribbled notations to become miraculously articulate in the old familiar way. Sordid troubles had filled his life many a time before and never dried up the spring of musical fancy which, rather, had found its strength in fending them off.

There could have been but one cause for Beethoven's despondency; it was the failure of vital reassertion through his art. His musical nature had not been deeply stirred since 1812. That year of the Seventh and Eight Symphonies had proved one of consummation, opening no further vista. No orchestral work of any consequence followed them. The F minor quartet of 1810, an autumnal piece, somber and ghostly in color, had seemed to bring to an end the high adventures of the four that had gone before. The fragmentary Sonata for Moritz Lichnowsky (Opus 90) of 1814 followed by five years the *"Lebewohl"* Sonata, and, like it, was an echo of a way he had left behind. Its slow movement, a fervid song in full-rounded phrases, little developed, was of an earlier Beethoven. The composer failed to follow it with another as if he could not go on in the old way, settle, as others had done, into a comfortable style for the rest of his life. It was for spirits less restless than his to stake and complacently

194

cultivate their gardens. His tumultuous vigor and full-voiced sentiment were too wild; the moment that produced them had a fluid vitality which could not be fixed. He could advance no further on the road of impulsive fervor, for he had passed his peak of hot-bloodedness. When the storm crisis began to subside, he stood for once mute and helpless, not knowing which way to turn. The years 1813, 1814, 1815, 1816, lay musically fallow. In the spring of 1817, his tragic plight, the lawsuits and kindred annoyances, called for retaliation in the powerful terms of his art. Music had always come to his rescue. For once it seemed to fail him.

Now he stood at a crossroad, impotent and confused, entirely without a sense of direction. The weight of his miseries had become unbearable for the lack of musical deliverance. There were sketches in his notebooks for what was to be the Ninth Symphony. He had every reason to push it ahead, taking the obvious road to wealth by way of London. But the sketches would not progress. Apparently, he was not ready for a symphony. He still grasped at the straw of an opera plan. His tragic surroundings seemed to crush out music altogether. He thought of flight, and the love of his nephew held him back. He turned again to the diary in an agony of indecision. His prayer for an answer is a prayer for the music that will not come:

"God help me, Thou seest me deserted by all men, for I do not wish to do wrong, hear my supplication, only for the future to be with my Karl, since no way can be found, O harsh fate, O cruel destiny, no, no, my unhappy condition will never end. Work during the summer for the journey, only thus can you carry out the great task for your poor nephew—make plans and remain cheerful for the sake of C.

"There is no salvation for you except to go away, only by that can you lift yourself up to the summits of your art again, while here you are sinking into vulgarity; and a symphony—and then away—away—away."

But the old faculty of resurgent growth had not died. The only explanation is that he had not been ready. Withdrawing more and more from converse with the world, he had been surrounding himself with his own thoughts and reflections. He had need of a new self-accounting, an instinctive re-adjustment, an altered horizon. There had to be a new subtilization and integration. There was no longer the conflict of battle in his veins; his mastery, when at last it was to re-assert itself, would have a new strength, but it would be a strength through moderation. The wooer, bidding for emotional response, was to be replaced by the introspective dreamer, oblivious of an audience, seeking inward light. The builder, with deepened skill, would devise structures more intricate because conceived in longer lines, in rising and falling curves so subtly molded that they were felt rather than directly perceived. Another would have wandered into the arid territory of abstruseness or intellectuality. Beethoven rarely strayed in that direction. In the shaping of his themes his efforts would tend as much as ever toward essential simplicity. So, his music would move clear of the precious or esoteric and remain universal.

He had already found the new way, but he had not recognized it. The change had showed itself in a piano sonata the year before—a medium in which he had broken no new ground since the *"Appassionata"* Sonata of 1806. The piano, favoring the extemporizing mood, had earlier served him for preliminary exploration when a reconstitution of his art was afoot and a symphony not yet to be attempted. The Sonata Opus 101, of 1816, was of this sort, music of a new close-knit, sinuous power. The quick fingers and receptive mind of the Baroness Dorothea von Ertmann, for whom he wrote it, caught something of its meaning; to most others, including the publisher Steiner, it was simply an enigma, a congregation of obscurities.

Now, other sketches leaped into life, filling page after page of the sketchbooks as Beethoven paced about Nussdorf and the other environs of Heiligenstadt. All other plans fell into the background, and even the symphonic notations were crowded out. The old compulsion was upon him again. Groping distractedly in the dark he had suddenly, unexpectedly, found his sense of direction. The new work continued its slow growth through the winter and another spring, fully engrossed its maker through the summer following, at Mödling, and was completed in the autumn of 1818. This sole notable product of two years of its

196

composer's life was still another piano sonata, pursuing the road which its predecessor had opened up, vast in proportions, far exceeding in length any sonata he had written. Beethoven was to name it the *"Hammer-Klavier"* Sonata because he had espoused a movement to give the instrument its German title. It was to reach far beyond the sonority or sustaining ability of the best instrument made, by whatever language it might be called. The first movement was symphonic in breadth and character, as if the composer, like a Titian or Michelangelo, were drafting vaster thoughts in a cartoon, fixing them in the definition of black and white. The *Adagio* seemed to probe the depths of suffering. It held the wistfulness of a lonely man who has given his heart to a child with the bitter result of injuring him and winning in return fear and contempt. There is alleviation in the *Adagio*, but it is momentary. The final fugue was released in strong assertion. He had found this release through Bach, but how different was its drive from the more static majesty of that master! "To make fugues," Beethoven once said to Holz, "requires no particular skill. In my study days I made dozens of them. But the fancy wishes also to assert its privileges, and today a new and really poetical element must be introduced into the old traditional form." The form goes upon his anvil in the B flat Sonata as it had in the A major Sonata, or the second 'Cello Sonata of 1815. But now he had acquired far greater pliability and concentrated power.

This was the strange end of an uncle's efforts to exploit his art for a nephew's salvation. The money needs—London and its pounds sterling—were forgotten. He had been led into the Sonata unawares by some impulse he could not have accounted for. A piano sonata had been furthest from his intentions. No one had asked for a piano sonata, least of all one like this. The result of his tremendous and protracted expenditure of energy was to be quite lost upon his own world.

CHAPTER NINETEEN

IT WAS in vain for Beethoven to try to enclose himself in the rarefied atmosphere which he had newly found. The bond that tied him to his miseries was too strong; the love of his nephew, grasping at his heart, was his undoing. He struggled long and hard in the autumn and winter of 1817 to make his lodgings in the house, *Zum grünen Baum,* in Landstrasse a place where a child could be received. In January, 1818, two years after Karl had been delivered into Giannatasio's hands, the boy was brought, with his chest of clothing, to a house which for all its master's intensive efforts was still little removed from the state of "shipwreck" he had once described.

We have the sorry spectacle of the mind and fancy which can embrace the universe becoming hopelessly tangled in a maze of petty struggles, even while the Sonata in B flat is occupying him. A missing pair of socks from the laundry and the possible theft involved, or the amount of meat a servant should be allowed and what it should cost—these and endless other questions harass the composer, become major issues—and remain unanswered. He forgets a meal time, tramps off and returns to find himself locked out of his own house. He accuses his servants of dishonesty, and they, tired of his abuse, take their revenge by lifting no finger to help him out of his poor confusion. The master of the noble and intangible world of the ideal becomes in a moment the slave of petty circumstance, a combatant in the sordid affairs of the scullery. He is always the loser. He is in the center of a nightmare in which the antagonists are phantoms evading his attack. He can never get to the bottom of their infamy for the good reason that most of it is imagined. If he

198

dismisses them, worse ones will take their places. In every detail of the picture there is suffering.

Beethoven took Karl to Mödling as early as May 19, 1818, together with two unpromising servants. His letter to Frau Streicher a month later is a remarkable document; it gives the impression of a turmoil of intrigue in which two "traitresses," one young, one "hoaryheaded," accept bribes from the mother and victimize the son, while Beethoven badgers him, trying to uncover the dark plots. "Everything is chaos," he wrote finally; "yet there will be no need to put me in a lunatic's cell." The good lady almost needed this assurance.

When the young artist August von Klöber went to Mödling to paint him, peace was outwardly restored. He found Beethoven giving his nephew a lesson upon the Broadwood piano he had just received from London, as a present from the firm of that name. Klöber had to shout into an ear trumpet to make himself understood, and yet he remarked that Beethoven seemed readily to detect by ear errors in the lad's playing. Beethoven could sense sound by the vibrations of a piano. Klöber's painting, which showed Beethoven with notebook and pencil in a Mödling landscape, the nephew sitting under a tree near by, has not survived. But a word picture shows the quick observation of the artist:

"Beethoven's household in Mödling was extremely simple as, indeed, was his whole nature; his garments consisted of a light-blue frock coat with yellow buttons, white waistcoat and necktie, as was the fashion at the time, but everything *negligée*. His complexion was healthy, the skin somewhat pockmarked, his hair was of the color of slightly bluish steel as it was already turning from black to gray. His eyes were bluish gray and very animated; when his hair was tossed by the wind there was something Ossianic—demonic—about him. In friendly converse, however, his expression became good-natured and gentle, particularly when the conversation pleased him. Every mood of his soul found powerful expression instantly in his features."

This picture, which says nothing of stress and tribulation, might reveal that tones were sounding in the composer's heart again—and so they were. The Sonata in B flat was in its last stages, and a still mightier project was already well begun. It was not the symphony; London must continue to wait indefinitely for that. It was a vast imagined chorus, shouting a *"Kyrie"* to the heavens. The chance news, a month or so before, that his Archduke was to be elevated to the Archbishopric of Olmütz started thoughts, unspurred by any commission or other expediency. The stirring missal text of the church was occupying the center of his plans. Again, it seemed, he had not known whither his developing spirit tended.

Beethoven had become again so deeply immersed in his music that even the nephew was for the time being forgotten. Karl was profiting by the lack of ordered supervision to take the upper hand and do what he pleased. His uncle had put him in a class of boys in charge of a village priest by the name of Fröhlich. Before June had passed Fröhlich had returned him to his uncle admitting that he could do nothing with him. Religious instruction left him openly bored. He disturbed the services in church, brought complaints from the neighbors by his conduct in the streets, and would soon demoralize the other twelve boys of the class. Most shocking of all, he reviled his mother, flagrantly "violating the Fourth Commandment." His uncle had permitted this, and had come to the priest to relate with relish that Karl had referred to his mother as a *"Rabenmutter,"* "raven mother." When Fröhlich took Karl aside and reproached him, Karl answered quite brazenly that he used such names about his mother to keep in good favor with his uncle; "He dared not tell him the truth because he would believe only lies."

As usual, open censure of Karl and failure to control him were enough to condemn anyone in Beethoven's eyes; the "spineless" priest was not spared. A tutor was found to instruct and prepare Karl for a public school in Vienna where the discipline would be stricter. Beethoven took the boy into the city in August for his examinations and entered him on November 6th. Now all seemed to run with a reasonable smoothness. Karl did well in his lessons, being quick and accurate, a born scholar, and was taught piano, drawing, and French on the side. Relations with the Giannatasios were resumed; there was music making. Beethoven began to talk of going to England in the spring.

The tranquillity was deceptive. On December 3rd, Beethoven

appeared at the Giannatasios' door, wild and unnerved. Karl had run away, and gone to his mother. Perhaps she had fled with him to Hungary to separate him from his uncle for once and all. Beethoven stood before his friends, agitated and bewildered, tears standing in his eyes, as Fanny, all sympathy, noted in her diary.

On the petition of the mother, the third she had made, the whole matter was brought up anew in the *Landrecht*. The magistrates had naturally inclined in favor of the famous artist and against the widow who had evidently been considered by her husband to be unreliable as the sole keeper of her son. The brand "adulteress" carried heavy connotations which Beethoven missed no chance to emphasize. At first they assumed that an unfaithful wife must necessarily be an untrustworthy mother. Yet this mother loved her son enough to agree willingly to provide half of his support from her meager funds with the doubtful recompense of a grudging permission to see him at infrequent intervals in the presence of a watchful stranger. These intervals had been reduced to one visit a month, and finally, when Beethoven went to Mödling, she was excluded altogether. Her affection and anxiety had taken the only course possible; she had gone to the servants of the Beethoven household for information about her boy, and probably had gained secret access to him. What she had learned justified her fears. He was being rapidly ruined, and poisoned against her as well. She heard, mistakenly, that Beethoven was planning to send Karl to a distant school and she protested before the court at the prospect of losing him altogether. This solution would have been the only possible one for the saving of Karl and the peace of mind of all concerned, but it was not the proposal of either guardian. Each wanted to keep the boy.

All three were examined at the *Landrecht*, and these facts came to light: Karl had been lonely with his uncle, having no companion. Beethoven had by turns coddled him, and suddenly in an outburst of emotion had threatened to throttle him, imposing impossible restrictions. Beethoven's moral advice did not prevent the boy from calling the servants insulting names (this might have been direct emulation) or from helping himself to coppers for the sweetshop. Beethoven dutifully knelt beside him in prayer twice a day; the effect of his religious instruction was only too plain in the testimony of the priest at Mödling. Johanna van Beethoven testified that her son had come to her "in fear of punishment and because he did not like to live with his uncle"; that she had kept him with her for a short time and then taken him voluntarily to the police station; that he had been ill-cared for at his uncle's house, and neglected, neither properly clothed nor washed.

At this point the case was referred by the state *Landrecht* to the lower court of the municipality of Vienna where it would naturally have been entered in the first place, had there not been a tacit acceptance of nobility in Beethoven's name. It was found that the Dutch prefix "van" bore no assumption of noble birth, as did the German "von." The tale that Beethoven pointed to his head and heart with the words "my nobility lies here and here" is not confirmed by the court records.

All parties concerned were called before the municipal court, and the pleas of each side listened to. Evidently this court was uninfluenced by Beethoven's world prominence and high connections, as it examined his qualifications to be a guardian. His written petition to the magistrates is a moving document, ringing in every sentence with his passionate devotion to the boy and his desperate fear of losing him to "vulgar and evil surroundings." Alas, Beethoven's devotion, already plain enough, was something else than his suitability. His ferocious attack upon the mother, the *Concupist* Hotschevar who had become her advocate, and upon the priest of Mödling, could have had but one effect upon the court: to convince them that to allow this petitioner his co-guardianship would result in shutting out the mother altogether, with her indisputable rights, and giving over the already intractable lad of eleven completely to the deafness, the irascibility, the fatuous affection, the disorderliness and incompetence of the well-meaning but half-mad uncle.

After several months of two-way tugging, friction and vexation, a decision was handed down on September 17, 1819. Frau van Beethoven's case was now looked upon with great leniency. Her sins of 1811 were considered as outlived. Beethoven, threatening to send the boy to school in another country, had intended to "pain the mother, tearing her heart out of her bosom." The magistrates gave no sign of knowing that she had recently given birth to an illegitimate child. It is difficult to judge, in the face of Beethoven's hot accusations, to what extent she was a menace to her son. Certain it is that she loved him enough to fight desperately for him, and if she indulged and pampered him, it was an instinctive weapon in that fight. The court decreed that the mother was to be co-guardian with Leopold Nussböck, a municipal official. Beethoven was ruled out.

Now Beethoven bent the whole force of his affection and determination upon regaining what had been taken from him. He engaged Dr. Johann Bach as advocate, and carried the case to the court of appeal. The winter season and spring months following were a succession of pleadings, bitter incriminations and intrigues which must have been thoroughly exhausting to Bach and to both courts, particularly those members of the Appellate Court who were singled out and told at length about the perfidy of the lower one. The marvel is that through it all, the *Missa Solemnis* progressed.

Whether because of the judicious directing hand of Bach or the sheer weight of his perseverance, Beethoven prevailed. On July 24, 1820, the Appellate Court reversed the lower decision and granted Beethoven joint guardianship together with his friend Councillor Peters, for whom he had asked.

Beethoven was as jubilant as if his troubles had ended. They had hardly begun.

CHAPTER TWENTY

THE WORRIES over Karl must for the time being be set aside, as we follow the composer in his pursuit of the developing Mass. Beethoven now showed an almost trance-like ability to step from one state of consciousness into another. This had become an absolute necessity. The nephew wandered about forgotten and the household remained askew as the imperious exigencies of the music filled every corner of the composer's mind.

Those friends who had reason to visit Beethoven at Mödling in the summer of 1819 were likely to find him wild in demeanor, roaring and writing, looking at them without seeing them. Now his mightiest concept, the *Missa Solemnis*, was in full progress. No labor he had undertaken required such concentration and application of the will to subdue. The subject was limitless, the media resistant and conflicting. A manner of presentation must be found. Schindler has described him in that year: "Beethoven was truly the boisterous, heaven-storming giant, and more particularly in the autumn, when he wrote the *Credo* with the exceedingly difficult fugue." Schindler has described a visit which he made in August to the Hafner house at Döbling, together with Johann Horsalka, a musician of Vienna:

"It was four o'clock in the afternoon. As soon as we entered we learned that in the morning both servants had gone away, and that there had been a quarrel after midnight which had disturbed all the neighbors, because as a consequence of a long vigil both had gone to sleep and the food which had been prepared had become unpalatable. In the living room, behind a locked door, we heard the master singing parts of the fugue in the *Credo*, singing, howling, stamping. After we had been listening a long time to this almost awful scene, and were about to go away, the door opened and Beethoven stood before us
204

with distorted features, calculated to excite fear. He looked as if he had been in mortal combat with the whole host of contrapuntists, his everlasting enemies."

The two friends found that he had eaten nothing since the day before, when, raging at the servants, he had driven them from the house.

Another interesting picture of Beethoven in the throes of the Mass, this one probably in its later stages, was related to Thayer by Professor Höfel, who remembered an incident when he was dining in a tavern some distance from Vienna. A police officer approached the commissioner who was of the party, and said:

" 'Mr. Commissioner, we have arrested somebody who will give us no peace. He keeps on yelling that he is Beethoven, but he's a tramp, has no hat, an old coat, etc.—nothing by which he can be identified.' The Commissioner ordered that the man be kept under arrest until morning. 'Then we will examine him and learn who he is.' Next morning the company was very anxious to know how the affair turned out and the Commissioner said that about 11 o'clock that night he had been waked by a policeman with the information that the prisoner would give them no peace and had demanded that Herzog, Musical Director in Wiener Neustadt, be called to identify him. So the Commissioner got up, dressed, went out and waked up Herzog, and in the middle of the night went with him to the jail. Herzog, as soon as he cast eyes on the man exclaimed, 'That *is* Beethoven!' He took him home with him, gave him his best room, etc. Next day came the burgomaster, making all manner of apologies. As it proved, Beethoven had got up early in the morning, and, slipping on a miserable old coat, without a hat, had gone out to walk a little. He got upon the towpath of the canal and kept on and on, seems to have lost his direction, for, with nothing to eat, he had continued on until he brought up at the canal-basin at the Ungerthor. Here, not knowing where he was, he was seen looking in at the windows of the houses, and as he looked so like a beggar the people had called a constable who arrested him. Upon his arrest the composer said, 'I am Beethoven.' 'Of course, why not?' (*Warum nicht gar?*) said the policeman. 'You're a tramp: Beethoven doesn't look so' (*Ein Lump sind Sie; so sieht der Beethoven nicht aus.*) Herzog gave him some decent clothes and the burgomaster sent him back to Baden, where he was then living, in the magisterial state-coach."

The *Missa Solemnis* dominated the composer's life for five years. In the course of its growth the Archduke was forgotten. His installation took place March 20, 1820, when the score was far from completed. It was not designed for a cathedral or congregation, or service of any sort. From the tremendous impact of the first *Kyrie* in choral unison to the tranquil personal conviction of the closing *Dona nobis pacem,* this music never gives the sense of filling out an expected pattern. One is reminded of the early Italian or German religious paintings where the fervor of the subject glows directly from the canvas, as if the artist in his intense preoccupation had forgotten his churchly or papal obligations, his pride of craft. So, the faith of Beethoven which transfigured his tones was direct, self-found, uninstructed. "Coming from the heart, may it again reach the heart," he wrote over his manuscript score, and not once does ecclesiastical convention intervene; neither does that familiar attribute of choral music, the calculated assault upon the ears. When the Mass makes its dramatic effect it does so simply because Beethoven felt his subject dramatically. Beethoven is not proclaiming a constituted gospel to a multitude. He is alone with his God. The *Missa Solemnis* is as personal, as solitary as the sonata which preceded it, or the quartets which were to follow.

Those who would like to prove the *Missa Solemnis* a Roman Catholic document point out that Beethoven led his nephew to the confessional, and that he accepted the last sacraments upon his deathbed. It is more significant that a devout man, brought up in the Roman Catholic faith, should have otherwise almost completely dispensed with the Church. The composer was indifferent to the ritual associations of the missal text. He had it translated from the Latin that he might weigh every word for its human, personal meaning.

Phrases written in the privacy of his notebooks show that he turned to thoughts of God in times of stress. His creed, his theology, may be guessed from transcripts in his own hand from the literature of his period. There is this sentence from Kant: "The moral law in us and the starry heavens above us." There is a paragraph, translated from the Hindu by Herder and carefully written out, which begins: "God is immaterial;

since He is invisible He can have no form, but from what we observe in His works we may conclude that He is eternal, omnipotent, omniscient, and omnipresent— The mighty one is He who is free from all desire, He alone; there is no greater than He."

Beethoven copied these sentences from Schiller's essay in Egyptology, *Die Sendung Moses,* and kept them, framed, upon his writing table:

"I am that which is—I am all, what is, what was, what will be; no mortal has lifted my veil . . .

"He is only and solely of Himself, and to this only One all things owe their existence."

This God, the God whom the indomitable tone creator faced in his despair, addressed in the privacy of his *Tagebuch*— this super-sectarian God is again addressed directly in the *Gloria* and *Credo,* in every page of the Mass. His concept had to be reconciled with a churchly form, and he wrote amidst his sketches:

"In order to write true church music, look through all of the monastic church chorals and also the strophes in the most current translations and perfect prosody in all Christian-Catholic psalms and hymns generally. Sacrifice again all the pettinesses of social life to your art. God above all things! For it is an eternal providence which directs omnisciently the good and evil fortunes of human beings. . . . Tranquilly will I submit myself to all vicissitudes and place my sole confidence in Thine unalterable goodness. O God! Be my rock, my light, forever my trust!"

It was probably the need for freedom in personal expression which kept Beethoven from probing more deeply into the restricting style of the early contrapuntists. Bach must surely have influenced him, for he had written his publisher for the then little known Mass in B minor, identifying it by a passage he remembered note for note, the bass of the *Crucifixus.* A principal difference in the two Masses is that Bach wrote in rounded amplitude, fulfilling traditional form to the utmost, while Beethoven, accustomed in any case to more pithy symphonic thinking, focused his emotions sharply to a point, and built with the special forcefulness which terseness can command. Beethoven shows the supreme effectiveness of the vivid word flung out once and for all, the sudden contrast between a resounding acclamation and subdued tenderness or mystery.

Taking, as he saw fit, the ingredients of the contemporary Mass, the chorus of fugal involutions, the alternating solo quartet, he used them quite in his own way for his own purposes. His choir, chanting its pious text in hushed simplicity, sometimes uttering words independent of the quartet above it, was anything but the traditional Gothic choir. It was almost a Sophoclean chorus, with its pervasive underground comment as of the people at large. The solo voices in turn intensify by their virtuosity. The orchestra more than accompanies, and is utterly unchurchlike. When the composer subordinates it to the voices, he is obeying nothing but his own clear purpose. The style is a mosaic of styles. Where a strong dramatic impact, where a line of recitative, serves the text, it is used. From another composer, this pastiche of the lay and churchly could have been a faltering and rather lame exhibition. The small fellows must stick to stylistic purity, for there lies their rudder, their unifier, their dependence upon the past. Beethoven could imperiously disregard the ritual proprieties. His inner conviction forged his own style, achieved his own unity. The *Missa* will outlast the objections of academic purists.

Of all Beethoven's double-dealings with publishers the crowning case is that of the *Missa Solemnis*. Never did an artist turn from his absorption in his most ambitious work to involve himself in such an accumulation of contradictory promises. "The letters," H. E. Krehbiel has written, as English editor of Thayer's *Life of Beethoven,* "have risen like ghosts to accuse him." If he was a sinner, he was at least a clumsy and ineffectual one. "Thank God," the composer once wrote in connection with the Mass, "I am a layman in all business transactions." A brief review of the correspondence over the Mass will incline the reader to agree with him.

On March 18, 1820, two days before the ceremony of installation of his friend as Archbishop of Olmütz, Beethoven wrote to the publisher Simrock offering the still uncompleted score for one hundred louis d'or with a promise of early delivery. More than a year passed and still the publisher had not received the score. On November 12, 1821, Beethoven wrote: "The Mass might have been sent before this, but it had to be carefully looked through." The composer had meanwhile raised his price by insisting upon a higher rate of exchange than that current in Germany. Putting Simrock off with further promises, he meanwhile wrote to the publisher Schlesinger in Berlin offering the Mass and demanding an early answer. Schlesinger accepted.

On July 26, 1822, Beethoven wrote to the firm of Peters at Leipzig, offering the Mass and observing: "In no event will Schlesinger ever get anything more from me; he has played me a scurvy trick, but aside from that, he is not among those who might have received the Mass." This did not prevent Beethoven from negotiating later with Schlesinger. On August 23rd, the publisher Artaria received an offer of the Mass at the same figure. "All that I can do is to give you the preference. Rest assured that I do not take a heller more from you than has been offered me by others. I could prove this to you in writing."

Simrock, still importunate, received from Beethoven on September 13, 1822, an astonishing letter. "The minimum that at least four publishers have offered me for the Mass is one thousand florins." Simrock in his generosity would surely not allow him to lose money on the work. Although Beethoven is under agreement with Simrock for a lesser amount and has accepted an advance, he is ready to do Simrock the favor of giving him the preference over the others, although for this larger figure. "I will at once send you," he adds, "a well-corrected score of the Mass which will suffice you for the engraving."

Needless to say, the score was not forthcoming. Two, not four, publishers had expressed themselves as willing to pay a thousand florins. Beethoven was no longer holding out for a price. He did not attempt to raise this figure. He tried to extract the thousand from Simrock, his all too patient friend in Bonn, and even set his brother upon his trail to obtain that amount from him. Meanwhile, he continued to involve himself in his own web of untenable promises. In November we find him writing to Peters that he would surely receive *a* Mass, for he had written two and

209

was trying to decide which one to send. Simrock was likewise informed that he would have a Mass by Easter. "You will surely receive one of these two grand Masses which are already composed." The second "already composed" mass consisted of a few notations in the sketchbook for a mass in C sharp minor. Beethoven hoped for an appointment as Imperial Court Composer to Austria, and was urged by Count Dietrichstein to compose a Mass for the Emperor, to facilitate the appointment. The Emperor's preferences, as described by Dietrichstein, were for short fugues and easy performability, which ruled out the Mass in D. Nothing came of the project or the second mass.

And now another scheme enters into the peddling of the Mass. In January and February, 1823, Beethoven signed and sent letters to every likely monarch of Europe, offering to deliver a manuscript copy of a "Grand Solemn Mass." The honorarium is fixed at fifty ducats in gold, to defray the "considerable expense" of copying. "The work in question, moreover, will not be published for the present." There were ten acceptances: the Courts of Russia, France, Denmark, Prussia, Saxony, the Duchies of Tuscany and Hesse-Darmstadt, the Princes Galitzin and Radziwill of Russia subscribed, and the humbler Cäcilia Society at Frankfort. One result was the first performance, which happened in Russia, and which Prince Galitzin brought to pass. Acceptances not at once forthcoming were encouraged by letters which Beethoven sent to powers near the throne: Goethe at Weimar, Cherubini in Paris, the Archduke Rudolph and von Könneritz in the Saxon cause. The hand-copied scores were slow in preparation, and brought protests from waiting ministers. There was now a new cause for delay in publication. A king would hardly be pleased to be told that the new Mass, for which he had paid fifty ducats and for which he was still waiting, had appeared in circulation in the shops.

Meanwhile, the hopes of the collected publisher-suitors were carefully kept alive. Pressed by Simrock, in March, 1823, to repay the advance he had received, Beethoven wrote: "Besides yourself, there are two other men who each desire a Mass. I am resolved to write at least three—the first is entirely finished, the second not yet, the third not even begun; but in view of them

I must have an understanding so that I may be secure in any case. You may have the Mass whenever you pay one thousand convention coin."

But Beethoven was not through increasing his list. He wrote Ries urging him to find an English purchaser. Diabelli in Vienna was approached, and became interested at once. He agreed upon the fee and received the score. When he insisted upon publishing it at once, Beethoven remembered his royal subscribers, and demanded that the score be returned. Diabelli threatened to sue, but did not. Beethoven waited until the greater part of a year had passed, and then wrote to two publishers on the same day (March 10, 1824) offering each a "new Grand Mass" at a thousand florins, and a "new Grand Symphony" at six hundred. They were Schott and Sons of Mayence, and H. A. Probst of Leipzig. Schott accepted at once and actually received the Mass, the Ninth Symphony, the Quartet in E flat, and some smaller pieces. He published the Mass in 1825.

One is taken aback by this record of procrastination, business coquetry and footless commitments. It is plain enough that Beethoven never understood the world of barter, nor learned the "ethics" which the necessity of equable give and take has created. He was a thorough blunderer, the very opposite of an artful schemer or an expert in the extraction of money. One can understand his readiness to slip out of his promise to Simrock when a higher fee was offered, but there was no sense in indefinitely increasing the list of expectants, unless he enjoyed the sweet taste of growing fame which brought one publisher after another to his feet, ready to take a long chance on an unseen mass. "They are scrambling for my works," he wrote to his brother in the summer of 1822. He was offering for sale a score which he was always expecting to be ready presently, and which he could not relinquish while a single phrase could be improved. Plays for time became a habit, and so did his acceptance of each prospective purchaser who came along. Never saying no, seldom candid, he fell into the way of false promises. Beethoven would have been astonished to behold his repeated transgressions marshaled into one cumulative indictment. He who errs habitually will be startled when the book of judgment lists line by line the sins of his years and adds them up to a damning total.

The piled-up duplicities cannot be explained away. There is his readiness to leave Simrock, his friend of Bonn days, suspended in mid-air for two years and more, only to desert him at last. There is his assurance to Zelter that if the *Singakademie* in Berlin wished *a cappella* music, the score could be altered accordingly. J. W. N. Sullivan, in *Beethoven: His Spiritual Development,* commends the honest recital of the whole case in Thayer's biography, but deplores the interjections of "pious horro." which surround it. "Beethoven's morality," writes Mr. Sullivan, "was of the noblest, though it was not identical with business morality." The morality of Beethoven, he points out, was that of the high-seeking and uncompromising artist who created the *Missa Solemnis* and not of the muddled man who sold it. This is momentarily reassuring, but it somehow remains inconclusive. Valiant arguments in defense of Beethoven are little better than sorrowful shakings of the head, if his strange ways are to be clearly accounted for. An objective search for causes is not served by an attempt to measure with the yardstick of social proprieties the genius who was before all others a law unto himself.

It would be more to the point merely to observe his actions as illustrating his character, his strange, twisted notions and odd ways. The traits, deep-rooted, go back to his childhood. One remembers the supersensitive boy who, unable to cope with the world, met it with supercilious defiance, or a sudden anger which sometimes could not distinguish between friend and foe. Now, deaf, aging solitude had enclosed him in a life of the imagination where hallucination became reality, and suspiciousness, long harbored, was magnified past all reasonableness. His ingrained obsequious manner, born of dependency, had grown into cynicism. Contempt lurked in his slighter friendships. Distrust had become a mania, and few escaped. The man who negotiated his Mass was a lonely dreamer who had grown to expect the worst from most men. He felt helpless in all things but music, and unable to cope with ordinary contingencies. "If I were only in London," he wrote to Ries in 1822, "what would I not compose for the Philharmonic Society! For Beethoven, thank God, can compose; of all else, he is incapable." His God-given function to compose was his service to the world, his one ability, his one loyalty. Let those who were money-blessed assure him a living, so that he might compose freely in the vein of his highest aspirations. That state of affairs never came to pass, though his patrons honestly tried to bring it about. What Beethoven failed to understand was that society was not so constituted as to give him an unassailable niche and entire artistic freedom. His patrons and his publishers were, no less than he, subject to misfortune, and this truth he never learned to accept. When his bank balance was discovered to have reached the vanishing point, the fault was theirs. It became his obsession that those around him were deserters of his cause. The publishers were "hell hounds who lick and gnaw at my brains," a species far down on his scale, a traditional foe who dragged his ideal creations through the market place. Steiner placed himself in the lowest rank of the damned by charging interest on a loan in "a most abominable manner." The Viennese public were fickle, flocking to the latest operatic effervescence from Italy. All men were found wanting.

There were times when those upon whom he depended, even those whom he loved, were looked upon with a distorting eye. His blind and unjust treatment required, so they learned to know, leniency and a long view. The long view is still called for as we read certain parts of the letters with their disingenuousness and abuse of friendly trust.

CHAPTER TWENTY-ONE

BEETHOVEN WAS now more seclusive than ever. He seldom showed himself in the streets of Vienna, and passers-by would turn their heads in surprise when a man hurried by in a long, shabby, green coat, pockets bulging with ear trumpet and notebook, the tousled silvery-gray hair waving in the wind. For the most part he lurked in his quarters, absorbed in deep matters, shy of visitors. In fine weather he fled to Hetzendorf or Baden, where it was even harder to hunt him out. Sir Julius Benedict, a young English pupil of Weber, visited Vienna in the autumn of 1823, and, asking to meet the famous Beethoven, was taken to Haslinger's music shop, where his attention was drawn to "a stout, short man with a very red face, small, piercing eyes, and bushy eyebrows, dressed in a very long overcoat which reached nearly to his ankles. . . . Notwithstanding the high color of his cheeks and his general untidiness, there was in those small, piercing eyes an expression which no painter could render." Sir Julius later saw him at Baden, and remembered him on account of "his white hair flowing over his mighty shoulders, with that wonderful look—sometimes contracting his brows when anything afflicted him, sometimes bursting out into a forced laughter, indescribably painful to his listeners. I was touched as if King Lear, or one of the old Gaelic bards stood before me."

Friedrich Rochlitz, respected editor of the *Zeitung* at Leipzig, stayed in Vienna through the previous summer, and waited for days until the moment should come when the composer might be approached with success. At length he met Franz Schubert, an obscure musician, then twenty-five, who worshipped Beethoven from afar. Schubert had sent the master some songs for approval, too shy even to ask for an interview, and although he

214

had had no direct answer, he was enraptured to hear later that Beethoven had been delighted with them. Schubert knew how Beethoven could be observed and told Rochlitz of the composer's usual tavern and hour of eating. Rochlitz sat at a table near by as Beethoven talked, loudly, volubly and without restraint. Later, the Leipziger was successful enough to accompany Beethoven on one of his long walks, and talk freely with him on many subjects. "He was really amiable, or if the word seems surprising I will say: the gloomy, unlicked bear is so winning and confiding, growls and shakes his hairy coat so harmlessly and curiously, that it is delightful, and one could not help liking him, even if he had had no more than a bear's abilities."

In a tavern, his grating voice could sometimes be heard by all present. The bassoonist Mittag has related that he once saw Beethoven alone at a corner table in such a place, lost in his thoughts. Suddenly he jumped to his feet and called to the waiter: "My bill!" "Already paid!" shouted the waiter in his ear. At another time, according to Zelter, who on a visit to Vienna observed him curiously, he insisted upon paying, although he had eaten nothing.

He could still hear certain musical tones when spoken words were entirely lost to him. Schindler has told how a "musical clock" was shown to him and made to play a portion of the Overture to *Fidelio*. Beethoven was pleased, and remarked: "Better than the performance at the *Kärntnerthor*." Perhaps the bell-like vibrations were more perceptible to him. But what trickled faintly through the hardened labyrinth of his left ear was of no use for practical purposes. When his overture, *The Consecration of the House*, written for the *Josephstadt Theater*, was performed at its opening on October 3, 1822, Beethoven, presiding at the piano, would have wrecked the performance, had not the *Kapellmeister* stood behind him unseen. Just a month later, *Fidelio* was revived at the *Kärntnerthor*, and Beethoven decided to lead it, in spite of the anxious hints of his friends. The first rehearsal had not progressed beyond the opening scene when things fell into confusion. Beethoven tended to drag his beat, and when the orchestra fell behind the singers he did not know that anything was wrong. Umlauf had to stop the performers several times, and each time Beethoven looked at him in surprise. Schindler tells the story:

"The impossibility of going ahead with the author of the work was evident. But how, in what manner inform him of the fact? Neither Duport, the director, nor Umlauf was willing to speak the saddening words: 'It will not do; go away, you unhappy man!' Beethoven, already uneasy in his seat, turned now to the right and now to the left, scrutinizing the faces to learn the cause of the interruption. Everywhere, silence. I had approached near him in the orchestra. He handed me his notebook with an indication that I write what the trouble was. Hastily I wrote in effect: 'Please do not go on; more at home.' With a bound, he was in the parterre and said merely—'Out, quick!' Without stopping, he ran toward his lodgings, Pfarrgasse, Vorstadt Leimgrube. Inside he threw himself on the sofa, covered his face with his hands and remained in this attitude till we sat down to eat. During the meal not a word came from his lips; he was a picture of profound melancholy and depression. When I tried to go away after the meal he begged me not to leave him until it was time to go to the theatre. At parting he asked me to go with him next day to his physician, Dr. Smetana, who had gained some repute as an aurist."

Dr. Smetana, like the rest, could do nothing for him. Never again did he look for a "cure" for his hearing.

Beethoven fled his town lodgings in the spring of 1823 because he had developed a high feud with the landlord over smoking flues and storm windows. Perhaps the landlord was trying to get rid of him by smoking him out. Beethoven was never a desirable tenant. He had been refused the Hafner house at Mödling in 1820 because the noisy altercations with servants through the summer before had aroused the neighbors to protest. The town landlord insulted Beethoven by hanging a "to let" sign on the house while he was still in possession. Schindler was instructed to get the police after him, which he dutifully did. Beethoven took flight to Hetzendorf and rented an attractive villa. But this landlord was too polite. He bowed deeply at every encounter until his tenant could not stand his obsequious manner and moved again. It was a bad summer for landlords. This one had rented his house with the stipulation that the shutters, which Beethoven did not need, should remain upon the windows.

It afterward appeared that the landlord knew of Beethoven's habit of writing memoranda upon the nearest object and counted on selling them.

Occupied as he was with music small and great, Beethoven did not relax his operatic ambitions. Opera was more than ever the main current, the musical high road of Vienna. Beethoven gave long and searching thought in 1823 to a possible operatic subject, as the letters and conversation books show. He found nothing acceptable until Grillparzer proposed the legend of Melusina, and this he turned over in his mind. But when Grillparzer visited him to discuss the plan, Beethoven shook his head over the opening. A hunter's chorus was indicated. "Weber used four horns—therefore I must have eight. Where will this lead to?" This amounted to saying that the fair Melusina, the sprite who married a mortal, was enticing him into Weber's province of the supernatural, where he neither belonged nor could compete. He conferred with Barbaja, who had a fine Italian troupe at the *Kärnthnerthor,* and at length told Grillparzer that the music was ready. The notebooks show nothing. The composer of the Piano Sonata, Opus 110, found no beginning for Melusina.

When Weber came to Vienna in 1823 to conduct his new opera *Euryanthe,* Beethoven received him with open arms. He had studied *Der Freischütz* and, according to Weber's son and biographer, struck the open score with his hand, exclaiming: "I would never have thought it of the gentle little man! Now Weber must write operas, nothing but operas, one after another and without polishing them too much. Casper the monster stands out here like a house. Wherever the devil puts in his claws they are felt." Any latent envy toward the younger composer, so successful in the field where Beethoven longed vainly to succeed, was overborne by the flash of genius which glowed from the Wolf Glen scene in the printed score. It was not so easy to be generous-minded toward Rossini, the rival who had need only to dangle an assemblage of nimble tunes to draw great quantities of applause and money. Gibes at Rossini in the course of light gossip on current musical affairs cannot be taken as outright condemnation. He spoke to Seyfried of Rossini as a "scene painter," and said: "If fortune had not given him a pretty talent and pretty melodies by the bushel, what he learned at school would have brought him nothing but potatoes for his big belly!" And to Freudenberg in 1824: "Rossini is a talented and a melodious composer; his music suits the frivolous and sensuous spirit of the times, and his productivity is so great that he needs only as many weeks as the Germans need years to write an opera." Rossini visited Vienna in the spring of 1822 when his *Zelmira* was produced, called on Beethoven and was courteously received. Beethoven warmly commended his *Barber of Seville,* and advised him to keep to comedies.

In the following April, there was another interesting encounter. Czerny brought his wonder pupil, Franz Liszt, to Vienna for a recital. Schindler led the boy, then eleven years old, to Beethoven, and urged him to favor the affair with his presence. The story that Beethoven lifted Liszt up and kissed him in public was born later in the imaginations of the pianist's publicists. Beethoven did not attend; it would have been useless in any case, for he could not have heard a note.

Following Beethoven in and out of Vienna, to Baden, to Oberdöbling in the summer of 1822 and to Hetzendorf in the summer following, one finds the usual string of worries and annoyances, which must have impinged upon the large works with which he was now almost constantly occupied. His eyesight bothered him, and the stomach troubles from which he was never long free deprived him of peace for work. Karl was now securely in his hands, placed at school, but with him in vacation periods. Karl must be supported, and music which took from one to five years to compose, and then merely baffled most people, only stood in the way of bills and tuition fees. This will account for the stream of *"Brodarbeiten"* which came from his pen, "bread works" impeding his deeper and more intensive projects. He wrote to Romberg of the "metallic recognition" which high art seldom receives in these days, and to his brother Johann: "If my health would only return I might yet be in clover" (literally, "reach a green branch"). He adds: "Were it not that my income brings in nothing I should compose only grand symphonies, church music, or perhaps quartets." But first, small matters must be cleared out of his path—piano variations, bagatelles

218

(*"Kleinigkeiten"*), which may have been first thoughts jotted down in the sketchbooks and turned forth as they stood. "Smearing" was his word for it.

The publisher Diabelli had proposed to him for variations a waltz tune of his own. Beethoven disliked Diabelli's silly jingle, a "cobbler's patch," he called it, but it had a malleable quality; to play with it diverted him, and ideas flowed faster than his pen. Variations piled up, one upon another, until Diabelli began to be alarmed lest he be kept waiting forever, or be handed a whole volume of them to print. Thirty-two were forthcoming. The theme was transformed again and again, dross became gold, the simpering rosalia, the "cobbler's patch," emerged in great beauty. The last collection of Scottish songs and variations went to Edinburgh, and when Schindler reported a current rumor that Beethoven had written himself out and could produce nothing better than folk-song arrangements, like the aged Haydn, Beethoven only smiled. "Wait a while," he said, "you'll soon learn differently."

The rumor shows how little the public knew of Beethoven's deeper currents. There was room in his thoughts, while the *Missa Solemnis* was developing, for three more piano sonatas, the last he was to compose. The Sonata Opus 109 was completed in 1820, Opus 110 in 1821, Opus 111 in 1822. Their close, flowing voices, their contrapuntal character pointed toward the string quartet, many years neglected. These, like all the important music he then wrote, came to their fruition laboriously, slowly and with much revision. Beethoven said to Rochlitz in 1822: "It is long since I have been able to bring myself to write easily. I sit and think and think. The ideas are there, but they will not go down on paper. I dread the beginning of large works. Once begun, it's all right."

He aimed still to compose two symphonies for London and an oratorio for the *Musikfreunde*. Goethe's *Faust* excited his imagination as a remoter possibility. While he still held back the manuscript of the *Missa Solemnis* in 1823, making endless last touches, the Ninth Symphony at last became his sole concern. He wrote to Karl from Baden on August 16th, "Today I really began my service to the Muses." Which means that the labor of development *in extenso* was under way. Once more everyday worries were cast aside for timeless imaginings; a world of jarring disharmony was shaken off that another world, pure, sane, clear, far-visioned, might be realized.

Eleven years had passed since the Seventh and Eighth Symphonies, years of what drastic change in the artist Beethoven! The sketchbooks as early as 1812 show scattered thoughts for further symphonies, which, however, never reached the forefront of his attention. He considered Schiller's *Ode to Joy* for a musical setting as early as 1793, but not in connection with a symphony. The theme for the *Scherzo* was the first note-for-note intimation of the symphony to come. It was written as the subject for a fugue in the fugal year of 1815. Sketches for the first movement, in 1817, were put aside for the *"Hammer-Klavier"* Sonata. In the next year his imagination was stimulated; the spell of the *Missa Solemnis,* newly begun, induced thoughts of a religious, a modal symphony, even a choral symphony. A Greek text was an alternate idea. He realized that German verses would not be appropriate for London, and he thought of two symphonies, one to be instrumental. The bold, disparate thoughts became diffused as they were pushed into the background by the all-absorbing *Missa Solemnis.*

When at last he was released from lingering anxieties over details of the Mass, the Symphony progressed no doubt the more rapidly for its long delay. Receiving from Ries in November, 1822, in behalf of the London Philharmonic Society, an offer of fifty pounds for a "manuscript symphony," the composer answered on February 5th that it would "soon be in London," adding three weeks later that he would send it at once on receiving a draft. One hopes that London had by then learned to discount Beethoven's promises. Only the first movement was then worked out—the *Adagio* theme for the slow movement was not even found. The score, although Beethoven worked continuously upon it, was not to be completed for more than a year. In the summer of 1823, he had qualms about a choral *Finale,* and indicated a theme for an instrumental *Finale* which was to be used later as the *Finale* of the Quartet in A minor. Deciding upon the

220

choral variations, he was in doubt at the last moment about how to introduce the choral text, after three long instrumental movements, into the wordless realm where the symphony had always dwelt. The mood of Schiller's exhortation to freedom and brotherhood lay already upon the music. A plausible transition remained obscure. "When he reached the development of the fourth movement," wrote Schindler, "there began a struggle such as is seldom seen. The object was to find a proper manner of introducing Schiller's *Ode*. One day, entering the room, he exclaimed, 'I have it! I have it!' With that he showed me the sketchbook bearing the words, 'Let us sing the song of the immortal Schiller, *Freude*.'" These words, so the sketchbooks show, were arrived at only after many trials, and were changed in their turn.

When Beethoven reached a solution to a problem of his art through inward travail, that solution, passing through stages of tentative groping, always became at last as striking and indisputable as if no other possibility could ever have existed. That point once reached, nothing was altered. "I change many things," said Beethoven to Louis Schlösser, a composer from Darmstadt, in the spring of 1823, when he was hard at work on his Symphony, "I discard and try again, until I am satisfied. Then, however, there begins in my head the development in every direction and, inasmuch as I know exactly what I want, the fundamental idea never deserts me; it arises before me, grows. I see and hear, and the picture in all its extent and dimensions stands before my mind in a single projection, and there remains for me nothing but the labor of writing it down." When once Beethoven had seen the picture of the *Finale* clearly before him, with its choral apotheosis, he put it down with direct and intensive utterance to the end.

It is specious to argue, as many have, that the introduction of the text is inverse or forced logic. There is no logic in tones except the plausibility which the composer's conviction creates. Beethoven never reached a conclusion with a surer sense of inevitability. The instrumental *Finale* which he earlier contemplated would have been more pleasing to the purists. A *Finale* on

221

the theme later to be used in the A minor Quartet would have sustained the elevation and other-worldliness of the Symphony. Its quality of swiftness and ethereal lightness, as if in flight, would have followed the *Adagio* with fine effect. Developed and concluded with more grandeur than in the Quartet, it would have rounded out a symphony more balanced and homogeneous than any symphony with a choral *Finale* could have been. But when Beethoven, tardily as usual, saw his way clearly, he knew that an instrumental rondo was simply what had occurred to him by the habit of convention. His aim had advanced beyond considerations of classical balance. It had become exploratory, upstriving. His heart demanded the sounding word, and must recall to proclaim it the battalions of human voices lately used in the *Missa Solemnis*. Again, as in that work, the idea controls, combines elements traditionally alien, and sweeping all else aside, soars to its close.

Beethoven was reluctant when his friends urged him to arrange a concert and introduce in Vienna both the *Missa Solemnis* and the new Symphony. Unfortunately, his reluctance seems to have had nothing to do with promises to London; his first thought for a preference was Berlin. He berated the Vienna public, and not unjustly, for his symphonies had not fared well in Vienna. His fame in the musical world had greatly increased, not by what he had written in the last decade, for he had written little that had been heard, but by what he had written years before. There was the Seventh Symphony in particular, the affecting sonatas and trios, and the opera *Fidelio,* now a steady repertory piece. Weber had recently revived it lovingly, and with success, at Prague. The connoisseurs in Berlin spoke of him; Parisians crowded to hear his symphonies under Habeneck; the eagerness of London for something new from him was plain enough.

In Vienna, the enchantment of distance was lacking. Many argued that since he was apparently crazy, his music must be crazy as well. With all this, there was something extraordinary in his aspect, something impressive. Reverberations of his fame came from foreign countries. The mere announcement of an

Akademie for the performance of a new symphony which his lone wrestlings had brought forth, would arouse curious interest as to what his latest wonder might be. A choral fantasia, yes, but a symphony with a chorus? Symphonies did not have choruses.

He wrote to Count Brühl in Berlin suggesting the combined first performances there of his new Mass and Symphony, and the Count replied favorably. This brought, in February, 1824, a long letter signed by thirty Viennese friends who designated themselves as "disciples and lovers of art," spokesmen from "the wide circle of reverent admirers surrounding your genius in this your second native city." They voiced a florid plea that the "grand, sacred composition" and the "new flower that glows in the garland of your glorious, still unequalled symphonies" be not allowed to be first made known elsewhere than in "the city of their birth." They regretted his "retirement from public life," and expressed their sorrow that *"the one* man whom all of us are compelled to acknowledge as foremost among living men in his domain, looked on in silence as foreign art took possession of German soil. . . . Appear soon among your friends, your admirers, those who venerate you!" The document gives the impression that his friends felt the need of giving encouragement to the now completely solitary Beethoven by bringing to performance the two scores the writing of which had kept him hidden from the world for the last six years. Count Moritz Lichnowsky was the promoter of the plea, and the signatures he obtained included the Counts Palfy and Fries, the Abbé Stadler, and Sonnleithner, all of whom had shown their devotion in the past. There were four publishers: Artaria, Diabelli, Steiner and Leidesdorf. At first Beethoven was angry, for the appearance of the petition in the *Theater Zeitung* gave rise to the rumor that he had prompted it in his own interest. Later Schindler, holding the letter in his hand, found him in his lodgings. He gazed out of the window a long while, as if moved, and then said: "It is very beautiful! It gives me great happiness!" Schindler agreed with his opinion, and he said: "Let us go for a walk." As they walked he did not speak.

The outcome was a decision to give the concert in Vienna

before the season had ended. But now there began a long succession of indecisions and delays over the arrangements. Which theatre, which conductor and singers, what prices? The conversation books show his friends gathered about, discussing points, urging him as tactfully as possible to make up his mind, as the time was growing short. But this he was unable to do. The habit of vacillation, or rather suspicious withdrawal from any commitment, had become fixed. The friends cornered him one after another or in groups, writing their advice, each doing his best to save the master from the ills of delay. There was good, faithful Schuppanzigh, "Milord Falstaff," whose girth continued always a subject for hilarity, and whom he continued to address in the third person. The Abbé Stadler enjoyed a surprising favor, considering that he was an old-schooler who found any music since Mozart, Beethoven's included, insupportable. The two could at least patch their quarrels by bringing up the subject of Mozart. Schindler's garrulity and stuffy ways sometimes goaded Beethoven to drive him violently from his presence. He would at such times brand him as a scoundrel to any who would listen. Schindler bowed his head and remained doggedly faithful, putting up with indefinite abuse for the privilege of remaining the great man's factotum number one. He clung always to his parasitic immortality and years later inscribed upon his visiting cards *"l'ami de Beethoven."*

The nephew, precocious and forward for his seventeen years, was always at hand with his own suggestions, and the adoring uncle was all too ready to listen to him. Karl never hesitated to nullify what progress the others had made toward an understanding, or to fan the flame of Beethoven's growing distrust of Schindler.

The encirclement of small spite and innuendo contained so much contradiction that it seemed as though Beethoven would never so much as fix a date for his concert. At last Lichnowsky, Schuppanzigh and Schindler, despairing of getting anywhere, made a little conspiracy to draw up an agreement and induce him to sign it as if it were a joke. The device was innocent, but it was also clumsy. They should have known their Beethoven better. When they had left the house Beethoven realized what they had been doing and sent the following notes:

"To Count Moritz Lichnowsky. I despise treachery. Do not visit me again. No concert."

"To Herrn Schuppanzigh. Let him visit me no more. I shall give no concert."

"To Schindler. I request you not to come again until I send for you. No concert."

The trio waited until the atmosphere had cleared and continued their preparations. The *Kärnthnerthor Theater* was at the last moment decided upon and May 7, 1824, as the date. Almost on the eve of the concert the censor forbade the inclusion of church ritual music in a theatre. The three numbers from the Mass which were performed (Beethoven, to avoid excessive length, omitted the *Gloria* and *Sanctus*) were listed as "hymns," and even then Moritz Lichnowsky had to use his influence to acquire permission. There were separate rehearsals for the singers and for the orchestra, but only two full rehearsals, a projected third being canceled to make way for a ballet rehearsal. The solo singers protested about their parts—to little avail—and the chorus, amateur singers, made representations to the composer about the high, sustained notes. Beethoven was immovable. The singers must soar to their altitude and hold it ringingly. The tonality, the circumstance, the climax exacted it. From the artistic requirement there was no appeal.

It is related that after the last rehearsal Beethoven, who had been much affected by the *Kyrie*, embraced the singers as they left the theatre. Only his eye had followed them—a doubtful guide. It can be imagined what would have emerged of the Mass and Symphony after two rehearsals by an inexpert chorus, an orchestra little better. The difficult *Credo* could hardly have given an impression better than shrillness, striving. As for the Symphony, what could the honest but unenlightened Umlauf have made of the dramatic impacts of the first movement, the lightning delicacy of the *Scherzo*, the tenuous, expressive lines of the slow movement? That was a day, be it remembered, when

225

a leader was literally no more than a time beater, for individual interpretation and the ways by which it is achieved—expressive nuance, adjusted contrast, fluency, the niceties of precision—these matters had not been invented, so far as orchestral playing was concerned. Surely it was better that Beethoven could not hear.

The house was crowded, except the Imperial box, which was empty. Beethoven's friends of course were at every hand, in orchestra and audience. Even Zmeskall, unable to walk, was carried to his seat in a sedan chair. Beethoven took his place beside Umlauf to give initial indications of tempo. The applause was loud and marked, and there was the air of something momentous taking place. When the *Scherzo* was reached the clear, rapid rhythm at once made itself understood; here at least was comprehensible music. An outburst of applause in the middle of its course almost compelled a repetition. The incident was taken by Schindler in conversation with Beethoven afterward as a praiseworthy exhibition of public discernment.

The accounts that have come down to us are friendly and prejudiced. Surely the affecting spectacle of the deaf composer in the midst of the orchestra had much to do with the applause. Mme. Ungher, the contralto, visited London many years later and made known to Grove an anecdote which that enthusiast promptly put upon paper:

"At the close of the performance an incident occurred which must have brought the tears to many an eye in the room. The master, though placed in the midst of this confluence of music, heard nothing of it at all and was not even sensible of the applause of the audience at the end of his great work, but continued standing with his back to the audience, and beating the time, till Fräulein Ungher, who had sung the contralto part, turned him, or induced him to turn round and face the people, who were still clapping their hands, and giving way to the greatest demonstrations of pleasure. His turning round, and the sudden conviction thereby forced on everybody that he had not done so before because he could not hear what was going on, acted like an electric shock on all present, and a volcanic explosion of sympathy and admiration followed, which was repeated again and again, and seemed as if it would never end."

226

The sense of triumph was short-lived. The accounting showed a profit of only 420 florins for Beethoven. At the tavern *"Zum Wilden Mann"* his wrath descended upon Schindler and Umlauf. He accused them in a loud voice of having cheated him. A second performance was arranged for May 23rd, a Sunday afternoon. Such initial expenses as the copying of parts need not this time reduce the net result. Solo airs were thrown in to entice the public and the truncated *Missa* was now reduced to the *Kyrie* only. The weather was fine, the spring at its full, and Vienna preferred to promenade in the Prater. The house was scarcely half filled, and the receipts showed a deficit twice as large as the former profit. This was the world's first acceptance of the intense labor of five years, of the two mightiest works of the mightiest composer of his century.

CHAPTER TWENTY-TWO

A LETTER from Neate, received by Beethoven in the new year of 1825, told him that the new Ninth Symphony, the "Characteristic Symphony" as it was sometimes called, had arrived and was about to go into rehearsal. Would he come and conduct it, and bring a new one with him? The acclamation of the English public, the Philharmonic Society in particular, and a fortune still awaited him. Since Beethoven had promised them exclusive possession of the Ninth Symphony for eighteen months, and had presented the Symphony in Vienna before they had received their copy, this was a heartening example of English good will. Beethoven resumed his discussions of an English visit, and continued to entertain the idea through the remainder of his life. He fell into the way of praising England and the English. Their government was a paragon, their taste was to be held up to the deplorable taste of Vienna. He spoke with such positiveness of a Tenth Symphony, a symphony for London, that Schindler and Holz came to believe, in the next year, that it was complete in his mind, and had only to be written down. The sketchbooks show no developed or identifiable sketches whatever. The Tenth Symphony remained in the category of a new opera or a new oratorio —plans which he never relinquished or ceased to discuss, but which never reached the point of a definite beginning or even an accepted subject.

Beethoven was not ready for another work of magnitude. Had he lived five or ten years longer than he did, he might have realized one or more of the far-flung schemes which now so strongly beckoned to him. Not an opera, surely, but perhaps a biblical oratorio based upon the Handelian manner which just now was taking a powerful hold upon his imagination.

228

These plans stood in abeyance in 1825 and 1826 because the composer's predilections were intimate, inwardly questioning, entirely quartet-wise. He was completely attuned to the succinctness and economy of four fluent voices which preferred to suggest large schemes rather than to proclaim them with tonal power. When the Ninth Symphony, in 1824, lay completed and at last ready for the copyist, quartets became Beethoven's whole tonal life; they were to remain so to the end. Galitzin, in St. Petersburg, did not have to press his commission for three. The first, in E flat, was ready in 1824, the second (in order of composition) in A minor and the third, in B flat, before the next year had ended. Recovering from an illness in May of 1825, he wrote into the A minor Quartet an *Andante* which, with its antique raised fourth, showed that his interest in the old church modes was still alive, and inseparable from religious thoughts. He wrote in a conversation book a title for this movement which was later changed: "Hymn of Thanksgiving to God by an Invalid on His Convalescence. Feeling of New Strength and Reawakened Feeling."

When the E flat Quartet was finished, Schuppanzigh's reassembled group at once met to try it out. The players struggled valiantly with their cryptic parts which they were entirely ready to take on faith, but which of course they found it extremely difficult to perform at all. Beethoven sat ferociously by, hearing nothing, following with hawklike intentness the fingers of the players and the movements of each bow. When afterward there was a general expression of disappointment by those who had heard it, Beethoven unreasonably blamed Schuppanzigh, and gave the parts to Böhm for two more morning performances at a coffee house in the Prater.

Sir George Smart, visiting Vienna in September, 1825, was fortunate enough to be present at the first performance of the A minor Quartet on September 9th. It was played before a group of friends at the rooms of Schlesinger in the inn *"Zum Wilden Mann."* Schlesinger had come from his father's publishing firm in Paris, and was on the alert for a good buy. About fourteen were there, including Beethoven's nephew, Czerny, the 'cellist Marx, the partner of Steiner, the Viennese publisher, and Böhm, leader of the rival quartet. Schuppanzigh was evidently restored to favor, for he, Holz, Weiss, and Linke were the performers. The new piece, Sir George remarked, was three-quarters of an hour long, and was played twice. He found it "most chromatic," which is interesting as an expert contemporary characterization. "Beethoven directed the performers, and took off his coat, the room being warm and crowded. A staccato passage not being expressed to the satisfaction of his eye, for, alas, he could not hear, he seized Holz's violin and played the passage a quarter of a tone too flat. I looked over the score during the performance. All paid him the greatest attention." The Quartet was played again, in the same rooms, two days later, before a larger company. Ten stayed for a dinner with wine. "No one could be more agreeable than he was—plenty of jokes. We all wrote to him by turns, but he can hear a little if you haloo quite close to his left ear." Beethoven, in a good mood, extemporized "for about twenty minutes in an extraordinary manner, sometimes very *fortissimo,* but full of genius. When he arose at the conclusion of the playing, he appeared greatly agitated."

In the autumn of 1825, Beethoven took lodgings on the second floor of the *Schwarzspanier Haus* overlooking the Glacis—destined to be the last of his many dwelling places in Vienna. "Steffen" von Breuning with his wife and child lived almost directly opposite in the *Rothes Haus,* which he rented from Prince Esterházy. The estrangement was patched up, and Stephan was much with Beethoven from that time. Beethoven often crossed the street to dine at the *Rothes Haus,* and formed a gallant friendship with Frau von Breuning, whom he would sometimes accompany on an errand, embarrassing her with his noisy, conspicuous ways. She graced his household with a helpful feminine eye and touch, but her daintiness in the partaking of food prevented her from accepting "coffee" in his rooms. Beethoven developed a great liking for the Breunings' small boy, Gerhard, whom he nicknamed *"Hosenknopf"* ("Trouser Button"), and, on account of his diminutive light-footedness, "Ariel." He liked to have the child about, watching his development and instructing him in the perception of beauty. Gerhard was as impressed as a child can be, and in his manhood wrote down his memories more clearly and accurately than some of the adult associates of Beethoven.

It is time to resume the history of Beethoven's misfortunes as guardian, a narrative now so entirely unrelated to his artistic life that the account must be kept separate. The settlement of the legal disputes and the establishment of Beethoven's entire rights brought no lasting peace to his perturbed spirit. The mother, excluded but never far away, remained to Beethoven an imagined source of danger. Peters, as joint guardian, was of little help. He could give advice, but Beethoven was already surrounded by conflicting advice, which only increased his indecision.

Karl and his uncle, alone together, were a tragic pair. There never could have been any real understanding between them. Beethoven, building proudly upon Karl's quick mentality, dreamed of a great career for the boy who bore his name. Thinking first of his musical training, he had written to Steiner months before the father's death, ordering the piano music which would make the best foundation. Czerny he had secured as his teacher, going over with him in great detail the course which should be taken. Karl had shown a certain keyboard glibness—apparently nothing more. He had a marked literary aptitude, and, sending him to the University of Vienna, Beethoven had fondly pinned his hopes on a distinguished academic career for him. Karl was particularly quick at languages. Beethoven thought of him as a classical scholar, a master of the art of letters such as he would have liked to be, if his rudimentary schooling had not prevented. With Karl, the situation was reversed. He had good educational opportunities but no training in concentration—nothing of that single road to mastery, the strongly motivated, patient following through. His alertness at grasping a subject, which made its impression upon bystanders, or saw him through an examination, led only to a cynical indolence, a disinclination to go on with it.

Karl announced in 1825 that he had had enough of the University. He would like to enter the army. When his uncle was entirely taken aback, he mentioned the business world. If a bookkeeper earned more than a professor of Greek, why struggle with a subject which was fifty times as hard? Not one of Beethoven's expectations for Karl was fulfilled, and not one of Karl's personal inclinations was comprehensible to him. To begin with, the normal being who wants nothing more than a comfortable berth in the world with as little work as possible was quite beyond the range of Beethoven's temperament.

Beethoven had no choice but to enter him, in the spring of 1825, in the Polytechnic Institute, where, at first, the reports of his studies were favorable. Living quarters were found for him in the house of Schlemmer, a government official, who had to listen to elaborate instructions about the importance of being watchful. When, in the summer, Beethoven moved to Baden, he had Karl there on Sundays and holidays. He put him hard at work as amanuensis, or at running errands, as if to keep him out of mischief. The trouble was that the young man approaching twenty was not to be kept out of mischief by the protestations of an uncle absurdly suspicious and pathetically easy to deceive, nor by Herr Schlemmer, who, leading his own busy life, could not be a constant nursemaid.

When Karl escaped from the exasperating supervision which denied him independence, freedom, a mind and will of his own, the privileges which nineteen craves more than all else, he sought pleasures in defiance of the sermons he had to listen to. His uncle's unjust reproaches and tirades on morality drove him further into the forbidden paths. Beethoven tried to restrain him by exacting written permission from Schlemmer when he went out at night. He skimped on pocket money and demanded an accounting for every penny. These were only irritations, which made Karl the more wily in covering his tracks. The lack of money drove him to cheaper and lower haunts. He applied his skill and wits to billiards, tried to acquire spending money by gambling. Beethoven put upon Schindler the unseemly assignment of spying upon him and even sent Johann upon investigations. When Beethoven learned that the boy had been seen in one of the lowest of dance halls, where women of the street were to be found, he was thrown into a panic and wished to go there at once. His advisers persuaded him that the discovery of Beethoven in such a place would cause a public sensation. So Beethoven sent Holz, who was himself only twenty-seven and adept in the sociabilities, to cultivate Karl's companionship. Holz reported that he drank with an air, but not sottishly. As for the art of harlotry, it was said that there was not one of that species in Vienna whom he did not know.

Now there were scenes between the two, heavy reproaches, insolently returned. Beethoven forbade him to see his mother, who, he was sure, had led him into all his evil ways. Karl had taken up with a companion called Niemetz. The mother liked this friend, which of course in itself proved his wickedness. Karl once brought Niemetz to Baden. and was subjected to unbearable humiliation as Beethoven burst out in a denunciation of both his friend and himself, in a public place. In a letter to Niemetz, Karl referred to his uncle as "the old fool." The tragic side of this piece of ingratitude is that it was largely true. Less forgivable is Karl's craftiness in pretending his love for his uncle, or, worse still, his readiness to plunge him into a storm of uncertainty and fear by absenting himself for days at a time, knowing that his reappearance would bring a rush of relief and love, and with it complete surrender.

A sheaf of letters from Beethoven to his nephew, preserved by Beethoven for later purposes of court testimony, have so survived. They are a heartbreaking record of mingled emotions—anger, suspicion, depression, blind love and cruel severity. If they had been contrived to fill a young man with insecurity and confusion, they could not have done so more effectively. The nephew is held accountable for his time; he is required to show a written receipt for expenditures as if the worst were always to be expected of him. When Beethoven suspects him of having seen his mother, he threatens to disown him, and abandon him to public scorn for having so treated his famous uncle. "If the agreement is broken, be it so. You will make yourself hated by all impartial persons who hear of this ingratitude." When he suspects the boy of having borrowed money from the servants he cries out, "My heart has suffered too much from your sly behavior," and prays to be rid of the "deceiving, abominable family which has been foisted upon me. May God hear my prayer, for I can never trust you any more. Unfortunately—your Father—or, rather, not your Father."

He writes in June, 1825, from Baden, after some unspecified "intrigue" of Karl, that he is faint from sickness. "Oh, do not grieve me further. The Man with the Scythe will not, as it is, fail to come soon."

But when in October Karl disappeared for several days he hurried to Vienna and Schlemmer's house. Karl was not there, and he left this letter:

"My precious son: Go no further— Only come to my arms, not a harsh word shall you hear. O God, do not rush to destruction. . . . You shall be received as lovingly as ever. What to consider, what to do in the future—this we will talk over affectionately. On my word of honor, no scolding, since it would in no case do good now. Henceforth you may expect from me only the most loving care and help. Do but come. Come to the faithful heart of your father." And he scrawls on the margin: "Only for God's sake come back home today. You might fall into who knows what danger. Hurry, hurry!"

He ends a letter of June: "Be my dear, only son, imitate my virtues, but not my faults." Who, least of all Karl, could have emulated the virtues of Beethoven? Small men are crushed in spirit by the proximity of great ones whose name and blood they bear. "I should not like to have spent so much," wrote Beethoven, "merely to have provided the world with an *ordinary man*." That reproach was the most humiliating of all. The mental vigor and expansiveness of the great Beethoven was oppressive to the petty one. The world, which meant the admirers of Beethoven who were always about, made Karl feel, even in their silence, that he was an ungrateful ne'er-do-well who repaid a great man's love by causing him anguish of spirit and dragging him down in health and creative energies. The uncle dominated the life of the boy, watched his every move, and bound him to submission because he was a minor, financially dependent, held by public opinion and by court decree. The love which Beethoven lavished upon him was a crushing weight which stirred in his heart nothing but bitter impatience. His growing sense of rebellion was as inevitable as the rebellion of a young animal which is confined and balked in its natural instincts.

234

So, in his twentieth year, he became adept in cajolery, and when confronted with inescapable discipline, plainly begrudged the filial respect which the period exacted. Karl writes in the conversation books: "You consider it insolence if, after you have upbraided me for hours undeservedly, this time at least, I cannot turn from my bitter feeling of pain to good humor. I am not so frivolous as you think. I can assure you that since the attack on me in the presence of this fellow I have been so depressed that people in the house have observed it. The receipt for the eighty florins which were paid in May I now positively know, after a search at home, I gave you; it must and no doubt will be found. If I continue to study while you are here it is not in a spirit of insolence, but because I believe that you will not be offended if I do not permit your presence to keep me from my work, which is now really piling up on me." The list of grievances continues. There were sudden outbursts as if he had caught the contagion of Beethoven's ungovernable temper. Once he grasped his uncle by the collar. But for the most part he sulked, or retorted in self-justification or self-pity.

This touching letter of Beethoven may have been the result of the violent scene just referred to:

"If for no other reason than that you at least obeyed me, all is forgiven and forgotten; more today by word of mouth, very quietly— Do not take a step which might make you unhappy and which would shorten my life. I did not get to sleep until three o'clock for I coughed all night long. I embrace you cordially and am convinced that you will soon cease longer to misjudge me; it is thus that I also judge your conduct of yesterday. I expect you surely today at one o'clock. Do not give me cause for further worry and apprehension. Meanwhile farewell!

"Your real and true Father. Do come— Do not permit my poor heart to bleed any longer."

The heart that overwhelms and destroys where it loves, bleeds at its own havoc; it brings threat of tragedy, and is helpless. The hard, furtive glance of Karl had become the glint which in a cornered animal means despair. Perhaps he could no longer keep covered an accumulation of transgressions with which the high-principled uncle could not be faced. There may have been a close and habitual understanding with his mother, or heavy gambling debts caused by insufficient pocket money, or an involvement of sex. What Karl's darker sins may have been will never be known; they were to be buried with him. It is sufficient that any of those mentioned would have affected Beethoven as a rending cataclysm, possibly resulting in repudiation and public scandal.

Near the end of July, 1826, Karl intimated to his uncle that he would be capable of destroying himself. In a panic, Beethoven went to Holz and took him to Schlemmer's house. Schlemmer confirmed their fears. Karl had made the same threat to him. Schlemmer had questioned him on his past, mentioning debts, but Karl would tell nothing except that something he had done was one of his reasons. These terrible words stand in a conversation book in Schlemmer's handwriting: "I found a loaded pistol in a chest, together with bullets and powder. I tell you this so that you may act in the case as his father. The pistol is in my keeping. Be lenient with him or he will despair."

Holz alone went in search of Karl, probably because Beethoven's presence would have pushed the "despair" which Schlemmer foresaw. Holz told the story to Dr. Reisser at the Polytechnic Institute and Reisser made light of it. "A pistol," he said. "The young comedy hero!" Holz knew Karl better than the professor did; the lad was probably not bluffing. Whether he would have the nerve to go through with it remained to be seen. Holz confronted Karl, and Karl coolly defied him. "What good will it do to hold me? If I can't get away from you today, I can at another time."

Schlemmer found and appropriated another pistol. Holz pointed out to Beethoven, who reproached him for letting Karl out of his sight, that he could not stand over him every second. If he was so persistent in his intention he would find his moment whatever steps were taken. If he were not allowed to have a pistol he would find another way. And Beethoven wrote fearfully in his conversation book: "He will drown himself!" They went to the house of Niemetz. Beethoven swallowed his pride and humbly asked of the young bounder, whom he had once roundly cursed, for any confidences he had had from Karl. Failing here, Bee-

236

thoven and Holz had planned to go to the police; perhaps he could be forcibly restrained. But while they were consulting Niemetz, Karl had quickly given them the slip. He was to be found nowhere. Beethoven spent Saturday night and Sunday morning in fruitless search and in an agony of doubt.

Karl, as it later developed, went to a pawnbroker and pledged his watch. He bought two pistols, powder and balls. He took a carriage to Baden, and spent the night in the empty house, writing letters. He wrote to Niemetz, and enclosed a note to his uncle. The next morning he followed the steps of one of Beethoven's favorite walks, through the Helenenthal to the ruins of Rauhenstein. Beethoven had lately been there. It was a spot idyllic enough to have given birth to that final beatification, the *Lento cantante* in D flat from the last quartet. All that Karl saw was that it was secluded enough for his purpose. He loaded the two pistols, held them to his temples, and pulled both triggers. Two shots rang out, shattering the peacefulness of a summer haunt sacred to a greater Beethoven.

A teamster drowsing behind his horse on this lazy Sunday morning of late summer (it was either July 30 or August 6th), saw the young man lying on the grass on the little hillock, his hair and face smeared with blood. The man was conscious, and gave his mother's address. The teamster carried him to his wagon and faithfully rumbled and jolted the whole distance to Vienna.

Beethoven, informed by the teamster, hurried wildly to the mother's house. The boy lay upon the bed, his hair still matted with blood. No doctor had yet been summoned. The mother believed the bullet had lodged in his skull. Beethoven's anxious inquiry brought only the old sullen hostility from Karl: "It is done. Now, only a surgeon who can hold his tongue. Smetana, if he is here. Do not bother me with reproaches and lamentations; what is done, is done." And Beethoven at once wrote a message to Smetana, who had doctored Karl as a lad:

"A great misfortune has happened to Karl accidentally by his own hand. I hope that he can yet be saved, especially by you if you come quickly. Karl has a bullet in his head, how, you shall learn—only quick, for God's sake quick!

"In order to save time it was necessary to take him to his mother's, where he is now."

Holz took the note, but meanwhile another surgeon had arrived and dressed the wound.

Karl had shown himself a novice at firearms. One pistol had missed him altogether, the other had grazed his temple, tearing the flesh but not penetrating the skull. Had he intended to kill himself? It is hard to say. There are degrees of intention. An intended suicide may unconsciously remove his coat before leaping, or choose a less turbulent place in the water beneath him, or dramatize his act, hoping to leave remorse behind him. Or, as he raises his pistol, the instinct which is the strongest in all things possessing life may stiffen his fingers with fear and spoil his aim.

When Beethoven had gone, Karl said: "If only he would leave off his reproaches. If only he would not come here again!" He did not want even to hear of his uncle, and threatened that if the name were mentioned he would tear off his bandage. Beethoven was not spared these remarks. When Karl was questioned later as to his reasons for shooting himself, he said that it was because he was "tired of life" and "weary of imprisonment." He said to the police magistrate who questioned him that he had shot himself because his uncle "tormented him too much," and added, "I grew worse because my uncle wanted me to be better."

The police took charge of the matter, for suicide was a penal offence. Beethoven found that Karl had stolen some of his books and sold them. He was in terror lest the police discover it and convict him of felony. Stephan von Breuning, whose councillorship was in the war department, urged that Karl be made a soldier. If he were put in a regiment, he would be free of Vienna and police supervision The vexed problem of guardianship, which had come up anew, would be solved. He would be under discipline, his actions ordered and accounted for. Nothing the boy could do, apparently, could alter Beethoven's reluctance to give him up, but this time he had no alternative. Karl readily agreed.

When it became necessary to find a place where Karl could go for a week or so, to recover from the evidences of his wound, meeting nobody, Beethoven at last saw fit to accept the many times repeated invitation of his brother Johann to visit his summer estate at Gneixendorf, an invitation which Beethoven, who could never get along with Johann, had persistently refused. The anecdote of Johann's card—"Johann van Beethoven, landowner" under which Beethoven wrote "Ludwig van Beethoven, brain owner"—perfectly describes their relation. Johann's pretentious absurdity always annoyed his brother. When he drove in the Prater in an open phaeton behind four horses and two footmen, Beethoven's friends joked over this laughable possessor of an illustrious name. Beethoven sometimes relied upon Johann's hard business sense, but would have avoided cultural topics. Karl writes in the conversation books in 1824 that he had seen his other uncle at a chamber concert. What was he doing there, Beethoven wanted to know, and Karl replied, "He wants to acquire taste; he is continually crying *bravo*." Holz tells that Johann listened to his brother's E flat Quartet a number of times, and hearing it once more mistook it for a new piece.

Beethoven's real aversion to Gneixendorf lay in the presence there of the sister-in-law whom he had once catapulted into the Beethoven family by trying to have her driven out of the town of Linz. He had wished to bring her before the police once more when, in 1823, during her husband's illness, she had openly paraded an affair with an army officer. Schindler had reported to Beethoven on the matter, probably with some exaggeration, for he delighted in discrediting Johann to his brother: "The woman, while her husband is lying ill, introduces her lover into his room, tricks herself like a sleigh horse in his presence, and then goes driving with him, leaving the sick husband languishing at home. She did this very often."

Beethoven could not bear the thought of being this woman's guest at Gneixendorf, and agreed to go only under Johann's assurance that she would be kept in the position of housekeeper, strictly in the background, and out of his way. Karl started for Gneixendorf with his two uncles on September 28th.

CHAPTER TWENTY-THREE

IT WAS a grotesque company, these three men who bore the name of Beethoven, journeying to the country estate on the Danube, enduring the two days of confinement in the monogrammed carriage of Johann. Karl was sullen in his corner, still with bandaged head. Johann was long and gaunt. Rawboned fingers, ill-concealed by white cloth gloves, rested upon bony knees encased in coffee-colored pantaloons. His ill-becoming foppishness was mocked by the baggy, frayed coat of his brother. Beethoven, haggard and drawn, must have been a picture of misery. Schindler has told how, after the calamity, he looked like a "broken old man of seventy." It must also have been a grim and silent trio. Written conversation with Beethoven would have been impossible in the jouncing vehicle. If the nephew and his other uncle had talked, Beethoven would have become suspicious. In any case, there were more subjects to avoid than to talk about.

Karl resented being treated as a wayward child under sufferance of good behavior. He looked upon Beethoven coldly as his enemy, to be endured because he had no other choice. Johann could hardly have felt warmly cordial toward the two troublesome relatives. His brother had at first refused bluntly to come. He looked upon Johann's wife as an object of iniquity to be compared with none, except perhaps his other sister-in-law. He relished the thought of her neither as hostess nor as a companion to Karl. Beethoven was a doubly ungrateful guest. He regarded Johann as a low schemer, and never hesitated to vilify him to his own nephew, calling him "Asinus," "pseudo-brother" and "unbrotherly brother."

The carriage turned out of Krems, passed the grubby little town of Gneixendorf ("The name," Beethoven once wrote, "sounds like an axle breaking"), and sprawled along a washed-out road through flat vineyards and meadows into "Wasserhof," the four hundred acres of the "landowner," and up to the two large houses which were his double country seat. The trees about the houses were almost the only ones to be seen. This Beethoven, choosing his site, had been less interested in streams, paths and peaceful groves than in arability, tenantry and a favorable ledger. His brother was consoled by a room with an open vista of the Danube. It reminded him of the Rhine of his childhood.

This retreat—any retreat—must have been a welcome relief to Beethoven. The crashing ruin of his attempt at guardianship had made him an object of public disapproval. He had vaunted his suitability, gone to the law, excluded the boy's own mother—and then made such a miserable failure of his responsibilities that he had driven his charge to suicide. What the world at large did not know was the extent to which he had sacrificed his art and his health in his frantic efforts to assure Karl's career. They could not have known that what at last drove Karl to his despairing deed was an uncle's love more infinite than his tragic clumsiness.

The nephew, in his own fashion, learned to make the most of his surroundings. His uncle, composing by day, locked in his room by night, was for the most part well out of his way. Uncle Johann showed common sense about him, and became more friendly. Johann's wife was kindly disposed toward him, praising his musical talent when he played duets with his composer uncle. The boy, of course, thrived on praise. He basked in the affluence of a propertied uncle who could not take the shortest drive without meeting tenants who stood bowing, hat in hand. The only trouble was that the uncle could not live up to the part. He looked too ludicrous for a lord of the manor, and spoiled the effect by penny-saving talk.

Karl went out of his way to be agreeable. He was solicitous to oblige by doing errands in Krems, the nearest town. He went oftener and stayed longer than necessary, until investigation showed that he had found soldier companions, a theatre, a billiard hall. Beethoven emerged from his room long enough to stir up a new cloud of dissension. Incapable of learning that hounding led to no good, he forbade Karl to leave the house, as if he were an irresponsible child. Karl was not averse to resuming the threat of drastic acts. The uncle, doting and fearful, found this unbearable and was ready to do almost anything to restore the nephew's good will. But Karl, taking refuge in righteous silence, wrote in the conversation book: "You ask me why I do not talk. Because I have had enough. Yours is the right to command; I must endure everything."

Karl felt fortified in his grievance because his uncle seemed, quite unreasonably, to oppose everyone around him. Johann he upbraided violently for not agreeing to cut off his lewd wife in his will, and leave all his property to his nephew. If Frau Beethoven overheard the excited roars, which she could not have missed if she were in the same house, she could hardly have been well disposed toward the brother-in-law who had once set the police on her and now wanted her disinherited.

The wearisome catalogue of troubles continues, but it does not tell everything. The life in creation had never lost its hold, nor paused except presently to renew itself with freshened vigor. Beethoven soon found his needed solitude at Gneixendorf as composition was upon him again. Sickness could not weaken, nor sorrow overwhelm him. The creating spirit never abated for a moment, nor relaxed its subtle, steeled control. The C sharp minor Quartet, written earlier in the year, was Beethoven's last prodigious tone structure. It was the final manifestation of the imagination which takes light of itself, expands, embraces, pervades all, until the result is extended beyond reason, but with a concise logic where not a note can be dispensed with.

That phenomenon was not to be repeated. The final catastrophe did not goad him to "take fate by the throat" once more and produce a colossus of defiance like the *Eroica,* or the *"Hammer-Klavier"* Sonata. But in the fading summer of 1826, an aging, sick man was delivered, as he had always been, from his despair. He entrenched himself still more deeply in his realm of tones, and excluded the vulgarities, hostile and painful thoughts which hedged him about. It was no mysterious power of trance or casting out, but the strength of the images which imperiously displaced a duller awareness. When Beethoven said,

"I am never alone when I am alone," he was speaking in sober fact.

The result, at Gneixendorf, was the Quartet in F major, and a swift new *Finale* for the earlier Quartet in B-flat major, replacing the fugue-finale which was to be published separately. The Quartet in F major thus became his final complete work. The music flows peacefully, rich in etched detail. All outward stimulus was lacking, but it was not needed. The inner source remained abundant. The melody of the *Lento cantante* is of a childlike simplicity, which pervades even the variations, as if at the end of the road the artist had found that complexity, elaboration and rhetoric were unessential. *"Süsser Ruhegesang, Friedengesang"* Beethoven wrote over it, and indeed its peacefulness is untouched by a single shadow.

Disputation, worry, ugly human pettiness could not encroach. Not even physical discomfort (for Beethoven was already suffering from the liver disorders from which he was never to recover). Now when the *raptus* was upon him he paid no attention to his surroundings, and did not even need his woods and streams. The simple country folk, who could not see the gleam in his eyes, the reflection of the inner life, took him for a half-wit. When he accompanied his brother on local visits people would not bother to speak to him. The mistress of one house, after serving the "landowner" from a crock of Gneixendorf wine, turned to Beethoven with the kindly remark: "Here, this man shall have some too!" Thayer picked up from two old peasants of Wasserhof years later a peculiar tale. They had respected Beethoven's position as brother to the landlord, but considered him mad, and kept a discreet distance. One of them was driving a pair of young oxen toward the manor house "when he met Beethoven shouting and waving his arms about in wild gesticulations. The peasant called to him: *'A bissel stada!'* (A little quieter) but he paid no attention. The oxen took fright, ran down a steep hill and the peasant had great difficulty in bringing them to a halt, turning them, and getting them back on the road. Again Beethoven came toward them, still shouting and waving. The yokel called to him a second time, but in vain; and now the oxen plunged toward the house where they were stopped by one

243

of the hired hands. When the driver came up and asked who the fool was who had scared his oxen, the man told him it was the proprietor's brother. 'A fine brother he is!' he answered."

If Beethoven became aware of these disturbances, which was seldom, he was angry. When the cook came in to make his bed and found him roaring and stamping she burst into laughter and was at once driven from the room. A servant was found, Michael Krenn, a vine dresser, with whom Beethoven came to a complete understanding. He learned to take Beethoven's strange ways for granted. After breakfast, which was at seven-thirty, Beethoven would roam the fields while Michael would straighten his room. He must have kept a protective eye on the master, too, for once a precious sketchbook was lost, and Michael found it. Beethoven would return to the house for dinner at about half-past twelve, go to his room, and roam again from mid afternoon until sunset. The routine continued, even through the rain and cold of the late season. The evenings he spent in his room, going to bed at ten. He would call Michael in and make him write out what had been said at dinner. Here at last was a servant whom he trusted, for Michael went to him several times with change he had dropped upon the floor. Once the rustic was sent on an errand to a near-by market and came back in dismay without the provisions, for he had lost the five florins. Frau von Beethoven discharged him. Beethoven was furious, paid the five florins and demanded the man's immediate reinstatement. From that time Beethoven never sat at table with the rest. Michael prepared his breakfast in his room, and brought his other meals on a tray.

The weeks at Gneixendorf multiplied until Karl's wound had long since healed, and almost two months had passed. Karl was becoming all too contented with his country life. His indolence was reasserting itself. Problems of police investigations, military examinations, inquiry into his character and past—these lay dormant at a safe distance in Vienna. Here he had found his own amusements and there were no duties. Johann was busy with the affairs of the estate. The lady of the house had by this time returned to Vienna, and as a consequence, Beethoven was less choleric. Karl got around him by the old trick which never failed—protestations of affection. When Beethoven insisted that it was more than time to return to Vienna, he wrote in answer: "The longer we are here the longer shall we be together, for when we are in Vienna I shall of course have to go away soon."

Breuning in Vienna urged that the young man be sent along to his new duties before he should get quite out of the way of them, and Johann, putting a straight case, pointed out to his brother that the time for listening to Karl's coaxings for delay was past. Wintry weather was setting in; the country house was thin-walled.

CHAPTER TWENTY-FOUR

UNCLE AND nephew at last set forth on the morning of the first day of December in some species of hired conveyance. Beethoven's statement to his doctor later that it was "the Devil's most wretched vehicle, a milk wagon," cannot be taken quite literally. Whatever it was, it was inadequate. Stopping for the night in some village tavern, Beethoven tossed upon the bed of an unheated room and toward midnight, again according to his account later reported by his doctor, "he experienced his first fever chill, a dry hacking cough, accompanied by violent thirst, and cutting pains in his sides. Feverish, he drank a quantity of ice-cold water, and longed helplessly for the first rays of morning light." Weak and miserable, he was helped into the exposed vehicle by his nephew, and by evening the two were back at the *Schwarzspanierhaus*.

Schindler, who disliked the nephew only less cordially than he did the brother, circulated the report that Karl left the prostrate Beethoven for days while he returned to his billiards, not even bothering to fetch a doctor. The conversation books give this piece of spite the lie. On December 4th, two days after their return, we find Karl patiently diverting the sick man by explaining to him the principles of multiplication which his schooling had never attained. There are pages of examples. On that day or the next, Karl wrote a note to Holz at his uncle's dictation. It was a light greeting to the effect that he would like to see his friend. He had "become sick and had thought it better to keep to his bed." Holz came, and immediately went in search of a doctor. The only one who was available at the moment and acceptable to the patient was Dr. Wawruch, assistant to Prof. Hildebrand at the General Hospital.

Wawruch found him, on December 5th, suffering from pneumonia, spitting blood, breathing with difficulty. The doctor, by his own account, relieved the inflammation of the lungs, saw him through the crisis. "On the fifth day he was able, in a sitting posture, to tell me, much moved, of the discomforts he had suffered." On the seventh day he felt well enough to get out of bed, walk about, and write business letters. Schindler tried to lay the cause of Beethoven's mortal illness upon the brother as well as the nephew. There is no proof of flagrant neglect in either case. Schindler's statement is probably untrue that Johann refused his brother the use of his closed carriage. The carriage would have been already in Vienna if it had taken Frau van Beethoven there.

Beethoven's lungs regained their old strength. But the lowering of his vitality opened the way for the intestinal disorders which had been bothering him for years. Nerve strain had undoubtedly aggravated his digestive troubles, and the excitement and shock when his nephew's misdeeds reached their climax must have had much to do with his bilious condition at Gneixendorf.

Jaundice now permeated his system. He suffered from violent intestinal pains. Dropsy caused a general swelling. Dr. Wawruch believed that the water must be drawn at once, and another doctor, called in for consultation, agreed. A surgeon, Seibert, from the hospital, inserted the tube and drew off a large quantity of fluid. Beethoven was impressed and compared the doctor to "Moses, striking the rock with his staff." Seyfried, who was not present, quoted Beethoven as saying, "better from my belly than from my pen," a remark which he may well have made, then or in retrospect.

This was on December 20th. "Five measures and a half" were taken. Beethoven enjoyed immense relief, and something like confidence in medical science. Two gifts arrived. The first was a ring from the King of Prussia, in acknowledgment of the Ninth Symphony. His Highness informed Beethoven by letter of his pleasure, and spoke of a diamond ring. When the box was opened the jewel was found to be no diamond, but only a "reddish" stone, of inferior value. This brought a proper tirade. The other present was wealth indeed. It was a set of the forty volumes of

Dr. Arnold's edition of Handel's works, sent by Johann Stumpff from London, according to his promise. Beethoven had often said that he placed Handel before any other composer. Taking renewed interest in life, too weak to compose but needing musical sustenance, he received them at the best possible moment. Gerhard von Breuning, Beethoven's "*Hosenknopf*," carried the heavy books one by one over from the piano to the bed, and Beethoven propped them against the wall and pored over the straight, sturdy, invigorating music. "I have long wanted them," said the composer to the boy, "for Handel was the greatest, the most skilled composer that ever lived. I can still learn from him." The magnificent oratorios set Beethoven dreaming of a "Saul and David" he had earlier planned, probably for the unfulfilled commission from the *Musikfreunde*. His acknowledgment to Stumpff told of his joy in the "royal present," a joy which his pen could not describe. He looked forward to his recovery, when once more he would be able "to soar through the air on Pegasus under full sail."

Schindler brought him a number of the songs of Schubert, and Beethoven was much excited by them. The diffident composer himself, under the wing of Hüttenbrenner, came in and stood at the bedside. It was too late for a real friendship to develop. Diabelli brought a present which delighted him: a picture he had just published of Haydn's birthplace. Beethoven showed it to the boy Gerhard and said: "Look what arrived today. It was in this little house that a great man was born!" "Trouser Button" in turn brought his schoolbook with pictures representing classical mythology, and the two turned the pages together as Beethoven related the tales he had always loved and often quoted. He was also in the mood to read, and he lost himself in novels of Sir Walter Scott, translations of which Johann fetched from the circulating library. He asked for Ovid's *Metamorphoses*. His thoughts may still have drifted toward an opera from antiquity.

The nephew, after many delays, left for Iglau to join his regiment on January 2nd. This was another boon for Beethoven, for the aggravations and arguments had continued as long as he was at Beethoven's side. A dutiful letter or two came from Iglau—and then nothing more. Beethoven never saw his nephew again

On the day after Karl's departure, Beethoven wrote a letter to Dr. Bach, naming Karl as his sole heir. The letter was not immediately sent because Breuning protested that the property should not be made accessible to the young wastrel in a lump sum. After delays and arguments, Beethoven had his way once more.

From this time the sick man had always at hand his circle of loyal attendants. The improvement in the composer's condition was only temporary; it became apparent in early January that a second tapping would have to be made. What confidence Beethoven had in Dr. Wawruch began to waver as he grew steadily worse in the face of a vast quantity of medicines. Wawruch was an amateur 'cellist, and an ardent admirer of Beethoven. Before taking up the medical profession he had studied for the priesthood. The patient, restless at his long confinement, did not want lofty sentiments or affectionate coaxing from his doctor; he wanted simply to be cured, and to return to his composing. When Wawruch was announced he would groan, "That ass!" and turn his face to the wall.

Dwindling faith in Dr. Wawruch was replaced by the idea that Dr. Malfatti, if anyone, could cure him. He sent Schindler to try his best persuasive powers. Malfatti, the uncle of Therese, had attended Beethoven in 1813. Beethoven had once called him names at least as impolite as those Wawruch now had to accept, and a long estrangement had resulted. Malfatti did not yield at once to the pleas of Schindler. He gave as his reason that he did not wish to interfere in Wawruch's case. "Tell Beethoven," he said, "that he, as a master of harmony, must know that I too am obliged to live in harmony with my colleagues." The unexpressed reason was that Beethoven had always been and notoriously remained an intractable patient. After two visits from Schindler, Malfatti at last came to the sick man on January 19th, and made his peace with him. His method was the exact opposite of what Wawruch's had been. The medicine bottles were banished, and caution with them. He allowed Beethoven small quantities of alcohol in the form of frozen punch. The cooling properties and gentle stimulation of the sherbet brought him relief, and revived his spirits and his hopes. He looked to Malfatti almost as a saviour. But the various experimentations of Malfatti seemed to increase the dropsical condition, and the ices, so Wawruch claimed, aggravated the weakened organs. Dr. Wawruch was retained, and Malfatti occasionally called in.

The Vienna colleagues, seeking to cheer or comfort Beethoven, went frequently in and out of the *Schwarzspanierhaus*: Schuppanzigh, Linke, Dolezalek, Piringer, Haslinger, Moritz Lichnowsky, Gleichenstein, Wolfmayer. Zmeskall, bedridden, sent his greeting. The word went across Europe that the great Beethoven was on his deathbed. The pianist Hummel hastened a journey to Vienna in order to be there before it was too late, and arrived on March 6th, with his wife and fifteen-year-old pupil, Ferdinand Hiller.

All past enmities were forgotten as Hummel, greatly moved, and the lad, awed and silent, entered the living room. The master was having a good day. He was sitting at the window "in apparent comfort." The first feeling of spring was in the air, and his long gray dressing gown was unbuttoned. Still, his appearance was a shock to Hummel who had last seen him in good health. He had had his fourth tapping a few days before. The sturdy frame was emaciated, the face sallow. Young Hiller carried away a vivid memory of the scene, and afterward wrote of it:

"He was unshaven, his thick, half-gray hair fell in disorder over his temples. The expression of his features heightened when he caught sight of Hummel, and he seemed to be extraordinarily glad to meet him. The two men embraced each other most cordially Hummel introduced me. Beethoven showed himself extremely kind and I was permitted to sit opposite him at the window. It is known that conversation with Beethoven was carried on in part in writing; he spoke, but those with whom he conversed had to write their questions and answers. For this purpose thick sheets of ordinary writing paper in quarto form and lead pencils always lay near him. How painful it must have been for the animated, easily impatient man to be obliged to wait for every answer, to make a pause in every moment of conversation, during which, as it were, thought was condemned to come to a standstill! He always followed the hand of the writer with hungry eyes and comprehended what was written at a glance instead of reading it."

250

Beethoven asked about the health of Goethe, whom they had just been visiting. He bemoaned his own condition: "Here I have been lying four months—one must at last lose patience!" He defended his nephew and complained of officialdom, which had made trouble over "a few trifles," and he closed this subject with the commentary: "Little thieves are hanged and the big ones allowed to go free!" He had little use for the government, and no more for the "present taste in art," which suffered from "dilettantism." He turned to Hiller and encouraged him in his musical studies, saying, "Art must be propagated ceaselessly." Then Hiller made bold to speak of the exclusive interest in Italian opera which he had found in Vienna, and Beethoven answered: "They say: '*Vox populi, vox dei.*' I never believed it."

A letter had come from Wegeler in February, bringing up fond memories, and suggesting a reunion at Bonn, to which his Eleonore added an endorsing postscript. Beethoven had written a nostalgic letter in October, apologizing for the tardiness of his answer: "I often compose an answer in my mind, but when I wish to write it down I usually throw the pen away, because I cannot write as I feel. I remember all the love which you have constantly shown me, for instance when you had my room whitewashed, and so pleasantly surprised me. It is the same with the Breuning family. . . . I still have the silhouette of your Lorchen, from which you will see that all the goodness and affection shown to me in my youth are still dear to me." His ambitions were very much alive: "If I ever let the muse sleep, it is only that she may awaken the stronger. I hope still to bring some great works into the world, and then, like an old child, to end my earthly career among good men."

Letters came from Moscheles and Stumpff, sent simultaneously from London, arriving in early March. Beethoven in his letter of acknowledgment to Stumpff had laid before him his financial situation due to his illness, which increased expenses and deprived him of the power to meet them "through the proceeds of my brain." He pointed out that "for a month and a half I have not been able to write a note. My salary suffices only to pay my semi-annual rent, after which there remains only a few hundred

251

florins." He hoped the Philharmonic Society might give a concert for his benefit.

The letters of both friends bore the news that the Society had at once convened and unanimously voted a loan to Beethoven of a hundred pounds "to be applied to his comforts and necessities during his illness." Schindler wrote to Moscheles that Beethoven's delight at receiving the gift was "like that of a child. . . . Numberless times during the day he exclaimed 'May God reward them a thousandfold!' " And Beethoven wrote, dictating with difficulty, offering "to compose either a new symphony, which lies already sketched in my desk, a new overture, or whatever else the Society shall wish." This was his last overweening promise. The merest fragments of sketches were afterward found, amid sketches for an overture on the letters of Bach's name.

Hummel visited him again on March 20th, bringing his wife, as Beethoven had urgently requested. He remembered her as a young and beautiful girl, and she in her turn, remembering his younger days, had avoided seeing him as he now was. "You are a lucky man," he had said to Hummel on his former visit. "You have a wife who takes care of you, who is in love with you—but poor me!" Now the two stood by his bed and had to lean over to catch his weak and disconnected words. Hiller reported his whispered words after the first greeting: "No doubt I shall soon be gone." Reverting to the noble conduct of the Philharmonic Society, he praised the English people as he had so long done, and "expressed his intention, as soon as matters were better with him, to undertake the journey to London. 'I will compose a grand overture for them, and a grand symphony.' . . . His eyes, which were still lively when we had seen him last, dropped and closed on this day, and it was difficult for him to rouse himself. It was no longer possible to pretend—the worst was to be feared.

"A hopeless picture was presented of the extraordinary man when we sought him again on March 23rd. It was to be the last time. He lay, weak and miserable, sighing deeply at intervals. Not a word fell from his lips; sweat stood upon his forehead. His handkerchief not being conveniently at hand, Hummel's wife took her fine cambric handkerchief and dried his face several times. Never shall I forget the grateful glance with which his broken eye looked upon her."

It was on that day that Beethoven signed his will of a single sentence, leaving his possessions without qualification to his nephew. There were other papers to be signed, and he had to be propped by pillows while his hand wrote the faltering letters. He turned to Schindler and young Breuning and said, with familiar irony: *"Plaudite amici, comœdia finita est!"* Wawruch made it clear that the time had come for the last sacrament, if he so wished it. He readily assented, and the rite was administered on the next morning (March 24th). He wrote his name for the last time, giving to Schott the rights of ownership of the C sharp minor Quartet. He spoke once more of writing his gratitude to the Philharmonic Society in London. At about one o'clock, a case of Rhine wine arrived from the firm of Schott in Mayence, and Schindler placed the bottles on the table beside the bed. Beethoven saw them and murmured: "Pity, pity—too late!" They were his last words.

Gerhard von Breuning has left the most vivid description of the last three days:

"During the next day and the day following the strong man lay completely unconscious, in the process of dissolution, breathing so stertorously that the rattle could be heard at a distance. His powerful frame, his unweakened lungs, fought like giants with approaching death. The spectacle was a fearful one. Although it was known that the poor man suffered no more, it was appalling to observe that the noble being, now irredeemably undergoing disintegration, was beyond all mental communication. It was expected as early as the 25th that he would pass away in the following night; yet we found him still alive on the 26th—breathing still more heavily, if that was possible, than the day before."

At three o'clock in the afternoon of March 26th, Anselm Hüttenbrenner called at the *Schwarzspanierhaus*. Several people were there: Schindler, of course; Johann van Beethoven and his wife; Stephan von Breuning and his son, Joseph Teltscher, the artist, who sat beside the raucously breathing figure on the bed, and began to make a sketch. Stephan made an outraged gesture of protest, and Teltscher quietly left. The constraint of helpless

253

waiting became oppressive to the ill-mixed company and induced restlessness. Breuning and Schindler walked out of the house and to the cemetery; the choice of a grave would fall on them. So it happened that when the end came only two were keeping vigil: Anselm Hüttenbrenner, small tradesman in the art of music, and Frau Johann van Beethoven, the hated sister-in-law.

Hüttenbrenner has left a strange account of Beethoven's death:

"Frau van Beethoven and I only were in the death chamber during the last moments of Beethoven's life. After Beethoven had lain unconscious, the death rattle in his throat, from three o'clock in the afternoon until past five, there came a flash of lightning accompanied by a violent clap of thunder, which garishly illuminated the death chamber. After this unexpected phenomenon of nature, which startled me greatly, Beethoven opened his eyes, lifted his right hand and looked up for several seconds with his fist clenched, and a very serious, threatening expression as if he wanted to say: 'Powers of Evil, I defy you! Away with you! God is with me! . . .' When he let the raised hand sink to the bed, his eyes closed half-way. My right hand was under his head, my left rested on his breast. Not another breath, not a heartbeat more!"

Here was a *finale* to warm the heart of romancers to come. It was not among the imaginative embroideries to be hunted down and exposed by the pitiless Thayer, for when Thayer had the account from Hüttenbrenner in 1860, the other witness was in her grave. Who can say that the power of will which had cast aside unendurable torture once and again to plunge into the world of tone and triumphantly change the face of his art, which had fought for four months the final interloper, would submit at last without a struggle? The storm was noted by all. When many whisper in awe that Nature itself has been thrown into convulsion by the passing of a man, we behold rumor become legend.

The next morning the three men who had been closest in the service of Beethoven through these last months met in the house where the body lay, to settle the important matter of his papers. The seven bank shares in particular must be found and handed over for the disposition of the estate. Breuning and Schindler searched everywhere, but in vain. Johann watched them in pointed silence, and remarked with an unpleasant smile that it was up to the two of them to produce the shares. Breuning, always quick to flare up, strode from the house. The two sought out Holz, for although Schindler had no love for Holz, he loved Johann still less. Holz, Beethoven had trusted with his important financial dealings when he trusted no one else. So the four, in whom Beethoven's enmities seemed to survive, met once more in the afternoon. Holz pulled out a nail in the composer's desk which released a secret drawer. In it they discovered three things: the bundle of bank notes, a letter written in pencil in Beethoven's hand, which was a passionate outpouring of love; the third secret treasure was a picture of Therese von Brunswick. This was Beethoven's legacy: to the world a riddle for eternity; to his nephew a small fortune, the purchasing equivalent today of about $15,000. Those to whom Beethoven had talked of his poverty, in particular the members of the London Philharmonic Society, felt taken aback, disillusioned that the great artist, the noble idealist, had falsely presented his circumstances and played upon their sympathy for gain. What they did not realize was that Beethoven, having set aside his windfall a dozen years before for his nephew, had come to regard it as inviolate, no longer belonging to him for his own use. The state of mind, born of his intense desire to assure the future of the boy, was lacking in accepted money sense but quite genuine. When Beethoven had told Schindler and Breuning of his intention to appeal to London for aid, these two had reminded him of his bank shares, and he had indignantly dismissed the idea of touching them. They were set apart for his nephew, and this closed the door to any thought of them for any other purpose.

The funeral, according to invitations drawn up by Breuning and Schindler and distributed at Haslinger's music shop, took place at three o'clock on the afternoon of March 29th. In the morning, crowds began to gather about the *Schwarzspanierhaus*, filled the square and the streets beyond. The weather was fine. The composer in death was looked upon, after the way of man, with greatly increased awareness and awe. According to contemporary accounts, confirmed in the memoirs of Seyfried and of Hiller, there was a concourse of twenty thousand people, which must effectually have blocked passageway in the Vienna of 1827.

Soldiers were called out to preserve order. The schools were closed. The coffin was placed in the court before the house and around it during the service stood Beethoven's colleagues and admirers in the arts—musicians, stage folk, poets, dressed in black, with white roses attached to crêpe bands on their sleeves. Seyfried led the choir through a *Miserere* and *Amplius,* an arrangement of his own, consisting of two of the composer's *Equali* for trombones, with vocal parts added. The coffin was borne to the Minorite Church in the Alserstrasse, with difficulty making its way through the pushing crowds. Eight *Kapellmeister* held the pall: Seyfried, Hummel, Kreutzer, Gyrowetz, Gansbächer, Würfel, Weigl, Eybler. The torchbearers included familiar faces: young Schubert, who had admired Beethoven at a distance, and others who knew him well: Czerny, Haslinger, Schuppanzigh, Linke, Bernard, Grillparzer, Piringer, Mayseder, Holz, Wolf-mayer, Streicher, Steiner, many others. His brother, Schindler, the Breunings, father and son, were caught by the surging people, and almost separated from the procession. As it passed Breuning's house, musicians within played the funeral march from the Piano Sonata Opus 26. Music of another was the last performed before his burial. In the parish house of Trinity Church the choristers sang a *Libera nos Domine* by Seyfried. A horse-drawn hearse bore the body to the cemetery at Währing. A poem by Castelli had been distributed at the house; another by Baron von Schlechta was distributed at the cemetery. Grillparzer had written a funeral oration, and this the actor Anschütz declaimed before the cemetery gate to the second multitude there assembled.

Compare this to a funeral procession of thirty-six years before, when a handful of friends, no more, followed the coffin of Mozart as it was borne from the chapel of St. Stephen's along the *Schulerstrasse* to the churchyard of St. Mark's. A sudden squall of snow and rain blew down the street, and sent the group scurrying for home, bent under their umbrellas. The remains of Mozart, in this same Vienna, were thrown into a pauper's grave, while no single bystander witnessed his interment. Yet Mozart had been accounted a famous man, the musical wonder of his age. In 1827, things were different. Now multitudes stood, heads

256

bowed, most of whom had never heard a note of Beethoven's music. Now, a great musician could command as much respect as any prince. The world had changed, and Beethoven had done much to change it, not by what he had exacted, but by a strange power in his music which lifted all men in spite of themselves.

THE WORKS
OF BEETHOVEN

INTRODUCTION

A GROWING intimacy with the works of Beethoven steadily increases one's impatience with the "three period" point of view. Not that it can be gainsaid. It is as old as Schindler. Von Lenz, who elaborated it in 1852, in *Beethoven et ses trois Styles*, like d'Indy, who was the last scholar to espouse and labor it, in 1911, were careful men, and so have been many others intervening—and since. Not only Beethoven, but any artist worth mentioning who has reached his span of years has had in some degree his three parts—his period of gradual self-extrication from habits of tradition, his full noontide of vigor, and his period of continual reapplication, where fine impetuosity is toned by mellowing judgment. The threefold view of Beethoven is indeed only too plainly justified. Even the two imaginary lines, neatly drawn across the highroad of his advance, are made plausible by the enormous acceleration of growth which throws a focus upon the year 1802, and the hiatus of the fallow years between 1812 and 1816.

The principal trouble with the triple category is its unserviceableness—its way of calling attention to the obvious and passing over as inconvenient points that are truly revealing. One of these is the consistency of Beethoven's growth, his continuous technical enrichment from first to last. Where Beethoven never fluctuated was in his musical ambition and his musical industry. Music continued always within him, even when it did not go down on paper. As the spirit's vision expanded, which it continued steadily to do, that vision was correspondingly implemented by developing craft. The chronology of his works shows an unbroken progress in the handling of form, transition and balance, harmonic variety. From his Bonn days, when he picked

261

up what scraps he could of the lore of counterpoint, until his final months, when he immersed himself in Handel, his power in the interplay of voices grew, finding its utmost fulfillment in the last quartets. This progress mocks at specious dividing lines. The works of 1806, of 1810, the Mass and piano sonatas of 1818-1820, the Ninth Symphony following, the final quartets—all are in regularly ascending steps of manipulatory skill.

The "otherworldliness" of the later works has been overdone. The increasing subtilization, the dynamic recession of the chamber music, is an indication of inward power and diversity rather than any aloofness. Beethoven could write for the expert musician or the man in the street, each in kind; nor did he ever lose touch with either. The legend that he became through his deafness a recluse, enigmatic, remote from the world, grew from a strange, lingering ear-blindness to the last quartets—an illusion now happily dispelled as their warm and human beauty has become generally apparent. The Ninth Symphony was not the music of a recluse; nor did Beethoven ever shut out the world from his art. His deafness inevitably affected his music, but it began to do so in his young manhood, when it was still only an apprehension, by sharpening his inward vision—a vision manifest in tones for all to know. In a sense Beethoven was a recluse; he was always one, from his brooding childhood; in another sense he was never a recluse, for he never ceased to crave friendship, love, public response.

One finds no downright change in Beethoven at any time in his life—only cumulative growth. Each epoch of his music contained all that had gone before. The increasing capaciousness allowed for wide variability—another circumstance embarrassing to the categorists. An access of new energy would bring a bold, even a prophetic work, and in its wake a reflective mood which would turn back to garner from the past. The lighter, hastily written works, bagatelles, songs, and the like, are often retrogressive, whether by desire to please average tastes or because what first occurred to him was apt to be conventional. At other times, while reverting to past ways, his highest qualities were awakened. The Piano Sonatas Opus 90 or 110 are thus behind their time, or the Eighth Symphony, the "Harp" Quartet or the Song Cycle *An die ferne Geliebte,* music where periodic regularities and the simpler harmonies of an earlier day abound.

This turning back upon himself no more than confirms the basic quality of Beethoven's growth as intensification, in which his early ideals are preserved. The composer who, on his death-bed, spoke in wondering admiration of Haydn, whom he might have looked down upon as technically superseded, was the composer who in his last work still cherished the classical ideal of beauty which had stood before him in his first. Opus 1 and Opus 135, as terminals in a full career, are less striking in their differences than in their similarity—the one is the reassertion of the other in enormously strengthened skill and in amplitude of conception. In the first trios almost the whole of Beethoven is implicit, in hint or vague outline. As in the working out of a single movement, so in the general course of his artist's growth one has the sense that he was laboring to uncover what was implicit in his nature, only waiting to be brought to light. The last quartet fulfills the specifications of the first trio—the classical concept of statement, development and return, the movements, repeats, *da capo,* etc., are still in good standing. There is an immense advance, but it is an advance in degree: suppleness, delicacy, point, conciseness of detail—and of course, depth, but not kind, of emotional experience. The voice handling in the *Lento* is no more intricate than the melodic ornamentation in the early slow movements, but it is infinitely more expressive, subtly intensifying a melody which is of the most elementary simplicity. Thematic simplicity was the composer's aim in the last quartet. As in his earlier music, a simple theme was usually arrived at by many sketches, as if the composer were striving against all that is weakening in complexity. Among the notations for the *Dona nobis Pacem* of the *Missa Solemnis* he wrote, *"immer simpler—durchaus simpel,"* and in the simplicity of that ending, as in the simplicity of the choral melody of the Ninth Symphony, lay music of universal, because universally comprehensible, beauty. Each could have come only from an artist whose heart remained that of a child—credulous, naïve, wondering, uncorroded by the guile of experience or expertness. The final quartets did not withdraw into a self-sufficient shell of the intellectual, the rare and remote. They could not, of course, be music for crowds, but their more personal, more delicate address is for all who seek beauty personal and intimate. The Cavatina of the B-flat Quartet comes to mind, which even its first hearers embraced, or the *Finale* of that Quartet, Beethoven's last music, and as gay and sociable as any he ever wrote! His last communication from the world of tones shows that world to be thoroughly ours—a world we enter with a reverence which is not alien and awed, but genuinely eager.

THE SYMPHONIES

SYMPHONY NO. 1 IN C MAJOR, OP. 21

Adagio molto; Allegro con brio
Andante cantabile con moto
Menuetto: Allegro molto e vivace
Finale: Adagio; Allegro molto e vivace

(The original manuscript of this Symphony has not been found, and there is no certainty as to when it was composed, but sketches for the *Finale* were found among the exercises in counterpoint which the young composer made for Albrechtsberger as early as 1795. It was on April 2, 1800, in Vienna, that the Symphony had its first performance. It was published in parts at the end of 1801. The full score did not appear in print until 1820. It is dedicated to Baron Gottfried van Swieten.)

The introductory *Adagio molto,* only twelve bars in length, seems to take its cue from Haydn, and hardly foreshadows the extended introductions of the Second, Fourth and Seventh symphonies to come. There once was learned dissension over the very first bars, because the composer chose to open in the not so alien key of F, and to lead his hearers into G major. The composer makes amends, with a main theme which proclaims its tonality by hammering insistently upon its tonic:

With this polarizing theme he can leap suddenly from one key to another without ambiguity. The second theme, of orthodox

265

contrasting and "feminine" character, seems as plainly designed to bring into play the alternate blending voices of the wood winds.

The theme itself of the *Andante cantabile* was one of those inspirations which at once took the popular fancy. The ready invention, the development of a fragment of rhythm or melody into fresh and charming significance, the individual treatment of the various instruments confirms what was already evident in the development of the first movement—Beethoven's orchestral voice already assured and distinct, speaking through the formal periods which he had not yet cast off.

The "Minuet," so named, is more than the prophecy of a *scherzo* with its rapid tempo—*allegro molto e vivace*. Although the repeats, the trio and *da capo* are quite in the accepted mold of the Haydnesque minuet, the composer rides freely on divine whims of modulation and stress of some passing thought, in a way which disturbed the pedants of the year 1800. Berlioz found the *Scherzo* "of exquisite freshness, lightness, and grace—the one truly original thing in this symphony."

It is told of the capricious introductory five bars of the *Finale,* in which the first violins reveal the ascending scale of the theme bit by bit, that Türk, cautious conductor at Halle in 1809, made a practice of omitting these bars in fear that the audience would be moved to laughter. The key progressions, the swift scale passages, the typical eighteenth-century sleight of hand, ally this movement more than the others with current ways. It was the ultimate word, let us say, upon a form which had reached with Haydn and Mozart its perfect crystallization, and after which there was no alternative but a new path. (See pages 68, 91.)

SYMPHONY NO. 2 IN D MAJOR, OP. 36

Adagio molto; Allegro con brio
Larghetto
Scherzo
Allegro molto

(Composed in 1802: the parts published in 1804, the score in 1820, first performed April 5, 1803, at the *Theater-an-der-Wien* in Vienna; dedicated to Prince Karl Lichnowsky.)

While Beethoven wrote the "testament," the secret confession of despair at his growing deafness, at Heiligenstadt in October, 1802, there lay upon his table the score, probably well advanced, of his serene and joyous Symphony in D major.

The Second Symphony is considerably more suave, more fulsome than the First. The success of the First had given Beethoven assurance, but, more important, the experience of it had given him resource. The orchestral colors are more delicately varied, making the music clear and luminous from beginning to end, giving the first movement its effect of brilliant sunshine, the *Larghetto* its special subdued glow, emphasizing the flashing changes of the *Scherzo* and the dynamic contrasts of the *Finale*. The Symphony draws to a consummation the classically rounded, sensuous tonal felicity of the quartets, Opus 18. It is the most striking and opulent achievement of the "pupil of Haydn." This manner of music could go no further—no further at least in the restless and questing hands of Beethoven. Indeed, beneath its constructive conformity, its directly appealing melody and its engaging cheerfulness, the Symphony was full of daring episodes threatening to disrupt the amiable course of orchestral custom. It seems incredible that this music, so gay and innocuous to us, could have puzzled and annoyed its first critics. But their words were unequivocal, one finding the finale an unspeakable monstrosity. This was the movement which shocked people most, although, strangely enough, the *Larghetto* was not always favored. Berlioz has told us that at a *Concert Spirituel* in Paris in 1821 the *Allegretto* from the Seventh was substituted for this movement—with the result that only the *Allegretto* was applauded. The first movement always commanded respect and admiration; in fact, one critic referred to it as "colossal" and "grand," adjectives made strange to us by what has followed. Probably the sinewy first theme, suddenly following the long and meandering introduction, elastic and vital in its manipulations, was found startling, and the second theme, which Rolland

267

has called a revolutionary summons to arms, surely stirred the
blood of Vienna in 1803:

There were also the rushing intermediate passages and the
thundering chords in the coda. Certainly Beethoven had never
used his ingenuity to greater effect. But it is the melodic abundance of the *Larghetto* in A major which first comes to mind
when the Symphony is mentioned. This movement reaches
lengths not by any involved ornamental development, but by
the treatment of its full-length phrases and episodes in sonata
form. Never had a movement generated such an unending flow
of fresh, melodic thoughts. As Beethoven for the first time turned
the orchestral forces on the swift course of one of his characteristic scherzos, with its humorous accents, the effect was more
startling than it had been in chamber combinations. The Trio
in particular plunges the hearer unceremoniously into F sharp,
whereupon, as suddenly returning to F, it beguiles him with a
bucolic tune. In the *Finale*, Beethoven's high spirits moved him
to greater boldness. Sudden bursts of chords, capricious modulations, these were regarded as exhibitions of poor taste. This explosive opening

coming instead of the expected purling rondo tune, had the effect
of a sudden loud and rude remark at a polite gathering. Success

had gone to the young man's head—this was going too far. A critic in Leipzig after the first performance of the Symphony there, compared the *Finale* to "a gross enormity, an immense wounded snake, unwilling to die, but writhing in its last agonies, and bleeding to death." (See pages 85, 88, 91, 120, 167.)

SYMPHONY NO. 3 IN E-FLAT MAJOR, "EROICA," OP. 55

Allegro con brio
Marcia funebre: Adagio assai
Scherzo: Allegro vivace; trio
Finale: Allegro

(Composed in the years 1802-1804, first performed at a private con‹ cert in the house of Prince von Lobkowitz in Vienna, December, 1804, the composer conducting. The first public performance was at the *Theater-an-der-Wien*, April 7, 1805. The parts were published in 1806, the score in 1820; dedicated to Prince Franz Joseph von Lobkowitz.)

The immense step from the Second Symphony to the Third is primarily an act of the imagination. The composer did not base his new power on any new scheme; he kept the form of the salon symphony which, as it stood, could have been quite incongruous to his every thought, and began furiously to expand and transform. He started his movements conventionally, as the sketch books show. The third movement first went upon paper as a minuet. Variations were then popular, and so were funeral marches. The opening phrase of the Symphony is, on its face value, an insignificant figure on the common chord. But no sooner was it defined than the mind, tonally possessed, began to build and reach. The exposition is a mighty projection of 155 bars, music of concentrated force, wide in dynamic and emotional range, conceived apparently in one great sketch, where the pencil could hardly keep pace with the outpouring thoughts. Traces of the classical exposition are recognizable; the pivot theme, created for the horns in E flat (a third horn is Beethoven's only addition to the classical orchestra in this Symphony) establishes the tonality, which does not give way to the dominant until the eighty-fifth bar, at which point at least four distinct thematic features have been introduced. The "second" theme proper which brings in B flat is to be less prominent than any of these, and less so than two further themes in its tonality (at bars 109 and 132). This exposition in full groups of thematic elements, each in distinct profile, is to become the way of the symphonies to follow —with the difference that the material laid forth in the *Eroica* is more widely varied, extending for example from this chain of outflung chords (from which incidentally the highest part will later furnish a marvelous bass):

to this *dolce* figure in the wood winds:

There are no periodic tunes here, but fragments of massive chords, and sinuous rhythms, subtly articulated but inextricable, meaningless as such except in their context. Every bar bears the heroic stamp. There is no melody in the conventional sense, but in its own sense the music is melody unbroken, in long ebb and flow, vital in every part. Even before the development is reached the composer has taken us through mountains and valleys, shown us the range, the universality of his subject. The development

270

is still more incredible, as it extends the classical idea of a brief thematic interplay into a section of 250 bars. It discloses vaster scenery, in which the foregoing elements are newly revealed, in their turn generating others. The recapitulation (beginning with the famous passage where the horns mysteriously sound the returning tonic E flat against a lingering dominant chord) restates the themes in the increased strength and beauty of fully developed acquaintance. But still the story is not told. In an unprecedented coda of 140 bars, the much exploited theme and its satellites reappear in fresh guise, as if the artist's faculty of imaginative growth could never expend itself. This first of the long codas is one of the most astonishing parts of the Symphony. A coda until then had been little more than a brilliant close, an underlined cadence. With Beethoven it was a resolution in a deeper sense. The repetition of the subject matter in the reprise could not be for him the final word. The movement had been a narrative of restless action—forcefulness gathering, striding to its peak and breaking, followed by a gentler lyricism which in turn grew in tension until the cycle was repeated. The movement required at last an established point of repose. The coda sings the theme softly, in confident reverie under a new and delicate violin figure:

As the coda takes its quiet course, the theme and its retinue of episodes are transfigured into tone poetry whence conflict is banished. Witness this emergence of a theme

from its more dynamic version in the exposition:

The main theme, ringing and joyous, heard as never before, brings the end.

The second movement, like the first, is one of conflicting impulses, but here assuaging melody contends, not with over-riding energy, but with the broken accents of heavy sorrow. The *legato* second strain in the major eases the muffled minor and the clipped notes of the opening "march" theme, to which the oboe has lent a special somber shading. The middle section, in C major, begins with a calmer, elegiac melody, over animating staccato triplets from the strings. The triplets become more insistent, ceasing only momentarily for broad fateful chords, and at last permeating the scene with their determined rhythm, as if the composer were setting his indomitable strength against tragedy itself. The opening section returns as the subdued theme of grief gives its dark answer to the display of defiance. But it does not long continue. A new melody is heard in a *fugato* of the strings, an episode of quiet, steady assertion, characteristic of the resolution Beethoven found in counterpoint. The whole orchestra joins to drive the point home. But a tragic *decrescendo* and a reminiscence of the funereal first theme is again the answer. Now Beethoven thunders his protest in mighty chords over a stormy accompaniment. There is a long subsidence—a magnificent yielding this time— and a return of the first theme again, now set forth in full voice. As in the first movement, there is still lacking the final answer, and that answer comes in another *pianissimo* coda, measures where peacefulness is found and sorrow accepted, as the theme, broken into incoherent fragments, comes to its last concord.

The conquering life resurgence comes, not shatteringly, but in a breath-taking *pianissimo,* in the swiftest, most wondrous *Scherzo* Beethoven had composed. No contrast more complete could be imagined. The *Scherzo* is another exhibition of strength, but this time it is strength finely controlled, unyielding and undisputed. In the Trio, the horns, maintaining the heroic key of E flat, deliver the principal phrases alone, in three-part harmony. The *Scherzo* returns with changes, such as the repetition of the famous descending passage of rhythmic displacement in unexpected duple time instead of syncopation. If this passage is "humorous," humor must be defined as the adroit and fanciful play of power.

And now in the *Finale,* the tumults of exultant strength are released. A dazzling flourish, and the bass of the theme is set forward simply by the plucked strings. It is repeated, its bareness somewhat adorned before the theme proper appears over it, by way of the wood winds. The varied theme had already appeared under Beethoven's name as the finale of "Prometheus," as a contra-dance, and as a set of piano variations. Was this fourth use of it the persistent exploitation of a particularly workable tune, or the orchestral realization for which the earlier uses were as sketches? The truth may lie between. The variations disclose a *fugato,* and later a new theme, a sort of "second subject" in conventional martial rhythm but an inspiriting stroke of genius in itself. The *fugato* returns in more elaboration, in which the bass is inverted. The music takes a graver, more lyric pace for the last variation, a long *poco andante*. The theme at this tempo has a very different expressive beauty. There grows from it a new alternate theme (first given to the oboe and violin). The principal theme now strides majestically across the scene over triplets of increasing excitement which recall the slow movement. There is a gradual dying away in which the splendor of the theme, itself unheard, still lingers. A *presto* brings a gleaming close. (See pages 86, 88, 90-92, 117-120, 192, 242.)

SYMPHONY NO. 4 IN B FLAT MAJOR, OP. 60

Adagio; Allegro vivace
Adagio
Menuetto: Allegro vivace
Allegro, ma non troppo

(Composed in 1806; first performed in March 1807, at the house of Prince Lobkowitz in Vienna; the parts were published in 1809, the score in 1821; dedicated to Count Franz von Oppersdorf.)

The Fourth Symphony sometimes escapes general notice because it is quite without the bold features of those which precede and follow. To assume that because it asserts itself less strikingly than others it is a lesser work would be to admit a sad ignorance of the manifold nature of its composer. He had his recesses, quiet and deep, where nostalgic beauty lingered in a special intimate sense, and this is one of them. It can be called a symphony of dreaming, the fixing in music of a mood of willing subjection to the affectionate regard of those about him, and response to it in an even, glowing tenderness, gently exuberant, as in the last two movements, touching passion, deep but without violence, as in the *Adagio*. Those devotees who are disposed, while not slighting the peaks of Beethoven, to linger in his fair valleys with a special delight, are all ardent champions of the Symphony in B flat. Berlioz described it as "generally lively, nimble, joyous, or of a heavenly sweetness." Thayer, who bestowed his adjectives guardedly, singled out the "placid and

274

serene Fourth Symphony—the most perfect in form of them all"; and Sir George Grove, a more demonstrative enthusiast, found in it something "extraordinarily *entraînant*—a more consistent and attractive whole cannot be. . . . The movements fit in their places like the limbs and features of a lovely statue; and, full of fire and invention as they are, all is subordinated to conciseness, grace, and beauty." Sir George was probably moved by the metaphor of Robert Schumann who, contemplating the Fourth Symphony as a companion to the Third and Fifth, called it "a slender Greek maiden between two Norse giants."

The significant points about its composition, of which little is known, are that it was written in 1806, in the summer of which year Beethoven stayed at Martonvásár with the Brunswicks, not lingering as usual near Vienna. Also that he probably laid aside his sketches for the Fifth Symphony to complete this one. Count Oppersdorf, the Hungarian nobleman who wished a symphony for his private orchestra, was promised the Symphony in C minor and received this instead, or rather the mere dedication of it, for he was scantily treated. The Count would scarcely have been pleased with it, even if he had been promptly and properly honored with the score, for the symphony was poles removed from the cheerful glibness of the eighteenth-century style. It was quite over the heads of its first hearers. Carl Maria von Weber, who in 1807 was a hopeful underling of twenty in a Silesian castle, aired his wit in print on the subject of this symphony. The young critic fancifully makes a violin complain, after a performance, that it had been compelled to "caper about like a wild goat" in order to "execute the no-ideas of Mr. Composer," while the first violoncello "(bathed in perspiration), says that he is too tired to speak and can recollect nothing like the warming he has just had since he was put through Cherubini's last opera." The orchestra attendant threatens to punish them with the *Eroica* if they are not quiet. "Clearness and force, spirit and fancy," he warns them, are of the past. The slow movement, Weber tells us, is "full of short, disjointed, unconnected ideas, at the rate of three or four notes per quarter of an hour," the *Finale* a mass of leaps from one

275

key to another in place of ideas—"on to the new note at once, never mind modulating! Above all, throw rules to the winds, for they only hamper a genius." A strange picture of a demure and unoffending symphony! Certainly it was an opinion which the rash young writer would later repent; what the words really prove is that the symphony was so ripe, so completely the composer's own, and so far afield from all custom that it appeared wayward and barren to the disgruntled conservatism of 1807.

The long opening *Adagio* has none of the broad chords or flourishes of the classical introduction; it is no meandering fantasia but a reverie, precisely conceived, musing upon its own placid theme in a somber minor which is soon to be banished. Incisive staccato chords establish at once the brightness of B flat major and the beat of the *Allegro vivace*. The subject matter of this movement is as abundant as that of the first movement of the *Eroica*, the exposition extending through 154 bars, unfolding one new thought after another in simple and inevitable continuity. The main theme, with its staccato notes, is taken up by the whole orchestra and then given humorously (and differently) to the bassoon over whispered trills from the violins:

It generates excitement in the violins and breaks with energetic syncopated chords which bring in the dominant key, and from the flute the graceful and lilting second subject, which suggests a *crescendo* in short chords and a new theme in canonic dialogue between the clarinet and bassoon. Another syncopated subject ends the section. The development plays lightly with fragments of the principal theme, and the little rhythmic figure which introduced it. The theme is combined with the second theme proper. There is a full recapitulation, more brilliantly written.

276

The *Adagio* devolves upon this theme:

cantabile

first heard from the strings and then from the full choirs in a soft *cantabile*. The accompanying rhythmic figure pervades the movement with its delicate accentuation, appearing by turn in each part of the orchestra, now and then in all parts at once, and at the last quite alone in the timpani. This until then merely reinforcing instrument is now used with special coloring. The movement takes its even, dreaming course with not a moment of full sonority. It sings constantly in every part—even the ornamental passages of traditional slow-movement development are no longer decoration, but dainty melodic tracery. No other slow movement of Beethoven is just like this one. What Wagner wrote of Beethoven in general can be applied to this *Adagio* in a special sense: "The power of the musician cannot be grasped otherwise than through the idea of magic. Assuredly while listening we fall into an enchanted state. In all parts and details which to sober senses are like a complex of technical means cunningly contrived to fulfill a form, we now perceive a ghostlike anima-tion . . . a pulsation of undulating joy, lamentation and ecstasy, all of which seem to spring from the depths of our own nature.

. . . Every technical detail . . . is raised to the highest significance of spontaneous effusion. There is no accessory here, no framing of a melody; every part in the accompaniment, each rhythmical note, indeed each rest, everything becomes melody."

The third movement is characterized by alternate phrases between wood winds and strings. The Trio, which in interest dominates the *Scherzo* section, makes a second return before the close, the first symphonic instance of what was to be a favorite device. The *Finale*, which is marked *allegro ma non troppo*, takes an easily fluent pace, as is fitting in a symphony not pointed by high brilliance. Its delightful twists and turns have an adroitness setting a new precedent in final movements. (See pages 113, 118, 120.)

SYMPHONY NO. 5 IN C MINOR, OP. 67

Allegro con brio
Andante con moto
{ *Allegro; Trio*
{ *Allegro*

(Completed near the end of the year 1807, and first performed at the *Theater-an-der-Wien*, Vienna, December 22, 1808, Beethoven conducting. The parts were published in April, 1809, and the score in March, 1826. The dedication is to Prince von Lobkowitz and Count Rasumowsky.)

Something in the direct, impelling drive of the first movement of the C minor Symphony commanded the general attention when it was new, challenged the skeptical, and soon forced its acceptance. Goethe heard it with grumbling disapproval, according to Mendelssohn, but was astonished and impressed in spite of himself. Lesueur, hidebound professor at the Paris Conservatoire, was talked by Berlioz into breaking his vow never to listen to another note of Beethoven, and found his prejudices and resistances quite swept away. A less plausible tale reports Maria Malibran as having been thrown into convulsions by this Symphony. The instances could be multipled. There was no gainsaying the forthright, sweeping storminess.

Even if the opening movement could have been denied, the

tender melodic sentiment of the *Andante* was more than enough to offset conservative objections to "waywardness" in the development, and the lilting measures of the *Scherzo* proper were more than enough to compensate the "rough" and puzzling Trio. The joyous, marchlike theme of the finale carried the symphony on its crest to popular success, silencing at length the objections of those meticulous musicians who found that movement "commonplace" and noisy—probably when their expectation of the usual polite rondo was violently upset. Louis Spohr complained on hearing the disreputable tones of trombones and piccolo in a symphony, but he could not resist Beethoven's uncanny touch in introducing a reminiscence of the *Scherzo* before the close. Even Berlioz, who was usually with Beethoven heart and soul, found repetitiousness in the *Finale*. After the magnificent first entrance of the theme, the major tonality so miraculously prepared for in the long transitional passage, all that could follow seemed to him lessened by comparison, and he was forced to take refuge in the simile of a row of even columns, of which the nearest looms largest.

It has required the weathering of time to show the Beethoven of the Fifth Symphony to be in no need of apologies, to be greater than his best champions ever suspected. Some of its most enthusiastic conductors in the century past seem to have under- or over-shot the mark when they attempted those passages which rely upon the understanding and dramatic response of the interpreter. Wagner castigated those who hurried over the impressive, held E-flat in the second bar, who sustained it no longer than the "usual duration of a *forte* bow stroke." He protested that "the life-blood of the note must be squeezed out of it to the last drop, with force enough to arrest the waves of the sea, and lay bare the ground of the ocean; to stop the clouds in their courses, dispel the mists, and reveal the pure blue sky, and the burning face of the sun himself." All this suggests that Beethoven may have suffered by two extremes in the matter of these *fermate*—from the italicizing Romantics, and from the too correct and brisk academicians.*

* Even many years later, Artur Nikisch was taken to task for over-prolonging those particular holds. Felix Weingartner, as recently as 1906, in

A rhythmic affinity between the movements can be pointed out:

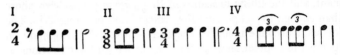

But the similarity (and it is nothing more) should be kept within the bounds of a superficial observation. Beethoven may not have been even aware of it—he was too deep an artist to pursue a unifying theory. A still greater mistake is to look upon the initial four-note figure with its segregating hold as more than a segment of the theme proper. Weingartner and others after him have exposed this fallacy, and what might be called the enlightened interpretation of this movement probably began with the realization that Beethoven never devised a first movement more conspicuous for graceful symmetry and even, melodic flow. An isolated tile cannot explain a mosaic, and the smaller the tile unit, the more smooth and integrated will be the lines of the complete picture. Just so does Beethoven's briefer "motto" devolve upon itself to produce long and regular melodic periods. Even in its first bare statement, the "motto" belongs conceptually to an eight-measure period, broken for the moment as the second *fermata* is held through an additional bar:

---

his "On the Performance of the Symphonies of Beethoven," felt obliged to warn conductors against what would now be considered unbelievable liberties, such as adding horns in the opening measures of the Symphony. He also told them to take the opening eighth notes in tempo, and showed how the flowing contours of the movement must not be obscured by false accentuation.

The movement is regular in its sections, conservative in its tonalities. Its very regularity, its incredible compactness, adds to its power which disrupted all contemporary notions of what a symphony was supposed to be.

The *Andante con moto* (in A flat major) is the most irregular of the four movements. It is not so much a theme with variations as free thoughts upon segments of a theme with certain earmarks and recurrences of the variation form hovering in the background. The first simple phrase of the melody requires twenty-two bars, with dreaming echoes and afterthoughts before the cadence finds its full close and point of repose. The whole *Andante* is one of delayed cadences. The second strain of the melody pauses upon the dominant and proceeds with an outburst into C major, repeats in this key to pause at the same place and dream away at leisure into E flat. The two sections of melody recur regularly with varying ornamental accompaniment in the strings, but again the questioning pauses bring in enchanting whispered vagaries, such as a *fugato* for flutes, oboes and clarinets, or a *pianissimo* dalliance by the violins upon a strand of accompaniment. The movement finds a sudden *fortissimo* close.

The third movement (*allegro,* with outward appearance of a *scherzo*) begins *pianissimo* with a phrase the rhythm of which crystallizes into the principal element, in *fortissimo*. This movement restores the C minor of the first and some of its rhythmic drive. But here the power of impulsion is light and springy. In the first section of the Trio in C major (the only part of the movement which is literally repeated) the basses thunder a theme which is briefly developed, fugally and otherwise. The composer begins what sounds until its tenth bar like a *da capo*. But this is in no sense a return, as the hearer soon realizes. The movement has changed its character, lost its steely vigor and taken on a light, skimming, mysterious quality. It evens off into a *pianissimo* where the suspense of soft drum beats prepares a new disclosure, lightly establishing (although one does not realize this until the disclosure comes) the quadruple beat. The bridge of mystery leads, with a sudden tension, into the tremendous outburst of the *Finale,* chords proclaiming C major with all of the power an orchestra of 1807 could muster—which means that trombones, piccolo and contra bassoon appeared for the first time in a symphony. The *Finale* follows the formal line of custom, with a second group in the dominant, the prescribed development section, and a fairly close recapitulation. But as completely as the first movement (which likewise outwardly conforms), it gives a new function to a symphony—a new and different character to music itself. Traditional preconceptions are swept away in floods of sound, joyous and triumphant. At the end of the development the riotous chords cease and in the sudden silence the *Scherzo*, or rather the bridge passage, is recalled. Again measures of wonderment fall into the sense of a coda as the oboe brings the theme to a gentle resolution. This interruption was a stroke of genius which none could deny, even the early malcontents who denounced the movement as vulgar and blatant—merely because they had settled back for a rondo and found something else instead. The Symphony which in all parts overrode disputation did so nowhere more tumultuously, more unanswerably, than in the final coda. (See pages 89, 116-118, 120-123, 191-192.)

SYMPHONY NO. 6 IN F MAJOR, "PASTORAL," OP. 68

Awakening of serene impressions on arriving in the country: *Allegro ma non troppo*
Scene by the brookside: *Andante molto moto*
{ Jolly gathering of country folk; *Allegro; in tempo d'allegro;* Thunderstorm; Tempest: *Allegro*
Shepherd's Song: Gladsome and thankful feelings after the storm: *Allegretto.*

(Completed in 1808; first performed at the *Theater-an-der-Wien*, in Vienna, December 22, 1808; dedicated to Prince von Lobkowitz and Count Rasoumowsky.)

After the tension and terseness, the dramatic grandeur of the Fifth Symphony, its companion work, the Sixth, is a surprising departure into relaxation and placidity. One can imagine the composer dreaming away lazy hours in the summer heat at
282

Döbling or Grinzing, lingering in the woods, by a stream or at a favorite tavern, while the gentle, droning themes of the Symphony hum in his head, taking limpid shapes. The Symphony, of course, requires in the listener something of this relaxation, a complete attunement to a mood which lingers fondly and unhurried. Those who look for dramatic contrasts, peaks of excitement in their music, will always find the "Pastoral," except for the storm episode, unsatisfying. Those who can drift without sense of urgency upon the current of Beethoven's placid stream in the *Szene am Bach* will readily accept the composer's thematic reiteration on account of the felicities of detail constantly unfolded—ever fresh and varied.

Opening in the key of F major, which according to the testimony of Schindler was to Beethoven the inevitable sunny key for such a subject, the Symphony lays forth two themes equally melodic and even-flowing. They establish the general character of the score, in that they have no marked accent or striking feature; the tonal and dynamic range is circumscribed, and the expression correspondingly delicate, and finely graded. There is no labored development, but a drone-like repetition of fragments from the themes, a sort of murmuring monotony, in which the composer charms the ear with a continuous, subtle alteration of tonality, color, position. One is reminded (here and in the slow movement) of the phenomena of floral growth, where simplicity and charm of surface conceal infinite variety, and organic intricacy.

The slow movement opens suggestively with an accompaniment of gently falling thirds, in triplets, a murmuring string figure which the composer alters but never forgets for long, giving the entire movement a feeling of motion despite its long-drawn melodic line. The accompaniment is lulling, but no less so than the graceful undulation of the melody over it. The episode of the bird-calls inserted before the three concluding measures has come in for plentiful comment, and cries of *"Malerei."* * The flute trill of the nightingale, the repeated oboe note of the quail (in characteristic rhythm) and the falling third (clarinet) of the

* *"Mehr Ausdruck der Empfindung als Malerei,"* "More an expression of feeling than painting" was Beethoven's inscription on the score.

cuckoo are blended into an integrated phrase in a pendant to the coda before its final rapturous cadence. Beethoven may have referred to these bars as a "joke" in a conversation with Schindler, but it was a whim refined so as to be in delicate keeping with the affecting *pianissimo* of his close. Perhaps his most serious obstacle was to overcome the remembrance among his critics of cruder devices in bird imitation.

The third movement is a *scherzo* in form and character, though not so named, and, as such, fills symphonic requirements, fits in with the "program" scheme by providing a country dance, and brings the needed brightness and swift motion after the long placidities. The Trio begins with a delightful oboe solo, to a simple whispered accompaniment for the violins and an occasional dominant and octave from the bassoon, as if two village fiddlers and a bassoonist (at a tavern in Mödling) were doing their elementary best.

There is a brief episode of real rustic vigor in duple time, a reprise, likewise brief, which rises to a high pitch of excitement, and is broken off suddenly on its dominant of F by the ominous rumble of the 'cellos and basses in a tremolo on D-flat. The storm is sometimes looked upon as the fourth of five movements. It forms a sort of transition from the *Scherzo* to the *Finale*, which two movements it binds without a break. The instrumental forces which Beethoven calls upon are of interest. In his first two movements, he scaled his sonority to the moderation of his subject, using only the usual wood winds and strings, with no brass excepting the horns, and no percussion. The *Scherzo* he appropriately brightened by adding a trumpet to his scheme. In the storm music he heightens his effects with a piccolo and two trombones, instruments which he had used in his symphonies for the first time when he wrote his Fifth. The trombones are retained in the *Finale*, but they are sparingly used. The timpani make their only entrance into the Symphony when Beethoven calls upon them for his rolls and claps of thunder; and he asks for no other percussion. Some have found Beethoven's storm technique superseded by such composers as Liszt, who outdid his predecessor in cataclysmic effects, and at the same time put the stamp of sensationalism upon chromatics and dimin-

284

ished seventh chords. Beethoven could easily have appalled and terrified his audience with devices such as he later used in his *Battle of Vittoria,* had he chosen to plunge his Pastoral Symphony to the pictorial level of that piece, mar its idyllic proportions, and abandon the great axiom which he set himself on its title page. Beethoven must have delighted in summer thunder showers, and enjoyed, so his friends have recorded, being drenched by them. This one gives no more than a momentary contraction of fear as it assembles and breaks. It clothes Nature in majesty always—in surpassing beauty at its moment of ominous gathering and its moment of clearing and relief. Critics, listening to the broad descending scale of the oboe as the rumbling dies away, have exclaimed "the rainbow"—and any listener is at liberty to agree with them.

The peace of contentment is re-established by yodeling octaves, peasantlike, from the clarinet and horn, which rise to jubilation in the *"Hirtengesang,"* the shepherd's song of thanks in similar character, sung by the violins. Beethoven first noted in the sketchbooks the following title for the *Finale:* "Expression of Thankfulness. Lord, we thank Thee"; whereupon we need only turn to Sturm's *Lehr und Erbauungs Buch,* from which Beethoven copied lines expressing a sentiment very common at the time: the "arrival at the knowledge of God," through Nature— "the school of the heart." He echoed the sentiment of his day in his constant praise of "God in Nature," but the sentiment happened also to be a personal conviction with him, a conviction which, explain it how you will, lifted a music of childlike simplicity of theme to a rapturous song of praise without equal, moving sustained and irresistible to its end. One cannot refrain from remarking upon the magnificent passage in the coda where the orchestra makes a gradual descent, serene and gently expanding, from a high-pitched *fortissimo* to a murmuring *pianissimo.* There is a not unsimilar passage before the close of the first movement. (See pages 118, 120, 123, 129.)

SYMPHONY NO. 7 IN A MAJOR, OP. 92

Poco sostenuto; Vivace
Allegretto
Presto; Assai meno presto; Tempo primo
Allegro con brio

(Completed in the summer of 1812,* first performed on December 8, 1813, in the hall of the University of Vienna, Beethoven conducting. The score and probably the parts were published in 1816; the dedication is to Count Moritz von Fries.)

It would require more than a technical yardstick to measure the true proportions of this Symphony—the sense of immensity which it conveys. Beethoven seems to have built up this impression by wilfully driving a single rhythmic figure through each movement, until the music attains (particularly in the body of the first movement, and in the *Finale*) a swift propulsion, an effect of cumulative growth which is akin to extraordinary size.

The long introduction unfolds two vistas, the first extending into a succession of rising scales, which someone has called "gigantic stairs," the second dwelling upon a melodious phrase in F major which, together with its accompaniment, dissolves into fragments and evaporates upon a point of suspense until the rhythm of the *Vivace* which is indeed the substance of the entire movement, springs gently to life (the *allegro* rhythm of the Fourth Symphony was born similarly but less mysteriously from its dissolving introduction). The rhythm of the main body of the movement, once released,

holds its swift course almost without cessation until the end. There is no contrasting theme. When the dominant tonality comes in the rhythm persists as in the opening movement of the

---

* The manuscript score was dated by the composer "1812; 13ten - -"; then follows the vertical stroke of the name of the month, the rest of which a careless binder trimmed off, leaving posterity perpetually in doubt whether it was May, June or July.

Fifth Symphony which this one resembles and outdoes in its pervading rhythmic *ostinato,* the *"cellule"* as d'Indy would have called it. The movement generates many subjects within its pattern, which again was something quite new in music. Even the Fifth Symphony, with its violent, dynamic contrasts, gave the antithesis of sustained, expansive motion. Schubert's great Symphony in C major, very different of course from Beethoven's Seventh, makes a similar effect of size by similar means in its *Finale.* Beethoven's rhythmic imagination is more virile. Starting from three notes it multiplies upon itself until it looms, leaping through every part of the orchestra, touching a new secret of beauty at every turn. Wagner called the Symphony "the dance in its highest condition, the happiest realization of the movements of the body in ideal form." If any other composer could impel an inexorable rhythm, many times repeated, into a vast music, it was Wagner.

In the *Allegretto* Beethoven withholds his headlong, capricious mood. But the sense of motion continues in this, the most agile of his symphonic slow movements (excepting the entirely different *Allegretto* of the Eighth). It is in A minor, and subdued by comparison, but pivots no less upon its rhythmic motto, and when the music changes to A major, the clarinets and bassoons setting their melody against triplets in the violins, the basses maintain the incessant rhythm. The form was more unvarying, more challenging to monotony than that of the first movement, the scheme consisting of a melody in three phrases, the third a repetition of the second, the whole repeated many times without development other than slight ornamentation and varied instrumentation. Even through two interludes and the *fugato,* the rhythm is never broken. The variety of the movement and its replenishing interest are astounding. No other composer could have held the attention of an audience for more than a minute with so rigid a plan. Beethoven had his first audience spellbound with his harmonic accompaniment, even before he had repeated it with his melody, woven through by the violas and 'cellos. The movement was encored at once, and quickly became the public favorite, so much so that sometimes at concerts it was substituted for the slow movements of the Second and Eighth Symphonies.

The third movement is marked simply *"presto,"* although it is a *scherzo* in effect. The whimsical Beethoven of the first movement is still in evidence, with sudden outbursts, and alternations of *fortissimo* and *piano*. The Trio, which occurs twice in the course of the movement, is entirely different in character from the light and graceful *presto,* although it grows directly from a simple alternation of two notes a half tone apart in the main body of the movement. Thayer reports the refrain, on the authority of the Abbé Stadler, to have derived from a pilgrims' hymn familiar in Lower Austria.

The *Finale* has been called typical of the "unbuttoned" Beethoven. Grove finds in it, for the first time in his music, "a vein of rough, hard, personal boisterousness, the same feeling which inspired the strange jests, puns and nicknames which abound in his letters." Schumann calls it "hitting all around" (*"schlagen um sich"*). "The force that reigns throughout this movement is literally prodigious, and reminds one of Carlyle's hero Ram Dass, who had 'fire enough in his belly to burn up the entire world.'" The second subject is in the martial rhythm which Beethoven used in his later works in moments of high elation: (See pages 119, 139, 156, 167, 172-173, 178, 183, 192, 194, 220, 222.)

SYMPHONY NO. 8 IN F MAJOR, OP. 93

Allegro vivace e con brio
Allegretto scherzando
Tempo di minuetto
Allegro vivace

(Composed in 1812, completed in October; first performed at the Redoutensaal, in Vienna, February 27, 1814; the score and probably the parts were published in 1816.)

The Eighth is sometimes spoken of as the "humorous" symphony, which is apt enough if one bears in mind that humor is far from confined to this one, and that Beethoven's humor in music was something deserving a name of its own. Except that his musical jokes seem to have been a result of overflowing high spirits, they are quite unlike the verbal ones with their frequent grossness, clumsiness, or cynicism. Moods in music are never to be matched by moods outside of it, and humor is no exception. It seems to consist in this Symphony of sudden turns in the course of an even and lyrical flow, breaking in upon formal, almost archaic periods. It is a sudden irregularity showing its head where all is regular—an altered rhythm, an explosion of *fortissimo,* a foreign note or an unrelated tonality. These incongruities the composer proceeds to justify by revealing them as integral to his scheme. Each becomes right and logical with use; indeed here lies the true individuality and charm of the Symphony. This is less like joking than divine play in that pure region of tonal thinking where grossness does not exist, where revelations of the highly charged fantasy are made obliquely, approached with deliberate mystification. If the Eighth Symphony is by its nature inferior to its more striking companion the Seventh (which it followed by four months), then lyric art is to be taken as less than the epic, Shakespeare's *As You Like It* as less than *Measure for Measure.* Beethoven's Eighth Symphony finds its maker in a state of mind which has turned from grandeur to a more personal, a more heart-warming exuberance. Melody and invention come pouring forth with an exceeding fertility; fancy is furiously alive.

The first movement opens squarely on the beat with a melody thoroughly delightful, but deceptively polite, with its twelve-bar period divided equally into three parts and ending on a neat cadence:

Another figure promises to be even more cadential, but at its repetition falls instead into a rhythm which is much to be used, and which, echoed by the strings on C sharp and A, brings in the second theme which starts upon D major, wanders engagingly, and winds up in C. Light staccato arpeggios announce a rhythm which breaks into a faster one, and in its first form finds a melody:

290

This is the basic rhythm of the opening theme; it is to introduce the development and again the coda on a light, wagging octave figure; indeed it is to pervade the movement. The development finds its complete thesis in the first-bar phrase of the theme. Indeed the composer needs nothing more, as in some of the most delightful pages of the Symphony he passes it about, throws it into the bass, and drives it through rising sequences into a triple *forte* statement of the theme. There is a full recapitulation and a coda which takes for its text the third-bar phrase of the same theme.

Berlioz wrote of the *Allegretto scherzando* that it "fell straight from heaven into the brain of its author, and was written in one stroke." But Berlioz was as deceived as all are by Beethoven's moments of apparent spontaneity; there were many sketches. This is the shortest of the symphonic slow movements, occupying eighty-one bars and less than five minutes in performance, consisting of a section repeated with varying detail, and a nine-bar coda. This canon which Beethoven wrote upon the theme gives the point of the story:

Since development would have labored the joke and trumpets and drums overridden its neat wit, all these are dispensed with, the

291

basses roaring out the explosive endings. The winds in light staccato chords imitate the ticking machine, while the strings play with the gay theme also found in the canon. Oulibicheff called this movement a travesty upon Rossini, and others, Berlioz conspicuously, could not reconcile themselves to the abrupt ending. But abrupt endings were Beethoven's point; there is no other kind in the Symphony, nor could anything have ended more abruptly than the first movement.

The third movement is most free from surprises. The themes are as naïve and thoroughly engaging as the Symphony of consistently engaging qualities calls for. Wagner was surely right in berating Mendelssohn for reading *Tempo di Menuetto* over the movement and taking it as fast as a *Ländler*. Its repose and easy *Gemütlichkeit* would be lost by hastening, and so would the bloom of its dainty coloring: the trumpet call which gives a lift to the opening phrase and the bassoons which give the last comment to the minuet proper; the horns and clarinets in the trio.

It is in the *Finale* that speed is in order, although probably neither Beethoven, Wagner or Mendelssohn would have approved the speed at which it is usually taken in our day. The opening theme gives material for most of the movement:

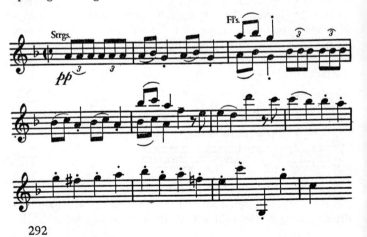

The triplets play at least as important a part as does the figure of rhythmic accompaniment in the *Allegretto*. The figure of the second bar is likewise to be the subject of much tossing about. It recalls the figure which opens the seventh bar of the Symphony and the one which is as ever-present in the *Allegretto* as plums in a pudding. There is still another fingerprint; the transitional octaves of the first movement here appear in a similar function. But here the bassoon and timpani (tuned in octaves) have them, and they wag in the even, common beat which the theme has established. This, as well as being the longest and most eventful movement, is the most unbuttoned. Commentators for years scratched their heads over it, feeling that this at last was carrying fun too far. The worst offense seems to have been the C sharp which bursts upon the scene unaccountably as the first theme is purring on C in the key of F. The trouble was that the composer failed to account for it, continuing blithely in the tonic key as if nothing had happened. Only in the recapitulation did he explain his C sharp by going into F sharp minor. Even reasonable men were disturbed. Sir George Grove, as recently as 1896, found the first and last movements "darkened by outbursts of unmistakable wrath." Needless to say, audiences of today sit before the terrible C sharps with entire equanimity. This movement has elements of a rondo—whether or not it is to be called one is quite inessential. The sections are preposterously unequal in length by literal count, and as beautifully and unerringly proportioned as Beethoven's music always is. The coda, if it must have a name, is almost as long as the whole remainder of the movement. It is in effect a second development, uncovering new material for the enhancement of the old. (See pages 119, 139, 167-169, 173, 183, 194, 220.)

SYMPHONY NO. 9 IN D MINOR, WITH FINAL CHORUS ON SCHILLER'S *ODE TO JOY*, OP. 125

Allegro, ma non troppo, un poco maestoso
Molto vivace: Presto
Adagio molto e cantabile

*Presto—Allegro assai—Presto—*Baritone Recitative—Quartet
and Chorus: *Allegro assai—*Tenor Solo and Chorus: *Allegro
assai vivace, alla marcia—*Chorus: *Allegro assai—*Chorus: *Andante Maestoso—Adagio, ma non troppo, ma divoto—Allegro
energico, sempre ben mercato—*Quartet and Chorus: *Allegro
ma non tanto; Prestissimo*

(Completed in 1824, first performed at the *Kärnthnerthor Theater,*
May 7, 1824; published in 1825 or 1826; dedicated to Friedrich Wilhelm III of Prussia.)

Themes which are gradually unfolded from mysterious mur-
murings in the orchestra—no uncommon experience nowadays—
all date back to the opening measures of the Ninth Symphony,
where Beethoven conceived the idea of building a music of indeterminate open fifths on the dominant, and accumulating a great
crescendo of suspense until the theme itself is revealed in the
pregnant key of D minor, proclaimed fortissimo by the whole
orchestra in unison. It might be added that no one since has quite
equaled the mighty effect of Beethoven's own precedent—not
even Wagner, who held this particular page in mystic awe, and
no doubt remembered it when he depicted the elementary serenity
of the Rhine in a very similar manner at the opening of the *Ring.*

The development in this, the longest of Beethoven's first movements, moves with unflagging power and majesty through many
an episode, many a sudden illumination from some fragment of
his themes. At the restatement of the main theme the orchestra
is flooded with the triumph of the D major long withheld. The
long coda, coming at the point where it would seem that nothing
more could be said on a much developed subject, calls forth new
vistas from the inexhaustible imagination of the tone magician
who needed little more than a simple chord upon which to erect
his vast schemes.

For the only time in his symphonies, Beethoven in this case
put his *Scherzo* second in order and before the slow movement. A
Scherzo it is in everything but name, with the usual repeats, trio,
and *da capo* (with bridge passages added). There is the dance-
like character of earlier *Scherzos,* and an echo of rusticity in the
trio, recalling the Sixth and Seventh. Yet all is lifted to the pre-
294

vailing mood of rarefied purity as this movement, like the others, adds a new voice to an old form. This *Scherzo* has been called "a miracle of repetition in monotony," by virtue of the incessant impact of its rhythm (associated with the kettledrums, tuned in octaves) which keeps a constant course through the most astonishing variety in modulation, color, counterpoint. The movement begins as a five-voice fugue, recalling the fact that Beethoven first conceived the theme as the subject for a fugue—the earliest of his sketches which eventually found its way into this symphony. The Trio continues the contrapuntal interest by the combination of two themes. The famous passage for the oboe against wind chords reminded Berlioz of "the effect produced by the fresh morning air, and the first rays of the rising sun in May."

The slow movement is built upon two themes whose structural relation lies principally in contrast: the first, *adagio* in B-flat, 4-4 time, the second, *andante moderato* in D major, triple time. After the almost static *adagio,* the second theme attains flowing motion in its melody, which Beethoven has marked *"espressivo."* This theme recurs in alternation with the other, but unlike the other is hardly varied, except in the instrumentation. The *adagio* theme undergoes variations of increasingly intricate melodic ornament like those by which Beethoven also lifted his last sonatas and quartets to such indescribable beauty.

The *Finale* opens with a frank discord, followed by a stormy and clamorous *presto* of seven bars. It is as if the composer, having wrested from his first three movements the very utmost drop that was in them, is still restless and unsatisfied. He must still advance upon his divine adventure, cast off his tragic or poignant moods, find some new expression, fulsome and radiant. A few measures of each movement are reviewed, and after each a recitative in the 'cellos and basses gives an answer of plain rejection; in the first two cases brusquely, in the case of the *adagio* softened by a tender memory. Beethoven's instruments seem on the very verge of speech. A hint of the coming choral theme is breathed in gentle accents by the wood winds, to which the recitative, now no longer confined to the strings, gives a convincing affirmative. Thereupon the theme in full is unfolded in its rightful D major. It is first heard in the utter simplicity of

295

the low strings in unison, *piano*. Gradually harmonies and instruments are added, until the exposition has been completely made, but not even yet has the composer left the instrumental field.

Once more there is the noisy *presto* passage, and the composer introduces words for the first time into a symphony. The baritone has this recitative:

"O Freunde, nicht diese Töne,	*"O brothers, these sad tones no longer!*
sondern lasst uns angenehmere	*Rather raise we now our voices,*
anstimmen, und freudenvollere."	*And joyful be our song!"*

There immediately follow the first three verses of Schiller's Ode, by the solo quartet and chorus:

Freude, schöner Götterfunken,	*Joy, thou spark from flame immortal*
Tochter aus Elysium,	*Daughter of Elysium!*
Wir betreten feuertrunken,	*Drunk with fire, heav'n born Goddess,*
Himmlische, dein Heiligthum.	*We invade thy halidom!*
Deine Zauber binden wieder,	*Let thy magic bring together*
Was die Mode streng getheilt;	*All whom earth-born laws divide;*
Alle Menschen werden Brüder,	*All mankind shall be as brothers*
Wo dein sanfter Flügel weilt.	*'Neath thy tender wings and wide.*
Wem der grosse Wurf gelungen,	*He that's had that best good fortune,*
Eines Freundes Freund zu sein,	*To his friend a friend to be,*
Wer ein holdes Weib errungen,	*He that's won a noble woman,*
Mische seinen Jubel ein!	*Let him join our Jubilee!*
Ja—wer auch nur eine Seele	*Ay, and who a single other*
Sein nennt auf dem Erdenrund!	*Soul on earth can call his own;*
Und wer's nie gekonnt, der stehle	*But let him who ne'er achieved it*
Weinend sich aus diesem Bund.	*Steal away in tears alone.*
Freude trinken alle Wesen	*Joy doth every living creature*
An den Brüsten der Natur;	*Draw from Nature's ample breast;*
Alle Guten, alle Bösen	*All the good and all the evil*
Folgen ihrer Rosenspur.	*Follow on her roseate quest.*
Küsse gab sie uns und Reben,	*Kisses doth she give, and vintage,*
Einen Freund, geprüft im Tod;	*Friends who firm in death have stood;*
Wollust ward dem Wurm gegeben,	*Joy of life the worm receiveth,*
Und der Cherub steht vor Gott.	*And the Angels dwell with God!*

The four line chorus (to the unused fourth verse) summons in Beethoven's imagination a marching host, and he gives it to proud and striding measures *"alla Marcia,"* adding piccolo, double bassoon, triangle, cymbals, and bass drum to his orchestra (again for the first time in a symphony). This is the verse, given to the tenor solo and chorus:

Froh, wie seine Sonnen fliegen	*Glad as burning suns that glorious*
Durch des Himmels prächt'gen Plan,	*Through the heavenly spaces sway,*
Laufet, Brüder, eure Bahn,	*Haste ye brothers, on your way,*
Freudig, wie ein Held zum Siegen.	*Joyous as a knight victorious.*

After the excitement of this variation, Beethoven allows himself to be alone with his instruments once more, and for the last time, in a double fugue. The chorus next sings (*andante maestoso*) the following short verse of far-flung import, calling upon three trombones to add to the impressiveness of the sonority:

Seid umschlungen, Millionen!	*Love to countless millions swelling,*
Diesen Kuss der ganzen Welt!	*Wafts one kiss to all the world!*
Brüder—überm Sternenzelt	*Surely, o'er yon stars unfurl'd,*
Muss ein lieber Vater wohnen!	*Some kind Father has his dwelling!*

A religious *adagio* in a mood of mystic devotion is the setting of the following verse:

Ihr stürzt nieder, Millionen?	*Fall ye prostrate, O ye millions!*
Ahnest du den Schöpfer, Welt?	*Dost thy Maker feel, O world?*
Such' ihn überm Sternenzelt!	*Seek Him o'er yon stars unfurl'd,*
Ueber Sternen muss er wohnen.	*O'er the stars rise His pavilions!*

But the key verse of the movement is the first: "*Freude, schöner Götterfunken,*" and this, with its chorus: "*Seid umschlungen, Millionen,*" is resumed by the quartet and chorus, and finally exalted to its sweeping climax in the coda, *prestissimo*. (See pages 89, 119, 193, 195, 211, 219-226, 229, 247.)

OTHER ORCHESTRAL MUSIC

OVERTURE TO COLLIN'S TRAGEDY *CORIOLAN,* OP. 62

(Composed in 1807, probably first performed at a subscription concert of Prince Lobkowitz in Vienna, March, 1807. Published in 1808 with a dedication to Court Secretary Heinrich J. von Collin.)

This overture has no aspect of a commission. It is really a concert piece, and was not in Beethoven's time, so far as is known, performed in connection with the play, which had been on the boards five years when it was written. Beethoven was undoubtedly drawn by the subject. He knew Collin, and had been attempting to collaborate with him in an opera. He knew Plutarch's account of the Roman General and Shakespeare's play —both were in his library. All three may have influenced his conception. Both dramatists took Plutarch's portrayal, the patrician warrior, a brave and reckless conqueror, retaliating scornfully when his contempt of the plebeian rabble aroused their enmity. Exiled, he joined the Volscians, the traditional enemy of Rome, and marched with them against his own people. In desperation, as Rome seemed about to fall, a delegation of women went out from the city, led by the mother and the wife of Coriolanus. They went to his tent and beseeched him on their knees to relent. The pride and determination of the soldier were at last subdued by the moving words of his mother, who pictured the eternal disgrace which he threatened to bring upon his own family. Coriolanus yielded and withdrew the forces under his command, thus bringing the anger of the Volscian leaders upon his own head. He was slain by them according to the version of Shakespeare; according to Collin he was driven to suicide. Collin's characters in action are more idealized and formalized, as if in the manner of the Greek tragedians. Coriolanus is a figure caught by fate, for he cannot in honor break his oath of fealty to the Volscians, a dilemma which must destroy him. The famous scene in which the inner struggle of honor, pride and love reaches its climax seems to be the direct subject of Beethoven's overture. The opening chords, proud and ferocious, implacable, limn Coriolanus in a few bold strokes. The second subject, gentle and melodious, seems to introduce the moving protestations of the mother. Shakespeare's far more human emotion in this scene must have touched the composer. The contrasting musical subject of Coriolanus recurs, at first resistant but gradually softening, until at the end there is entire capitulation.

It is not hard to see in Coriolanus the figure of Beethoven himself. The composer must have felt strangely close to the Roman noble infinitely daring, the arch individualist, the despiser of meanness and ignorance who, taking his own reckless course, yielding to none, at last found himself alone in the world, clad in an armor of implacability which only one power could penetrate—the tenderness of feminine persuasion. (See page 114.)

"WELLINGTONS SIEG, ODER DIE SCHLACHT BEI VITTORIA" ("WELLINGTON'S VICTORY, OR THE BATTLE OF VITTORIA"), OP. 91

    1 The Battle
           March: "Rule Britannia"
           March: "Marlborough"
           Battle
    2 Victory Symphony
           Intrada: *Allegro con brio*

(First performed December 8, 1813, in celebration of the victory of

July 27, 1813. Published in 1816, and dedicated to the Prince Regent of England, later George IV.) (See pages 171-174, 177, 191.)

OVERTURE IN C MAJOR, OP. 115

(Composed in 1814 "for the name day of our Kaiser"—October 4th. First performed December 25, 1815, and published 1825, with a dedication to Prince Anton Heinrich Radziwill.) (See page 192.)

OVERTURE IN C MAJOR, *"DIE WEIHE DES HAUSES"* ("THE CONSECRATION OF THE HOUSE"), OP. 124

(Composed in late September, 1822; for the opening of the Josephstädter Theater, October 3, 1822. Published in 1825, dedicated to Prince Nicolaus Galitzin.) (See page 215.)

ORCHESTRAL WORKS
WITHOUT
OPUS NUMBER

TWELVE MINUETS
TWELVE GERMAN DANCES

(Composed in 1795, for a Benefit Ball in the small Redoutensaal, Vienna, November 22, 1795; published in the same year in piano arrangement.)

TWELVE CONTRADANCES

(Composed in 1802; published in 1803.)

ELEVEN VIENNESE DANCES

(Nottebohm does not list these dances, but Hugo Riemann edited them in 1907 as composed in the summer of 1819, at Mödling, for performance by a village band. They consist of Waltzes, Minuets, and *Länderer*.)

ALLEGRETTO IN E-FLAT (*"GRATULATIONS —MENUET"*)

(Composed in 1822; published in 1835.)

PIECES FOR MILITARY BAND

TWO MILITARY MARCHES (1809, 1816)
POLONAISE (1810)
ECOSSAISE (1810)

The "Jena" Symphony, so called, was brought to general attention in 1911 by Prof. Fritz Stein of the University of Jena, where he had found it in the archives of the College of Music. It was in C major, and consisted of manuscript parts, on two of which the name of Beethoven was written in pencil, in an unknown hand. Prof. Stein conjectured that Beethoven may have sent the Symphony to Jena from Bonn in his student years. Its authenticity, however, has been widely doubted.

THE CONCERTOS

PIANO CONCERTO NO. 1 IN C MAJOR, OP. 15

Allegro con brio
Largo
Rondo: Allegro

(Composed in 1797; first performed at Prague in 1798; published in 1801; dedicated to the Princess Odescalcchi.)

The Concerto in C major, the second in order of composition, is almost as Mozartean as its predecessor, numbered as second. Nothing Beethoven wrote is closer to Mozart than these two concertos. What Mozart had done in matching the two mediums must have held the destined successor in a sort of reverential awe.* But it was not the awe of constraint. The concertos tell, rather, of whole-hearted acceptance, warm idealization. In the two concertos Mozart's custom of a long orchestral exposition is closely imitated. The delayed entrance of the soloist is similarly effective as a free, pliable, individual voice—a device as dramatic as the first entrance of the principal actor in a play after dialogue to whip up suspense. Listening to this orchestral exposition, one

* Beethoven was at an Augarten concert with John Cramer, the pianist-composer, when Mozart's Concerto in C minor (K.491) was being performed. A fresh theme in the rondo brought from Beethoven the exclamation—"Cramer, Cramer! We shall never be able to do anything like that!" "As the theme was repeated and wrought to a climax," says Thayer who had the anecdote from Cramer's widow, "Beethoven, swaying his body to and fro, marked the time and in every possible manner manifested a delight rising to enthusiasm." This happened in 1799, while Beethoven's C major Concerto still lay in manuscript.

can almost build up an illusion that it is Mozart indeed. Yet there are signs, and as the movement progresses the signs multiply: characteristic rising scales, twists of modulation. But there is another change—more pervasive, and more intimate. Beethoven's instruments begin to sing as Mozart's had; but in the very act of imitation the degree of incandescence is raised, the line broadened. This is particularly true of the C major Concerto, which reaches a greater point of glow than the one in B flat. The orchestra is freer, as in the *Largo,* where the second strain (given to the orchestra and designed for it) finds an impassioned pulse. The horns are used already with a special sense in this Concerto, and in the slow movement the clarinet stands out as it had not before. The orchestra is not yet liberated, but it is perceptibly finding itself. The Concerto is forward- as well as backward-looking, tapping at the door of happy discoveries to come and bringing to pass even through the fulfillment of formal expectations the spell of the poet Beethoven.

The rondo is built upon a theme in delightful irregularity of phrase, first set forth in a light staccato by the piano. A second theme, in the dominant key, given out by the strings, has been identified with the Austrian folksong *"In Mantua in Banden der treue Hofer sass":*

But the first theme holds the rudder, rondo fashion. Theme and episodes are carried out in the usual give and take of solo and *tutti.* (See pages 49, 61, 67, 73-74.)

PIANO CONCERTO NO. 2 IN B FLAT MAJOR, OP. 19

Allegro con brio
Adagio
Rondo: Molto allegro

(Composed in 1794, first performed March 29, 1795, in Vienna; revised in 1800 and published in 1801; dedicated to Carl Nikl, Noble of Nikelsberg.)

This was Beethoven's earliest orchestral score which he saw fit to publish. His dissatisfaction with it, several times expressed, may have had most to do with the piano part to which, it is believed, his several revisions were confined. Certainly it is not an inept work; each movement speaks with smooth assurance. More likely the composer's dissatisfaction came from a realization that it falls short of Mozart's superb concertos, which it plainly copies, and at the same time falls short of the warmer voice its composer knew he could find, and was indeed about to find in the concerto which shortly followed.

In a word, the Concerto in B flat, with its good measure of grace and charm, is rather too meek for Beethoven. The orchestra steps forward to take its alternate place, wood winds echoing strings, and discreetly steps into the background to make way for the soloist. The orchestra's principal function in the first movement is to announce themes which the pianist proceeds to embroider. In the *Adagio,* the embroidery sometimes weighs upon rather than enlivens the melodic line. Before the close of this *Adagio* the soloist and *tutti* have a brief dialogue which is more experimental than forceful, but which clearly points the way of concertos to come. The final rondo is gay and inconsequential. Reversing the order of the first movement, the piano states the subjects, which the orchestra takes up in turn. (See pages 48, 67, 73.)

PIANO CONCERTO NO. 3 IN C MINOR, OP. 37

Allegro con brio
Largo
Rondo: Allegro

(Composed in 1800, first performed at the *Theater-an-der-Wien*, April 5, 1803, the composer playing the solo part. Published in 1804; dedicated to Prince Louis Ferdinand of Prussia.)

The technical advance, the power and breadth of the C minor Concerto, composed only a year after the final revision of the one in C major, is proof of Beethoven's rapid development in orchestral resource at this time. The piano part, no longer treated in restricted, harpsichord style, as in the first two concertos, attains stature and sweep in its first measures. But first there is a considerable exposition by the orchestra and here too we are conscious of expansion of field—symphonic forcefulness and range of expression. This opening subject is made known in the strings:

Upon a C minor cadence the soloist enters with three furious C major scales, which, however, introduce the initial subject in its proper minor. The pianist brings in a new subject in E flat minor and repeats the regular "second" subject, equally lyrical, in E flat major. The same rushing scale passages, now in D major, introduce the development, which begins with a quizzical play upon the repeated fourths of the initial theme. After indeterminate bars, the theme settles into G minor. Twice, but without success, the orchestra tries to lead the theme into the major, so sounding its first half under a long piano trill. The cadenza for this, as for each of the first four concertos, is written separately. The *Largo,* in E major, seems earlier in style. The first theme, if found in one of the early piano sonatas, might

306

have seemed quite in place. It is stated by the piano, sung in turn by the muted strings. A second theme is more ornamentally treated by soloist and orchestra. A third theme is carried by the wood winds over piano arpeggios. There is a reprise, and short cadenza *"con gran espressione"* before the close. The rondo brings back the C minor tonality and (according to formula) more than once, despite some remarkable vagaries. A presto *coda* derives a fresh theme from the labored one and, in a rush of C major, carries the movement to a close. (See pages 49, 73, 87.)

PIANO CONCERTO NO. 4 IN G MAJOR, OP. 58

Allegro moderato
{ *Andante con moto*
{ *Rondo vivace*

(Composed 1804, 1805 or 1806; first performed at the house of Prince Lobkowitz, in Vienna, in March 1807, first publicly performed at the *Theater-an-der-Wien*, December 22, 1808, the composer as soloist. Published in 1808; dedicated to the Archduke Rudolph.)

The Fourth, being a soft-spoken concerto, was for many years overlooked, passed by for the more striking Third or Fifth; it has at length (and permanently) come into its own. Disregarding the usual requirements of flash and display in the first movement of a concerto, Beethoven builds the initial *Allegro* on gently melodic material, through which the piano weaves its embroidery. The solo instrument opens quietly with a five-bar phrase of the first theme, as if to claim its place in the sun, whereupon the orchestra proceeds alone, and according to precedent, with the full exposition. The development, with voices of solo and orchestra blended, brings in its course two further themes, each lyrical in character.

The *Andante con moto*, which has no like in the literature of concertos, contains within its seventy bars a message whose import words cannot convey. It consists of a dialogue between the string choir and the piano. The former states a short, im-

307

perious phrase in octaves, *forte* and *staccato;* it is a recitative, and yet it is more. The piano answers with a melody of indescribable tenderness. The two opposing voices continue their alternate phrases, but before the soft plea of the piano, increasingly irresistible, the austerity of the strings is gradually mollified, until it capitulates altogether, subsiding into a breathless *pianissimo.* The last whispering suspended chord of the piano is swept away as the *vivace* theme of the rondo (further brightened by the restoration of the major mode) is delivered *pianissimo* by the strings, with its sprightly answering theme in the piano. The *Finale* follows a more usual course to a brilliant conclusion. (See pages 108, 114, 121.)

PIANO CONCERTO NO. 5 IN E FLAT MAJOR, "EMPEROR," OP. 73

Allegro
{ *Adagio un poco mosso*
{ *Rondo: Allegro ma non tanto*

(Completed in 1809, first performed at Leipzig by Johann Schneider, probably in 1810. Published in 1811 with a dedication to the Archduke Rudolph.)

The "Emperor" Concerto failed unequivocally when it was first performed in Vienna in February, 1812. The fault was not with the piece, which had done well at Leipzig, nor with the soloist, who was Beethoven's devoted and talented pupil Karl Czerny. It was no doubt the audience, which called itself the "Society of Noble Ladies for Charity," and, loudly applauding three living tableaux, paid little attention to the new piece by Beethoven. Castelli's *Thalia,* a contemporary periodical, gave this reason: "Beethoven, full of proud confidence in himself, never writes for the multitude; he demands understanding and feeling, and because of the intentional difficulties, he can receive these only at the hands of the connoisseurs, a majority of whom is not to be found on such occasions."

The assemblage at this concert, probably in the mood for light diversion, no doubt missed altogether the very different voice of Beethoven which underlay its expected aspect of thundering chords, cadenza-like passages in scales, trills, arpeggios, forms which in lesser hands are so often the merest bombast. They failed to see that, accepting the style which custom had dictated to him, Beethoven had transformed it into something quite different, had written his signature into every measure. The three emphatic chords from the orchestra in the introduction, each followed by solo passages of elaborate bravura, establish at once a music of sweeping and imperious grandeur unknown to any concerto written up to 1812, and beside which the dignity of emperors or archdukes loses all consequence.

There follow almost a hundred measures in which the orchestra alone lays forth the two themes and develops them in leisurely amplitude. The piano from this point assumes the first place, and makes the themes, so symphonically cast, now primarily its own. The solo part traverses elaborate figures which, however, never obscure the thematic outlines, but unfailingly intensify them and enhance the development. Beethoven writes his own cadenza into the score, and, by explicit direction, forestalls weakling interpolations. The slow movement (in B major) is short, like that of the G major concerto, and like that illustrious predecessor consists of a sort of duologue between orchestra and piano. Here the muted strings intone their noble and tender theme, which the piano answers with a *pianissimo* passage of its own, in gently descending triplets. The free, searching improvisation of the piano ascends by trills in half-steps, arousing a sense of expectancy which is resolved as it clarifies at last upon the theme of the orchestra. The piano sings the theme in a full exposition. Wood winds and strings are then softly blended with a dreamy and constantly shifting figure from the piano. The music dies away upon a mysterious sense of anticipation, and over a sustained note of the horns the piano gives a soft intimation, still in the *adagio* tempo, of the lively rondo theme which immediately follows. The piano takes the thematic lead in this finale, which is long, and brilliantly developed. (See pages 108, 123, 138-139.)

CONCERTO FOR VIOLIN IN D MAJOR, OP. 61

Allegro, ma non troppo
Larghetto
Rondo

(Composed in 1806, first performed by Franz Clement at the *Theater-an-der-Wien* in Vienna, December 23, 1806. Published in 1809 with a dedication to "his friend" Stephan von Breuning.)

The autograph score bears this punning and polyglot inscription: *"Concerto par Clemenza pour Clement, primo Violino e direttore al theatro di Vienna Dal L. v. Bthvn."* Why Clement did not finally receive the dedication we are not told; Beethoven had good reason to favor the leader of the violins at the opera. The score, according to accounts, was not completed until the last moment, and Clement, receiving the solo part too late for the final rehearsal, played the concerto "at sight." To have accomplished such a feat, or at least to boast of having accomplished it would have been Clement's way. He took pride in feats of musical memory, and, having been exploited as a boy wonder at the age of nine, was not beneath tricks to catch applause. At the concert where he played Beethoven's Concerto he edified all present with a fantasia of his own in which he held the instrument upside down.

The five introductory taps on the drum:

become the basic pattern of the entire movement. Its very commonness, squarely measuring off the bar, lends to its serviceability, makes its omnipresence natural, and gives the whole context a downright, on-the-beat character. The rhythm is inherent in two phrases of the main theme and the last phrase of the second theme. It is echoed between phrases in the accompaniment. It is double-quickened, used in transitional passages. The movement is one of those in which some early hearers failed to distinguish between reiteration and repetitiousness. The themes, profusely set forth, are similar in character, but endlessly variegated in the placid, untroubled course of the whole.

The *Larghetto* is subdued by mutes upon the strings; and only three pairs of instruments to match them—clarinets, bassoons and horns. The voice of the solo instrument continues in graceful lines of ornamental tracery in a musing half light. Only for a few measures in the middle section does it carry the melody. The *Rondo* theme is tossed from the middle to the high range of the instrument and then picked up by the orchestra. The horns have a theme which peculiarly belongs to them. As the development progresses the brilliance drops away to dreaming again as fragments are murmured and the delicate colorings of the horns, or bassoon, or oboes have their passing enchantments. In short, a concerto without dazzling qualities, with a solo part which asks taste, discernment in expression, and warm response. The concerto was long neglected, and when it belatedly came into its own, it came to remain. (See page 114.)

CONCERTO FOR PIANO, VIOLIN AND VIO· LONCELLO WITH ORCHESTRA, OP. 56

> *Allegro*
> { *Largo*
> { *Rondo alla Polacca*

(Completed in 1804; published in 1807; dedicated to Prince von Lobkowitz.)

The Concerto is far earlier in style than its year would suggest. Schindler conjectured that the piano part was written for the use of the Archduke Rudolph, who was then sixteen, and hardly a pianist of brilliance. (See page 108.)

OTHER WORKS
FOR SOLO INSTRUMENT
WITH ORCHESTRA

ROMANZA FOR VIOLIN AND ORCHESTRA IN G MAJOR, OP. 40

(Composed in 1803, and published in the same year, without dedication. This single slow movement is without tempo indication.)

ROMANZA FOR VIOLIN AND ORCHESTRA IN F MAJOR, OP. 50

("Two violin adagios with orchestral accompaniment" were offered for publication by Karl van Beethoven in 1802, although the Romanza in G major was apparently not completed. Opus 50 was published in 1805 [without dedication]. It is an *adagio cantabile*.)

RONDO IN B FLAT MAJOR FOR PIANO AND ORCHESTRA (WITHOUT OPUS NUMBER)

(This rondo is believed to have been intended for the Piano Concerto in the same key. It was completed by Czerny and published in 1829.)

Fantasy for Piano, Chorus and Orchestra in C minor, Op. 80. (For description, see page 329.)

MUSIC FOR THE STAGE

FIDELIO, OPERA IN TWO ACTS, OP. 72

OVERTURE
ACT ONE

ACT TWO

16 Finale (Prisoners, Townsfolk, Leonore, Marcelline, Florestan, Rocco, Pizarro, Fernando) *"Heil! Heil! Heil sei dem Tag" "Wer ein holdes Weib errungen"*

Beethoven began to compose his opera in 1803. He intended to call it *Leonore,* but it was performed, November 20, 1805, as *Fidelio, Oder die eheliche Liebe,** the title which has persisted. In the first revision, for the performance which took place March 29, 1806, the three acts were made two by combining the first and second—the original second act began with the March, No. 6. Various shortenings were made, and three numbers were omitted, which three is uncertain. The second revision, begun in March, 1814, for the revival of May 23, 1814, is the ultimate version. The first version had included three numbers subsequently omitted in one revision or the other: a trio after No. 2, a duet after No. 8, and a duet between Leonore and Florestan before their famous duet, No. 15. Principal changes in the final version were in Leonore's recitative, No. 9; the second chorus of the prisoners, in No. 10, which was added in place of a stock finale by the principal characters; the last, and visionary portion of Florestan's air, No. 11, which was added, and the *Finale,* No. 16, which was rewritten.

What is now known as Overture *Leonore* No. 2 was played at the first production; the Overture "No. 3" was written for the second production of 1806; for the revival of 1814 Beethoven wrote what is still called and still used as the Overture to *Fidelio.*

In its manner of setting forth, *Fidelio* is an example of the contemporary custom of the *Singspiel:* a series of ensemble numbers, duets, trios, quartets, interspersed with solo arias wherein each of the five principal singers is given one opportunity to declare himself, passages of spoken dialogue to speed lighter matters or to facilitate dramatic disclosures by the direct clarity of speech. There are other portions of the dialogue which call for musical intensification, where the feelings of Leonore or Florestan under the stress of their predicament exact from the composer his utmost in emotional depiction. Here the expedient is used of recitative over a running orchestral commentary. This commentary is usually far more expressive than the declamation

* *Fidelio, or Conjugal Love.*

it supports. The solos of Leonore and Florestan and Pizarro are highly dramatic. Only the ensembles with their combined asides interrupt the action and formalize the naturalistic, homely tale of the jail keeper's family. The piece ambles along inconsequentially through its first four numbers, while the audience enjoys the more musical than dramatic appeal of the coloratura air of Marcelline, or the quartet following, where canonic imitation delightfully fulfills itself, or the air in which Rocco the jail keeper and would-be father-in-law relates in buffo style how true love is built on a sound budget. We are not greatly concerned over his peasant philosophy except when, by the contrast with what is implied and shortly set forth, it throws a nobler concept of love into bolder relief. The librettist and composer keep the tone light as Marcelline indifferently teases her hopeless suitor (Jaquino) and nurtures maidenly but ardent sentiments for her father's hired assistant. This assistant is Leonore, known as "Fidelio," and disguised as a man in doublets and boots. She has ingratiated herself with this family with the secret purpose of finding out whether her suspicion is justified that her husband may be imprisoned there. She is cautious and self-possessed; for a long while the audience has no more than hints of her intent. She has Rocco as completely fooled as his daughter. He greatly favors this smart "lad" as a son-in-law and is inclined to indulge him. The dilemma grown from the disguise is hazardous to "Fidelio's" plans, but helpful too: Rocco is easily coaxed into revealing the secret of an unnamed prisoner who is slowly starving to death in a deep cell; the old man even allows "Fidelio" to accompany him into the cell. Until this point "Fidelio" shows no strong feeling. She must play her part; she cannot discourage Marcelline; she does not yet know whether the miserable victim of the political ambition of another is her husband.

With the first entrance of Pizarro the atmosphere becomes taut with his horrifying intentions. Now apprehension for both Florestan and his all-daring wife never relaxes its hold upon the listener. Agitated figures accompany Pizarro's air, sinuously chromatic, as dreadful as the composer knew how to make them, and the musical portraiture of the ruthlessly self-seeking Governor of the Prison is to be sustained. He commands sentries

315

to mount the tower and warn him of the approach of the Minister of State, who must never know that he (Pizarro) is illegally confining Florestan here to save his own threatened reputation. He orders Rocco to kill the prisoner, and when Rocco recoils decides to do it himself. Rocco is told to dig open a disused cistern in Florestan's cell so that the body can be disposed of. Leonore's horror as she learns of this, and her determination to save her husband inspire her famous aria, which so far is the high point of tension in the opera. Leonore persuades Rocco to allow the prisoners a glimpse of the sun and sky in the prison yard. The episode serves several purposes. It is a graphic reminder of the condition of the single doomed prisoner who must remain in his darkness; it furnishes a dramatic finale as the ragged, bloodless skeletons, blinking in the light of day, sing their weird, insubstantial and piteous chorus.

That chorus prepares the way for the opening of the second act, the scene which discloses Florestan in his dungeon cell. Other composers, Weber or Cherubini, might have contrived more striking and sensational effects. Beethoven did not need expertness in theatrical cunning. The hero and heroine and their predicament were now so actual to him that he found the way simply and directly as no other could have done. The scene comes to life, even to plausible life, and remains through generations of ripening musical stagecraft one of the most exciting in all opera. There is a lugubrious introduction, drum taps which tell of prison damp, and, as the curtain rises, the aria of Florestan, where, in a sudden radiance of F major, hope builds a vision of restoration through Leonore. Rocco enters with Leonore, who must assist in the horrible task of digging her husband's grave. They find Florestan sleeping, and Leonore fears at first that he is dead. She cannot discern whether the emaciated form, scarcely visible in the darkness, is really Florestan. There is an agitated duet in A minor between Leonore and the old man as they pursue their dreadful task, and a scene of spoken recitative where Florestan wakens and asks for a drop of water, which Rocco dares not give him. Leonore must still remain unrecognized, but succeeds in putting in his hand a crust of bread.

Pizarro enters, reveals his identity, and draws a knife, pre-
316

pared to put an end to the spark of life which still remains in his victim. Leonore throws herself upon Florestan with the ringing words:

"First kill his wife!"

The rest echo in astonishment: "His wife?" This electrifying scene is in the form of a melodrama with recitative. Pizarro is about to attack them both with his dagger when Leonore draws a pistol from her doublet and holds him at bay. The stressful music ceases, and from the silence there sounds clearly, at a distance, a trumpet call. It is the signal which Pizarro himself had ordered, warning of the approach of the Minister. Now, instead of protecting him, it proclaims his doom and the liberation of those he has oppressed. The number closes with music of flooding relief, and leads to a jubilant duet between the reunited pair. The finale, which shows the prison square, is a chorus of rejoicing in the spirit of the codas in the second and third overtures. The prisoners are freed, Pizarro delivered to justice, and Leonore instructed by the Minister publicly to unlock the chains of Florestan. (See pages 98-106, 110-111, 114, 117, 119, 129, 133, 174-178, 183-184, 191, 215, 222.)

THE OVERTURES TO FIDELIO

The record of the four overtures is in line with the revisions of the score itself. For the first production of *Fidelio* in Vienna, November 20, 1805, Beethoven wrote the superb overture which later came to be known as "Leonore No. 2." Rewriting the overture for the second production in the year following, using similar material, he gave it different stress, a greater and more rounded symphonic development. The result was the so-called "Leonore No. 3." When again the opera was thoroughly changed for the Vienna production of 1814, Beethoven realized that his fully developed overture was quite out of place at the head of his opera, and he accordingly wrote a typical theatre overture, soon permanently known as the *Fidelio* overture, since it was publicly accepted and became one with the opera. There remains to be accounted for the so-called Overture to "Leonore No. 1." This was discovered and performed the year after Beethoven's death, and it was immediately assumed that this was an early attempt, rejected by Beethoven in favor of the one used at the initial performance. However, Seyfried propounded the upsetting theory that this posthumous overture was the one which Beethoven wrote for an intended performance at Prague in 1808, a performance which never took place. Nottebohm, studying the sketches, agreed with him, and the judicious Thayer, supporting them, created an authoritative front which prevailed for a long time. This, of course, would place the debated overture as the third in order, a point of view highly embarrassing to those who had set forth the evolution of the three overtures from the simpler "No. 1." Of more recent writers, Paul Bekker (1912) was inclined to believe that the "No. 1" is after all the early work it was originally supposed to be, and Romain Rolland (1928) took the same stand, citing as additional authority Josef Braunstein's "excellent work, *Beethoven's Leonore-Ouvertüren, eine historisch-stilkritische Untersuchung* (1927), which enables us at last to correct the errors in which, following Seyfried and Nottebohm, criticism had become entangled." This is a convenient theory, supported by the evidence of the music itself, and dispelling the rather lame arguments that Beethoven could have shortly followed his magnificent "No. 3" with such a compromise, whether for the limitations of the Prague theatre orchestra, or for any other reason. The *Fidelio* Overture which he wrote in 1814 had no tragic pretensions. It was a serviceable theatre overture, preparing the hearer for the opening scene of Marcelline with her ironing, and her *Singspiel* suitor. The Overture No. 3 is sometimes played between the two acts, sometimes between the last two scenes, which of course is a choice of anticipating or repeating the climax as it occurs in the opera.

The Overture to Leonore No. 3 retains all of the essentials of its predecessor, Leonore No. 2.* There is the introduction, grave and songful, based upon the air of Florestan: *"In des Lebens Frühlingstagen."* The main body of the Overture, which

---

* A variant upon the "No. 2" Overture, with alterations apparently in Beethoven's own hand, was discovered in 1926, in the files of Breitkopf and Härtel at Leipzig.

begins with the same theme (*allegro*) in both cases, rises from a whispering *pianissimo* to a full proclamation. The section of working out, or dramatic struggle, attains its climax with the trumpet call (taken directly from the opera). In the "No. 2," the coda of jubilation, introduced by the famous string scales of gathering tension for the outburst, follows almost immediately the trumpet calls of deliverance—surely the inevitable dramatic logic, even though it went directly against the formal convention which required a reprise at this point. Beethoven, more closely occupied in the "No. 2" with the events of the opera itself, omitted the reprise, following the trumpet fanfare with a soft intonation of Florestan's air, a sort of hymn of thanksgiving, as if the joy of the freed prisoner must be hushed and holy in its first moments. The melody is suspended on its final cadence, and the last three unresolved notes, hovering mysteriously, become the motto of the famous string passage in which the emotion is released.

Beethoven sacrificed this direct transition in the "No. 3" Overture. He evidently felt the need of a symphonic rounding out, and accordingly inserted a full reprise, delaying the entrance of the coda of jubilation which dramatic sequence would demand closely to follow the trumpet fanfare. But the subject had developed in Beethoven's imagination to a new and electrifying potency. The fanfare, simplified and more effectively introduced, is now softly answered by the joyful theme of Florestan and Leonore used at that point in the opera (and not used in "No. 2"). The composer, with that ability to sustain a mood which is beyond analysis, keeps the feeling of suspense, of mounting joy which allows the listener no "let down" before the triumphant climax of the coda. The air of Florestan is worked in at the end of the reprise, but in tempo, as the music moves without interruption to its greatly expanded and now overwhelming coda. The "third Leonore Overture" shows in general a symphonic "tightening" and an added forcefulness. The introduction eliminates a few measures, the development many measures, in which music of the greatest beauty is discarded. Beethoven, having thus shortened his development, evens the total length by adding the reprise and enlarging the coda. (See pages 103-104, 175, 215.)

EGMONT, INCIDENTAL MUSIC TO GOETHE'S TRAGEDY, OP. 84

> *Overture*
> *Song of Clärchen (Die Trommel gerühret)*
> *Entr'acte (Act I)*
> *Entr'acte (Act II)*
> *Song of Clärchen (Freudvoll und Leidvoll)*
> *Entr'acte (Act III)*
> *Entr'acte (Act IV)*
> *Clärchen's Death*
> *Melodrama*
> *Symphony of Victory*

(Composed in 1810; first performed in connection with the drama at the *Hofburg Theater*, Vienna, May 24, 1810. The Overture was published in 1811, the remaining numbers in 1812.)

Beethoven must surely have been attracted by Goethe's likable hero—the champion of liberty and of the independence of his people, who met death on the scaffold under an unscrupulous dictator, while his courage lived on in the unconquerable spirit of his subjects.

Without going into musical particularization, it is easy to sense in the overture the main currents of the play: the harsh tyranny of the Duke of Alva, who lays a trap to seize Count Egmont in his palace and terrorizes the burghers of Brussels, as his soldiery patrol the streets, under the decree that "two or three, found conversing together in the streets, are, without trial, declared guilty of high treason"; the dumb anger of the citizens, who will not be permanently cowed; the noble defiance and idealism of Egmont which, even after his death, is finally to prevail and throw off the invader. All the thoughts of Clärchen are for the great Count Egmont, her secret lover. Her two songs, in different scenes, are thoughts of him. The "melodrama" occurs in the final scene. Egmont, treacherously seized and condemned to public execution, lies asleep in his cell. A vision appears to him in the form of the Goddess of Freedom. Her face is that of Clärchen. She tells him that his death will secure the freedom of the provinces. The "symphony of victory" is heard as he marches away to his death. It is identical with the close of the Overture. (See pages 139, 142, 146, 151, 192.)

DIE RUINEN VON ATHEN, INCIDENTAL MUSIC TO A PLAY (*"NACHSPIEL"*) BY AUGUST VON KOTZEBUE, OP. 113

Overture
1 Chorus: *"Tochter des mächtigen Zeus"*
2 Duet: *"Ohne Verschulden"*
3 Chorus of Dervishes: *"Du hast in deines Ärmels Falten"*
4 *Marcia alla turca*
5 Music Off-Stage
6 March with Chorus: *"Schmückt die Altäre"*
7 Recitative and Aria (*"Will unser Genius"*) with Chorus: *"Wir tragen empfängliche Herzen im Busen"*
8 Chorus: *"Heil unserm König!"*

(Composed in 1811 for the opening of the Theatre in Pesth and performed there—together with the *King Stephen* music—February 9, 1812. The Overture was published in 1823, the music complete in 1846. The March with Chorus, No. 6, was rewritten for the opening of the *Josephstädter Theater* in Vinena, and performed there together with the Overture "The Consecration of the House" on October 3, 1822. This revision was published as Opus 114 in that year.) (See pages 173, 192.)

"KÖNIG STEPHAN, ODER UNGARNS ERSTER WOHLTÄTER" ("KING STEPHEN, OR HUNGARY'S FIRST BENEFACTOR"), INCIDENTAL MUSIC TO A PLAY (*"VORSPIEL"*) BY AUGUST VON KOTZEBUE, OP. 117

Overture
1 Men's Chorus: *"Ruhend von seinen Thaten"*

321

2 Men's Chorus: *"Auf dunkelm Irrweg"*
3 Victory March
4 Women's Chorus: *"Wo die Unschuld"*
5 Melodrama
6 Chorus: *"Eine neue strahlende Sonne"*
7 Melodrama
8 Ghostly March and Melodrama with Chorus: *"Heil unserm König!"*
9 Final Chorus: *"Heil unsern Enkeln!"*

(Composed, together with the music for *The Ruins of Athens*, for the opening of the Theatre in Pesth, February 9, 1812. The Overture was published in 1826; the music complete in 1864.) (See page 192.)

DIE GESCHÖPFE DES PROMETHEUS ("THE CREATIONS OF PROMETHEUS") BALLET, OP. 43

Overture: *Adagio; allegro molto con brio*
1 Introduction *(Allegro non troppo; Poco adagio)*
2 *Adagio*
3 *Allegro vivace*
4 *Maestoso; andante*
5 *Adagio*
6 *Un poco adagio; allegro*
7 *Grave*
8 *Marcia: allegro con brio*
9 *Adagio*
10 *Pastorale: allegro*
11 *Andante*
12 *Maestoso*
13 *Allegro*
14 *Andante*
15 *Andantino*
16 *Finale: allegretto*

(Composed in 1800; first performed in March, 1801, at the Imperial Court Theatre in Vienna; published in 1802; dedicated to the Princess Karl Lichnowsky.)

Salvatore Vigano, Milanese dancer and designer of ballets, decided in 1800 to pay tribute to Maria Theresa, the second wife of the Emperor Francis, and ordered Beethoven to provide music for an allegorical piece on Prometheus, the Greek God who, according to the first programme, led people out of their ignorance, and refined them by means of the arts and sciences. The *"Geschöpfe,"* variously translated as the "Creatures," "Creations" or "Men" of Prometheus, were two statues which he brought to life and "through the power of harmony made sensitive to all the human passions." In the ballet he leads them to Apollo, who submits them to instruction in the arts and graces by the muses. The ballet had a pronounced success, and survived numerous performances. (See pages 74, 96, 192.)

STAGE MUSIC WITHOUT OPUS NUMBER

RITTERBALLET

(Composed in 1790. The Ballet, which contains eight numbers, was published in Breitkopf and Härtel's complete edition, in 1887.) (See page 24.)

TRIUMPH-MARSCH IN C MAJOR FOR KUFFNER'S TRAGEDY ("TARPEJA")

(Composed in 1813 for a performance March 26, 1813; published in a piano arrangement, 1819.)

GERMANIA'S WIEDERGEBURT ("GERMANIA'S REBIRTH"), FINAL CHORUS FROM TREITSCHKE'S PLAY *"GUTE NACHRICHT"* ("GOOD TIDINGS")

For Bass with Chorus and Orchestra

(Composed in 1814, and performed with the play at the **Kärnthnerthor Theater,** April 11, 1814. Published in piano arrangement in June.)

323

"ES IST VOLLBRACHT" ("IT IS FULFILLED"), FINAL CHORUS FROM TREITSCHKE'S PLAY *"DIE EHRENPFORTEN"* ("THE TRIUMPHAL ARCH")

For Bass with Chorus and Orchestra

(Composed in 1815, and performed with the play at the *Kärnthner-thor Theater,* July 15, 1815. Published in piano arrangement, July 24th.)

MUSIC TO FRIEDRICH DUNCKER'S DRAMA, *LEONORE PROHASKA*

(Four numbers; composed in 1815.)

CHORUS FOR THE FESTIVAL PLAY, *DIE WEIHE DES HAUSES*

(Text by Carl Meisl; set for solo and chorus, with orchestra: composed in 1822.)

CHORAL WORKS

MISSA SOLEMNIS IN D MAJOR FOR ORCHESTRA, CHORUS AND FOUR SOLO VOICES, OP. 123

Kyrie: Assai sostenuto (Mit Andacht); Andante assai ben marcato; Tempo primo
Gloria: Allegro vivace; Larghetto; Allegro
Credo: Allegro ma non troppo; Adagio; Andante; Allegro; Grave
Sanctus: Adagio (Mit Andacht); Allegro pesante; Presto; Preludium: Sostenuto ma non troppo; Benedictus; Andante molto cantabile
Agnus Dei: Adagio; Allegretto vivace; Allegro vivace; Tempo primo

(Composed 1818-1823; first performed at St. Petersburg, Russia, April 6, 1824; published 1826 with a dedication to the Archduke Rudolph of Austria.)

The *Missa Solemnis,* written at a high level of intense feeling, was not designed with any thought of average receptivity. The tension is too unrelieved, the moments of brilliance, vivid delineation, affecting tenderness, too fleeting for ready assimilation. There is a marked absence of broad and telling effects to capture the casual attention of the lay public—tunefully-built, reiterative choruses in the Handelian manner, melodious solo numbers for variety and relief. Beethoven does not linger to drive a point home so roundly, so obviously, that all may follow. He makes his points succinctly, with a direct thrust, in a score which is too compact, too rich in inner detail to attain that comforting if sometimes dubious quality known as "box-office appeal."

Beethoven wrote at the top of the opening *Kyrie,* "Mit

Andacht," and the same words appear over the *Sanctus.* That direction might well stand for the whole score. Each page, when faithfully performed, clearly reflects the intense devotion of its writer. There is an orchestral introduction, a choral ejaculation of the word (*"Kyrie"*) linked and carried into lyric expression by the solo voices, chanted words by the chorus, and contrapuntal development, at length subsiding into a *pianissimo* *"Eleison."* In these features the main characteristics of the *"Missa"* are already laid down. The solo quartet, in a flowing *andante,* soon joined by the chorus, gives the intervening *Christe.* The *Kyrie* returns in different modulation and treatment, dying away in a prayerful coda.

In the *Gloria* the orchestral forces (without trombones) and the chorus in upstriding phrases first disclose the full force of the composer praising his God. The resounding tumult suddenly falls away as the chorus begins its rhythmic chant, *"et in terra pax hominibus."* The *Laudamus te* is accompanied by the *Gloria* figure in the orchestra in a *fortissimo* unison; the *adoramus te* brings a dramatic *pianissimo*—and then again the glorification. The music conforms phrase by phrase to the text, and yet remains musical logic, self-contained and inevitable. A *cantabile* interlude introduces the *"Gratias agimus,"* a hymn of thanksgiving which the *"Domine Deus"* soon dispels, the words set against the *Gloria* motto in the orchestra. At the words *"Pater omnipotens,"* the might of God summons a sustained chord, blazing with organ and orchestra, trombones included.

But again, at the mention of Christ as Son of God there is a long *diminuendo* to the expressive *Larghetto* of the *Qui tollis,* the plea of humanity for Christ's absolution, accentuated by the choral lamentation, *"Miserere."* The *Quoniam,* brief and majestic, ushers in the great fugal return of the *Gloria,* the climax of the movement. The *fugato* is not worked out to the uttermost ends of the form, but seized upon, turned abruptly to heightened dramatic purposes by a master hand. Concision lends new strength and a *presto* Coda ends all. This cumulative peak is to be rivaled only by the final fugue of the *Credo.* The *Gloria* is the only movement which does not end *pianissimo,* save the very close of the Mass.

The *Credo* is by far the longest, the most comprehensive movement. The music, like the text, holds heaven and earth, is a panorama of the Christian faith. The motto of the repeated word, *"Credo,"* is a striking profile, terse, Beethovian. The strong and confident music becomes *piano* for three arresting bars at *"et invisibilium,"* for three more at *"ante omnia saecula."* As Christ descends to earth the music becomes humbly devotional; his descent is described by the literal descent of voices and instruments in unison octaves. The *"Et incarnatus"* is in complete contrast. The tenor solo sings of Christ's birth by the Virgin Mary in a mystic *adagio,* in the remote, old-churchly intervals of the Doric mode. Fluttering string figures, trills from the flute give the music the light, delicate colors, the tender virginal piety of an early Florentine painting. The other solo voices enter, the chorus chants the words in *pianissimo,* and then *Et homo factus est* is briefly set forth in the mortal, earthly major of D.

The *Crucifixus,* an *adagio espressivo,* is dramatic, concentrated, moving. The solo voices sing the first phrase, the chorus enters with a soft undercurrent, *"sub Pontio Pilato passus est."* The orchestra here develops a melody at once anguished and tender. Tchaikovsky would have seized upon such a kernel of expressive songfulness and expanded it into a whole movement. Beethoven tells his message in eleven bars—and is done. There is a brief, hushed pause after *"sepultus est,"* and the *"Et Resurrexit"* is accomplished in a sudden outburst of the chorus unaccompanied. The *"et"* is a short, explosive ejaculation. The six words are delivered in six measures. If the phrase had been even once repeated, the magnificent effect would have been much lessened. The *"et ascendit"* is as literal as the descent had been, and almost as brief. The word, *"judicare,"* is announced by the solo trombone, unaccompanied; "the quick and the dead" get further literal description. The final words of the *Credo, "et vitam venturi saeculi, Amen,"* become the subject of the most extended fugal treatment in the Mass. It is a music of formidable choral difficulty, of superb architecture, and tremendous effect. The chorus at last gives out two *Amens* in a *fortissimo* staccato, and then, over the softly rising scales of a sustained *pianissimo,* the word floats into silence.

The opening words of the *Sanctus* are confined to a short *adagio* by the solo quartet. In half voice, over tremolo strings, they intone the rhythmic syllables. Then the quartet continues with the *"Pleni sunt coeli"* in the elaboration of a short *fugato,* to rushing passages in the orchestra. The *Osanna* is a presto, again fugal and short. An orchestral *"Preludium"* of great beauty, the longest instrumental passage in the Mass, ushers in the *Benedictus.* The orchestration is subdued, supported by the deep organ pedal, until suddenly the high voices of the solo violin with two flutes break in like a ray of light, and gently descend as the choral basses sing once, in a rhythmical *pianissimo, "Benedictus qui venit in nomine Domini."* The symphony continues with a beatific, extended melody by the violin solo. The other solo voices take up the melody, the chorus adding now and again its rhythmic chant. The chorus, at last assuming the lead with a renewed *"Osanna,"* brings a tranquil close.

The *Agnus Dei* opens *adagio,* the bass solo taking the first strain, darkly and tragically, the other soloists presently entering. The chorus is heard in a poignant undercurrent, the *"Miserere"* similar in stress of syllable, but not otherwise, to the earlier use of the word. The chorus once more replaces the single singers, and first delivers the *"Dona nobis pacem,"* which Beethoven has labeled "Prayer for inward and outward peace." The movement is restless and agitated. It breaks off and the orchestra in a passage full of suspense gives a suggestion of distant drums and trumpet, like the threatening tread of an army. The alto solo, then the tenor, repeats *"Agnus Dei"* as an anguished prayer: "Lamb of God, who takest away the sins of the world, have mercy!" The chorus gives out one *"Miserere nobis,"* now a loud cry. The quartet takes the words, and then the chorus. There is a sense of wild struggle; then at last the music becomes increasingly confident. A hauntingly beautiful phrase for the chorus, which has occurred once before (unaccompanied), near the beginning of the movement, recurs twice at the very end. The theme, entirely undeveloped, has an indescribable beatific charm. It effectually dispels at the last moment the still lingering threat of the timpani. It is indeed the answer to the plea "for inward peace." (See pages 108, 110, 131, 200, 203-212, 219, 222-223, 225, 227.)

FANTASY IN C MINOR FOR PIANOFORTE, CHORUS AND ORCHESTRA, OP. 80

Adagio; Finale (Allegro; meno allegro; Allegretto ma non troppo)

(Composed in 1808; first performed December 22, 1808; published July, 1811, with a dedication to "His Majesty Maximilian Joseph, King of Bavaria." The author of the text is unknown.) (See pages 121, 122.)

CHRISTUS AM OELBERGE ("CHRIST ON THE MOUNT OF OLIVES"), ORATORIO FOR THREE SOLO VOICES, CHORUS, AND ORCHESTRA, OP. 85

Introduction, Recitative and Air (Jesus)
Recitative and Air (Seraph with Chorus of Angels)
Recitative and Duet (Jesus, Seraph)
Recitative (Jesus) Chorus of Soldiers and Young Men
Recitative (Peter, Jesus) Trio (Jesus, Seraph, Peter, with Chorus)
  Chorus of Angels

(Completed in 1800; first performed April 5, 1803, at the *Theater-an-der-Wien* in Vienna. Published in 1811, without dedication. The text is by Franz Xaver Huber.) (See pages 74, 87, 116, 152, 191-192.)

MASS IN C MAJOR, FOR FOUR SOLO VOICES, CHORUS AND ORCHESTRA, OP. 86

> *Kyrie: Andante con moto assai vivace*
> *Gloria: Allegro con brio*
> *Credo: Allegro con brio*
> *Sanctus: Adagio*
> *Benedictus: Allegretto ma non troppo*
> *Agnus Dei: Poco andante*

(Composed in 1807; first performed September 8, 1807, at the estate of Prince Nicolas Esterházy. Published in 1812, with a dedication to Prince Ferdinand Kinsky.) (See pages 116, 117, 121.)

ELEGISCHER GESANG ("ELEGIAC SONG") FOR FOUR VOICES, WITH STRING QUARTET, OP. 118

(Composed in 1814 in memory of the wife of the Baron von Pasqua-lati, Beethoven's landlord and friend, to whom the score is dedicated. Published in 1826.) (See page 183.)

OPFERLIED ("SONG OF SACRIFICE") FOR SOPRANO WITH CHORUS AND ORCHESTRA, OP. 121B

(Composed probably 1822; first performed in Vienna, April 4, 1824; published in 1825, without dedication. The text is by Friedrich von Matthisson.)

BUNDESLIED ("SONG OF FELLOWSHIP") FOR TWO SOLO VOICES, CHORUS AND WIND INSTRUMENTS, OP. 122

(Composed probably in 1822; published in 1825 without dedication. The text is from Goethe.)

DER GLORREICHE AUGENBLICK ("THE GLORIOUS OCCASION"), CANTATA FOR FOUR SOLO VOICES, CHORUS AND ORCHESTRA, OP. 136

Chorus: Allegro ma non tanto
Recitative (Leader of the People, Genius) and Chorus
Recitative and Air (Vienna) with Chorus
Recitative, Cavatina (Prophetess) and Chorus

330

Choral Works

Recitative and Quartet *(Vienna, Prophetess, Genius, and Leader of the People)*
Chorus *(Men, women, and children)*

(Composed in 1814, first performed November 29, 1814, in Vienna; published in 1836 with the inscription: "Performed before the highest royalty and nobility at the Vienna Congress, in 1814." The text is by Dr. Aloys Weissenbach. The Cantata also appeared in 1836 with a different text, under the title: *"Preis der Tonkunst."*) (See pages 177-178.)

WITHOUT OPUS NUMBER

CANTATA ON THE DEATH OF KAISER JOSEPH II (1790)

(Published in Breitkopf and Härtel's complete edition, 1887.)

CANTATA ON THE CORONATION OF LEOPOLD II (1790)

(Published in Breitkopf and Härtel's complete edition, 1887.)

"GESANG DER MÖNCHE" (SONG OF THE MONKS) FROM SCHILLER'S WILHELM TELL, FOR THREE MEN'S VOICES

(The manuscript was inscribed, "In memory of the sudden and unexpected death of our Krumpholz on May 3, 1817"—Wenzel Krumpholz died May 2, 1817. Published 1839.)

WORKS FOR INDIVIDUAL VOICES WITH ORCHESTRA.

SCENE AND ARIA, *"AH! PERFIDO!"* FOR SOPRANO WITH ORCHESTRA, OP. 65

(Composed in 1796, published in 1805 with a dedication to the Countess von Clary.)

"MEERESSTILLE UND GLÜCKLICHE FAHRT" ("CALM SEA AND PROSPEROUS VOYAGE"), FOR FOUR VOICES WITH ORCHESTRA, OP. 112

(Beethoven made this setting of Goethe's poem in 1815, in which year it was performed on December 25th. It was published in 1823, with a dedication to Goethe.)

TRIO, *"TREMATE, EMPI, TREMATE,"* FOR SOPRANO, TENOR AND BASS WITH ORCHESTRA, OP. 116

(Composed in 1802, first performed in 1814, and published in 1826.)

WITHOUT OPUS NUMBER

TWO AIRS FOR BASS AND ORCHESTRA, *PRÜFUNG DES KÜSSENS, MIT MÄDELN SICH VERTRAGEN*

(Composed in 1790; published in Breitkopf and Härtel's complete edition.)

332

TWO AIRS FOR VOICE AND ORCHESTRA FROM UMLAUF'S *DIE SCHÖNE SCHUSTERIN*

(Composed in 1796; published in Breitkopf and Härtel's complete edition.)

AUF DIE VERBÜNDETEN FÜRSTIN (TEXT BY C. BERNARD), CHORUS AND ORCHESTRA

(Composed in 1814; published in Breitkopf and Härtel's complete edition.)

OPFERLIED (TEXT BY MATTHISON), FOR THREE SOLO VOICES, CHORUS, AND SMALL ORCHESTRA

(Derived from Op. 121b; published in Breitkopf and Härtel's complete edition.)

FOLK SONG ARRANGEMENTS

THE FOLLOWING songs were arranged for one or two voices (sometimes with small chorus), with accompaniment of pianoforte, violin, and violoncello. All were made by commission of George Thomson of Edinburgh. Only the first collection bears an opus number. All were written between 1810 and 1816.

TWENTY-FIVE SCOTTISH SONGS, OP. 108

TWENTY-FIVE IRISH SONGS

TWENTY IRISH SONGS

TWELVE IRISH SONGS

TWENTY-SIX WELSH SONGS

TWELVE SCOTTISH SONGS

TWELVE FOLK SONGS OF VARIOUS NATIONS

(See page 166.)

THE SONGS WITH
PIANOFORTE

THOSE WHO look in the songs of Beethoven for a complete transformation of what was then a rudimentary *genre* are disappointed. The enrichment of means, the sudden challenge so often found in his instrumental works, are missing. Certainly the songs are to be evaluated by their best, for many were quickly written to fulfill a commission or pay a compliment; almost half of the seventy-seven songs with piano accompaniment were not published under opus numbers (it must be added that this unhonored group contains a few treasures). It was largely a matter of whether the poet and his text touched the imagination of the composer.

When a text touches his sympathy, his mastery of the expressive power of the voice finds its own in a way that puts that mastery quite beyond doubt. But the sense is never dispelled that the medium is resistant—the imagination fettered, the musician unable to range freely and release his full powers within the narrow field. E. T. A. Hoffmann, contemporary expert in romanticism, wrote in 1813: "Beethoven, who is more the Romantic than any composer who has existed, is for that reason less successful with vocal music. Such music shuts out the possibility of indefinite longings, for words present sentiments already fixed and experienced." The words may move him, they may fit the lyric line, but when the point comes where in instrumental music development would carry him to the heart of the matter, the contingencies of text and form obstruct and bind him. The piano cannot become an expressive instrument in its own right; for the most part it must stay in the background, with elementary rippling chords and echoing phrases, as if deferring to each inflection of the voice.

The *Lied* was not yet a freely developed form. The popular, sentimental variety in the salons had not been lifted to anything more elaborate than a melody in the folk song style which was simply repeated for each verse. Beethoven's were no more than this in many cases, but sometimes the supreme melodist takes hold, and in a little song such as the tender *Die Liebe* of Lessing, or the humorous *Der Kuss*, works his magic.

Songs in the declamatory, quasi-theatrical style are convincing in the case of the second setting of *An die Hoffnung* from Tiedge's *Urania*, but others, like *Liebes-Klage*, or several on Italian texts bespeak little more than the sedulous pupil of Salieri. The popular *In questa tomba oscura* seems to borrow its ready and effusive sentiment from the theatre. *Adelaide*, still more popular, has been unduly condescended to by the learned appraisers. If it is effusive, it is quite genuinely so; its strophic regularity is part of its charm, and so is the graceful, unusually pianistic accompaniment. The setting of Matthison's *Andenken* is an instance where sentiment pervades a simple form and finds its end almost entirely through the voice, little pauses, vocal turns, dramatic tensions becoming the distinctive features.

Another instance is the set of six little religious verses by Gellert. The first is a brief prayer, the last (*Busslied*) an extended one, where the music closely reflects the poet's thought, rising from the anguish of self-castigation to the glowing rapture of faith. The fourth song, *Die Ehre Gottes in der Natur*, is familiar, with its majestic chords, its melodic beauty clothed in simplicity. Schubert drew from this, as from the dramatic third song, *Vom Tode*. In these songs the subject moved the devout Beethoven. In the love songs of Goethe it was the subject and the poet as well, for Goethe in almost every case elicited the best from Beethoven. *Neue Liebe, neues Leben*, or *Mit einem gemalten Band* or the *Mailied* are more or less strophic, reaching heights of classic and lyric art. The song of Mignon, or the *Wonne der Wehmuth* (*Trocknet nicht, Thränen der ewigen Liebe!*) have intense dramatic expression, the second breaking the metrical line as each phrase is musically thought. There is a liberation in style otherwise rare in the songs—the voice and the piano speak in a true duet as between two individuals. It is the test of ground breaking in the two songs that the piano part could be played alone and have meaning throughout. Songs like these opened the road for the future masters of the *Lied* form.

Two late songs, *Resignation* and two settings in one from Bürger, *Seufzer eines Ungeliebten—Gegenliebe,* plainly stirred something in the lonely Beethoven. The same may be said of the set of songs by Jeitteles—*An die ferne Geliebte* of 1816—where again the hopeless lover speaks and turns to the beauty of nature about him. The result was a song cycle of six poems—a precedent for Schumann and others. The songs are continuous, the piano accomplishing the modulations and changes of mood in a few bars of transition in each case. The text is closely followed by the musician, with changes of tempo many and free. In the last song, the lover makes his full heart's declaration in an *andante cantabile,* and returns to the closing line of the first song—a significant binding touch. The cycle, as an extended and various text, can be called the composer's most subtly balanced and integrated handling of the song style.

AN DIE HOFFNUNG ("TO HOPE"), OP. 32, FROM TIEDGE'S *URANIA*

(Published in 1805.)

ADELAIDE, OP. 46, POEM BY MATTHISON

(Published in 1797; dedicated to the poet.) (See pages 67-68.)

SIX SONGS, OP. 48, FROM GELLERT

1 *Bitten* (Prayer)
2 *Die Liebe des Nächsten* (Love of our Neighbor)
3 *Vom Tode* (Death)

4 *Die Ehre Gottes in der Natur* (Nature's Praise of God)
5 *Gottes Macht und Vorsehung* (God's Might and Bounty)
6 *Busslied* (Penitence)

(Published in 1803; dedicated to Count von Browne.)

EIGHT SONGS, OP. 52

1 *Urians Reise um die Welt* (Urian's Journey Around the World) from Claudius
2 *Feuerfarb'* (Flame Color) from Sophie Mereau
3 *Das Liedchen von der Ruhe* (Little Song of Repose) from Wilhelm Ültzen
4 *Mailied* (May Song) from Goethe
5 *Mollys Abschied* (Molly's Farewell) from Bürger
6 *Die Liebe* (Love) from Lessing
7 *Marmotte,* from Goethe
8 *Das Blümchen Wunderhold* (The Flower Wondrous Fair) from Bürger

(Published as a collection in 1805, the first four at least being early compositions.)

SIX SONGS, OP. 75

1 *Mignon,* from Goethe
2 *Neue Liebe, neues Leben* (New Love, New Life) from Goethe
3 *Es war einmal ein König,* from Goethe's *Faust*
4 *Gretels Warnung* (Gretel's Warning)
5 *An den fernen Geliebten* (To the Distant Beloved) from C. L. Reissig
6 *Der Zufriedene* (Contentment) from C. L. Reissig

(Published as a collection in 1810; dedicated to Princess Kinsky.) (See page 147.)

FOUR ARIETTAS AND A DUET, OP. 82

1 *Hoffnung* (Hope)
2 *Liebes-Klage* (Love Lament) from Metastasio

328

The Songs with Pianoforte

> 3 *Stille Frage* (The Lover's Question), *Arietta buffa,* from Metastasio
>
> 4 *Liebes-Ungeduld* (The Impatient Lover), *Arietta assai serioso,* from Metastasio
>
> 5 *Lebens-Genuss* (Life's Delight), for Soprano and Tenor, from Metastasio

(Published in 1811.)

THREE SONGS, OP. 83, FROM GOETHE

> 1 *Wonne der Wehmuth* (Sweetness of Melancholy)
> 2 *Sehnsucht* (Longing)
> 3 *Mit einem gemalten Band* (With a Colored Ribbon)

(Composed in 1810, published in 1811; dedicated to the Princess Kinsky.) (See page 147.)

DAS GLÜCK DER FREUNDSCHAFT (THE JOY OF FRIENDSHIP), OP. 88, FROM LÖSCHENKOHL

(Published in 1803 without opus number; in 1804 with opus number, and with German and Italian text.)

AN DIE HOFFNUNG (TO HOPE), OP. 94, FROM TIEDGE'S *URANIA*

(Composed probably in 1816; published in 1816; dedicated to the Princess Kinsky. The setting is entirely different from Op. 32.)

AN DIE FERNE GELIEBTE (TO THE DISTANT BELOVED), OP. 98, SONG CYCLE, FROM A. JEITTELES

> 1 *Auf dem Hügel sitz ich spähend*
> 2 *Wo die Berge so blau*

339

3 *Leichte Segler*
4 *Diese Wolken in den Höhen*
5 *Es kehret der Maien*
6 *Nimm sie hin denn, diese Lieder*

(Composed and published in 1816; dedicated to Prince von Lobko-witz.)

DER MANN VON WORT (THE MAN OF HIS WORD), OP. 99, FROM F. A. KLEINSCHMID

(Published in 1816.)

MERKENSTEIN, OP. 100, FOR TWO VOICES, FROM J. B. RUPPRECHT

(Composed in 1814, published in 1816.)

DER KUSS (THE KISS), ARIETTA, OP. 128, FROM C. F. WEISS

(Composed in 1822, published in 1825.)

SONGS WITHOUT OPUS NUMBERS

SCHILDERUNG EINES MÄDCHENS (PORTRAIT OF A MAIDEN)

(Published in 1783.)

AN EINEN SÄUGLING (TO AN INFANT) FROM WIRTHS

(Published in 1784.)

DER FREIE MANN (THE FREE MAN) FROM G. C. PFEFFEL

(Composed about 1790, revised about 1795, published 1806.)

The Songs with Pianoforte

OPFERLIED (SACRIFICIAL SONG) FROM MATTHISON

(Composed at the latest 1795, published 1806.)

ABSCHIEDSGESANG AN WIEN'S BÜRGER (PARTING SONG OF THE CITIZENS OF VIENNA) FROM FRIEDELBERG

(Published in 1796.)

KRIEGSLIED DER OESTERREICHER (AUSTRIAN WAR SONG), WITH CHORUS, FROM FRIEDELBERG

(Published in 1797.)

ZÄRTLICHE LIEBE (TENDER LOVE) FROM HERROSEN

(Published in 1803.)

LA PARTENZA (THE FAREWELL) FROM METASTASIO

(Composed at the latest, 1798; published, at first with Italian text only, 1803.)

DER WACHTELSCHLAG (THE CALL OF THE QUAIL) FROM S. F. SAUTER

(Composed probably 1799; published 1804.)

ALS DIE GELIEBTE SICH TRENNEN WOLLTE (WHEN LOVERS PART)

(Translated by Stephan von Breuning from a French opera text; published in 1809.)

341

IN QUESTA TOMBA OSCURA (IN THIS DARK TOMB) FROM G. CARPANI

(Composed in 1807; published in 1808.)

ANDENKEN (REMEMBRANCE) FROM MATTHISON

(Published in 1810.)

SEHNSUCHT (LONGING) FROM GOETHE

(Four settings of the poem. The first was published in 1808, the four in 1810.)

LIED AUS DER FERNE (SONG FROM A DISTANCE) FROM C. L. REISSIG

(Composed in 1809; published in 1810.)

DER LIEBENDE (THE LOVER) FROM C. L. REISSIG

(Published in 1810.)

DER JÜNGLING IN DER FREMDE (THE YOUTH IN A STRANGE LAND) FROM C. L. REISSIG

(Published in 1810.)

AN DIE GELIEBTE (TO THE BELOVED) FROM J. L. STOLL

(Composed in 1811, published in 1814; a second setting, composed not earlier than 1812, was published about 1840.)

DER BARDENGEIST (THE SPIRIT BARD) FROM F. R. HERRMANN

(Composed in 1813; published in 1814.)

DES KRIEGERS ABSCHIED (THE WARRIOR'S FAREWELL) FROM C. L. REISSIG

(Composed in 1814; published in 1815.)

SEHNSUCHT (LONGING) FROM C. L. REISSIG

(Composed in 1815 or 1816; published in 1816.)

DAS GEHEIMNIS (THE SECRET) FROM WESSENBERG

(Composed in 1815; published in 1816.)

RUF VOM BERGE (CALL FROM THE MOUNTAIN) FROM TREITSCHKE

(Composed in 1816; published in 1817.)

SO ODER SO (THIS WAY OR THAT) FROM CARL LAPPE

(Composed and published in 1817.)

RESIGNATION, FROM PAUL GRAF VON HAUGWITZ

(Composed in 1817; published in 1818.)

ABENDLIED UNTER'M GESTIRNTEN HIMMEL (EVENING SONG BENEATH THE STARRY HEAVENS) FROM HEINRICH GOEBLE

(Composed and published in 1820.)

SEUFZER EINES UNGELIEBTEN UND GEGENLIEBE (DESPONDING AND RESPONSIVE LOVE) FROM G. A. BURGER

(Composed about 1795; published in 1837.)

DIE LAUTE KLAGE (THE LOUD LAMENT) FROM HERDER

(Composed probably in 1809; published in 1837.)

GEDENKE MEIN! (THINK OF ME!)

(Published posthumously in 1844.)

These songs, not listed in Nottebohm's Thematic Catalogue, are published in the supplement of Breitkopf and Härtel's edition of the complete works:

> *Ich, du mit flatterndem Sinn*
> *Merkenstein* (for solo voice)
> *Der Gesang der Nachtigall*
> *Lied (für Frau von Weissenthurn)*
> *Lied aus Metastasio's Olimpiade*
> *An Minna*
> *Trinklied*
> *Klage*
> *Elegie auf den Tod eines Pudels*

344

THE
STRING QUARTETS

BEETHOVEN TURNED to the string quartet three times in his life, each time briefly and intensively, and each time wrote a group of them. The six of Opus 18 were published in 1801 as his entrance into the field hallowed by Mozart and Haydn. In the summer of 1806 he composed the three of Opus 59 for Count Rasoumowsky. There followed the Quartets Opus 74 of 1809 and Opus 95 of 1810. Not for fourteen years did he write another, and then having completed the Ninth Symphony he composed his last five, working upon them until his mortal illness overtook him. The division into "early," "middle" and "late" is, needless to say, extremely convenient for the proponents of three periods.

SIX STRING QUARTETS, OP. 18

(Completed from sketches made through several years and published in two sets of three in the summer and autumn of 1801; dedicated to Prince von Lobkowitz.)

Beethoven's first venture in the form of the string quartet was a step as circumspect as he had made by his thirty-first year. The Quartets of Opus 18 were certainly an accumulation, the result of holding back. The very abundance of musical ideas which sparkle through the twenty-four movements are an indication of that, for Beethoven at no other time in his life composed full-length works by sixes, as Haydn had. He had long been attending the quartet parties of Prince Lichnowsky and of Emanuel

Aloys Förster, a master in the difficult form, from whom he may have had guidance. But self-instruction was his way. He may have made sketches as early as 1794. Certainly he did the greater part of his labor of composition in 1799, when the sketchbooks overflow with themes of all but the Fourth and Sixth. Some of his themes were bright bits of melody such as his predecessors had conjured up with characteristic ease and dispatch. But Beethoven probably planned even his gayest rondo themes with scrupulous care and an eye to their possibilities, as their working out shows.

It has been said that these six are inferior to their models, less suave and ripened than the quartets of Haydn and Mozart which they outwardly imitate. Certainly no one, not even Beethoven, could have borrowed that elegant investiture of a closing century and worn it with the consummate grace of those two who had made it so completely a part of their natures. The brocaded coat, already slightly outmoded, does not encase these broader shoulders quite so comfortably. The wonder is that Beethoven wears it with the success that he does. In the first place, he has made himself completely at home in the medium. He handles the sonorities of the instruments smoothly and with effect. The texture, at its best, is richer, less often content with using the inner voices for chord making. But the old-time air of formal correctness hangs over them. The component sections are ushered in obviously, with a flourish, phrases balanced, cadences underlined. There are moments when one asks whether the composer of the piano sonatas Opus 10 and 14 has relapsed into cautiousness, or whether the masters gone before have hypnotized him and subdued the rising undercurrent of individual assertion. It would be nearer to the truth to say that the quartets under which he had grown up had been taken far too closely to his heart for summary casting out. They had become part of himself because he still belonged more to the past than to the future. The first-movement form suited him admirably; the slow movement could long expand from within without breaking the outward mold; the traditional *gigue* finale appealed to the still young effervescence of his invention. When certain quartets, such as the one in G major, begin in the old graceful manner, the hearer is intrigued by an exuberance which is genuine and vital, no weak copy of another's style. But the course of development presently sets the imagination alight until the new strength of the Beethoven to come has suffused the score. It is the combination of surface charm and youthful innovation which gives the six quartets their special appeal. (See page 68.)

STRING QUARTET IN F MAJOR, OP. 18. NO. 1

Allegro con brio
Adagio affettuoso ed appassionato
Scherzo: Allegro molto
Allegro

The Quartet in F major was not the first in order of composition. Beethoven chose it to open the set, perhaps, because the opening *allegro con brio* was a brilliant challenge. Beethoven at once threw down a gauntlet, a fragment of a theme in unison, with a rhythmic twist:

It is inconspicuous enough on its face but becomes a unit for manipulation which, linked with itself in many repetitions, tossed back and forth between the instruments and built into sequential lines can become closely integrated discourse. The theme was arrived at laboriously through eleven pages of the sketchbooks, until it was stripped at last to a bare rhythmic kernel, which in itself implied a movement. Mozart had done this sort of thing to a degree (the first movement of the G minor symphony is an obvious example), but here Beethoven is unmistakably advancing upon a road of his own. One can already foretell the close pattern of another *allegro con brio* in C minor, to open a symphony seven years later (at this early moment the First Symphony is in hand). The Quartet plumbs no depths, but it opens a

347

way. Louis Spohr, a contemporary quartet specialist, was as completely won by this *tour de force* as he was destined to be puzzled by the Fifth Symphony in its time. The slow movement, an *adagio* of extended melody, drenched in D minor, is evidence at once of the abrupt mood changes which are to characterize Opus 18. The first phrase of the melody, sung by the leading violin over triplet chords which burden the air with melancholy, extends through twelve 9/8 bars. *"Adagio affettuoso ed appassionato"* stands above it, and the composer is true to his promise as, after three tragic pauses, he reaches his *fortissimo* climax. His friend Amenda has told us that Beethoven mentioned having in mind the tomb scene from *Romeo and Juliet,* an appropriate thought, whether the story be true or not. But the mood becomes tenuous when dissected by the fine-spun and extended treatment of elaborate subdivision into sixteenth notes. A rather too well-behaved *Scherzo* rises to individuality in the Trio with its staccato octaves and drone bass. The final *allegro* matches the brilliance of the first movement, a more conventional pattern giving way to episodes which forget to be formal, and so gain in charm.

STRING QUARTET IN G MAJOR, OP. 18. NO. 2

> *Allegro*
> *Adagio cantabile*
> *Scherzo: Allegro*
> *Allegro molto, quasi presto*

This quartet is sometimes identified in Germany as the *"compliments Quartett,"* a misleading tag, since, after bowing its way in rather stiffly,

the music proceeds to relax and establish its true character— pliant, singing, forceful in rhythmic accent or modulation. The *Adagio cantabile* is no sooner fully stated than it gives way unexpectedly to a swift and light *allegro,* growing from the cadential figure. The *Andante* returns for a brief development, the melody in the bass, and ends with a *pianissimo* reminiscence of the interruption. This bold stroke had no precedent. Learning could not justify it, but the effect is magic. In the *Scherzo,* the lingering earmarks of the minuet have quite vanished. The *Finale,* "*quasi presto,*" starts off upon a theme of most uncourtly gaiety, and proceeds accordingly. Beethoven applied his favorite expression, "Unbuttoned" ("*Aufgeknöpft*") to this movement.

STRING QUARTET IN D MAJOR, OP. 18, NO. 3

Allegro
Andante con moto
Allegro
Presto

The Quartet in D major is believed to have been the first in order of composition, which might account for a prevailing sense of formality. The title "complimentary" would better describe this than the one in G major. The tender and wistful theme which opens the *Andante con moto* promises an emotional tension which is not realized, for the second theme, with its eighteenth-century sprightliness, forbids sentimental indulgence. The third movement, labeled merely "*Allegro*" is minuet-like, and its trio in the minor has an antique flavor. The *Presto* in 6/8 rhythm is, despite its formal obedience, the most individual of the four movements.

STRING QUARTET IN C MINOR, OP. 18, NO. 4

Allegro ma non tanto
Andante scherzoso, quasi allegretto
Menuetto: Allegretto
Allegro

The Fourth Quartet is the only one of the six in which the minor mode prevails. The opening movement strikes a new note, in which the expected light-heartedness is conspicuously absent. The theme is warmly fluent, serious, gradually rising to passionate eloquence:

This sort of thing has long since become a commonplace. At that time, as an opening for a quartet, it was utterly unheard of. The movement, pursuing its ardent course dramatically to the end, must have created a considerable impression in its day. Nothing could be more abrupt than the cheerful staccato theme of the *Andante scherzoso* in C major, which follows. Beethoven, as elsewhere in Opus 18, plays for contrast between movements, as if he enjoyed roughly dispelling a mood he built up. He had not yet learned to draw together a succession of movements by the reaching and encompassing power of a generating mood. After the grave opening movement he presents a lively *"quasi allegretto"* which rises from a show of contrapuntal skill into a delightful play of fantasy. The minuet (so called) restores the minor mode, takes a chromatic course, and pauses for a rather slight trio. The final rondo is as bright and insouciant as the rondo in the *Pathétique* Sonata in the same minor tonality, which, since it is a *finale* in the eighteenth-century *genre,* is hardly surprising.

STRING QUARTET IN A MAJOR, OP. 18, NO. 5

> *Allegro*
> *Minuetto*
> *Andante cantabile con Variazioni*
> *Allegro*

The A major Quartet has been described as conspicuously "Mozartean" by Joseph de Marliave in his book on Beethoven's Quartets, this writer pointing to a passage in the *Finale* which seems to him a "deliberate imitation." The spirit of Mozart indeed hovers over all six quartets; it is felt in the adroit manipulation of the voices, but more directly still in the lilting episodic fragments which bob up continually, principally in the finales. They have a distinct flavor of Italian opera, and it may well be questioned whether Beethoven's frequent Italianisms in this formative period did not come to him in large part by way of Mozart. The Minuet, by exception, is the second movement (the Fourth and Fifth Quartets are the only ones with minuets so called). The *Andante cantabile* falls back upon the then popular form of a theme with variations, and in the fifth and last of them rises to expressive heights. The finale has another of the "small unit" themes, identical in rhythm, be it noted, to the opening motto of the C minor Symphony. The movement is accordingly close-knit, and fluent in every part.

STRING QUARTET IN B FLAT MAJOR, OP. 18, NO. 6

Allegro con brio
Adagio ma non troppo
Scherzo: Allegro
La Malinconia: Adagio—Allegretto quasi allegro

The last quartet uncovers, in its *Finale,* the only really tragic page in the six, yet, as if to preserve the traditional sense of balance, the Quartet opens with a skipping, inconsequential theme, and continues with an *Adagio* which with its melodic beauty is grave and reserved. The *Scherzo,* for all its simplicity, is forward-rather than backward-looking. One can feel Schubert in its naïveté, and the opening chords of the Trio might, if time ran backwards, have been lifted from that composer. The *Finale* is a development of the conception of the slow movement of the G major Quartet with its interrupting *allegro,* except that here the rapid movement, breaking in with the most violent contrast Beethoven could imagine at the time, strongly prevails. The introductory *adagio* is entitled: *"La Malinconia: Questo pezzo si deve trattare colla più gran delicatezza"* ("Melancholy: this portion must be played with the greatest delicacy"). The direction indicates Beethoven's uneasiness to entrust it to green hands —and it must have seemed strange indeed to its first players. A weird *pianissimo* phrase several times repeated,

leads to chains of modulations dark and alien. The music, mysterious and suspensive, was written, it should be remembered, long before Romantics had spoiled the force of macabre effects and diminished seventh chords by wallowing in them. The silence is shattered by the rushing perpetual-motion theme of the *"Allegretto quasi allegro."* The *Finale* proper is interrupted twice by brief reminiscences of the *adagio* phrase, but re-asserts itself the more strongly, increasing to a *prestissimo* conclusion.

THREE STRING QUARTETS, OP. 59

(Completed in 1806, first performed in February, 1807, in Vienna, and published in January, 1808. Dedicated to Count von Rasoumowsky.)

The first page of the F major Quartet of Opus 59 shows a vastly matured Beethoven as compared with the composer of Opus 18. Six years had elapsed—and what a six years! He had composed the *Eroica, Fidelio,* many sonatas, including the *"Appassionata."* * In other words, he had strengthened his hand in each other form, while the string quartet had once more to await a belated turn. The three came in close succession, composed in the summer of 1806 from sketches traceable two years earlier. The result was a strong and confident beginning and carrying through. Now the time had passed when he could have tossed forth lively scraps of tunes for mere juggling purposes, or otherwise preserved the old forms except in sheer nostalgic delectation. The current is broad and deep, vigorously independent, calling forth the full tonal capacity of four stringed instruments when his thoughts tend to symphonic proportions. His manipulatory power, enormously increased, welds and tightens, liberates, builds. The fancy takes any sort of flight it wills, and is richly various. The advance of Opus 59 upon Opus 18 is reflected in the attitude of contemporary quartet players. Having long cherished the earlier six for their thematic and structural eighteenth-century clarity, they supposed that Beethoven was

* The String Quintet, Opus 29, preceded these (1802).

either perpetrating a joke on them or had quite lost his musical sanity.

The three quartets of Opus 59 are in their way the subtlest, the most viable and deeply personal expression of what is called Beethoven's "second period." They are highly varied, as if the composer's cumulative abstention from what must have been in many ways his most beloved medium must find recompense in every expressive aspect of the nature which had lately found power, joy and bitter anguish past all dreaming. (See pages 69, 111, 112, 113, 115-117.)

STRING QUARTET (NO. 7) IN F MAJOR, OP. 59, NO. 1

Allegro
Allegretto vivace e sempre scherzando
Adagio molto e mesto
Allegro

The Quartet in F major can be called the full-rounded, the completely realized expression of what the composer worked toward in his early quartets. It consummates rather than breaks new ground. The first movement starts with an agreeable warm serenity upon a simple but characterful melody:

The sonata form is treated throughout with a forcefulness which puts the string quartet on a new plane of breadth and symphonic suggestion. The movement ends with a fine coda, another imple-

354

ment of eloquence acquired by Beethoven since 1801! For his second movement, an *Allegretto scherzando,* Beethoven finds the sonata form again to his purpose (indeed he uses this form in each of the four movements—an unprecedented procedure). The rhythmic motto and the principal theme, made known in a staccato *pianissimo,* become the groundwork for a kaleidoscopic interplay of airy fantasy, prismatic changes and sudden humorous conceits. The *Allegretto scherzando* of the Eighth Symphony was not to be written for six years. This one, similar in its humor, swifter and longer, is correspondingly richer in detail. The *Adagio* is constructed on two singing themes, developed quite simply in alternation in the different registers of the instruments. The technical accounting could be more detailed; it would give no remote idea of the deeply penetrating power of the movement, which lies in the intense beauty of the themes, and in the pathos of the intervening passages which analysis cannot show. One recalls the lover's melancholy of the *Adagio* in the First Quartet; but here the mood, instead of thinning out under subdivision, probes continuously deeper. It is akin to the most successful of the Goethe songs to come, with the difference that the fullness of heart, there only glimpsed, is here completely unburdened. The lamentation is not wild, but nobly, quietly moving. Even behind the tragic accents there is a firm serenity. With his four string voices, Beethoven has found one of the most impassioned of all his slow movements. The spell lingers as the violin soars and descends to a trill, cut across by the opening phrase of the *Finale*. Beethoven fulfills his obligation to Count Rasoumowsky by introducing a "*Thème Russe,*" so labeled, as his principal subject. The treatment brings to bear the composer's skill and ingenuity; it is interesting and effective. When the movement has ended one feels that Beethoven has played with the rhythmic possibilities of the tune rather than preserved its peasant gaiety, as he might have done with an Austrian tune. (See pages 69, 113, 116.)

STRING QUARTET (NO. 8) IN E MINOR, OP. 59. NO. 2

Allegro
Molto adagio
Allegretto
Finale: Presto

The Second Quartet is less frequently performed than its pred-ecessor because it is less grateful for display purposes, and less immediately understandable. The key of E minor from Beetho-ven is in itself a storm signal, and the exposition of the opening movement with astringent chords and interrupting pauses, fore-tells the conflict which is felt in the development, where harsh, restless passages are overcome and at last integrated with a fluent whole. Now Beethoven, ordering his movements, has pro-gressed beyond the simple, eighteenth-century idea of balance by contrast. Sudden reaction was a part of his nature, expressed in his music; but here reaction had far deeper causes than va-riety. The restlessness in the first movement conditions the res-olution of the movement which follows. The *Adagio,* the high point of the Quartet, banishes troubled thoughts with a special quietude quite without precedent in the quartets until that time. D'Indy spoke of the "deep religious calm" of the opening chords,

remembering perhaps religious passages in the last quartets which are for a moment suggested. But here the ardent Beethoven still gently makes his presence felt in the even, endlessly unbroken line of the melody, which brings to mind the *Adagio* of the B flat Symphony of the same summer. Holz has told (it should be remembered that he did not yet know the composer in 1806) that Beethoven conceived the movement under the domination of a starry night at Baden; indeed an expanse of heaven could well have induced such all-embracing contemplation as this. The placid spell of the coda was not to be broken by a jaunty *scherzo* movement. Instead, the composer leads his hearers into an *allegretto, pianissimo,* which preserves some of the gently undulating character of what has gone before. The second (and last) Russian theme which Opus 59 was to contain is worked into the Trio as a simple accompanied melody. Now, a brilliant close is called for, and taking a lively tune of the rondo type in C major, Beethoven achieves one of his most masterful and striking finales.

STRING QUARTET (NO. 9) IN C MAJOR, OP. 59 NO. 3

> *Andante con moto; Allegro vivace*
> *Andante con moto, quasi allegretto*
> *Menuetto: Grazioso*
> *Allegro molto*

Having completed his quartets in F major and E minor, Beethoven was apparently through with deep matters for the time being. The first and last movements of the Quartet in C are for he most part surface music, a jubilant display of power. The second movement is no probing *adagio* but a lightly treading *"quasi allegretto."* In the third movement, as if resting from psychological explorations, Beethoven reverts to a *"Menuetto grazioso."* For the first time in a quartet Beethoven puts an introduction before the opening movement. *Pianissimo* chords and shifting modulations lead to the bright main theme, rhythmic and staccato. This, broken up in development, is woven closely with other fragments into a most engaging movement. The *"Andante con moto, quasi allegretto"* floats on a light 6/8 rhythm, in a quizzical vein, with the somber cast of a prevailing A minor:

The graceful little movement is in a sense simplicity itself, but to define its character has bothered the wise men. A. B. Marx, the ponderous German biographer, found it "curiously strange" (*"seltsam fremder"*), and Marliave has written of "a lament so bitter that one seems to hear a cry of sorrow from an unseen world." D'Indy is content with the milder (and more convincing) observation that it "searches many shadowy corners." The Minuet, while following structural prescription, is anything but square cut; its rhythmic subtlety has little suggestion of the dance. A coda leads directly into the *Finale,* a fugue in C major, which rushes tumultuously, though controlled by an iron hand, to its resounding close. Years were to pass before Beethoven would use the fugue form for deeply expressive purposes. This one, if not much more than a *tour de force,* is proof enough of his skill with a fugue in 1806. Its effectiveness is such that conductors after Beethoven's death often attempted it with a full string orchestra. (See page 113.)

STRING QUARTET (NO. 10) IN E FLAT MAJOR, "HARP," OP. 74

> *Poco adagio; Allegro*
> *Adagio ma non troppo*
> *Presto*
> *Allegretto con Variazioni*

(Completed in 1809; published in December, 1810; dedicated to Prince von Lobkowitz.)

This Quartet is one of the works where Beethoven is content to rest in the satisfaction of ways tried and tested, disinclined to become venturesome or involved. The long and particularly delightful introduction sets the pace of the first three movements, which dwell for the most part in full, consonant chords, drawing from the instruments the greatest tonal effulgence. The first movement exults in broad and vigorous sonorities, only to fall away into the dreaming arpeggios which have given the Quartet its popular title of the "Harp" Quartet. The *Adagio* is the last of the slow movements in the quartets where passionate ardor openly speaks. Rich harmonies under a single, singing voice prevail. This is one of the special treasures of the quartets, to be placed beside the slow movement of Opus 59 No. 1. The *Scherzo* movement makes its chords with swift insistence in a presto springing with energy. The Trio alters the rhythm from 3/4 to a virtual 6/8 by doubled bars, an idea which was to be used in the *Scherzo* of the Ninth Symphony of years to come. Both *Scherzo* and Trio are repeated, and the first part, making its third appearance with modifications, dreams its way into a *pianissimo* bridge, which leads into an unexpected but altogether delightful *finale*—an *allegretto* theme with six variations. The variations are free and sometimes complex in their working, straying from the theme in an unclassical and advanced technique which more than any other movement bespeaks the advanced year of 1809. (See page 138.)

STRING QUARTET (NO. 11) IN F MINOR, OP. 95 (*QUARTETT SERIOSO*)

> *Allegro con brio*
> { *Allegretto, ma non troppo*
> { *Allegro assai vivace, ma serioso*
> *Larghetto espressivo; Allegretto agitato*

(Completed in October, 1810; published in December, 1816; dedicated to "his friend, Court Secretary, Nikolaus Zmeskall von Domanovetz.")

No other quartet of Beethoven has such a strongly distinguishing character. Its pages are branded with its style almost as clearly as the pages of *Tristan*. The harmonic scheme is remarkably chromatic for its time; the modulations are restless and abrupt. Until the end it is cast in somber colors which the prevailing minor mode accentuates. The tempi, until the concluding *Allegro,* are moderate. It is so concise, or rather concentrated, in its expression, quite lacking extensive development, that it becomes the shortest of them all. The opening theme, rapped out in a *forte* unison, is abrupt and hard, uncompromisingly minor:

Thus the trend of the movement is set. Sudden major scales assault the gloomy harmonies, but without avail. The atmosphere is by no means cleared by the *Allegretto,* which takes the place of a slow movement. Although it bears the signature of D major, that bright key has little opportunity to assert itself. Heavy, descending short notes from the 'cello foretell trouble. A mournful theme suggests a wailing phrase to the viola, the instrument which is to suffuse each movement with its special dark coloring:

A device upon which Beethoven leans heavily throughout the quartet should be noted: the melodic half-tone lapse from the sixth degree of the minor scale to the fifth, a veritable accent of lamentation. It is again the viola which leads with the mournful theme of a brief *fugato*. As the movement dies away the *scherzo*, or what serves for a *scherzo*, asserts itself with a strong, abrupt rhythm. The Trio, an austere melody with a weird accompanying figure, makes a second brief appearance in the minor. In a short introduction to the agitated last movement the most poignant note is the viola's falling half-tone plaint (before mentioned). The main body (*allegretto agitato*) is troubled and restless, the minor accents of the themes set against stormy figures. The movement subsides, as if from exhaustion, until a light and swift *allegro* sweeps away the last F minor chord with the relief of F major. So the quartet closes with a sudden rush of liberation, a jubilation of major scales which are entirely characteristic of Beethoven. D'Indy calls this coda an "error of genius" a "Rossinian operatic *finale*"—which seems a strange remark. With all respect to the scholarship of this invaluable analyst, one feels that the composer never wrote a tumult of major runs with a surer sense of dramatic necessity. (See pages 140, 194.)

STRING QUARTET (NO. 12) IN E FLAT MAJOR, OP. 127

> *Maestoso: Allegro*
> *Adagio, ma non troppo e molto cantabile*
> *Scherzando vivace*
> *Finale: Allegro*

(Completed in 1824; probably first performed in March, 1825, in Vienna; published in March, 1826, dedicated to Prince Nicolaus von Galitzin.)

The Quartet in E flat is a worthy portal of the incredible last five, which can be considered as on a technical level, having been composed almost without interruption through the last three years of Beethoven's life. Fourteen years had elapsed since the Quartet in F minor of 1810. The Quartet in E flat shows at once that it was a far more fully equipped Beethoven who was returning to the form of his ultimate choice. In a technical sense at least, if not in other ways, the five quartets can be looked upon as the crown of all that he did, and all that had gone before as a preparation. The hand was always learning. The final piano sonatas had put tradition-bound construction in a state of flux; the *Missa Solemnis* had probed the four-part counterpoint which the quartets would further exploit; the Ninth Symphony lifted the scherzo and the slow movement to a new plane of eloquence, and those roads the quartets would likewise further pursue.

It would be effrontery to attempt to convey by ambitious adjectives the inward nature of this Quartet. It moves for the most part lightly and delicately, aware of the medium which is unequaled in its possibilities for delicate detail. The first movement, *Scherzo,* and *Finale* in turn maintain a reiterative rhythm (only momentarily relieved), which serves to accentuate the abundant resource of development. The first movement opens with a six-bar introduction of broad chords, *maestoso,* in duple rhythm, which, recurring at the beginning and near the end of the development, affords contrast and has the function, well-remembered from the composer's past, of boldly bringing in a new key. This is a movement of even unfoldment, in which what ought to be called the exposition, manipulating the main theme even in its setting forth, working in episodes by imitation, but never disclosing a second theme in a contrasted key, merges with the development proper. The much-worked theme remains subtly productive, and in the coda furnishes a mere three notes for a stroke of magic. There follows what is to be the last of the long slow movements, save for the "Song of Thanksgiving" in the A minor Quartet. Comparisons are of course quite futile, but it is possible, while under the mystic spell of this slow movement, to tell oneself that there can be no other. The theme bears a 12/8 signature, is in a regular rhythm, which the lower voices maintain in an "accompaniment" which, to use class-room parlance, is both vertical and horizontal. The first of the five variations brings motion and fresh expressiveness in the independent treatment of the four voices. Never had polyphony been bent to greater eloquence. An *andante con moto* follows, the melody, now single, acquiring a new beauty in thirty-second notes, over (and later under) light *pizzicato* chords. The effect is a propulsive animation within gravity; a paradox only music could achieve—and in music, only Beethoven! The third variation is again a many-voiced *Adagio* (in E major) upon a transformation of the theme, the fourth, by contrast once more, an (almost) monodic form, over rising staccato triplets. There are a few bars developing four notes of this most plastic of themes before the final variation, wherein the first violin wanders high in sixteenth notes, touching altitudes sacred to Beethoven. A reminiscence of the staccato triplets brings the end. The adroit variety of style and tempi (achieved by note values), the changing contours of the theme through which it continues to make its identity felt defeat any sense of *longeur* in one of Beethoven's longest movements. "One seems to have lingered," wrote Schumann while under its spell, "not fifteen short minutes, but an eternity."

The *Scherzo* is likewise one of Beethoven's longest in that form. A few broken bits of themes—a four-note figure, an inversion of it, and the figure with a trill which accompanies it— these suffice as building materials for the lightest and airiest, the most scintillating of structures. The little galloping rhythm is incessant, sometimes gathering to pounding strength, twice pausing for the interpolation of a 2/4 phrase. The Trio, a surface-skimming *presto,* gives the variation of an even, triple beat. The rhythm of the *Scherzo* is the motto of the quartet. It is found in the introductory *maestoso* of the first movement; it is the rhythmic basis of the *adagio* theme of the second. It is necessarily absent from the *Finale* (after the insistence of the *Scherzo* any further use of it would have been impossible). The

363

Finale (the tempo unspecified, but customarily played rapidly) is in common time. The main theme, like that of the first movement, does not strike the hearer at first but acquires character with dissection and persistent use. At last the composer puts his theme into a 6/8 rhythm, *presto,* for a zephyr-like close. (See pages 211, 229, 239.)

STRING QUARTET (NO. 13) IN B FLAT MAJOR, OP. 130

> *Adagio ma non troppo; Allegro*
> *Presto*
> *Andante con moto ma non troppo, poco scherzando*
> *Alla danza tedesca: allegro assai*
> *Cavatina: Adagio molto espressivo*
> *Finale: Allegro*

(Composed in 1825, the second and ultimate *Finale* in November, 1826; first performed, with the original fugue *Finale* March 21, 1826, in Vienna; published posthumously May, 1827, dedicated to Prince Nicolaus von Galitzin.)

Only in this Quartet has Beethoven left a work of sonata proportions with six separate and developed movements. The usual four movements are to be found, but between the slow movement (an unusually animated *Andante*) and the *Finale* he has inserted a German dance which resembles a second scherzo, and a *Cavatina* which is a second slow movement, this time grave and sustained in character. The first movement is in itself unusual. It is Beethoven's most fully realized effort to oppose sections of contrasted tempo, and by alternation to bring about the modification of one by the other. The conflict of opposite themes was a much-favored method. The conflict of a slow introductory section and the *Allegro* proper was of course far more unwieldy; he had attempted it in the *Pathétique* Sonata

364

and the Sonata Opus 109 with indeterminate results. A quiet and contemplative *adagio* of thirteen bars is interrupted by the *Allegro*, which, after a few more bars in the first tempo re-enters and takes full possession, dramatically bringing in elements from the *Adagio* portion. As the development begins, and again before the coda, snatches from the *Adagio* again and again bring the music to a pause. But the *Allegro* prevails with this call which has been its proclamation throughout:

The *Presto* is a wisp of a movement, lasting, on account of its speed, about a hundred seconds. It opens *pianissimo*, and proposes what might be a peasant dance, if it were not of lightning agility, and adroitly shadowed by B flat minor. The Trio, in the tonic major, increases the swiftness by a 6/4 instead of a 4/4 signature within the same beat. A fanciful bridge brings back the first portion with trills and other new touches added. The *Andante con moto*, labeled *"poco scherzando,"* is in the evocative key of D flat, beginning with the promise of a sustained slow movement. After two bars, however, it breaks up into an accompaniment of staccato sixteenth notes over which develops a fantastic duet in light animation. The character of this extraordinary movement, the most unusual of the six, is a sort of delicate, insubstantial activity, the interwoven themes sometimes giving way to *pianissimo* passages in *pizzicato*. The discourse constantly engenders new thoughts, sometimes producing prominent melodies, such as a softly wistful passage introduced by the first violin under the direction *cantabile*. The *alla danza tedesca* is a brief *da capo* movement on a simple dance tune, set simply, but with the light restraint and sense of remotenesss from reality which pervades the Quartet.

There follows the *Cavatina*, an *adagio* of no more than sixty-six bars, which without ornamental development delivers its

365

message of passionate sadness with completeness and the utmost persuasion. This is the one movement of sustained sentiment in a Quartet of staccato filigree, subtle accentuation and dainty half-lights. The first violin seems to hold the burden of the melody throughout, as if to justify the name *"Cavatina,"* but the voices beneath, subdued, are none the less richly eloquent in motion:

A middle section is hinted as the lower strings hold the tonic E flat in *pianissimo* triplets. But the 'cello drops to D flat, the violin sounds an unearthly G flat, and there begins, faintly and brokenly, a melody in the eerie key of C flat major, which changes to its relative A flat minor. Beethoven has written over this passage *beklemmt* ("anguished"). The passage is like a ghost of the *Adagio* in the *"Hammer-Klavier"* Sonata. But in eight awed measures, scarcely audible, it has given its message of suffering. The initial melody returns to close, *pianissimo*, this movement of tender elegy.

The grave introductory bars of the fugue movement with which he originally intended to close this Quartet would have followed the *Cavatina* with beautiful effect. Deciding, in the next year, to write a new *finale*, he completed at Gneixendorf in November, 1826, what was to be his last composition. It was a swan song, smiling and fulsome, a final proof that heavy sickness, misery and drab surroundings could not encroach upon the serene spirit and the firm hand. Never did the composer more engrossingly turn a slight theme to forms of serious beauty, warming from playfulness to sentiment. Its character is that of the second, third and fourth movements—light-hearted, with a special, delicate, veiled beauty. How follow the silence after the luminous close of the *Cavatina* with measures of dance-like gaiety? Beethoven does not brusquely sweep the heavy mood aside with a sudden rondo as he might have done in his youth. The refrain in C minor, discreetly subdued, takes quiet possession over staccato octaves from the viola. Phrases of set lengths, with repeats, give the suggestion of a rondo, but there is an extended sonata development, with various changes of mood, and inexhaustible fantasy. (See pages 229, 243, 264.)

GROSSE FUGUE FOR STRING QUARTET IN B FLAT MAJOR, OP. 133

*Overtura (Allegro)—Fuga (Allegro)—Meno Mosso e moderato—
Allegro molto e con brio*

(Composed in 1825 as the finale of the String Quartet, Opus 130; published separately and posthumously, May, 1827, as *"Grande Fugue tantôt libre, tantôt recherchée"*; dedicated to Rudolph, Archduke of Austria.)

The "Great Fugue" which Beethoven first intended as the *finale* of the Quartet in B flat would, as the sixth movement of that already extensive work, have reached into lengths far beyond contemporary listening capacities. When the Quartet had been performed, Beethoven's friends, so we are told, were as baffled by the fugue as they were entranced by the *Cavatina*. They urged him to write a more understandable *finale,* and when Artaria offered to publish the fugue separately in such a case, Beethoven reluctantly consented. D'Indy has argued for the restoration of the fugue to its proper position, from which it was ousted by the pressure of others, on the grounds that it is a blood relative to the earlier movements—the first movement in particular. Courageous players have on occasion so performed the

367

Quartet. The stand is arguable. Beethoven, who knew his own mind, had elsewhere turned to the tense and concentrated logic of a fugue as the culmination of a succession of not too weighty movements (the Piano Sonatas Opus 101 or 109, the last 'Cello Sonata, Opus 102). He conceived his first fugue subject in this his favorite joyous *alla marcia* rhythm (found in the Sonata Opus 101, the A minor Quartet and indeed in the *Andante* of the Quartet to which this fugue belonged).

And yet it is possible to wonder whether Beethoven, following practical advice, did not really reach the same decision quite by himself on aesthetic grounds. Having completed the fugue, he may have realized that he had in the heat of his subject exceeded his aim of writing a properly terse *finale* to a long quartet. What may have started out to be pointed summation had grown into an exhaustive and involved piece of music, no mere fugue *finale,* but three fugues erected upon a single theme, and bound by an introduction and a coda. The *Grosse Fugue,* wherever it may belong, is a work of self-standing proportions.

Fifteen minutes of fugal writing must be considered alien to any sonata scheme. The listener who is accustomed to variety in color and dynamics, the alleviations of frank chords and melodies, will not be drawn by lengths of discourse which, however eventful as counterpoint, are as sheer sonority unrelieved and lacking in ebb and flow. Beethoven does not wrap his voices in velvet as he had done, for example, in the *Cavatina.* In full pursuit of an idea, he forfeits the tonal amenities. At times the spacing is wide, the high range of the violin strained, the subtle rhythmic variation less noticeable than the insistent beat of the long and devious subject of the first fugue. These forbidding aspects are gradually forgotten as the contrapuntal adventures of the theme itself, with its striking physiognomy, are set forth.*

The introduction is marked *"Overtura,"* and like an overture it is a preliminary digest of what is to follow:

* The theme compares, note for note, with the theme which introduces the A minor Quartet, Opus 132 (where, however, it is set in suave harmonies). The fugue theme of the C sharp minor Quartet, Opus 131, is also chromatically similar. Beethoven worked upon the three quartets simultaneously.

It is nothing more than the bare exposition of the all-pervading theme in each of the principal forms it is to assume: in majestic bar lengths, in diminution and altered rhythm as it is to appear in the third fugue, and in quarter notes as in the second fugue, with the accompanying figure of that fugue. The ubiquitous theme is played in the bass as countersubject to the subject of the first fugue:

The second fugue offers the contrast of *pianissimo,* in G flat, *meno mosso e moderato.* It opens with the theme in double diminution (sixteenth notes), and proceeds with a weaving second subject in the same note value. The third fugue, *Allegro molto e con brio,* states the theme rhythmically, and combines it with a new subject, beginning with a trill. The moderate section interrupts it, and reappears again fleetingly just before the coda begins. The theme by this time has been stretched and compressed, inverted, divided up, combined with itself. In the coda, the inexhaustible Beethoven presents it in further guises, but in harmonic clothing at last. (See page 108.)

370

STRING QUARTET (NO. 14) IN C SHARP MINOR, OP. 131

Adagio ma non troppo e molto espressivo—Allegro molto vivace—
Allegro moderato—Andante ma non troppo e molto cantabile—
Presto—Adagio quasi un poco andante—Allegro

(Completed in 1826; published in April, 1827, dedicated to the Baron von Stutterheim.)

Holz has related having once said to Beethoven that in his opinion the Quartet in B flat was the greatest of them all. Beethoven replied: "Each in its way. Art demands of us that we shall not stand still. You will find a new manner of voice treatment, and thank God here is less lack of fancy than ever before." At a later time he declared the C sharp minor Quartet to be his greatest. When the manuscript was delivered to Schott and Sons in August, the publishers were much upset to find this inscription upon it in the composer's handwriting: *"Zusammengestohlen aus Verschiedenem diesem und jenem"* ("A putting together of various stolen odds and ends"). Unable to perceive that the remark and not the score itself was Beethoven's little joke, they wrote to him in alarm, and had to be explicitly reassured that it was really "brand new." Perhaps he was referring to the seven movements, played without a break, a plan which in other hands would certainly have sounded like a putting together of odds and ends. The balanced structure of this Quartet, the beauty of its two connecting movements, with their undeveloped treasure, the remarkable unity which binds its many elements—these have been an unending subject of admiration.

The seven numbered movements are easily conceived in terms of the conventional four. The opening fugue, which far exceeds in length and importance any usual introduction, can be taken as an introduction. The following *Allegro molto vivace* can be looked upon as the first movement, the eleven bars of the *Allegro moderato* as a bridge passage leading into the *Andante* with variations, the fully developed slow movement. The *Presto* is distinctly a scherzo, the *Adagio* of twenty-eight bars, another episode, bringing a short relief of slow tempo between the swift scherzo movement and the *Allegro finale* which follows.

In the unfolding of the great fugue, the process of the intellect is always subservient to that of the heart. It is long and devious, but sustained, constantly revelatory. Strangely enough (considering its success) this was Beethoven's only fugue in slow tempo. The sorrowful mood is dispelled by the *Allegro molto vivace* in D major—"the return to life," Paul Bekker has called it, "to joyful thought and emotion, an *incarnatus est* in the human rather than the religious sense." A bridging movement of a few measures with a violin cadenza introduces the long slow movement (in A major), a theme with six very free variations. The theme

was called by Wagner, who wrote at length about this Quartet, "the blessed incarnation of innocence." The variations are a marvel of melodic resource, the theme much transformed—often disappearing altogether. The *Presto* (in E major) is closer to the orthodoxy of a *scherzo*. The short *Adagio* between the *Presto* and the last movement is another gentle hymn of faith, contemplative, giving the pause of mystery with which Beethoven would linger over a pending disclosure. The final *allegro* is brilliant and jubilant. It has the impulse of militant triumph which recalls the finale of the *Eroica,* the march episodes from the Ninth Symphony or the A minor Quartet. (See pages 242, 253.)

STRING QUARTET (NO. 15) IN A MINOR, OP. 132

Assai sostenuto; Allegro
Allegro ma non tanto
Molto Adagio: Canzona di ringraziamento in modo
  lidico, offerta alla divinitá da un guarito
Alla Marcia, assai vivace; Allegro appassionato

(Completed in 1825, probably before the Quartets Opus 130 and Opus 131; first performed November 6, 1825, in Vienna; published September, 1827, dedicated to Prince Nicolaus von Galitzin.)

The minor mode prevails, save in the scherzo-like second movement, and the close of the *Finale.* The programme clue which Beethoven wrote over the slow movement "Song of thanksgiving to the Deity by a convalescent, in the Lydian mode," has over-stimulated certain commentators. The slow movement was probably written on his recovery from an illness in the spring of 1825, but sketches for the other movements antedate that illness. The *finale* theme appears among the sketches for the Ninth Symphony in 1823, intended as a finale for the Symphony, and thoughts of a "religious song in a symphony in the old modes" was noted in 1818 while the *Missa Solemnis* was occupying him. The work upon the A minor and B flat quartets in 1825 is so closely inter-mingled that the *alla Tedesca* which went into the latter, may have been contemplated for the former. This drift of plans shows the busy continuity of the artist's musical state of mind as the succession of quartets progressed.

The first movement is a remarkable piece of constructive integration. One may lay a finger upon the main theme, introduced by a flourish of the first violin and to be persistently worked, a lyric theme of the second group in a contrasting F major over a triplet accompaniment. Boundaries of the usual three sections can be faintly discerned. But these observations are not even the beginning of an approach to the core of the matter. Beethoven seems to have followed the general trodden path quite absent-mindedly and only because the problem which engrossed him, taking its own form, did not come into conflict with habits of structure. The sustained introductory chords, where anguish seems stilled in faith, are the basic spirit of the movement as they recur, shadow-like, making their harmony subtly felt. The outward voice of the movement is that of the principal theme

which has the same characteristic plaint of the falling half tone from sixth to dominant noted in the F minor Quartet. The 'cello gives out this F-E in the second bar of the four-note introductory motto; the violin passage which ushers in the theme poises on it. The theme repeats it twice and sends it into sequential repetitions until the tension breaks with a *forte* unison descent upon a rhythm which has grown from it. These few bars can be taken as a characteristic link in the chain of events which comprise the whole movement. Plaints gather into an outburst of passionate energy, which in turn gives way to the calm of the introductory motto chords or the clear and healing major of the second theme. The principal theme engenders many episodes which are a part of itself, and which are combined with it closely and organically. In place of an orthodox development there is what might be called a second exposition, which is not repetitious,

but vital and generative. The second movement, in a relieving
A major, is in *scherzo* form with repeats and *da capo*. The trio,
which does not recur, is in the character of a German dance, the
tune carried by the violin in its high range.

Over the *Molto Adagio* Beethoven wrote—"*Heiliger Dankge-
sang eines Genesenen an die Gottheit, in der Lydischen Tonart*"
(translated into Italian in the printed score), and over the alternate *Andante*—"*Neue Kraft Fühlend.*" * The *Adagio* section occurs three times, treated as a varied chorale on its recurrences.
The intervening *Andante* occurs twice, elaborated on its second
appearance. The five-part song form is suggested, or indeed the
scherzo and trio with its double alternation. The *Andante* serves
as a foil for the *Adagio* because of its melodic flow after the
almost static chords of the *Adagio* as it is first heard. The fresh
D major, following the modal harmonies, gives a sense of restoration similar to the F major of the first movement. The chords of
the *Adagio* have a remote, mystic, ethereal quality, far different from those which opened the Quartet, the modal harmonies
(equivalent to F major with the fourth raised to B natural) giving a special coloring:

The placid, motionless chant is beautifully conveyed by the four
instruments. As it returns, the four voices move alternately, with
a suggestion of antique choral counterpoint. The minimum note
value is the eighth; when the *adagio* returns once more, to end
the movement, it is the sixteenth. This last section is marked "*Mit
innigster Empfindung*" ("With the most intimate feeling"). The
hushed spell of this close is quite beyond description. It is a high
point in all the quartets—in all the music of Beethoven. A march

* With a sense of renewed strength.

movement (in A major) of twenty-four bars in two repeated sections is music of joyous summoning. The Ninth Symphony is recalled, and the impression is strengthened as there follows an agitated recitative, full of anticipation. The finale, the theme of which was sketched two years before, and intended for the Ninth Symphony, is set in a rondo, a form Beethoven had long ceased to use. Its use here is understandable; the composer wished to make this theme dominate, not only by rich fragmentary manipulation, but by dramatic returns in toto and in the now dramatically important A minor tonality.* These returns are made the more effective by the sudden preliminary hushing of the other voices. A long *crescendo* leads to the final *presto,* and the sounding of the theme at last in the joyous A major. Descending unison octaves, just before the final cadence, are a last reminiscence of the Ninth Symphony. (See pages 220, 222, 229.)

STRING QUARTET (NO. 16) IN F MAJOR, OP. 135

Allegretto
Vivace
Lento assai, cantante e tranquillo
Grave ma non troppo tratto; Allegro

(Completed at Gneixendorf, October, 1826; published posthumously, September, 1827; dedicated to "his friend" Johann Wolfmayer.)

The last quartet, written at Gneixendorf in the waning summer of 1826, is brief in duration, slight in conception—no companion in stature for the four that preceded it. It would seem that after the intensive explorations of the C sharp minor Quartet, the composer was ready to let his skill and fancy play upon the surface of his art. Fragments of themes, wilfully angular, perhaps casually arrived at, become the subjects of contrapuntal working in the first and last movements. The slow movement is far from

* The F to E interval, which links the recitative with the finale in a single *adagio* bar, is reiterated by the second violin through the entire statement of the theme, giving it its poignant minor character.

casual. It alone rouses the composer to his true and familiar grandeur. It recalls the *Cavatina* of the B flat Quartet by its brevity, position and character, and indeed the F major Quartet is content to reflect upon past ways. It falls back into the regular four-movement scheme, lately departed from. The first movement is novel in capricious details of the working out, and no less so the *vivace* which follows, with its light play upon the off beat in a triple rhythm. In the Trio, the swift dance of shifting chords gives a fleeting reminiscence of the scherzo of the Ninth Symphony. A dominant-tonic figure of the theme becomes a driving *ostinato* which insists furiously upon A major while the first violin skips wide and high above it. The wisest of musicians were for years puzzled by this delightful caricature of a drone bass. The "*Lento assai, cantante e tranquillo*" is in D flat major, the key which Beethoven spoke of as the key for sentiment. The melody, as simple and diatonic as could be imagined, conquers at once before it has been gilded by a single rare harmony or ornamentation. But presently it is richly harmonized, and the intensity is increased by a moving episode of no more than ten bars in the enharmonic C sharp minor. Two short (and indescribable) variations restore the tranquillity of the opening. Beethoven could write the shortest as well as the longest of slow movements—and with equal success.

Upon the manuscript, at the head of the last movement, stands this legend in the composer's script:

The question is put by the 'cello and viola in rising sequences, while diminished seventh chords of F minor echo the insistent interrogation. This caprice, lightly conceived, seems to haunt the music for the moment. The man who was tragically harassed and mortally ill may have asked himself whether he must accept the inevitable and may then have brushed aside morbid thoughts as music in the restored major rose within him, and the inverted motto took full possession of the *Finale.* Music, strong and confident was always his answer to dark questionings. Even this episode recalls the past—the *"malinconia"* of the early B flat Quartet in Opus 18. But here the flooding relief of the major is far more skillfully handled. In this, as in most of the *finales* of the final quartets, the joyous close is the more affecting by its combination of tumultuous speed and delicate dynamic restraint. (See pages 237, 243, 263.)

THE VIOLIN SONATAS

Of the ten sonatas for Violin and Pianoforte, the first eight were written in the space of four years—between 1799 and 1802. The last two at least were written for the immediate use of violinists—the Ninth (the "Kreutzer" Sonata) for Bridgetower in 1803, and the last for Rode as late as 1812. Not one of them bears a dedication which could be called intimate. Apparently, then, Beethoven came to the point of writing a violin sonata (or a 'cello sonata, for that matter) only in fulfillment of a distinct and advantageous demand and not by the personal inclination which so often led him into a new piano sonata, symphony or quartet. The duo combination did not seem to beckon. One has often the feeling while listening to the violin sonatas that one instrument is deferring to the other. Sometimes progress is retarded while the second instrument is allowed to repeat, in concerto style, what the first has played. But these moments, fortunately, are few. More often the marriage is as happy and fruitful as marriages are supposed to be. In parts of all the sonatas, and all of some of them, the themes become inherent to both instruments, and the texture becomes a silken, variegated whole as, imagination alight, the composer rears his structures of tone.

THREE SONATAS (NOS. 1, 2, 3), OP. 12 (IN D MAJOR, A MAJOR, AND E-FLAT)

1 *Allegro con brio*
  Tema con variazioni: Andante con moto
  Rondo: Allegro

2 *Allegro vivace*
  Andante più tosto allegro
  Allegro piacèvole

3 *Allegro con spirito*
  Adagio con molt' espressione
  Rondo: Allegro molto

(Composed—probably—in 1798; published January, 1799; dedicated to "Antonio Salieri, First *Kapellmeister* of the Imperial Court at Vienna.")

Beethoven seems to have set out to write two sonatas in the grandest manner he then new, opening each with broad flourishes and sweeping runs, giving the violinist, incidentally, plenty to do. Between the two, as if to show that he was not the full-time slave of display, he placed a sonata, simple, tuneful, full of fresh, youthful spirit and entirely charming. The first movement of the Sonata in A major waltzes gaily on bright, lilting fragments of melody which might have tumbled from an opera of Mozart, where they would have been woven around a singer's voice. The slow movement plays upon its melody in a light-rhythmed *allegretto,* and in an A minor which is quizzical rather than grave. The finale carries the same gently skimming mood into a rondo in the original key. A sonata which makes no attempt to capture the hearer by an onslaught of sound, and captivates him instead. The first Sonata of the set proceeds, after a first movement which adds new brilliance and strength to the gallant style, with an orthodox set of variations, the third in the minor. The rondo has the rich invention Beethoven could unfailingly summon in this form, even in his earlier years, and with which he also plentifully dressed the rondo the third Sonata. This Sonata has for its middle movement an *adagio* where elegance warms to sentiment, and rises at the close to dramatized emotional expression. (See page 73.)

SONATA IN A MINOR (NO. 4), OP. 23

Presto
Andante scherzoso, più allegretto
Allegro molto

(Composed in 1800; published October, 1801, dedicated to Count Moritz von Fried.)

The sketches for the first two movements coincide with those for the Piano Sonata, Opus 22, and the first and last of the String Quartets, Opus 18. The minor mode pervades the first movement, but plaintively rather than darkly. Both theme groups (the second in the dominant minor) are continuously fluent, drawing the two instruments into an intimate and inseparable duet. The development is remarkably fertile. The middle movement, a playful *Andante*, banishes the elegiac cast with a clear A major. It begins upon an elementary tune with piquant rests, which the violin presently fills in.

For a second section, a lively staccato theme furnishes a *fugato* in three parts. The development alternates and combines the two with great charm. The *Finale* is a rondo, devolving upon a fluent A minor melody which seems to wish to recapture the mood of the first movement. But the movement becomes active and urgent. A curious episode is built upon a succession of whole-note chords which prove to be a framework for sinuous filling in.

SONATA (NO. 5) IN F MAJOR, OP. 24

Allegro
Adagio molto espressivo
Scherzo: Allegro molto
Rondo: Allegro ma non troppo

(The Sonata appeared in the same year as the one previous, and with the same dedication. In fact it was at first intended as Opus 23, No. 2, and so put out.)

Those who cherish the easier violin sonatas for home performance find the one in F major particularly rewarding. It opens in this wise:

and runs a fairly simple course, in evenly rippling figures, uncovering lesser excitements, delightful always. There is not a shadow upon its bright surface, which will account for the title *Der Frühling* which has been popularly bestowed upon it in Germany. Its amiable acceptance of the four-movement convention, and its tonality which rivals D major as the sunny key, brings to mind the "Pastoral" Sonata for piano, which closely followed it. A characteristic piece of humor in the opening movement is the portentous warning of a second theme in G minor or C minor, the theme suddenly emerging in a gleaming and triumphant (and prescribed) C major. The slow movement sets a romantic song in B-flat in the daintiest of figurations. The *Scherzo,* in minimum size of eight-bar lengths, is based on a naïve staccato tune. The rondo is a stream of moderate current and sparkling twists.

THREE SONATAS (NOS. 6, 7, 8), OP. 30 (IN A MAJOR, C MINOR, AND G MAJOR)

(Composed in 1802 and published in May, 1803, with a dedication to the Czar Alexander I of Russia.) (See page 85.)

SONATA IN A MAJOR, OP. 30, NO. 1

Allegro
Adagio
Allegretto con variazioni

The opening of the A major Sonata is not so directly taking as the second subject, but it improves with acquaintance in a development brilliant and adroit. The *Adagio* grows from a broad, songlike melody of tender beauty, lightly animated by a rhythmic accompaniment:

The *Finale* is a set of six variations upon an *allegretto* theme developed in the classical manner, and at last transformed from common to 6/8 time. This *Finale* replaced one which Beethoven set aside as inappropriate and subsequently used for the "Kreutzer" Sonata.

SONATA IN C MINOR, OP. 30, NO. 2

Allegro con brio
Adagio cantabile
Scherzo: Allegro
Finale: Allegro

The C minor Sonata can be called the most treasure-laden of them all, the nearest to Beethoven's true inner grandeur (not excepting the "Kreutzer" Sonata, which is easily conceded to be the most brilliant). This, the writer believes, is not a minority opinion among those who know both. The C minor Sonata has stature by its combination of opposite qualities, which reveal with remarkable completeness the Beethoven in whom thoughts of the *Eroica* were first stirring. C minor, it has often been observed, was always a key of conflict with Beethoven, a tonality to which he turned with a special seriousness. As music of stormy undercurrent mingles with episodes of engaging tranquillity, it brings to mind the Piano Sonata in D minor, Opus 31, No. 2, which was composed simultaneously. The opening bars:

have little meaning until the figure in sixteenth notes is revealed in eloquent forcefulness, rumbling threateningly in the bass or multiplied into a storming accompaniment. In wonderful contrast is this theme (militant if you wish), a confident and resilient assertion of E-flat major—

As the development begins, the notes first quoted step forward into full, swinging power, until the opposing concept is brought forward, correspondingly reinforced in sonority. The struggle continues at length and with rich results, thundering at last to its C minor close. The two middle movements are in complete and dramatic contrast to the outer ones—entirely idyllic. The *Adagio cantabile*, the most winsome slow movement in all the violin sonatas, sings in tender sentiment which is unfailingly enhanced by such elaborations in accompaniment as rising staccato arpeggios, and feathery scales. The *Scherzo* takes a blithe path—and is closed upon by the menace of the deep staccato notes which open the *Finale*, and the mysterious descending chords which open the door of C minor once more. The movement has moments of stark drama, rising in the final presto to a climax of ferocity.

SONATA IN G MAJOR, OP. 30, NO. 3

Allegro assai
Tempo di Menuetto
Allegro vivace

The third Sonata, in G major, is insubstantial, even superficial by comparison. The first and last movements are gay and brilliantly effective, the middle one, by contrast, delicate and thinly scored. None of the Sonata is what Beethoven once or twice referred to as music "from the heart." This opening figure in the first movement—

appearing in many guises, roaring in the bass, or whispering in the treble, is characteristic of points of excitement, such as flashing scales, or the passage of driving trills which opens the development. There follows a slow-paced movement in "minuet tempo," a movement of transparent simplicity. Except for a graceful triple beat and a form which is a loose and extended version of the trio and return, it has no aspects of a minuet. The alternate sections are in E-flat and a languorous G minor. This lingering over tenuous, reiterative measures might wear too thin, did not the master hand lay upon them a hypnotic charm of antique grace notes. The rondo is headlong and sparkling, giving the violinist plentiful opportunity to show his sleight of hand. The composer, having used up his little theme in the formal rounds, plays tricks with it, such as throwing the rhythm out of place, or pausing upon a well-hammered G major to drop suddenly into a *pianissimo* in E-flat.

SONATA (NO. 9) IN A MAJOR, OP. 47

Adagio sostenuto: Presto
Andante con variazioni
Finale: Presto

(Composed in 1803; first performed about May 24, 1803, at an Augarten concert by Bridgetower, Beethoven playing the piano part; published in 1805 with a dedication to Rudolph Kreutzer.)

"Written in a very *concertante* style" runs the subtitle, "as that of a concerto." The young mulatto violinist Bridgetower,* who came to Vienna in early 1803 and impressed Beethoven, although Beethoven had not met him, seems to have been the motive of this unusual "concerto" sonata. Beethoven evidently offered to provide a sonata for Bridgetower's morning concert at the Augarten in May, and accompany him in its performance.

---

* The name seems to have baffled German understanding. Held, writing memoirs, mentions him as "Bridgethauer," and Beethoven, in a letter, writes "Brishdower." Schindler refers to him as an "American ship captain," which seems to be no closer to the truth than that he lived in England. George Augustus Polgreen Bridgetower was born in Poland of a Polish (or German) mother and a father who was referred to sometimes as an "African" and sometimes as an "Abyssinian Prince." The boy caused such a sensation as a violin prodigy in England that he was inducted into the Royal band at Brighton. He advertised himself as a pupil of Haydn, a claim which scholars take the liberty of doubting. He was twenty-four when he encountered Beethoven.

But, laying himself out with a piece in the full bravura manner, he had great difficulty getting it ready in time.

Czerny said that the first movement was "composed in four days," but the truth probably was that a partly written movement was hastily completed in four days, the violin part written in readable copy with all speed by Ries, the piano part indicated here and there. Bridgetower performed the variations also from manuscript. Only the *Finale,* long since written out for use in the Violin Sonata, Opus 30, No. 1, was ready in full and adequate notation. According to Bridgetower's memorandum upon his copy of the score, Beethoven performed the slow movement with such "chaste expression" that it was encored. Bridgetower also tells that as they rehearsed he echoed the pianist's cadenza in the repeat of the exposition of the first movement, whereat Beethoven leaped up and embraced him, shouting, *"Noch einmal, mein lieber Bursch!"* One can imagine other and stronger words at this piece of presumption. The two quarreled, and when, after a delay, the Sonata appeared in print, the dedication had gone to Rudolph Kreutzer, the prominent Parisian violinist. Kreutzer, it is said, never played the Sonata in public.

It is one of the surest signs of Beethoven's surpassing resourcefulness that when he was by necessity stage conscious, writing broadly for a performer before a multitude, the result did not fall into the hollow glitter elsewhere found under such circumstances. Passage work, of which each player has an ample share in the give and take of the "Kreutzer" Sonata, sings warmly in heroic lines, as if something of the *Eroica,* then his main concern, had crept into it. The slow introduction (the only one in the violin sonatas) sets the expansive mood. The cluster of themes and episodes are all exploited to the full, and countered by a hymn-like succession of harmonies in static whole notes. The variations proceed formally, each in a set decorative pattern, one favoring the pianist, another the violinist. There is no opportunity for the personal revelation which occurs in the slow movements of the C minor Sonata, or the Sonata to follow. The overelaboration, with something less than supreme genius to direct it, could easily have fallen from molten beauty into cold rigidity. The final *Presto,* in full sonata form, would obviously

388

have overbalanced the first two movements of the earlier Sonata in the same key, for which it was at first intended. Beethoven, according to Ries, had found the *Finale* "too brilliant" for this position, and wrote to supplant it the variations which appeared when the score was published.* (See page 87.)

SONATA (NO. 10) IN G MAJOR, OP. 96

Allegro moderato
Adagio espressivo
Scherzo: Allegro
Poco allegretto

(Composed in 1812; first performed by Pierre Rode and the Archduke Rudolph on December 29, 1812, at the Palace of Prince Lobkowitz; published in July, 1816, with a dedication to the Archduke.)

Pierre Rode, the celebrated violinist, visiting Vienna in 1812, and, as Spohr then wrote, plainly past his prime, was the occasion of this (probably quickly written) Sonata. Beethoven felt obliged to explain to the Archduke in a letter that he had been "embarrassed" by the necessity of avoiding "rushing and resounding passages," which were not in Rode's style. He might have said, more truly, that they were not then in his own, as the inward character of the music proved, and as music to follow would confirm.

If there were any reason to compare this belated Sonata with the "Kreutzer" Sonata of nine years earlier, the contrast would be far more striking than could ever be explained by the varying styles of two violinists. The Sonata in G major does not sing in exultant sonorities under the fingers. Neither player is favored with "passages." The pianist's portion is rewarding only insofar as he studies delicate inflections and achieves them with a special understanding (such as the Archduke could scarcely have had). The violinist, deprived of the spotlight, must be content to weave

* The three Sonatas, Opus 30, were announced in publication a few days after Bridgetower's concert.

his way in the general texture, as if he were playing in a string quartet. But these are negative virtues. It is a light-hearted Sonata, with themes of delicate charm, such as this opening motto

which subtly pervades the first movement, although seldom appearing note for note. The restrained beauty of the *Adagio*, defined in light tracery, and the airiness of the *Scherzo*, which never touches the ground, cannot be conveyed by quotation. The theme of the *Finale* is simplicity itself—

Its course is held back before the close by a long *adagio* episode which without literal reminiscence strives to re-establish the mood of the slow movement. A. Eaglefield Hull, who considers this "the most intimate of all the violin sonatas," calls it "not really characteristic of the master's latest style, which does not commence until Opus 106." This seems like a case of cutting the man to the cloth of theory. The G major Sonata is as characteristic of the "latest style" Beethoven as the Piano Sonata, Opus 78, written three years before, is characteristic, and as the "Archduke" Trio, which immediately preceded the Violin Sonata, is not. (See page 108.)

THE
VIOLONCELLO SONATAS

Beethoven seldom turned his hand to sonatas for violoncello and piano. He certainly had inducement to write them: He always had 'cellist friends about him, some of them fine players, who would have welcomed sonatas from him and made the most of them—Doležalek, Zmeskall, the Krafts, father and son, and later Linke. Yet until 1809, when he wrote the A major Sonata for Gleichenstein, there were only the two extremely youthful works which he had contrived for the King of Prussia when visiting Berlin in 1796. Once more, as late as 1815, he added another pair (Opus 102), this time for the Countess Marie von Erdödy. The total of five, therefore, are distributed at three widely separated points in his life—Opus 5 very early, Opus 69 at the full tide of his middle career, and Opus 102 at a time when he had quite ceased to concern himself with duo sonatas.

One can only conclude that the problem of carrying a mono-chrome tenor voice interestingly through a succession of movements did not attract him. With his growing mastery, he went far toward solving that problem.

TWO SONATAS (NOS. 1 AND 2), OP. 5 (IN F MAJOR AND G MINOR)

1 *Adagio sostenuto; Allegro*
   Allegro vivace

2 *Adagio sostenuto ed espressivo; Allegro molto, più tosto presto*
   Rondo: Allegro

(Composed in 1796, and performed by Beethoven and Duport, the Court 'Cellist, before the King of Prussia in the royal palace at

Berlin; published February, 1797; dedicated to the Emperor Wilhelm II of Prussia.)

The two Sonatas follow the identical plan of a long *Adagio* introduction, followed by two fast movements. It would seem that the composer could not see his way to attaining sufficient color variety from the 'cello through the lengths of a regular slow movement, and took this expedient for providing the instrument with the slow melody for which it is best fitted. The result is in each case introductory pages of considerable beauty where the 'cello attains its highest point of eloquence, and a sonata proper in an unrelieved sprightly tempo more suited to the keyboard style. The introduction to the first of the sonatas is a wandering fantasia with melodic elements. The *allegro* proper is for the pianist—a first movement in the vivacious salon manner, where the solo 'cellist has the leavings—a scrap of tune or a filling in. The second Sonata is more favorable to the instrument, as if the composer were already more at home with his materials. The introduction becomes more than preluding; it exceeds the already unprecedented length of the first introduction, and develops melody as if a true slow movement were taking shape. The main *Allegro* is likewise more fruitful for the 'cello, the second group of subjects being manifold and lyrical in character. The rondos seem tailored rather to the pleasures of a monarch than to the subtler possibilities of a violoncello. (See page 49.)

SONATA (NO. 3) IN A MAJOR, OP. 69

Allegro, ma non tanto
Scherzo: Allegro molto
Adagio cantabile; Allegro vivace

(Composed in 1809; published in April, 1809, with a dedication to "my friend, the Imperial Court Councillor, Baron von Gleichenstein.")

The Sonata proves that in the course of thirteen years the composer had acquired far more understanding of the 'cello, or, to put it perhaps more accurately, had found the way to write music which more fully exploited its range, color and graces. In the very opening bars the instrument takes the center of the stage, commanding but not usurping the attention with an unaccompanied theme which is part of its nature, and which will sound strikingly dramatic on the piano:

The movement preserves this balance between instruments, between animation and melody. The 'cello is seldom merely a doubling or a superfluous voice. The mean style is a reticent accompaniment about which play the independent melodies of each instrument. The *Scherzo* contributes to the charm of this unclouded Sonata with a specimen of Beethoven's wizardry with the merest wisp of a tune:

The last two notes continue in a dreaming *ostinato* and furnish the Trio. There follows the regular periodic melody of what promises to be a regular slow movement. But it is not developed.

393

Beethoven has merely found a more appropriate position for an *adagio* introduction—before the *Finale*. The *Finale* is a sonata movement, melodic throughout, lightly and still transparently written for the piano.

TWO SONATAS (NOS. 4 AND 5), OP. 102 (IN C MAJOR AND D MAJOR)

1   *Andante—Allegro vivace*
    Adagio—Tempo d'andante—Allegro vivace

2   *Allegro con brio*
    { *Adagio con molto sentimento d'affetto*
    { *Allegro fugato*

(Completed in August, 1815; published in 1817 with a dedication to the Countess Marie von Erdödy.)

"Two free sonatas" runs the title. They are free in the ordering of movements, just as the Piano Sonata, Opus 101, written immediately before these, is free. Having in his 'cello sonatas until then tried an introduction at the beginning and before the finale, Beethoven in the C major Sonata puts an introduction in both positions. In the final Sonata he tries a full-length slow movement at last. The result justifies the venture. The two Sonatas resemble the Violin Sonata Opus 96 in finding their substance in a concentrated, finely pointed style, sometimes intellectualized, where idiosyncrasy has free play. The deaf man has lost much that he has had of the virtuoso's point of view. His imagination develops delicate sensuous beauty, sometimes tonal power, but the idea, often conceived in manifold voices, has first control. The two Sonatas are restrained in scope, quite without thought of display. That they were intended for intimate home performance at the Erdödys' by his friend Linke,* who was tutor to the Erdödy children, may have had something to do with this.

* Linke, who had often nobly served Beethoven in the Schuppanzigh Quartet, was the subject of much punning, *"linke"* meaning "left." *"Lieber Linke und Rechte,"* Beethoven called him, and he wrote to Jedlersee suggesting that Linke play on his left bank of the Danube until the population should be "drawn to his side."

The *Andante teneramente* of the first Sonata begins with a gentle theme, *dolce cantabile,* which seems born for the soft-spoken tenor voice. Rhapsody replaces development, and leads, after two pages, into the *Allegro vivace*. In its striding rhythmic theme, the piano is favored, but only intermittently, for the second theme is of the 'cello's kind. The end of the movement brings the only pause, and an *Adagio,* of anticipatory character, ushers in, surprisingly enough, the theme of the *Andante* which began the Sonata. This again is illusory, for after seven measures the *Finale* makes a whispering entrance. It is notable for bridge passages in which the 'cello softly sounds open fifths as if groping for a tonality.

The second Sonata of course dispenses with an introduction, for a slow movement is to come. The lively figure of the opening movement lends itself to close and varied working. The *Adagio con molto sentimento d'affetto* is in D minor, with a long middle section in D major. The melody as it stands is sparingly used; the 'cello sings it only once. But the melodic invention is abundant and marvelously expressed in the duet which it maintains with the piano. The whole movement is ethereally light, at once tender and remote. In the finale, which follows without break, the 'cello adds a fourth voice to a *fugato,* which, however industrious, is light-footed until the close. (See pages 183, 197.)

THE TRIOS

FOR PIANO, VIOLIN AND VIOLONCELLO

After choosing three Trios for his Opus 1, of 1795, Beethoven left this combination for piano and strings untouched until 1808, when he wrote the two of Opus 70. Once more, in 1811, he wrote the "Archduke" Trio, Opus 97, which in itself would give a lusty answer to the suggestion that he may have been disinclined toward this medium.

THREE PIANO TRIOS, OP. 1 (IN E-FLAT MAJOR, G MAJOR, AND C MINOR)

1 *Allegro*
Adagio cantabile
Scherzo: Quasi allegro assai
Finale: Presto

2 *Adagio; Allegro vivace*
Largo con espressione
Scherzo: Allegro
Finale: Presto

3 *Allegro con brio*
Andante cantabile con variazioni
Menuetto: Quasi allegretto
Finale: Prestissimo

(Completed and published in 1795; dedicated to Prince Karl von Lichnowsky.)

Beethoven put his best foot forward in his Opus 1, and did it in a way that could not have failed to place him in high and popular standing. The blending of the instruments, the smooth handling of the form, the clearly wrought themes—all of them first-rate of their kind—not least, the confident boldness of the innovations—these qualities bespeak the hand of a young master who has been in no hurry to declare himself. The threefold result could stand indisputably beside its models.

The gay eighteenth-century infectiousness of the first two Trios at least could not have been denied. The third borrows some of the clouded wistfulness which Mozart had found in the minor mode, and emerges with the intimations of a new and more serious voice.

The opening movement of the Trio in E-flat establishes at once that the composer can carry his hearers into alien keys at least as adroitly as Haydn; he can also plunge with dramatic abruptness into a new key; those who were at first taken aback by this soon learned that they would have no choice but to reconcile themselves to it. The theme of the *Adagio cantabile* could have been written by Haydn, but not its development. The *Scherzo* is not remarkable as a *scherzo* of Beethoven; it is extremely interesting as his first. The *presto Finale* dances blithely on an irresistible up-skipping theme.

The second Trio, in G major, offers Beethoven's first known use of a slow introduction, to which the *Allegro vivace* which follows offers a perfect foil. The chromatic passage which brings in the close of the exposition was something quite unheard of in the year 1800. The *Largo con espressione* is Beethoven's first fully developed slow movement in the affecting singing style; the first "song without words," it could be called. The gates are opened wide to sentiment and to lengths untold. But it is not a minor song; E major is the prevailing key. A *Scherzo* in D major, again more historically than musically interesting, is followed by a *presto Finale* even more dancing and sparkling than that of the first Trio. It should be noted that in all three *Finales* of his Opus 1, Beethoven spurns the rondo for the first movement form, with its richer possibilities.

It is not surprising that Haydn took exception to the C minor Trio rather than the others. The exterior is not at particular odds with custom, but the key is prophetic, and indeed a Beethoven to come, forceful and earnest, the melodious poet of sentiment, is already discernible. The first and last movements show this rather than the *Andante cantabile,* a theme in B-flat with five variations in the manner Beethoven then so well knew, and the pleasing minuet. The opening movement and the final *prestissimo,* each alternate between a plaintive minor and a brighter major theme. Each begins with striking introductory measures which will serve later for abrupt and emphatic modulations. These may have been the first tentative steps which would lead to the terse "motto" theme and its compact power in development. (See pages 47, 48, 66.)

TWO PIANO TRIOS (NOS. 4 AND 5), OP. 70 (IN D MAJOR AND E-FLAT MAJOR)

1   *Allegro vivace e con brio*
    Largo assai
    Presto

2   *Poco sostenuto; Allegro ma non troppo*
    Allegretto
    Allegretto ma non troppo
    Finale: Allegro

(Completed by the end of 1808; published in 1809; dedicated to the Countess Marie von Erdödy.)

The two Trios, Op. 70, show an immense stride from Op. 1. The composer seems to rejoice in the form, although he chose it so seldom. He now writes far more brilliantly for the piano. The sustaining instruments are more pliable and eloquent. The combination can achieve a ringing sonority. The D major Trio proclaims its virtuoso character at once in the flamboyant octaves of its opening theme. But it has not the life-affirming, fluent inevitability of the "Emperor" Concerto, which is of its year. The difference is one of character as well as degree. A certain restless uneasiness, a probing of dark corners, suggests rather the F minor Quartet, which shortly followed. This quality finds full expression in the slow movement, in a melancholy which sounds hollow and almost forbidding, the usual stream of sensuous melody sometimes lapsing. A weird figure which might be described as a soulless cry is repeated in many forms without cessation throughout the movement:

Nottebohm shows that this figure appears among Beethoven's sketches for the opening scene of the witches in *Macbeth*. As if he still had that scene in his mind as he wrote the Trio, he increases the eerie effect by light tremolo chords in the piano, these, too, almost without cessation. The hollow desolation of this wan music has given the work the title, *"Geister"* (Ghost) Trio. The music several times gathers to a despairing climax, which falls away as the tremolo breaks into long descending scales. The composer is hard to recognize in this curious venture into morbidity.

What stands out at once in the Trio in E-flat is the third movement, *Allegretto,* in scherzo form. The theme has a folkish purity which is enhanced by its entirely simple setting forth. Schubert might have written it, and also that part of the alternative section where the piano holds a dialogue by alternation with the mated strings. A whimsical connecting passage and an equally curious chain of soft modulations, bringing the return of the first section, stand out delightfully against the diatonic purity about them. The Trio is engaging throughout, unruffled by any sign of trouble or violence. The tempi are moderate, an *allegretto* with variations upon another simple tune serving for a slow movement. The first movement begins and ends with

399

antique flourishes in a slower tempo. The *Finale* is as light-hearted as the *Scherzo,* but, it must be admitted, a little dry by comparison.

PIANO TRIO (NO. 6) IN B-FLAT MAJOR, OP. 97

Allegro moderato
Scherzo: Allegro
$\begin{cases} Andante \ cantabile \ ma \ però \ con \ moto \\ Allegro \ moderato \end{cases}$

(Completed in March, 1811; published in 1816, dedicated to the Archduke Rudolph.)

The last Trio (known as the "Archduke" Trio) is not, technically speaking, more brilliant than its two predecessors, nor more skillfully made as an ensemble or as a musical construction. Its true superiority makes itself felt in the powerful, straightforward inevitability of the musical current, while its special skill is evident in the result—in the way the instruments are made to build a sonority suggesting far more than three—the way, too, that the discourse achieves its transitions and its sweeping impulsion. This, in a word, was the heroic Beethoven. He was too full of his subject to concern himself with the play of ingenuity or the cultivation of personal idiosyncrasy. These were privileges of chamber music, and Beethoven was not in the mood of chamber music. The B-flat Trio is designed for virtuosos, a platform and a multitude. The piano part has a dozen traits of the concerto style, and indeed the Trio is so closely in the vein of the Fourth and Fifth Piano Concertos that it can in parts be almost thought of as a sixth. It has the same expansive grandeur which Beethoven found in broadly singing themes, and similarly weaves an imperious spell with piano figures upon elementary harmonies. The second theme of the opening movement is significantly reminiscent of the opening of the Fourth Concerto (it is even in the same tonality):

A swift *Scherzo,* in the composer's best vein, follows. The *Largo* is a series of five variations on a hymn-like theme, which, according to Beethoven's unique way, is endlessly illuminated by decorations, each proving anew that the simple wholeness of the song was not the measure of its content. The coda at last breaks the theme up into melodic pieces which coalesce into one of the finest pages of the Trio. The slow movement is linked with the final rondo, a circumstance which recalls that the *Scherzo,* with its similar tempo, would have been out of place in this position. One is also reminded of the rondos of the Fourth and Fifth Concertos, which this much resembles in character, with the difference—if the sacrilege be permitted—that it has a better theme. (See page 108.)

WITHOUT OPUS NUMBER

PIANO TRIO IN E FLAT

(In three movements; published posthumously, in 1830.)

PIANO TRIO IN B FLAT

(In one movement; composed in 1812; the manuscript inscribed to "his little friend, Maximiliane Brentano." Published in 1830.)

(For trios in other combinations, see pages 407-408.)

CHAMBER MUSIC
FOR VARIOUS
COMBINATIONS

QUINTET IN C MAJOR, FOR TWO VIOLINS, TWO VIOLAS AND 'CELLO, OP. 29

Allegro moderato
Adagio molto espressivo
Scherzo: Allegro
Presto

(Composed and published in 1801; dedicated to Count Moritz von Fries.)

When Haydn was asked why he did not write string quintets, he answered, with surely a grain of irony or petulance: "Because I was never commissioned to write them." Beethoven had no such reason, as is proved by the publishers' eagerness to put out his one real venture in that combination. Why he only once conceived a full-length work for string quintet is the more puzzling because he had the numerous, surpassing examples of Mozart, and because his own sounded so eminently well. The additional viola in Opus 29 gives body to the bass, often doubling the 'cello, solidifies chords and enriches the combined sonority.

But the principal interest in Opus 29 is the appearance of what has aspects of a quartet to fill in the curious gap between Opus 18 and Opus 59. It is far in advance of the former and noticeably short of the latter. A certain old-time strictness of phrasing lingers in the first movement; the main theme of the *Adagio* has a Mozartean elegance. The scoring keeps a classical simplicity and transparency. But the progress of the first movement, starting with a grace warm and flowing—

moving adroitly to boldness of musical thinking, suggests the opening movement of Opus 59 to come. The slow movement and the *Scherzo* could be called matured dalliance with old forms. But the *Finale* brings definite innovation. It seems to follow out a striking figure of accompaniment in the slow movement, a rapid flutter of repeated notes. Now the lower strings extend this flutter into a stormy agitation of sixteenths (by which the piece is sometimes called the "Storm" Quintet). Against it are the lightning flashes of darting scales from the first violin, later alternating with the 'cello. Twice the *presto* is interrupted by a section of eighteen bars (*Andante con moto e scherzoso*) first in A major, and at last in the tonic key. (See pages 87, 92.)

SEPTET IN E-FLAT MAJOR, FOR VIOLIN, VIOLA, HORN, CLARINET, BASSOON, VIOLONCELLO AND DOUBLE BASS, OP. 20

(First performed April 7, 1800, in Vienna, and published 1802; dedicated to the Empress Maria Theresa.)

> *Adagio; allegro con brio*
> *Adagio cantabile*
> *Tempo di menuetto*
> *Tema con variazioni*
> *Scherzo: allegro molto e vivace*
> *Andante con moto; Presto*

There are several recorded instances of Beethoven's impatience with the persisting popularity of his Septet. When Neate, in 1815, told him that it was a great favorite in England, Beethoven swore, and wished it could be destroyed. Cipriani Potter, making a similar remark two years later, had a similar answer. He did "not know how to compose" when he wrote the Septet, said Beethoven. He was "writing something better now." That something was the *"Hammer-Klavier"* Sonata.

Beethoven's annoyance is quite understandable. A suite composed in a mood of light effervescence, gratifying popular expectancy by amiably conforming to eighteenth-century custom, is well enough if taken in kind. But when it is taken solemnly to heart and held up as if in reproach as the ultimate model, then the artist who had lived to probe fresh possibilities chafed at being expected to return to a dead century and remain there. What Beethoven may not have remembered when he made his impatient expostulations was a gratifying quality in the Septet over and above its harmonic or stylistic complacence. A true master of the distinguishing charm of wind voices matches the clarinet, bassoon and horn, and sets them in the reciprocal company of the string quartet. Each group has an illustrious and pleasantly voluble leader: the clarinet for the one, the first violin for the other. In alternate phrases the wind and string groups offset each other with a charm exceeded only by the solos for each wind instrument in the *Adagio,* or the viola solo in the trio of the *Scherzo,* or the still recurring color discoveries in the set of variations in miniature. Beethoven also failed to figure the gratefulness of the sheer melodic exuberance, which never once lags. The Septet had a full right to stand on its own direct charm, comparisons aside and apart from considerations of progress. The music is quite unclouded until the last movement, when an introductory *Andante* in march time brings in an almost funereal E-flat minor. The *Presto* following is more serious than what has gone before, with shadows of minor several times crossing its bright surface. (See pages 67, 91.)

DUOS

SONATA FOR PIANO AND FRENCH HORN IN F MAJOR, OP. 17

(Probably first played by Beethoven and Punto in 1800; published in 1801, with a dedication to the Baroness von Braun.)

———

TWELVE VARIATIONS FOR VIOLIN AND PIANO, ON THE AIR *"SE VUOL BALLARE"* FROM MOZART'S "THE MARRIAGE OF FIGARO"

(Published in 1793 and dedicated to Eleonore von Breuning.)

RONDO IN G, FOR VIOLIN AND PIANO

(Probably written in 1794, when it was sent to Eleonore von Breuning. Published in 1808.)

SIX GERMAN DANCES, FOR VIOLIN AND PIANO

(Published in 1814.)

———

TWELVE VARIATIONS FOR PIANO AND VIOLONCELLO, ON A THEME FROM MOZART'S *THE MAGIC FLUTE,* OP. 66

(Published in 1798.)

TWELVE VARIATIONS FOR PIANO AND VIOLONCELLO, ON A THEME FROM HANDEL'S *JUDAS MACCABAEUS*

(Published without opus number in 1797; dedicated to Princess Christiane von Lichnowsky.)

406

SEVEN VARIATIONS FOR PIANO AND VIOLONCELLO, ON A THEME FROM MOZART'S *THE MAGIC FLUTE*

(Published in 1802, with a dedication to Count von Browne.)

THREE DUOS FOR CLARINET AND BASSOON

(Published in 1815, without opus number.)

TRIOS

STRING TRIO IN E-FLAT, OP. 3

(Composed in 1796; published 1797. This Trio is in the nature of a serenade, in six movements.)

SERENADE FOR VIOLIN, VIOLA, AND VIOLONCELLO, IN D MAJOR, OP. 8

(Published in 1797.)

THREE STRING TRIOS (IN G MAJOR, D MAJOR, AND C MINOR), OP. 9

(Published in 1798. The dedication, to the Count von Browne, bears elaborate compliments in French, concluding: "the author has the rare satisfaction of presenting to the first Maecenas of his Muse, the best of his works.")

TRIO FOR PIANO, CLARINET, OR VIOLIN, AND VIOLONCELLO, IN B-FLAT MAJOR, OP. 11

(Published in 1798, and dedicated to the Countess von Thun.) (See page 73.)

SERENADE FOR FLUTE, VIOLIN AND VIOLA, IN D MAJOR, OP. 25

(Composed in 1797, published in 1802.)

TRIO FOR PIANO, CLARINET OR VIOLIN, AND VIOLONCELLO, IN E FLAT MAJOR, OP. 38

(Published in 1806; a transcription by Beethoven of the Septet, Op. 20.)

FOURTEEN VARIATIONS FOR PIANO, VIOLIN, AND VIOLONCELLO, IN E MAJOR, OP. 44

(Composed in 1803 and published in 1804.)

TRIO FOR TWO OBOES AND ENGLISH HORN, IN C MAJOR, OP. 87

(Composed in 1794; published in 1804.)

VARIATIONS IN G MAJOR, FOR PIANO, VIOLIN, AND VIOLONCELLO, OP. 121A

(The theme is from a song *"Ich bin der Schneider Kakadu"* from Wenzel Muller's opera, *Die Schwestern von Prag*. The variations were published in 1824.)

QUARTETS

THREE QUARTETS FOR PIANO AND STRINGS (IN E-FLAT MAJOR, D MAJOR, AND C MAJOR)

(Composed in 1785; published in 1832, without opus number.)
408

THREE EQUALI FOR FOUR TROMBONES, IN D MINOR, D MAJOR, AND B MAJOR

(Composed in 1812; the score of the first two was published in 1827 as an arrangement for four-part male chorus and four trombones; text: *Miserere* and *Amplius,* made by Seyfried and sung at Beethoven's funeral; without opus number.) (See page 256.)

QUINTETS

QUINTET (FOR TWO VIOLINS, TWO VIOLAS, AND VIOLONCELLO), IN E FLAT MAJOR, OP. 4

(A transcription of the Wind Octet, Op. 103; published in 1797.)

QUINTET FOR PIANO, OBOE, CLARINET, HORN, AND BASSOON, IN E-FLAT MAJOR, OP. 16

(First played at a concert of Schuppanzigh in Vienna, April 6, 1797; published in 1801, dedicated to the Prince von Schwartzenberg. Sometimes played in a quartet arrangement for piano and strings.) (See page 51.)

Quintet for Strings in C Major, Op. 29. (For description, see page 403.)

QUINTET FOR STRINGS IN C MINOR, OP. 104

(Transcribed by the composer in 1817 from the Piano Trio of 1795, Op. 1, No. 3.)

FUGUE FOR STRING QUINTET (TWO VIOLINS, TWO VIOLAS, AND VIOLONCELLO), IN D MAJOR, OP. 137

(Composed in 1817, published posthumously, in 1827.)

SEXTETS

SEXTET FOR TWO CLARINETS, TWO HORNS AND TWO BASSOONS, IN E-FLAT MAJOR, OP. 71

(An early work of unknown date, published in 1810.)

SEXTET FOR TWO VIOLINS, VIOLA, VIO-LONCELLO AND TWO HORNS OBBLIGATI, IN E-FLAT MAJOR, OP. 81B

(An early work of unknown date, published in 1810.)

SEPTET

Septet for Violin, Viola, Horn, Clarinet, Bassoon, Violoncello and Double Bass, in E-Flat Major, Op. 20. (For description, see page 404.)

OCTETS

OCTET FOR TWO OBOES, TWO CLARINETS, TWO HORNS AND TWO BASSOONS, IN E-FLAT MAJOR, OP. 103

(The original version of the Quintet, Op. 4, of 1797; published in 1832.)

RONDINO IN E-FLAT MAJOR, FOR TWO OBOES, TWO CLARINETS, TWO HORNS AND TWO BASSOONS

(Attributed to the Bonn period; published in 1829 without Opus number.)

410

The following miscellaneous pieces are included in the supplement of Breitkopf and Härtel's complete edition:

SIX LÄNDLER FOR TWO VIOLINS AND BASS

MARCH FOR TWO CLARINETS, TWO HORNS, AND TWO BASSOONS

TRIO FOR CLAVIER, FLUTE AND BASSOON

SONATINA FOR MANDOLIN WITH PIANO

ADAGIO FOR MANDOLIN WITH PIANO

THE
PIANOFORTE SONATAS

No DEPARTMENT of Beethoven's music so well reveals the form-exploring composer as do the piano sonatas. His habit of extemporization largely accounts for it. We are told how he would return to his piano from one of his walks, aflame with an idea, or how he would sit at a keyboard, wherever he might be, and in a state of dreaming fantasy allow his thoughts to take tangible shape through his fingers. The piano sonatas may well have been the most important outcome of such moments, and in them one is not surprised at first finding a growing sense of movement-succession.

When Beethoven wrote his first four piano sonatas in four movements he was plainly presuming to lift them to the importance of trios or quartets. Composers until then had never ventured to detain an audience with more than three movements of piano solo.* The main *allegro* and a *presto* close were often enough. Sometimes there was a slow introduction, usually a slow movement between. Mozart and Haydn each kept the three-movement plan, Haydn in his last years (which were contemporary with Beethoven's Opus 2 and Opus 7) further elaborating the slow movement, as if anxious to keep abreast with Beethoven.

But Beethoven, having set a precedent for four movements, presently showed a preference for three. The tendency was not a

---

* Minuets were sometimes used in easy sonatas, where with their slower tempo they would sometimes replace the rondo *finale*. Haydn occasionally substituted a minuet for a slow movement. Dussek or Hummel in late works extended sonatas to four movements, with a "*scherzo*" or "*scherzoso*," showing the desire, but not the ability, to emulate Beethoven.

reversion. Pianists who paraded their own sonatas had aimed merely at showing their paces: brilliant passage work, the ornamental singing tone, and the swift *ad captandum* bid for applause. Beethoven was impelled from four movements to three by other reasons. His piano was to him a more personal, less formally constricted mode of expression than the larger media, where he saw fit carefully to lay out the fourfold aspect of a subject. Sometimes the intent of a sonata brings this four-movement amplitude; more often Beethoven moves directly, with a dramatic and concentrated awareness, from first movement to intermediate movement to *finale*. The first is searching, anticipatory, setting opposing elements in conflict. The slow movement finds quietude through emotional introspection; the finale is the clear, unequivocal answer, the ringing assertion, joyous or triumphant. This finale was the peak of tension and the *dénouement,* which by that circumstance moderated the emphasis of the middle movement. It likewise obviated a minuet or *scherzo* as a third movement, which in Beethoven's more concentrated sonatas would have been a deviation, a delay of the pressing answer. Even the middle movement of three became the link of the first and last, with an intermediate function, a lyrical relaxation through which the memory of the opening movement and the sense of suspense must not be dissipated. For this interlude, a *scherzo* sometimes sufficed (Opus 10 No. 2, 14 No. 2, 27 No. 2, 101, 109, 110), affording relief between more serious matters, recalling, perhaps, Shakespeare's light interludes. Sometimes, when a perceptible integration of the first and last movements was required, an extended slow movement, the vehicle for Beethoven's deepest sentiments, was eliminated!

When he used a full-length slow movement, it either took the full center of the stage so that the *finale* became an afterthought, a dropping away, or broke the thread of continuity with its elaborations (Opus 31, No. 1). This was the evident reason for the substitution of a short movement for a long one between the closely connected outer movements of the *"Waldstein"* Sonata and of the short slow movements, similarly placed, in the *"Appassionata"* and *"Lebewohl"* Sonatas. Except in Opus 106, Opus 109, and the last Sonata of all, Opus 111, the slow movement in all its rich beauties was never reinstated. In Opus 109 and Opus 111,

413

Beethoven amazed his contemporaries by putting the slow movement at the end, making it the crux of all, the peaceful rather
than the vociferous culmination. After his Fourth Sonata, of
1797, four movements became the exception, two or three the rule,
and, if brief or introductory movements are considered as ap-
pendages, two movements can be called the ultimate basic plan.
The effort which had its complete fruition in the two movements,
fluent, balanced, perfectly integrated, of Opus 111, is clearly
observable through the course of the thirty-two sonatas.

The piano sonatas are the closest and most continuous reflection which we have of the composer's development, extending
from his childhood with few breaks until the year 1822. Beethoven's first published music was the set of three sonatas written for
his Elector at the age of twelve, and published (in 1783) without
opus number. The little sonatas fall stiffly into the contemporary
keyboard style, showing here and there that their author was
indeed the Beethoven to come. A fragmentary "Easy Sonata" in
C, which he sent to Eleonore von Breuning from Vienna in 1790
(but had written earlier) has much grace and romantic charm.

In the seven years between 1796 and 1802, Beethoven wrote
the bulk of his sonatas for the pianoforte—the first twenty of
them! Not one of these years failed to produce at least one from
his pen, and in the year 1802 alone five were published. This
means, of course, that there was a great demand for them, and
the young pianist was careful not to let this demand languish
ungratified. Indeed, no call was unheeded, whether for variations,
songs, chamber music in any combination, and the record shows
about eighty-five works as having been composed in this period.
But the piano sonatas offer the most personal record of growth.
The successful virtuoso speaks in them, the performer who exults
in his finger mastery and works his magic to subdue all; the extemporizer, the dreaming artist puts his best findings on paper.
The lover declares himself in tones—the language which the fair-
est and haughtiest cannot withstand. The variety of the titled
dedications proves that the act of public compliment was often
something else than sentimental, but also that Beethoven did not
lack patrons and the attention of their wives and daughters. Some
of his sonatas fell gratefully under their fingers, but others, the

"grand sonatas," so-called by the publishers, were plainly for concert talents; these their composer could with luck be induced to play at an elegant gathering, in his fiery fashion, for the delight of all.

THREE SONATAS (NOS. 1, 2 AND 3), OP. 2 (IN F MINOR; A MAJOR; C MAJOR)

1 *Allegro*	2 *Allegro vivace*
Adagio	*Largo appassionato*
Menuetto: Allegretto	*Scherzo: Allegretto*
Prestissimo	*Rondo*

3 *Allegro con brio*
Adagio
Scherzo: Allegro
Allegro assai

(Published in March, 1796, dedicated to "Mr. Joseph Haydn, Doctor of Music.")

Like the Trios, Opus 1, which they followed by a year in publication, the Sonatas, Opus 2, may have been withheld by their self-testing composer; indeed their composition probably coincided in part with that of the Trios. In the dedication, Beethoven pays his respects to "Mr." Haydn as an Oxford Doctor, but he will not include the phrase "pupil of Haydn" as Haydn would like; he will not openly admit that he has really learned anything from him. Nevertheless, the involuntary homage is there; it lies in the music, and so shows itself as very ungrudging indeed. The way the three Sonatas linger in the old patterns means only that the patterns were still entirely agreeable to him. He liked the introductory theme which was a sort of arpeggio flourish useful in development (an inheritance from Clementi). The *adagio* theme of the First Sonata, and even its treatment, are wholeheartedly Haydnesque. The minuet of the First is also derivative in style, like the rondo finales of the Second and Third. The music in no way suggests timid conformity, but eager liking. The rondo, which he was eventually to shed as unsuitable, still strongly attracted him. It fitted his fresh exuberance, which could build brightly exciting structures from the bricks and mortar of ready invention and upspringing tunes. In first movements the virtuoso favored octaves and running passages, tailored to his own supple hands.

The final *prestissimo* in F minor of the first Sonata of Opus 2 is its most striking movement by its impulsion which overrides light brilliance and foretells the storms of years to follow. The development brings mid-relief in a new *dolce* melody. The second Sonata, in A major, is outstanding in the *"Largo appassionato"*

typical of many slow movements to come, with its shadows of grandeur, its harmonic weightiness and eloquent bass, its rhetorical short chords, and ornamentation. There had been rhetoric in music before, but not the voice of passion as here. The last Sonata is the most brilliant and most developed of the three. The second theme of the opening movement was salvaged from an unpublished piano quartet, written in Bonn in 1785. An adroit, modulatory theme, more than worthy of a boy of fifteen, and well worth saving! The *Adagio* is a love song, more content to dream upon its thesis than to probe it. The *Scherzo*, like the one in the previous Sonata, is less a disrupting innovation than a happy discovery of a new movement type, already a confirmed trade-mark of Beethoven.

SONATA IN E-FLAT (NO. 4), OP. 7

> *Allegro molto e con brio*
> *Largo, con gran espressione*
> *Allegro*
> *Rondo: poco allegretto e grazioso*

(Published in October, 1797, dedicated to the Countess Babette von Keglevics.)

That this Sonata was published alone as a "Grand Sonata" would indicate concert stature. It has longer lines and fuller development in the first movement, and a rondo of greater brilliance. The *Largo con gran espressione* carries further the emotionalism of the *Largo* in the A major Sonata. In the middle portion there is an unheard-of attempt at musical imitation of the broken accents of grief: dissolving sighs, short chords, exaggerated alternations of *fortissimo* and *pianissimo*—tense pauses. The peaceful conclusion shows already the last revealing touch which Beethoven could put into a coda.

THREE SONATAS (NOS. 5, 6, 7), OP. 10 (NO. 1 IN C MINOR, NO. 2 IN F MAJOR, NO. 3 IN D MAJOR)

1 *Allegro molto e con brio*
  Adagio molto
  Finale: prestissimo

2 *Allegro*
  Allegretto
  Presto

3 *Presto*
  Largo e mesto
  Menuetto: allegro
  Rondo: allegro

417

(Published in September, 1798; dedicated to the Countess von Browne.)

In his Opus 10, Beethoven first finds his plan of three movements in sonatas. The step is tentative; as always, he imposes no outer reform but feels his way gradually from within. The composer reaches toward integration and singleness of character, while the mood which dominates him shows him the way. The tempi find a new adjustment between movements. He tends to keep the old key relationships, but binds with them more firmly and strongly.

The first Sonata contains a long slow movement of weighty and tragic import. Beethoven introduces its A-flat major with a movement in C minor, in an unusually serious vein. After the last chord of subdued dreaming in the magic coda of the *Adagio,* any idea of a disrupting *scherzo* is dismissed. He aims at dramatic contrast by breaking in with the subject of the *prestissimo* closing movement, *piano,* with ominous implications in the sudden C minor. The *Finale* is a sonata-form movement, brief and tense, without let-down. Its course is withheld for a moment, before the close, for a reminiscent *adagio* phrase.

The second Sonata finds a different three-movement plan. This time the expected slow movement is omitted, and the *Scherzo,* as middle movement, is modified to an *allegretto,* flowing melodiously in a gentle F minor. The returning refrain is written out and freshly developed (a new departure!). The Trio maintains the lyric mood, variety being reserved for the short *Finale* on a single canonic theme, this time clearly and ringingly gay.

The third Sonata spreads out four movements once more, and sets forth a *Largo* which is the most deeply probing and anguished music its composer had written until then:

It is his first slow movement for the piano in the minor. It further explores what Beethoven has several times tried in his piano sonatas, a path which he may have developed in his soul-searching moments of improvisation. It could be called the imitation in music of convulsive emotion. A minuet follows, but it is no perfunctory opening of a ballroom door upon the last dissonant chords of pain which have just ended a remarkable confession. It is rather a bit of placid melody in a gently rhythmic tempo. This in turn contrasts with the final rondo. (See pages 67-68.)

SONATA *PATHÉTIQUE* (NO. 8) IN C MINOR, OP. 13

Grave; Allegro molto e con brio
Adagio cantabile
Rondo: Allegro

(Published in 1799; dedicated to Prince Karl von Lichnowsky.)

As if to follow up his success as poet of melancholy, Beethoven took a bold step; he dedicated a sonata to his patron Prince with a mournful descriptive title, *Pathétique*.* The Sonata is more significant by its innovations, by the road it opens, than by what it accomplishes musically. It is a proclamation of prevailing character in a sonata, even though it fails to carry out its promise. It could not conceivably have done so. Clementi and Dussek had labeled slow movements *"patetico,"* but carefully wrapped them in surrounding cheerfulness. It would not have been in Beethoven's nature to carry pathos through a sonata, even if his Prince could have found so strange a thing acceptable. Pathos in the salon was something discreetly veiled, quickly covered. Beethoven until then had never presumed to open a movement in a minor tonality without immediately counterpoising a major episode. A minor sonata must have a major slow movement. To open the *Pathétique* Sonata with a C minor introduction, proceed with the principal *Allegro* in the same tonality, and uncover a second theme in E-flat minor was going very far indeed! The introduction, *grave,* indulges unrestrainedly in chromatic shifting chords and sighing phrases. It becomes the mood-pivot of the movement by recurring twice to bring in the development and the final cadence. The main body of the movement alternates between a theme which is a long rise and fall upon a chain of resolutions, and upon a theme which is a succession of plaintive falling intervals. These indeed were "accents of woe" unrelieved. The *Adagio cantabile* which follows, in A-flat major, is a song in grave, formal phrases; the rondo wears a correct but unconvincing mourning veil of C minor. The Sonata made its obvious appeal, had its great vogue among the lovers of music and sentiment, and was frowned upon with equal consistence by the sterner academicians. Time has proved neither judgment to be entirely just. Beethoven deliberately assuming the tragic mask seems to have become a little stilted and conscious of his attitude. The first movement never becomes molten; the slow movement, as gracefully and chastely beautiful as a Greek statue, is to the *Largo* of the Sonata preceding as marble is to flame. (See pages 67, 68, 74.)

* This was the only sonata, save the *Lebewohl* Sonata, Opus 81a, to which Beethoven gave a title.

TWO SONATAS (NOS. 9 AND 10), OP. 14 (IN E MAJOR AND G MAJOR)

1 *Allegro*
   Allegretto
   Rondo: Allegro commodo

2 *Allegro*
   Andante
   Scherzo: Allegro assai

(Published in 1799; dedicated to the Baroness von Braun.)

The first Sonata later appeared in a transcription for string quartet by Beethoven himself, under protest and probably in the realization that in any case nothing could stop the flood of arrangements which the publishers put out to supply every home combination, most of them bungling as well as unsuitable.

Beethoven held to his three-movement plan in his Opus 14. The middle movement of the first is another singing *Allegretto,* in *da capo* form; the second has an ostensible slow movement which nevertheless floats in a light animation of staccato chords, a melody quite without tears:

It is in the form of short variations, unelaborated. The opening movements of each show Beethoven's increasing power to reach out and articulate his elements into long lines, weave his detail into a close and continuously flowing pattern. The second ends in a sonata-form movement which is labeled "scherzo" by virtue of the impishly scampering theme.

SONATA IN B-FLAT MAJOR (NO. 11), OP. 22

Allegro con brio
Adagio con molt' espressione
Menuetto
Rondo: Allegretto

(Published in 1802; dedicated to the Count von Browne.)

Beethoven offered the B-flat Sonata to Peters in Leipzig with the remark (translated literally): "This sonata, my dear brother, has washed itself." * Whether or not this bit of exuberance has any special significance, it is worth noticing that the Sonata presents the orthodox four movements, opens the first with what sounds like an eighteenth-century flourish

but turns out to be something far different, and that each movement (excepting the *Adagio*) opens with a rather conventional theme and proceeds to play fast and loose with it. The Sonata was

---

* Tovey translated *hat sich gewaschen* as "takes the cake," and quoted as similar Stevenson's pleased announcement of his *The Master of Ballantrae* as "a howling cheese."

cut out for popularity, with show passages certain to please the self-exhibiting virtuosos, who must accept certain bold excursions in consequence. The *Adagio* is rather self-consciously ornamental in its melody, resulting in what must be called surface music if compared to certain slow movements gone before. But it plants ideas from which John Field and Chopin will profit in nocturnes to come.

SONATA (NO. 12) IN A-FLAT MAJOR, OP. 26

> *Tema con variazioni: Andante*
> *Scherzo: Allegro molto*
> *Marcia funebre sulla morte d'un eroe*
> *Allegro*

(Composed in 1801, published in 1802; dedicated to Prince Karl von Lichnowsky.)

The Sonata begins with a set of five variations, following a precedent which Mozart had set with his Sonata in A major (K. 331). These variations are a fine example of a form then much exploited by Beethoven apart from the Sonata. The *Scherzo* is placed before the funeral march as if in correct deference to the imaginary "hero." It has been told that Beethoven heard Paër's successful opera *Achilles* in 1801, and, struck with the funeral march in that piece, expressed his intention to do something similar. There is a resemblance between the two, which again might be no more than a lugubrious convention of funeral marches which both composers followed. It should be remembered that *Die Geschöpfe des Prometheus* was composed in 1801, and shortly afterwards the variations upon the theme from the ballet which again would provide the finale for the *Eroica* Symphony, work upon which shortly followed. Anything further removed from the orchestral *Marcia funebre* would be harder to imagine than this one for the piano. It is pompous and cold, telling of the external trappings of death. The Trio imitates the roll of drums and the cannon salute, as if the composer were witnessing the funeral rites of some stranger in a public square. The solemn ceremonial is dismissed by a decidedly cheerful rondo.(See page 256.)

TWO SONATAS, *QUASI UNA FANTASIA* (NOS. 13 AND 14), OP. 27 (IN E-FLAT MAJOR AND C-SHARP MINOR)

1   *Andante*
Allegro molto vivace
Adagio con espressione
Allegro vivace

2   *Adagio sostenuto*
Allegretto
Presto agitato

(Probably both composed in 1801; both published in 1802. The first Sonata was dedicated to the Princess Josephine Sophie von Liechtenstein, the second to the Countess Giulietta Guicciardi.)

    The phrase *Quasi una Fantasia* is not a challenge; it is a declaration of adherence to a method, now clear enough for formulation, which Beethoven would increasingly apply to his Sonatas, and in some degree to all of his instrumental works to come. There would have been little point in labeling each of his piano works as "in the manner of a fantasia," more, perhaps, in sometimes dropping the word "Sonata" altogether.

    But this is a mere matter of names. What the two Sonatas of Opus 27 plainly aim for is inward fusion through progressive continuity. Beethoven was attempting to break down the boundaries of movements which were too divisional for the mood poet. Wishing to bind the movements into an unbroken flow, he inserts the warning *attacca* as each ends and another begins. But he has not yet come to the device of withholding his cadence. Beethoven seems also to be in search of a position for his slow movements. The *Adagio* of the first Sonata leads into the *Finale* as an introduction, and not as a distinct movement. The Sonata in E-flat opens with an *Andante,* which is little developed; after the *Scherzo* there begins what promises to become a slow movement, which, however, after twenty-three bars turns out to be the introduction to an exciting *Finale*.

The Sonata in C-sharp minor finds a more successful plan. This Sonata has attracted more than its share of attention and more praise than its comparative worth by its romantic implications and the sobriquet "Moonlight" tagged to it by the critic Rellstab.* Beethoven is reported to have had no special fondness for this Sonata, partly perhaps because it eclipsed others in the public attention. Whatever its worth, which is certainly considerable, it is significant through its fortunate (but not permanent) solution of the slow-movement question. The almost formless introductory slow movement (Bach-like preluding which in its course develops a theme) is followed by an *allegretto* interlude and a *finale* which is the peak of all, and which is altogether remarkable. It is the first of the tumultuous outbursts of stormy passion which Beethoven was about to let loose through the piano sonatas. It is music in which agitation and urgency never cease, even when they are an undercurrent to the melodic passages. The poet of passion has taken complete possession at last, his turbulence erasing for the time being all memories of the rollicking rondo *finale* from which a tempest had grown. (See pages 64, 146.)

SONATA (NO. 15) IN D MAJOR, OP. 28

> *Allegro*
> *Andante*
> *Scherzo: Allegro vivace*
> *Rondo: Allegro ma non troppo*

(Composed in 1801; published in August, 1802; dedicated to Joseph Edler von Sonnenfels.)

Of the four Sonatas of the year 1801 (the others were Opus 26 and the two of Opus 27) this was the only one in four movements.

* Rellstab associated it with Lake Lucerne, as if that lake, which of course Beethoven never saw, had a special brand of moonlight!

In fact, it was the last piano sonata to follow the traditional four-movement succession. The composer was for the last time in a formally compliant mood. The mood is also relaxed and playful, moving in a leisurely course upon a light surface, musing dreamily and posing no problems. Cranz, a later Hamburg publisher, named it the "*Sonata Pastorale,*" a title acceptable enough if we make the inner reservation that this is by no means the only sonata with pastoral qualities. The dreamily persistent tonic pedal of the first movement would support the idea, but the grave and polished beauty of the *Andante* would not. A carefree staccato episode in D major relieves it.

The Scherzo proposes humorous notes of bar length in descending octaves which become the bars of waltzing measures. The Trio offers a little four-measure snatch of tune which is played eight times, with only the last two notes changing, while the humorist provides much harmonic activity beneath. The rondo dances blithely upon a clumping, quasi-clumsy bass, a trait at last which is unquestionably peasant-like.

THREE SONATAS (NOS. 16, 17 AND 18), OP. 31 (IN G MAJOR, D MINOR, AND E-FLAT MAJOR)

(All three Sonatas were probably composed in 1802; the first two were published by Nägeli in Zurich in 1803 as Opus 29, all three were published by Simrock in 1805 as Opus 31; they are without dedication.)

The Pianoforte Sonatas

The first two Sonatas appeared in Nägeli's series, *"Repertoire des Clavecinistes,"* a series which had also included the *Pathé-tique* Sonata. That the second of them, at least, was utterly un-suited for the harpsichord does not seem to have bothered the publishers, who were loath to admit that Beethoven had long ceased to write harpsichord sonatas, although that instrument still stood in many homes. Cappi published Opus 31 in 1805 as *pour le clavier ou pianoforte.** It was Nägeli who infuriated Beethoven by sending him proofs of the G major Sonata with an "improve-ment" of his own—the addition of a tonic phrase resolving a hanging dominant in the coda of the first movement:

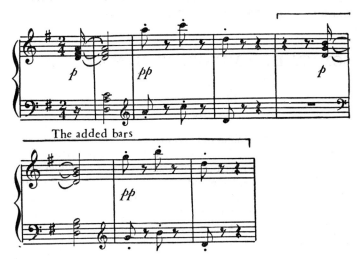

The added bars

Beethoven quickly eliminated the four bars, but errors persisted, and he sent the two to Simrock, ordering him to reprint them with the line: *"édition très correcte."* (See page 85.)

* Opus 31 were the last of Beethoven's sonatas to bear the double title. Until then, all had been so designated except Op. 14, 22 and 28, which had been announced simply as "for the pianoforte."

SONATA IN G MAJOR, OP. 31, NO. 1

Allegro vivace
Adagio grazioso
Rondo: Allegretto

The first Sonata is far more slender in substance than the one which is to follow, but it is none the less fanciful and engaging. The *Adagio grazioso* (a curious title!) is laden with a smothering abundance of trills and what might be called coloratura passages, which (an occurrence rare with Beethoven) sometimes fill in where depth of feeling is lacking. The Sonata ends in a rondo which jogs along winningly at an *allegretto* pace.

SONATA IN D MINOR, OP. 31, NO. 2

Largo; Allegro
Adagio
Allegretto

The Sonata in D minor offers something far different than surface dalliance. It has been compared to the *"Appassionata"* of four years later, and even the idle imagination of Schindler saw a kinship in these two. He asked Beethoven what they meant and Beethoven answered: "Read Shakespeare's *Tempest*." Schindler does not tell us whether he obeyed his master's command. His quotation of it has sent many a commentator thumbing the pages of the play, as if to discern one sonata or the other in the lines of Prospero or Miranda or Ariel. The blunt and unpoetical truth could well be that Beethoven as yet knew only the title (the plays were then appearing one by one in German translation), and readily applied it to the two sonatas which are as tempestuous in character as the play is otherwise.

It is surely an error to regard the D minor Sonata, as some have done, as an earlier and lesser, a half-realized *"Appassionata."* It is similar in the ground swell of the first movement, the darkly agitated passages, the part restoration of peacefulness by the slow movement, and the more positive answer of the swift and

428

brilliant finale. But this earlier sonata is more contained; it has no traffic with the violence which is forceful at the expense of lustrous, singing sonority. It runs smoothly and fancifully under the fingers—passion with the strength of an ardor that glows. The *largo* of the single questioning arpeggio chord,

is at first answered by agitated passages, and then takes shape as the main theme, a sequential melody rising from the bass and curving plaintively above its accompaniment. This music has a special enchantment of melancholy which the F minor Sonata with its plunge and abandon must by its very nature sacrifice. The movement, insistently questioning, breaks twice into eloquent recitative passages, the first instance of an expressive resource to be used in later works. The *Adagio* is the partial, but not the final answer. It is far more prominent and assertive than the slow movement of the Sonata in F minor to come. The final *Allegretto,* on the other hand, is less assertive than the later *Finale.* Its graceful, weaving figure for the two hands is release through power that is sinuous and adroit, quite in keeping with the whole.

SONATA IN E-FLAT MAJOR, OP. 31, NO. 3

Allegro
Scherzo: Allegretto vivace
Menuetto: Moderato e grazioso
Presto con fuoco

429

The third Sonata establishes in its first phrase and maintains throughout a light and fanciful character, as if there were no such things as passions and solemn sentiments. The quizzical first bar which is to lead obliquely into the tonic E-flat becomes the charming and ubiquitous feature of the whole movement:

The Sonata is the last in four movements, excepting Opus 106, and these four are by no means orthodox. Three (the minuet is the exception) are in sonata form. The tempi of the first three are moderate and subtly adjusted—an easy-going *allegro,* a vivacious *scherzo* which is in reality no scherzo at all, and a slow minuet. The *"scherzo"* is full of humor, with sudden alternations of loud and soft, the minuet a delicate song. The *Presto con fuoco* bursts in upon the placid scene with dazzling effect, proclaiming its joyous theme in one of Beethoven's irresistible final movements.

TWO EASY SONATAS (NOS. 19 AND 20), OP. 49 (G MINOR, G MAJOR)

1	*Andante*	2	*Allegro ma non troppo*
	Rondo: Allegro		*Tempo di menuetto*

(Published in 1805; without dedication.)

The two little Sonatas of Opus 49, relics of a polite past, are conspicuously out of place between the manifold treasures of Opus 31 and the imperious onslaught of the "Waldstein" Sonata to follow. Some have placed their date of composition as early as 1796, which would put them just after Opus 2. This would prove that Beethoven had not intended to publish them, and account for the appearance of the minuet theme from the second in the Septet of 1802. He evidently at that time merely lifted a good theme from a discarded sonata. The two, far easier to perform than Opus 2, may have been written for a pupil. It is believed that Beethoven's brother Karl, in a quiet way he had, sent them to a publisher in the realization that what more could play more would buy. Beethoven's annoyance can be imagined at the appearance in 1805, two months before the "Waldstein" Sonata, of two works some nine years old, abandoned and forgotten, duplicating a minuet otherwise used. But the great usefulness and occasional charm of the two Sonatas compels the gratitude of posterity for the business acumen of Karl van Beethoven.

SONATA (NO. 21) IN C MAJOR, OP. 53

> *Allegro con brio*
> *Introduzione (Adagio molto)*
> *Rondo: Allegretto moderato*

(Composed in 1804; published in 1805; dedicated to Count von Waldstein.)

The two Sonatas which reach the highest point of stormy power both belong to the summer of the year 1804, the momentous year in which the *Eroica* was completed. The C major Sonata appeared in print in the following spring, dedicated to the Count Waldstein, the patron of the last years at Bonn; the *"Appassionata"* was not ready until two years later. The excitements of the "Waldstein" Sonata are more external, although the piece was certainly not written, as later events might indicate, as a vehicle for aspiring performers riding toward fame. Each Sonata consists of two movements of violent tumult, with a relieving slow movement between. It is hard to believe the tale that Beethoven was persuaded by "a friend" to substitute for the long *Andante* * at first intended for the "Waldstein" Sonata the short *Adagio* which now

* This *Andante* was published separately in 1806 as the *"Andante Favori."*

431

introduces the finale. Beethoven certainly needed no anonymous "friend" to tell him that the long and elaborately ornamented slow movement went beyond its function of a point of repose, and would have quite dissipated what was also a point of suspense. The first movement is one of implacable violence, as of a natural storm. The gathering convulsions and chromatic scales of the "Pastoral" Symphony are anticipated. The melody which lay in Beethoven's heart as the answer to this storm rises to jubilant radiance in the theme of the rondo, which gleams forth with such complete enchantment. This *pianissimo* moment is the most exciting of an exciting sonata—after delay in the intricate byways of the *"Andante favori"* it would have been quite lost. (See pages 94, 133.)

SONATA (NO. 22) IN F MAJOR, OP. 54

In tempo d'un Menuetto
Allegretto

(Composed in 1804; published, without dedication, in 1806.)

The little two-movement Sonata in F major is almost like an interlude between the two towering ones. It has the signs of an improvisation, an adventure of the straying fancy. Such adventure was of course more likely than not to uncover unexpected and happy possibilities. Beethoven begins upon a theme which might serve for a minuet

In tempo d'un Menuetto

develops it with a plastic sense of reiterative balance, but without a definite repeat. Instead of a melodic trio, he embarks upon an essay in staccato octaves, or sixths in contrary motion. The minuet returns, then, briefly, the staccato octaves, and the minuet, further embroidered. Beethoven seems to be finding, as if by accident, the plan of the twice appearing trio which was to become his preferred scheme for his *da capo* movements. The *allegretto* is a sort of *perpetuum mobile,* speeding brightly upon a single theme to its end.

SONATA (NO. 23) IN F MINOR, OP. 57

Allegro assai
Andante con moto
Allegro ma non troppo

(Probably begun in 1804, certainly completed in 1806, published in February, 1807; dedicated to "his good friend" Franz von Brunswick.)

It must be admitted that the title *"Appassionata"* which the publisher Cranz in Hamburg gave to the Sonata in F minor might have been worse. This is the most voluminously described of the Sonatas; paragraphs, whole chapters, have been lavished upon it. If the word images are extravagant, extravagance is not out of place, for the Sonata is the tonal embodiment of extravagance. The first and last movements know no restraint except that which directs the utmost power. The artist has laid bare his emotional nature so completely, so startlingly, that the rhapsodists are wisest who do not compete with him. A popular conception of Beethoven seems drawn in its terms—a figure of gigantic grandeur, with the nobly furrowed brow, shaken by every violent, and moved by every tender emotion. Those who knew Beethoven in the flesh would perhaps not have recognized him in this picture. But no one can say that the Sonata in F minor is not the faithful mirror of its composer. The very strength of the music makes it evident that it must be so. Nor can anyone who stands before this music deny that the man who has been this way, who has left these traces in dots and lines dreamed in mighty terms, was nobly visioned, was swept in turn by sharp suffering, terrifying gusts of fury and a prodigious exultant strength. The storms of the first movement have the vitality and directness of genuine experience.

As in the "Waldstein" Sonata, Beethoven had the need of a slow movement between two turbulent ones. But here the contingency is quite different. The tale of violence, ending in a dark *pianissimo*, as it began, is a tale unanswered. The composer turns inward again, and more deeply, to the peace which he could always find in his heart. A theme of grave and gentle harmonic beauty moves quietly and evenly through simple variations, without modulation. Furious, implacable chords crash in upon it, and the returning music of turmoil becomes headlong and driving. There is not the expected returning major, the close of joyous liberation. All that consoles in this Sonata is its prayer-like *Andante,* and its sense throughout of abundant, unshakable strength. (See pages 94, 112, 134, 196.)

SONATA (NO. 24) IN F-SHARP MAJOR, OP. 78

Adagio cantabile; Allegro, ma non troppo
Allegro assai

(Composed in October, 1809, published in December, 1810; dedicated to the Countess Therese von Brunswick.)

As if the *"Appassionata"* Sonata had received the utmost which, in the full-blooded vigor of his most fertile years, he could pour into music for the piano, Beethoven turned away from Sonatas, devoting himself to orchestral music. In the ten years that followed the *"Appassionata,"* only four were forthcoming, and these had more beauty and lyric charm than substance. Not one

of them could have been called, by the most sanguine of publishers, *"Appassionata."* They were the Sonata in F-sharp, dedicated to Therese von Brunswick, the Sonatine in G major, Opus
79, and the two "programme" Sonatas—the "Farewell" Sonata
and the one in E major, dedicated to Count Moritz Lichnowsky
on the occasion of his engagement to be married.

The first of them, the Sonata in F-sharp, is a sonata in miniature (its two movements with repeats are played in less than nine
minutes). It has met with undue condescension and neglect. Lenz
called it "a piece which shows the hand of Beethoven and not his
genius—two uninteresting movements of a wearying monotony."
Later writers did not go so outrageously astray. Some have
pointed to it as proof that Therese von Brunswick, to whom it
was dedicated, could not have been the "immortal beloved" because it has neither stormy passion nor a slow movement. Virtuosos have passed it by for its lack of ostentation, amateurs for
its difficulty. It has deserved better treatment, and one confidently
predicts that it will outlast its detractors. The fact that it is one
of the least brilliant gems among the variegated thirty-two does
not prevent it from being one of the rarest and most beautiful.

If a sonata is to be measured by its dedication (an unsafe cri-
terion), then it can be pointed out that Beethoven made his really
intimate love avowals in the greatest secrecy, and that the
"Moonlight" Sonata with its stormy confession addressed to a
wide public was as suitable to the worldly Giulietta Guicciardi as
the fine and delicate Sonata in F-sharp major was suitable for the
special sensibility, musical discernment, intelligence, intimate
understanding, of Therese. Beethoven once expressed his preference for the F-sharp major Sonata over the irrepressible one in
C-sharp minor, the favorite of too many others. The preference is
not surprising. When he made the remark he had left behind his
broad and thunderous ways, was turning his fantasy inward and
cultivating a freshly expressive delicacy of detail, shading by
modulation, melodic alternation, or new byways in figuration. He
addresses Therese characteristically, with musing, tender, but
unimpassioned sentiment. The Sonata is for the elect; it avoids
the obvious, plays lightly with fragments in a succint way that

requires active attention. Even the key seeks the untrodden path.
Both movements pivot upon F-sharp, but ceaselessly tap strange
tonalities, touching frequently upon the minor. The four-bar
Adagio leads directly into the principal melody, simple and
charming in its bare statement:

The repetition of the exposition and development sections are
justified by the direct pithiness of each. The second movement is
slightly faster. Its theme suggests a *scherzo,* its form a rondo, but
with plain elements of sonata development. The movement is several things in one. No sonata Beethoven wrote is more closely at
one in character, or more perfect in realization. Its special fra-
grance is captured and maintained only by the subtle and reverent
artist. If music, which must find its own in understatement, without effusion or climax, without benefit of the conquering virtuoso
and the multitude, is to be prized—then this Sonata can hold its
place among the most treasurable of them all. (See page 138.)

SONATINE (NO. 25) IN G MAJOR, OP. 79

> *Presto alla tedesca*
> *Andante espressivo*
> *Vivace*

(Published in 1810, without dedication.)

This little piece was no early work brought forth after its time, as Opus 49 had been. It was composed in 1809 from sketches which first appear in the key of C major, and over which Beethoven wrote, *"Sonate facile ou Sonatine."* The three movements are short, little developed and without pretension. If Beethoven intended the work for beginners, it must be said that his first movement upon a little rustic waltz was of the sort to lead them unawares into deep waters. The *alla tedesca*

is nothing else than an Austrian peasant Ländler of the sort which Beethoven had composed before and would use again. (The *Alla danza tedesca* in the String Quartet in B-flat, Opus 130, is built upon an inversion of this theme.) Indeed the Ländler sets the style for the three movements, which are of plain folkish suggestion. It has been pointed out that the *Andante* might pass for one of the sugar-and-water Venetian Gondolier's Songs from Mendelssohn's *Songs Without Words*. It might *almost* have passed for Mendelssohn.* There is also the difference that it is a small point of dalliance with Beethoven, which foretells a large

* It would be an interesting occupation to search the Sonatas for premonitions of Romantic piano composers to come. These are clearly to be found: Schubert, Schumann, Mendelssohn, Chopin, Liszt.

part of Mendeissohn. The Sonata was probably written quickly. What it obviously lacks is gestation, just as it obviously possesses mature skill and ready invention.

SONATA (NO. 26) IN E-FLAT, OP. 81A *

(*DAS LEBEWOHL, DIE ABWESENHEIT, DAS WIEDERSEHEN*)

Adagio; Allegro
Andante espressivo (*In gehender Bewegung, doch mit Ausdruck*)
Vivacissimo (*Im lebhaftesten Zeitmaasse*)

{Composed in 1809, published in 1811; dedicated to the Archduke Rudolph of Austria.)

Beethoven here used German tempo indications for the first time, as if matching the titles. The publisher rendered the titles (Farewell—Absence—Return) in French, according to the custom of the day, whereupon Beethoven protested that *Les Adieux* was far less personal than *Lebewohl*—"the one is said in a hearty manner to a single person; the other to a whole assembly, to whole towns." His intention was unmistakably personal. The Archduke Rudolph fled Vienna (with his kind) on May 4, 1809, before the French invaders. Beethoven remained, and at once sketched out the music of farewell: "Dedicated to and written from the heart for his Imperial Highness." The slow movement was actually written during his absence, and the joyous pages of restoration after his return to Vienna in October.

The programme is most delicately handled. The syllables of *Lebewohl* are inserted above the three notes of the motto in the introduction, which is to recur in the following *allegro*, an expression of tender regret at the departure of the loved one:

---

* The Sonata acquired its strange opus number because of Beethoven's insistence upon chronological order. While Simrock held it, Breitkopf and Härtel put out the Opus numbers 75 to 85. Opus 81 from this publisher, the Sextet for Strings and Horns, accordingly became Opus 81b.

The brief *Andante* (in the relative C minor) is a monologue of inconsolable loneliness. There are remarkable recitative passages. The music becomes urgently questioning until the plaintive opening figure, reaching upward and suspended there, is shattered by a loud chord of the dominant major. There is released a tumult of rushing chords and breathless staccato notes. In the face of such a tide no one can question the composer's complete sincerity. Whatever the true cause, this was music "from the heart," music of release in his best vein. He never wrote programme music more vividly descriptive than this "characteristic" Sonata, as it was then called. (See pages 108, 137, 194.)

SONATA (NO. 27) IN E MINOR, OP. 90

Mit Lebhaftigkeit und durchaus mit Empfindung und Ausdruck
Nicht zu geschwind und sehr singbar vorzutragen

(Completed in August, 1814; published in June, 1815; dedicated to Count Moritz von Lichnowsky.)

Beethoven dedicated this Sonata to his patron, Count Moritz Lichnowsky, the surviving brother of Karl, upon his engagement to Fräulein Stummer, an opera singer at the Hoftheater. In a letter from Baden, dated September 21st, and addressed to his "Worthy honored Count and friend," Beethoven discloses that

439

"Soon a sonata of mine will be published, which I have dedicated to you. I wished to surprise you, for the dedication had long been intended, but your letter of yesterday forces me to make this known to you." He speaks warmly, but with a certain formality, of friendship and indebtedness, protests disinterestedness, and warns the Count that "anything in the nature of a present" in return would only pain him.

The Sonata is like the *Lebewohl* Sonata in that the correct gesture and the genuine expression of affection are both present, and hard to disentangle. Beethoven told Schindler that the Sonata was a love story; the first movement was the "struggle between the head and the heart," the second, "communion with the beloved." Purged of its blunt humor and restored to the plane of the music, this might be interpreted as the not too troubled anticipations of courtship and the felicity of understanding in the mutual pledge. The betrothal of a friend, even a formal friend, would have been enough to stir memories of personal experience, and to arouse music as easily.

The subject, of course, precluded extremes of tempo or emotion. The two-movement scheme, the form of intimate expression, was called for. The first movement shows a moderate animation, a not too restless romantic questing; the second, the peaceful, consonant idyll, at the slightly slower pace which allows the music to sing but not to drag. The music meets the circumstance. Beethoven had not written a piano sonata for five years. His skill at subtle handling had increased. But fresh investigation was not expected here. The Sonata cultivates leisurely, rounded periods, meets conventional expectations, but enlivens from within. The first movement hovers in and out of E minor, dwelling upon B minor for a second subject. The second movement is a rondo in a clear and placid E major. It is built upon a sixteen-bar song whose charm is its utter simplicity. The four strophes, the repeated phrases, the tonic returns at length which the form requires would put a strain upon the patience without the endless varieties of detail which renew and freshen the naïve discourse. (See pages 183, 194.)

PIANO SONATA (NO. 28) IN A MAJOR, OP. 101

Etwas lebhaft, und mit der innigsten Empfindung
Lebhaft, marschmässig
Langsam und sehnsuchtvoll; Geschwind, doch nicht zu sehr und mit
Entschlossenheit

(Composed probably in 1815 and 1816; published February, 1817, as *"Sonate für das Hammer-Klavier"*; dedicated to the Baroness Dorothea Ertmann.)

The space of only a year between Opus 101 and its predecessor, Opus 90, seems surprising as the two are compared. Each is as subtly handled as its ripe year would suggest, but the earlier one, with its easy sentiment, and leisurely amplitude, is backward-looking, while the A major Sonata shows the composer on his mettle. Fantasy, while lightly lyrical, can reach boldly toward a new expressive mold. Perhaps the dedications are a sign of what Beethoven thought of each—the first as suitable for a Count in love, the second for the far more expert and discriminating Dorothea von Ertmann.* The Sonata in F-sharp major (Opus 78), though written in 1809, six years before, is decidedly more akin to Opus 101, and this little Sonata, be it remembered, was dedicated to the sensitive intellectual, Therese von Brunswick. Like this one, and unlike the sonata which complimented the affianced Count Moritz Lichnowsky with commodious periods of romantic melodiousness, Opus 101 draws carefully aside from all ruts of comfortable custom and takes a distinctive course, cultivating conciseness. The first movement occupies two pages. The

* Beethoven's "Dorothea-Cäcilia," as he called her, was accounted a pianist of great distinction, a bond which helped to cement a long friendship. Mendelssohn, meeting the Baroness and her military husband years later as an elderly couple, had this anecdote from her which he related in a letter: "When she lost her last child, Beethoven at first did not want to come into the house; at length he invited her to visit him, and when she came he sat himself down at the pianoforte and said simply: 'We will now talk to each other in tones,' and for over an hour played without stopping. She remarked: 'He told me everything, and at last brought me comfort.'"

second, "marchlike," but by no means heavily shod, is soon over by its tempo. The *Adagio* consists of nineteen measures. The *Finale*, with its fugal development, is a movement of normal length—and more than normal moment. As in Opus 27, 53, 57, or 81a, the finale is the substance and climax toward which the earlier movements lead. Beethoven makes his points with delicacy and constant variation, never lingering over them; it is a sonata, in a word, which asks for alert listening. The usual segments of sonata form can be discovered in the first movement, but they are not rhetorically ushered in; the articulation is so close that the joints are scarcely perceived. The movement is a fluent whole, its melodic idea continuously changing, maintaining its character by a constant rhythm.* There is no contrasting theme. The dominant serves to bring in a syncopation of the rhythm. The second movement replaces the usual *scherzo* with the first of the "march" episodes to which Beethoven would twice again turn in his last years:

Lebhaft Marschmässig
Vivace alla Marcia

The rhythm has a resemblance to the key rhythm of the first movement, but its swiftness changes graceful pulsation to springing activity. Only the Trio, with its canonic imitations, relieves the rhythmic persistence. The *Adagio* is introductory, but instead of mere chordal harmonies proposes a melodic phrase of great beauty in A minor, with a *gruppetto* which, with the economy and

---

* It was surely in such movements as this that Wagner found his delightful expedient of using a rhythmic *ostinato* as a loom for unbroken melodic strands and a constant variegation of color.

directness characteristic of the whole Sonata, develops in a few measures a momentary intensification of the until now even mood. A cadenza suggests a new disclosure, but first makes a parenthetical, dreamy allusion to the opening of the Sonata, with a hold after each phrase.*

But the poetic reflections are swept aside. The *Finale* proper puts its proposition with hard clarity and vigorous assertion. This was not a fugue *Finale,* with its problem of style contradiction still to be solved, but a regular sonata-form movement with a fugue planted in the development. The hybrid justifies itself with exciting results. The exposition, in double counterpoint, predicts weighty doings, which presently come to pass. Tovey once aptly remarked that the fugue style and the sonata style are as different as a court trial and a stage scene. The one is a closely worded, narrowly conditioned procedure; the other free and open for the interplay of contrast, stress and subsidence, every device of which drama is made. But a highly charged trial scene placed within a play, and cunningly set off, becomes its crux. So, too, a fugue within a sonata movement. This fugue in four voices, having excitingly clinched its contrapuntal argument, gives way to a free recapitulation and coda, where chordal clarity returns with heightened effect. (See pages 196-197.)

PIANO SONATA (*"GROSSE SONATE FÜR DAS HAMMER-KLAVIER"*) NO. 29 IN B-FLAT MAJOR, OP. 106

> *Allegro*
> *Scherzo: Assai vivace*
> *Adagio sostenuto: Appassionato e con molto sentimento*
> *Largo; Allegro risoluto*

(Composed in 1818 and 1819; published September, 1819; dedicated to the Archduke Rudolph of Austria.)

* The direct reference to an earlier movement was an innovation. A similar incident is to be found in the C major 'Cello Sonata, Opus 102, written at the same time.

The *Hammer-Klavier* * Sonata makes itself known in its first two bars as a tremendous and violent resurgence of power:

Beethoven produced nothing even comparable to it as an on-slaught upon the piano, save the *"Appassionata,"* which, it should be remembered, was completed twelve years before. When the "Emperor" Concerto of 1809, the *Egmont* Overture of 1810, the "Archduke" Trio of 1811, and the Seventh Symphony of 1812 have been named, one looks in vain in the ensuing years for another of those explosions of flooding power. After 1812, Beethoven had composed only scattered small pieces, such as the last two 'cello sonatas, or the song cycle *An die ferne Geliebte,* or the piano sonata, Opus 90—delicate music, almost precious. His friends began to wonder whether the fires had been so subdued by the weight of trouble and advancing age that they would never flare up again. The answer was a sonata which was a sudden release of a strength so long gathered that it overflowed into immense lines and resulted in the most vastly conceived, far-flung

* The tag name *"Hammer-Klavier"* could as well have belonged to the Sonata, Opus 101. Readily falling in with the patriotic movement toward the use of the German language in place of the then unpopular Italian, Beethoven used the (by no means common) translation of the name of the instrument, and, in the case of Opus 101, German tempi for the movements. He forthwith relapsed into the customary Italian directions for tempi.

work he had yet written for the piano. Only the *Eroica* Symphony could have been compared to it in stature, and the *Eroica*, it should be remembered, was another sudden release of strength, goaded by duress of suffering, breaking in upon a relaxed and lyrical period.

The *Hammer-Klavier* Sonata is certainly more bold in innovation than its predecessor, but the composer, as before when the content exceeded all bounds, relied upon the compass of custom in the broad outline. The opening movement discloses a conspicuous theme of contrasting *cantabile* character, and repeats the exposition. The *Scherzo* has the traditional trio with a melody over triplets, and a *da capo*. The *Adagio* is in sonata form with clear road signs of a reprise and coda, their progress following the ornamental variation style of slow movements. The *Finale* (introduced by a circuitously modulating *largo*) is a fully developed fugue traversing every known device of the academics. Since this general staking out tells nothing whatsoever of the real character of the terrain, it need not be further pursued. The character of the Sonata can be called an uncompromising vigor which, knowing nothing of persuasion, speaks with a direct force of conviction, imparting a tremendous sense of inevitability. When Beethoven high-handedly cuts Gordian knots with sudden unexpected modulations, no one thinks of questioning. The first movement is rampant, hurling great chords, ranging all over the keyboard, as if Beethoven's imagination were liberated by the new Broadwood piano with its hard and brilliant action which had been sent from England to his Döbling quarters, much to his delight. But the Sonata is not grateful to pianists, imposing as it can be made to sound. The fingers are unmercifully twisted by the rich polyphonic writing.* The *Scherzo* intervenes as a point of repose between the weighty concentration of the first movement and of the *Adagio* to follow. The order was doubly obligatory, for no scherzo could have broken the silence

---

* The symphonic magnitude of this Sonata led Felix Weingartner to make an orchestration of it. But the texture is only thickened by the orchestral medium.

445

after that deeply troubled music.* One feels in the *Scherzo* a plain blood kinship with the first movement. A certain wayward-ness, a strong-minded "intellectuality" in part explains it, and indeed persists through the entire Sonata. It has been pointed out that the first three movements bear the motto shape of a rising and falling third, and that Beethoven added to the *Adagio* the present introductory bar with its rising third after he had dispatched the copy to the publisher, preserving, instinctively perhaps, the inter-movement unity:

The point may be well taken—it certainly does not need labor-ing.

* And yet Beethoven gave Ries permission in a letter to London to omit the fugue finale and end the Sonata with the *Scherzo!* This consent to a piece of outrageous mutilation, involving, of course, the destruction of bridges, could only have been made with a sense of passing inconsequentiality and comforting distance. Only once in the remainder of his life would Beethoven resume the old order of slow movement—scherzo: This was in the String Quartet in E-flat, Opus 127.

The *Adagio,* in F-sharp minor, lasts twenty minutes—it is the longest of the slow movements *—long because it came from a full heart. Who will explain all that lay upon his spirit as he wrote the slow-moving chain of heavy chords, with their dissonant inner voices, and their abrupt, perturbing modulations? It is inward, soul-searching music without a doubt, its color sometimes dark and haunted, sometimes peaceful, as in the D major of the "second" theme, which probes deeply into the bass. The sinuous figures in thirty-second notes climb to the highest register of the piano and give a strange sense of dreaming upon a remote altitude. But the music holds a steady course, never gathering to a great climax of tension as he would earlier have done. Agitation can assault but no longer ravage his deep peacefulness. We recognize the believer in whom thoughts for a Mass were beginning to assemble. In the coda a repeated high F-sharp in a long crescendo brings one moment of frenzied doubt, which is answered as the initial theme, now restored to the greatest simplicity, falls away into silence. The movement, ending, leaves both desolation and resignation. The heaviness cannot be brusquely swept aside. The composer dreams his way through a *Largo,* a fantasia of uncertainty and expectancy, hinting ambiguous tonalities, making deceptive starts upon a fast tempo, hovering at last upon high trills as the point of disclosure is reached. There could have been only one answer to the *Adagio* of lengths and depths—a tremendous life assertion, an overriding return of vitality and will power which nothing can stem. Beethoven in the year 1818 could have ended this Sonata with nothing else than a fugue. The fugue is in three voices, carried out, according to the indication on the score, "with a certain freedom." The freedom would be the introduction at will of episodes, the unrelenting pursuit of every fugal involution to the bitter end, with a disregard for asperities where another would have steered into smoother waters of thirds and sixths. The variously combined devices which descend even to the *cancrizans,* or mirror-wise presentation of the subject, need not

* Only the slow movement of the Quartet in A minor, Op. 132, is close to it in length.

be called a note pattern for the eye. It shows rather the imagination which will take any proposition whatever, and turn it into tonal sense. The many complexities will baffle the uninstructed listener, but the product of constructive power, as an outburst of prodigious strength, will command his admiration. (See pages 108, 110, 197-199, 206, 220, 242.)

PIANO SONATA (NO. 30) IN E MAJOR, OP. 109

Vivace, ma non troppo
Prestissimo
Andante con Variazioni: Gezangvoll, mit innigster Empfindung

(Completed in 1820, the last two movements composed simultaneously with the Credo of the *Missa Solemnis;* published in November, 1821; dedicated to "Fräulein Maximiliane Brentano.")

The *"Hammer-Klavier"* Sonata is unique among the last five in having three peaks of about equal eminence, so far as emphasis is concerned. The rest have each a single peak, and that always at the end. Plainly, Beethoven had settled into the two-movement plan as the most desirable for a piano sonata.* The Sonata Opus 109 is as clearly a *"Sonata quasi una fantasia"* as any which Beethoven wrote.

The first movement seeks to combine two apparently irreconcilable sections, one *vivace,* the other *adagio,* by alternate juxtaposition, the *vivace* occurring at the beginning, middle and end, the *adagio* twice in between. By this order, any sense of a slow introduction is destroyed. The rhapsodist dreams upon a flowing chord interplay of the two hands, a pattern always developing, pausing only twice to admit wandering measures of slow

---

* The insertion of a scherzo-like movement between the two as a sort of intermezzo does not alter this general scheme, nor does the insertion of a brief slow movement as introduction to the finale. Of the thirteen sonatas which followed the Sonata in E-flat, Opus 31, No. 3, of 1802, only the *"Hammer-Klavier"* has four movements.

chords, arpeggios and scales.* The *prestissimo* is a sort of swift interlude, which passes on a gust of E minor for the hearer, but reveals loveliness of melodic voice twining, when closely examined. The finale breaks another precedent. Beethoven had never before closed a work with slow movement.† He was to close his last sonata with an *adagio molto*. This marvelous set of variations, surely the richest of the many Beethoven wrote for the piano, shows its promise in the beautiful theme itself, expressive in the voice motion of its quartet-like setting forth:

* Romain Rolland has observed that Beethoven's autograph score indicates a closer continuity than the printed editions. The manuscript shows single, not double, bar lines at the abrupt transitions in the first movement, and at the end: *"attacca il prestissimo."* The last two variations of the finale are unnumbered.

† The Violin Sonata Opus 30, No. 1, and the String Quartet Opus 74 have each a variation finale, but the theme is in *allegretto* tempo, the Quartet having a swift conclusion.

The first variation crystallizes the theme into new and songful shape over chord accompaniment (it is to be continuously altered to circumstance, not resuming its exact original form until the final statement). The second variation is a *"leggieramente,"* the third a speeded up dissertation upon the climbing bass voice over which the theme was first heard. The fourth and fifth break it up into flowing figures in alternate or combined voices, again suggesting the string quartet. The last variation becomes chordal again, holding a dominant pedal almost throughout. The slow tempo is restored, and so is the substance of the theme, which loses itself in a long gathering climax of trills and arpeggios. At last, and with telling effect, it is reconstituted in all its simplicity. (See page 219.)

PIANO SONATA (NO. 31) IN A-FLAT MAJOR, OP. 110

> *Moderato cantabile, molto espressivo*
> *Allegro molto*
> *Adagio, ma non troppo; Fuga: Allegro, ma non troppo*

(Completed December 25, 1821; published in 1822, without dedication.)

A clear and simple harmonic style was only momentarily met in the Sonata Opus 109. In his Opus 110, Beethoven seems, for the time being, to have forsworn counterpoint. The Sonata opens in long, sinuous melody, crystal clear over the simplest harmonic pulsations:

The Sonata is to sing its way, in apparent simplicity, up to the very threshold of its final fugue. But the simplicity is deceptive. A single line of melody, when a master is at work, does not preclude subtlety and craft. The first movement of the Sonata in A-flat is so adroitly joined that one is scarcely aware of themes or sections. In place of a definable "second" theme is a passing F minor where the feeling becomes taut. The second movement dances gracefully in and out like one of the earlier scherzos. Its coda leads into an *Adagio* and recitative, and drops softly into an *Arioso dolente* which is a harmonized song where utter simplicity reigns supreme. The *Arioso* is more than an introduction, for it is to return at equal length. It is another trial of sections in complete contrast, alternately interlaid. The foil is a fugue, fully worked, which gives way to the *Arioso,* now an impassioned G minor, this in turn subsiding in broken ac-s. The fugue returns on an inversion of its subject. Do these oppositions of the fugal and the monodic achieve psy-fusion? Somehow, inexplicably, they do. Disparate ntained within the dreaming imagination which ata has occupied while a mass lies in abeyance. masculine contingent in this contest which end, but it is modified by the opposing rmony. The last page resolves into sus- oth chords. (See pages 217, 219.)

PIANO SONATA (NO. 32) IN C MINOR, OP. 111

Maestoso: Allegro con brio ed appassionato
Arietta: Adagio molto semplice cantabile

(Completed January, 1822; published in 1823, a dedication to the Archduke Rudolph indicated and removed.)

The last of the piano sonatas could be called the rounded consummation, the tested and proven realization of the two-movement sonata. The two movements have no intermezzo, cadenza or connecting bridge whatsoever. They are deeply connected inwardly, and in point of order. The first is furiously energetic, a magnificent exhibition of power. The fugued development is Beethoven's most thoroughly effective application of fugal ways to dramatic ends within the sonata style. The second movement, the *adagio "Arietta"* with variations, is the answer to violence and conflict in the remote and restrained contemplativeness of his last works. Von Lenz called the two movements "Resistance —Resignation" or "Sansara—Nirvana." The description is just —indeed the Sonata is wide enough to be read in many terms, such as, for example, the successive conflict and resolution fundamental in Beethoven's character. It epitomizes the bulk of his works, the first movement standing for those of the *"Appassionata"* * years, the second the lofty final slow movement which this is one, and which could not bespeak more unr bly a man who in tones had found his peace with his God. Schindler tells us that he asked the there was to be a finale, and that Beethoven had not had time to write a third move Schlesinger, and his father, both asked letters—sonatas did not end *adagio*. Ha been left with the copyist by mistake answered the Schlesingers with the had used upon Schindler; apparen them at all.

The introduction opens wit

* Note Beethoven's direction,
452

the merest fragments recur twice in the body of the movement. A chain of modulations leads to a bass trill upon which
is suddenly born the main theme, rapped out in octave unison:

A second theme in C major makes little headway against the
imperious and stormy C minor. But suddenly the music rushes
and breaks upon a high note, falls away in staccato chords
which reach C major, placid and contained. There is no need
for introduction to the *Arietta* in that key. The master has
subdued his demon miraculously and completely with a few
measures at the close of the first movement and fully prepared
the gentle entrance of the ethereal theme:

ARIETTA

It is one of the themes which is not a distinct melody in itself, but, with its four voices, all melody. Its little rhythmic inflection is the very kernel of the variations to come. The theme is for the most part calm and chaste, even in its variations. At the beginning of the second section a momentary A minor shows stronger feeling, and this strain, too, is made much of later on. The variations progress in figures of increasingly minute subdivisions, which expand at last into dreaming arpeggio chords, through which the theme is occasionally felt as a wraith of chord successions. This ending, with its prolonged trills and its exploration of the heights of the instrument, suggests the final variation of Opus 109. But here the road is still further pursued. The last Sonata of the thirty-two ends upon a quietly ecstatic C major, a plane worlds removed from all trouble. (See page 219.)

PIANO SONATAS WITHOUT OPUS NUMBER

THREE SONATAS (E-FLAT MAJOR, F MINOR, D MAJOR)

(Published in 1783, under the title: "Three sonatas for piano, written for and dedicated to my most gracious Lord the eminent Archbishop and Prince of Cologne, Maximilian Friedrich, by Ludwig van Beethoven, aged eleven years." Each sonata is in three movements.) (See page 61.)

EASY SONATA IN C MAJOR (FRAGMENTARY)

(Beethoven presented the manuscript to Eleonore von Breuning in 1796, with a dedication to her. It consisted of an *Allegro* and a part of an *Adagio,* which Ferdinand Ries completed by adding eleven bars when the score was published in 1830.) (See page 66.)

Two Sonatinas (in G major and F major), published as Beethoven's after his death, are not accepted as authentic.

MISCELLANEOUS WORKS FOR PIANO SOLO

VARIATIONS

SIX VARIATIONS ON AN ORIGINAL THEME, IN F MAJOR, OP. 34

(Composed in 1802; published in 1803; dedicated to the Princess Odeschalchi.)

FIFTEEN VARIATIONS (IN E-FLAT MAJOR), ON A THEME FROM THE BALLET *DIE GESCHÖPFE DES PROMETHEUS*, OP. 35

(Composed in 1802; published in 1803; dedicated to Count Moritz von Lichnowsky.)

SIX VARIATIONS IN D MAJOR (ON THE MARCH FROM *DIE RUINEN VON ATHEN*), OP. 76

(Composed about 1809; published 1810; dedicated to "his friend Oliva.")

SIX THEMES WITH VARIATIONS, OP. 105

(Composed in 1818–1819 for G. Thomson in Edinburgh; five Scottish and one Austrian theme; for piano solo or piano with flute or violin.)

TEN THEMES WITH VARIATIONS, OP. 107

(Composed in 1818–1820 for G. Thomson in Edinburgh; six Scottish, two Tyrolian, one Swiss, and one Russian theme; for piano solo, or piano with flute or violin.)

THIRTY-THREE VARIATIONS (IN C MAJOR) ON A WALTZ BY A. DIABELLI, OP. 120

(Begun in 1821 or 1822; completed in 1823 and published by Diabelli in June of that year. Dedicated to Frau Antonie Brentano.)

The "Diabelli" Variations, like the Thirty-two Variations in C Minor (of 1806–1807), are an outstanding instance where a theme of no consequence but of eminent serviceability became so firmly implanted in Beethoven's mind that it could not be released until it had fulfilled itself through about as many forms and paces as he could conjure up. There is hardly anywhere in music such an instance of prodigious results from small beginnings. Hans von Bülow, in his edition of the piano music of Beethoven, has called the Variations the *"Mikrokosmos* of Beethoven's genius. Indeed," he has written, "the whole image of the world of tone is outlined here, the whole evolution of musical thought and sound fantasy from the most contained contemplation to the most abandoned humor—an unbelievably rich variety." In the warmth of his enthusiasm Bülow defends the theme itself against those who have unwarrantably "scorned" it. But the best he can say about the tune is somehow not very encouraging. Its "melodic neutrality," he finds, protects it from becoming "outmoded." It is a "quite pretty, elegant (*geschmack-voll*) little fragment." But Beethoven himself called it a *"Schus-terfleck."*

The "cobbler's patch" theme becomes a harmonic skeleton, a convenient container. The metamorphosis is so free that a theme from Mozart's *Don Giovanni* (*Notte e giorno faticar*), made on the same formal pattern, quizzically provides the twenty-second variation without causing the least sense of incongruity. The

456

variance in tempo is as great as that of mood, which is by turns martial, grave, scherzo-like, solid or gay. The twenty-ninth variation ventures into the tonic minor. The thirty-first, a *largo molto espressivo* with ornamental scale passages, is "deeply and tenderly conceived," in the words of Bülow, and "could be called a reincarnation of the Bach *adagio,* as the double fugue that follows similarly resembles a Handelian *allegro.*" The final variation begins as a *tempo di minuetto,* "the rebirth of the Haydn and Mozart era," making the three successive variations a compendium of the history of music, "a picture of the whole musical universe re-enacted." This final variation leaves the sense of a minuet behind, to wander in more ethereal regions where whispering arpeggios somehow recall the last pages of the final Piano Sonata. If it is a leave-taking of the piano, or, as Schumann has called it, a "farewell to the listener," it is a reluctant and a lingering one.

VARIATIONS WITHOUT OPUS NUMBERS

NINE VARIATIONS (IN A MAJOR) ON A THEME OF PAISIELLO (FROM *"DIE SCHÖNE MÜLLERIN"*)

(Published in 1795; dedicated to Prince Carl von Lichnowsky.)

SIX VARIATIONS (IN G MAJOR) ON A THEME OF PAISIELLO (FROM *"DIE SCHÖNE MÜLLERIN"*)

(Published in 1796.)

TWELVE VARIATIONS (IN C MAJOR) ON A MINUET FROM THE BALLET *"LE NOZZE DISTURBATE"* BY J. J. HAIBEL

(Published in 1796.)

TWELVE VARIATIONS (IN A MAJOR) ON THE RUSSIAN DANCE FROM THE BALLET *"DAS WALDMÄDCHEN"* BY PAUL WRANITZKY

(Published in 1797; dedicated to the Countess von Browne.)

SIX EASY VARIATIONS (IN F MAJOR) ON A SWISS SONG

(For Piano or Harp. Published in 1798.)

EIGHT VARIATIONS (IN C MAJOR) ON A THEME FROM THE OPERA *"RICHARD LÖWENHERZ"* BY GRÉTRY

(Published in 1798.)

TEN VARIATIONS (IN B-FLAT MAJOR) ON A THEME FROM THE OPERA *"FALSTAFF"* BY ANTONIO SALIERI

(Published in 1799; dedicated to the Countess Barbara Keglevics.)

SEVEN VARIATIONS (IN F MAJOR) ON A THEME FROM THE OPERA *"DAS UNTER-BROCHENE OPFERFEST"* BY PAUL WINTER

(Published in 1799.)

EIGHT VARIATIONS (IN F MAJOR) ON A THEME FROM THE OPERA *"SOLIMAN II"* BY F. X. SÜSSMAYR

(Published in 1799; dedicated to the Countess von Browne.)

SIX EASY VARIATIONS (IN G MAJOR) ON AN ORIGINAL THEME

(Composed probably in 1800 and published in 1801.)

SEVEN VARIATIONS (IN C MAJOR) ON THE "FOLK SONG," *"GOD SAVE THE KING"*

(Published in 1804.)

FIVE VARIATIONS (IN D MAJOR) ON THE "FOLK SONG," *"RULE BRITANNIA"*

(Published in 1804.)

THIRTY-TWO VARIATIONS (IN C MINOR)

(Composed in 1806–1807; published in 1807.) (See page 114.)

EIGHT VARIATIONS (IN B-FLAT MAJOR) ON THE SONG: *"ICH HAB' EIN KLEINES HÜTTCHEN NUR"*

(Date of composition unknown; published in 1831.)

OTHER WORKS FOR PIANO SOLO

ATELLES, OP. 33

uncertain; published in 1803.)

S (THROUGH THE TWELVE
P. 39

mpleted in 1789, published in 1803.)

TWO RONDOS (IN C MAJOR AND G MAJOR), OP. 51

(The first was published in 1797, the second in 1802. The second was dedicated to the Countess Henriette von Lichnowsky.) (See page 64.)

FANTASY IN G MINOR, OP. 77

(Composed at the latest in 1808, and published in 1810; dedicated to Count Franz von Brunswick.) (See page 138.)

POLONAISE IN C MAJOR, OP. 89

(Composed in 1814, published in 1815; dedicated to the Empress Elizabeth Alexievna of Russia.)

TWELVE NEW BAGATELLES, OP. 119

(Nos. 7–11 were published in 1821 as *"Kleinigkeiten"*; Nos. 1–11 were published in Paris in 1823 as *"Nouvelles Bagatelles faciles et agréables"*; the twelfth was added in a publication of 1828.)

SIX BAGATELLES, OP. 126

(Composed in 1823, inscribed *"Kleinigkeiten"*; published in 1825.)

RONDO A CAPRICCIO IN G MAJOR, OP. 129

(Published in 1828 without Opus number, and with this inscription: "This capriccio, posthumously discovered, bears this inscription the manuscript: *'Die Wuth über den verlornen Groschen, ausget in einer Caprice'"* ["Anger at the loss of a penny, abated caprice"].)

PIANO WORKS WITHOUT OP

RONDO IN A MAJOR

(Published in 1784 in a collection: "Bou Piano.")

SIX MINUETS

(Published in 1796.)

SEVEN *"LÄNDLERISCHE TÄNZE"*

(Published in 1799.)

SIX *"LÄNDLERISCHE TÄNZE"*

(Composed and published in 1802.)

ANDANTE IN F MAJOR

(Composed in 1804, and first intended for the Sonata Opus 53. Published in 1806 as *"Andante pour le pianoforte."* The title *"Andante favori"* was used by a later publisher.) (See page 133.)

MINUET IN E-FLAT MAJOR

(Published in 1805.)

PRAELUDIUM IN F MINOR

(Published in 1805.)

DEUTSCHER TANZ (ALLEMANDE) IN G MAJOR

(First appeared as the last in a set of six German Dances for Violin and Piano, in 1814. Published for Piano solo in 1855.)

KLEINES STÜCK ("LITTLE PIECE") IN B-FLAT MAJOR

(Composed in 1818, published in 1824.)

LETZTER GEDANKE ("LAST THOUGHT"), IN C MAJOR

(Published in 1840 as "Beethoven's last musical thought," transcribed from a sketch for String Quintet.)

KLAVIERSTÜCK ("FÜR ELISE"), IN A MINOR

(See page 141)

———

Included in the supplement of Breitkopf and Härtel's complete works are:

Two Bagatelles
Allegretto
Lustig-Traurig
Six Ecossaises
Ecossaises in E flat and G
Waltzes in E flat and D
Allemande in A

Listed in Nottebohm's **Thematic Catalogue** as "spurious or doubtful works" are the following, all for Piano Solo: *"Alexandermarsch"* in F major, a *"Pariser Einzugsmarsch"* in C major, a *"Trauermarsch"* in F minor, a set of ten waltzes, and the waltz in F major published in 1838 as *"Abschieds-Gedanken"* (translated as "Farewell to the Piano").

WORKS FOR PIANO
(FOUR HANDS)

SONATA IN D MAJOR, OP. 6

(Published in 1797.)

THREE MARCHES (IN C MAJOR, E-FLAT MAJOR, AND D MAJOR), OP. 45

(Published in 1804, with a dedication to the Princess Esterházy.)

WITHOUT OPUS NUMBER

VARIATIONS (IN C MAJOR) ON A THEME OF COUNT WALDSTEIN

(Published in 1794.)

SIX VARIATIONS (IN D MAJOR) ON THE AIR "ICH DENKE DEIN"

(Written in 1800 in the family album of the Countesses Josephine Deym and Therese Brunswick; published in 1805.)

INDEX OF NAMES

(IN THE "LIFE OF BEETHOVEN")

465

Index of Names

Fries, Count Moritz, 92, 223
Frimmel, Theodor von, 130
Fux, Joseph, 45

Galitzin, Prince Nicolas von, 210, 229
Gaveaux, Pierre, 98
Giannatasio del Rio, Cajetan, 162, 186, 188, 189, 190, 193, 198, 200
Giannatasio del Rio, Fanny, 162, 188, 190, 201
Gleichenstein, Baron Ignatz von, 128, 140, 141, 143, 144, 250
Gluck, C. W. von, 18, 24, 71
Goethe, Christiane von, 150, 152
Goethe, J. W. von, 28, 56, 70, 109, 128, 139, 142, 146-154, 162, 210, 219, 251
Grétry, A. E. M., 3, 24
Grillparzer, Franz, 128, 217, 256
Grove, Sir George, 130, 226
Guicciardi, Giulietta, 61, 63, 64, 65, 79, 160, 161
Gyrowetz, Adalbert, 139, 256

Habeneck, F. A., 122, 222
Handel, G. F., 15, 39, 56, 127, 248
Hartl, Joseph, 139
Haslinger, Tobias, 180, 214, 250, 255, 256
Haydn, Joseph, 33-34, 36, 38-48, 68-70, 99, 116, 123, 131, 191, 193, 248
Herder, J. G. von, 28, 206
Herzlieb, Minna, 150
Hevesy, André de, 130, 162
Hiller, Ferdinand, 250, 251, 255
Hoffmeister and Kühn, 66, 73
Holz, Carl, 197, 228, 230, 236, 238, 246, 255, 256
Homer, 28
Honrath, Jeannette d', 30
Hotschevar, Jacob, 202
Hummel, Johann Nepomuk, 49, 58, 170, 172, 250, 252, 256
Hüttenbrenner, Anselm, 253, 254

Jahn, Otto, 20, 65

Kalischer, Dr. A. C., 161
Kanka, Dr. Johann, 179, 184
Kant, Immanuel, 71, 206
Kees, Hofrat von, 39
Keglevich, Barbara, 61
Kinsky, Prince Ferdinand, 39, 124, 139, 158, 166, 167, 174, 182-184
Klöber, August von, 199
Klopstock, F. G., 28, 127, 128
Koch, Babette, 30
Kotzebue, A. F. von, 192
Kraft, Anton, 38
Kraft, Nicholas, 38
Krehbiel, H. E., 161, 208
Krumpholz, Wenzel, 60, 87, 133

La Mara (Marie Lipsius), 65, 161
La Roche, Maximiliane, 146
Latronne, Louis, 184
Lessing, G. E., 28
Lichnowsky, Prince Karl, 38, 39, 41, 46, 50, 55, 68, 83, 89, 94, 102, 107, 120, 133, 134, 158, 178, 179
Lichnowsky, Princess Marie Christine (von Thun), 38, 103, 115
Lichnowsky, Count Moritz, 38, 40, 183, 194, 223, 224, 225, 250
Liechtenstein, Baron Carl A., 107
Linke, Joseph, 115, 180, 183, 230, 250, 256
Liszt, Franz, 218
Lobkowitz, Prince, 40, 55, 56, 107, 110, 111, 120, 122, 124, 138, 139, 166, 174, 179, 183, 184
Lucchesi, Andrea, 13, 18, 19
Ludwig, Emil, 149

Malfatti, Anna, 140, 141, 143, 144
Malfatti, Dr., 140, 249, 250
Malfatti, Therese, 140, 141, 142, 143, 144, 150, 155, 158
Mälzel, Johann Nepomuk, 169, 170, 171, 172, 173, 174, 183

467

Index of Names

MODERN LIBRARY GIANTS

A series of sturdily bound and handsomely printed, full-sized library editions of books formerly available only in expensive sets. These volumes contain from 600 to 1,400 pages each.

THE MODERN LIBRARY GIANTS REPRESENT A SELECTION OF THE WORLD'S GREATEST BOOKS

MISCELLANEOUS